BLEACH
VOL. 54: GOODBYE TO OUR XCUTION
SHONEN JUMP Manga Edition

STORY AND ART BY
TITE KUBO

Translation/Joe Yamazaki
Touch-up Art & Lettering/Mark McMurray
Design/Kam Li
Editor/Alexis Kirsch

BLEACH © 2001 by Tite Kubo. All rights reserved. First published
in Japan in 2001 by SHUEISHA Inc., Tokyo. English translation rights
arranged by SHUEISHA Inc.

The rights of the author(s) of the work(s) in this publication to be so
identified have been asserted in accordance with Copyright, Designs and
Patents Act 1988. A CIP catalogue record for this book is available from
the British Library.

The stories, characters and incidents mentioned in this publication are
entirely fictional.

No portion of this book may be reproduced or transmitted in any form
or by any means without written permission from the copyright holders.

Printed in the U.S.A.

Published by VIZ Media, LLC
P.O. Box 77010
San Francisco, CA 94107

10 9 8 7 6 5 4 3 2 1
First printing, January 2013

www.viz.com

PARENTAL ADVISORY
BLEACH is rated T for Teen and is recommended
for ages 13 and up. This volume contains
fantasy violence.
ratings.viz.com

THE WORLD'S
MOST POPULAR MANGA
SHONEN JUMP
www.shonenjump.com

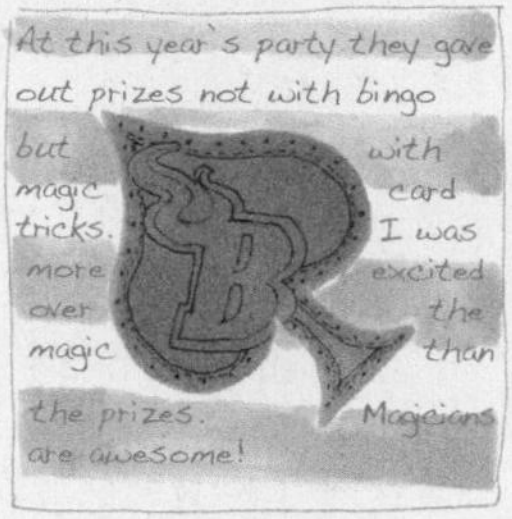
At this year's party they gave
out prizes not with bingo
but with
magic card
tricks. I was
more excited
over the
magic than
the prizes. Magicians
are awesome!

I received a break at the beginning of the year, so for the first time I was able to attend the New Year's party while not working. It was the best one! It's so nice to come home and not have work waiting for me.

-Tite Kubo

Bleach is author Tite Kubo's second title. Kubo made his debut with *ZOMBIEPOWDER.*, a four-volume series for *Weekly Shonen Jump*. To date, *Bleach* has been translated into numerous languages and has also inspired an animated TV series that began airing in the U.S. in 2006. Beginning its serialization in 2001, *Bleach* is still a mainstay in the pages of *Weekly Shonen Jump*. In 2005, *Bleach* was awarded the prestigious Shogakukan Manga Award in the *shonen* (boys) category.

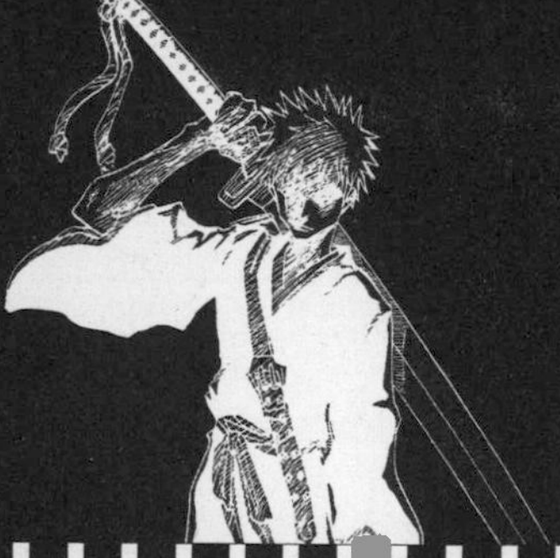

If you can say that your heart doesn't change
Then that is strength

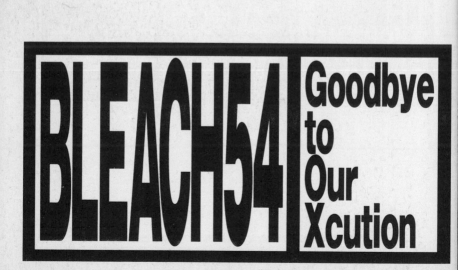

BLEACH54

Goodbye to Our Xcution

STARS AND

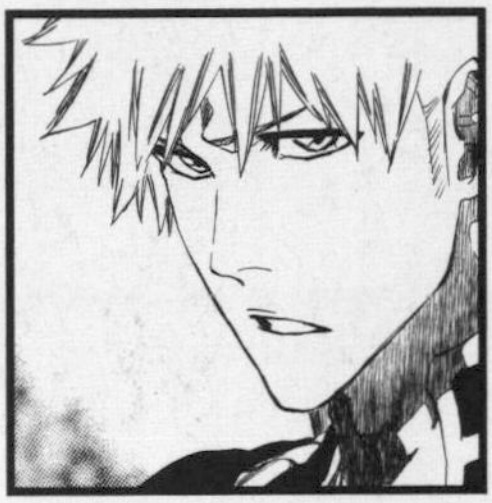

銀城空吾
Kugo Ginjo

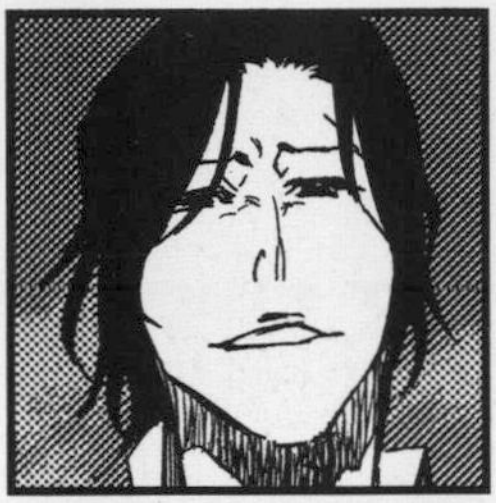

Ichigo Kurosaki
黒崎一護

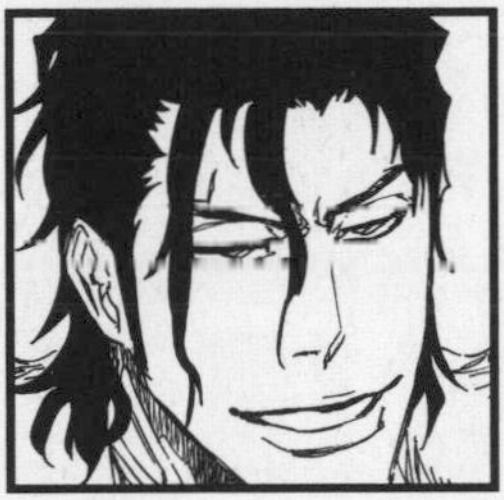

Shukuro Tsukishima
月島秀九郎

plot

Ichigo Kurosaki meets Soul Reaper Rukia Kuchiki and ends up helping her eradicate Hollows. After developing his powers as a Soul Reaper, Ichigo enters battle against Aizen and his dark ambitions! Ichigo finally defeats Aizen in exchange for his powers as a Soul Reaper.

With the battle over, Ichigo regains his daily life. But his tranquil days end when he meets Ginjo, who offers to help Ichigo get his powers back. But it was all a dark plot by Ginjo and his partner Tsukishima! As Ichigo sinks into despair after his powers are robbed from him once again, Rukia and the Soul Reapers from the Soul Society come to the rescue! With his true powers back, Ichigo now faces off against Ginjo!

BLEACH ALL

朽木ルキア
Rukia Kuchiki

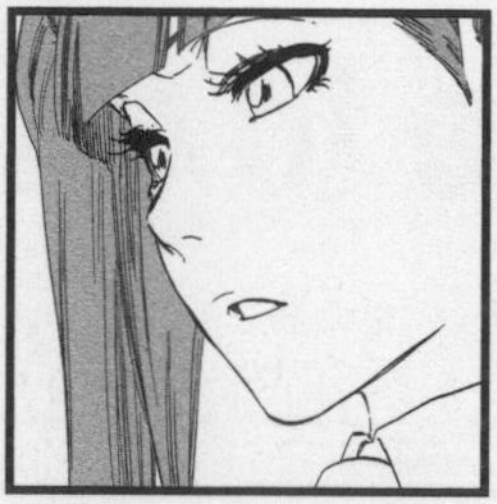

獅子河原萌笑
Moeh Shishigawara

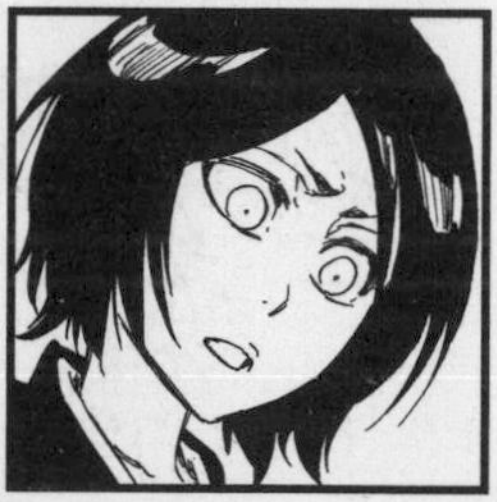

Riruka Dokugamine
毒ヶ峰リルカ

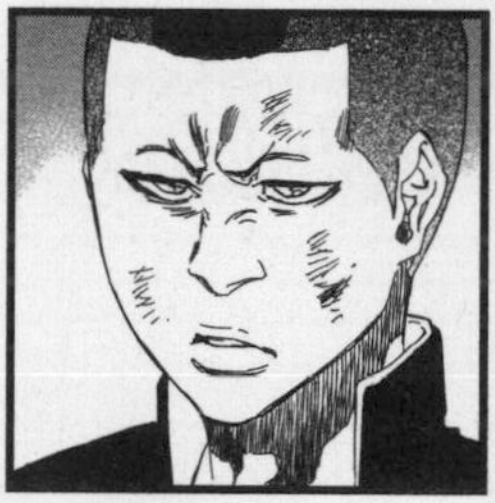

STORIES

BLEACH54

Goodbye to Our Xcution

Contents

470. Pray for Predators		7
471. Pray for Predators 2		27
472. Razoredge Requiem		47
473. Enemies in the Dark		67
474. beLIEve		87
475. Shades of the Bond		107
476. THE LOST		127
477. THE LOST 2		147
478. THE LOST 3		167
479. Goodbye to Our Xcution		187

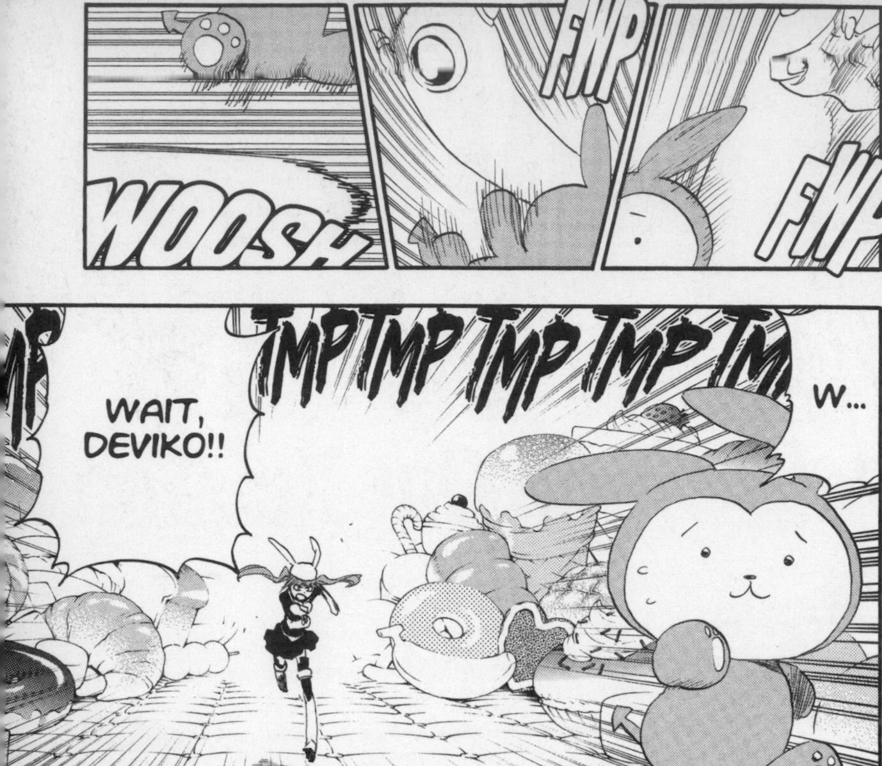
FWP
FWP
WOOSH
W...
TMP TMP TMP TMP TM
WAIT, DEVIKO!!
MP
WHO'S DEVIKO ?!
THIS IS RABBIT PLUSHIE! AT LEAST CALL ME RABBIKO!!
IT'S NOT A RABBIT! IT'S A DEVIL !!
LOOK AT THE TAIL! YOU'RE SO STUPID!!
CRAP ...
I DON'T UNDER-STAND HOW I ENDED UP LIKE THIS, BUT...
...I'M GLAD SHE'S SLOW!
I NEED TO FIND A PLACE WHERE I CAN HIDE AND COME UP WITH A PLAN...

470. Pray for Predators

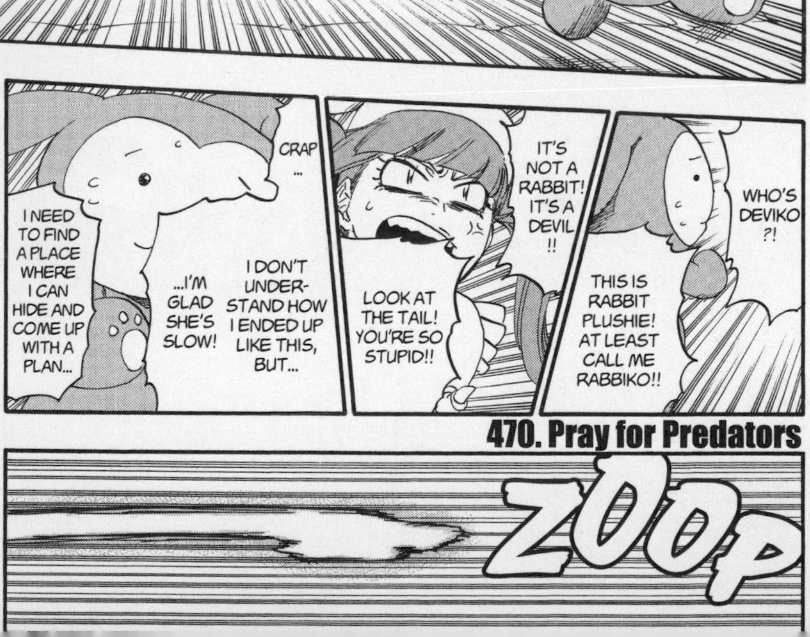
ZOOP

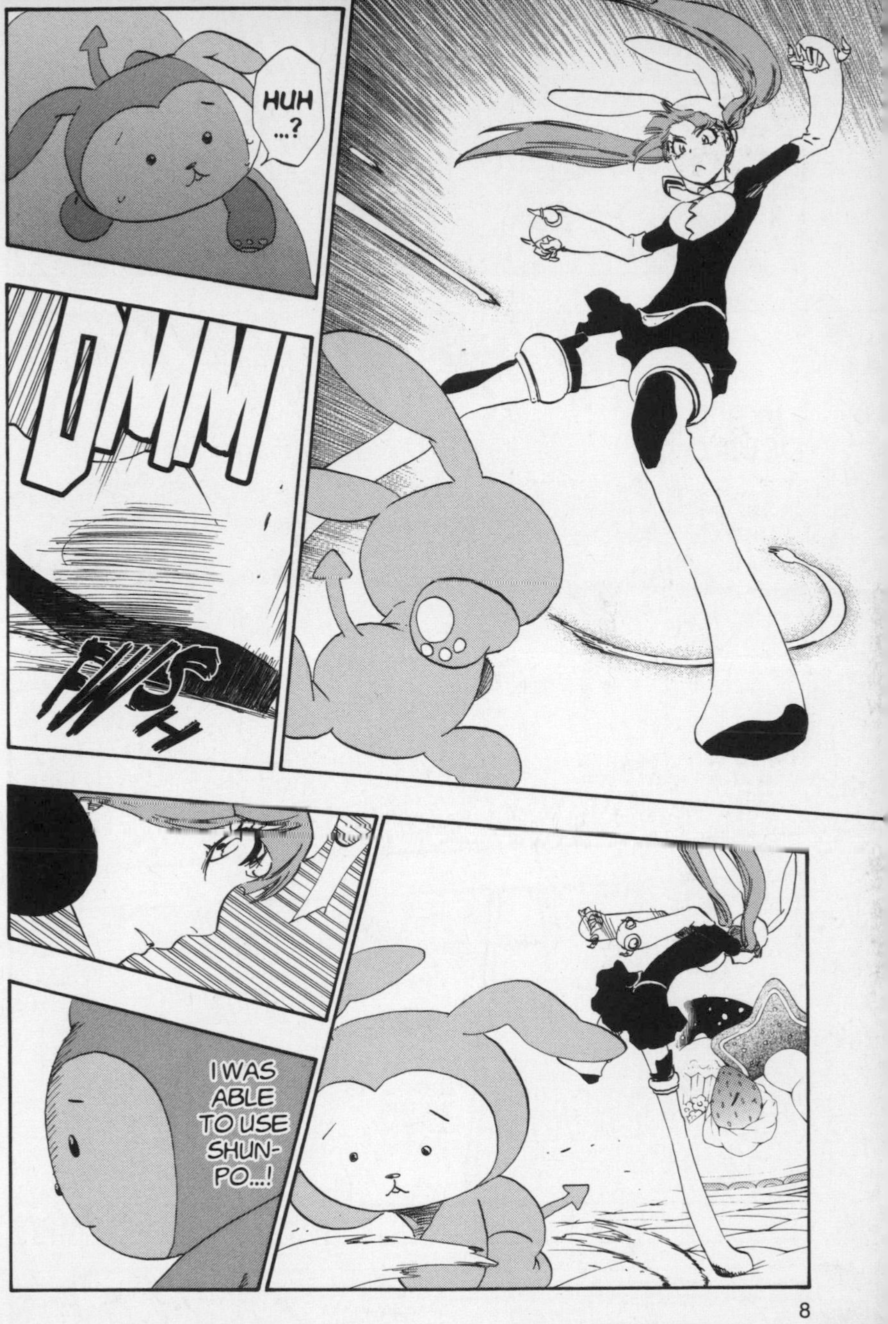
HUH ...?
DMM
FWSH
I WAS ABLE TO USE SHUN-PO...!

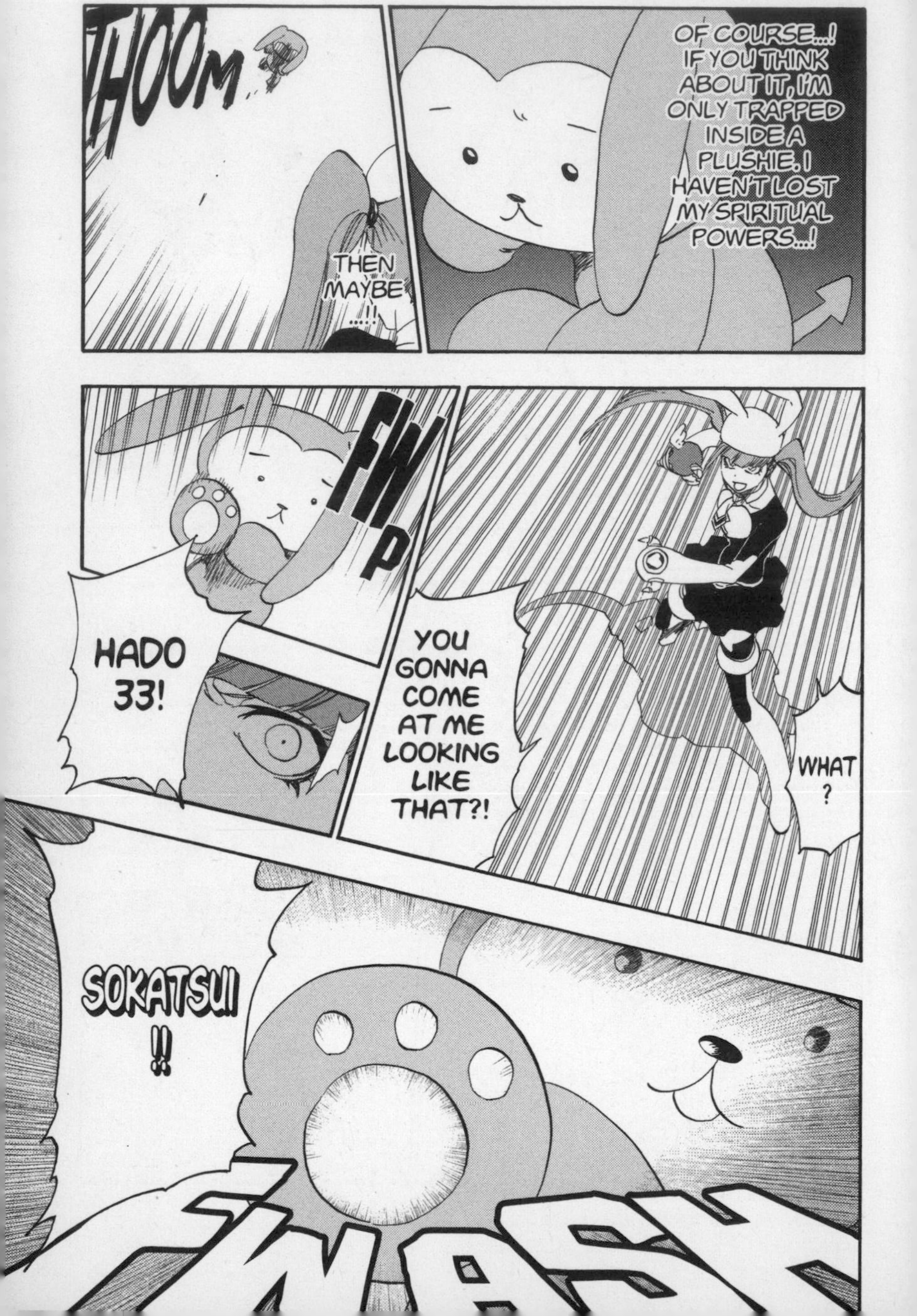
OF COURSE...! IF YOU THINK ABOUT IT, I'M ONLY TRAPPED INSIDE A PLUSHIE. I HAVEN'T LOST MY SPIRITUAL POWERS...!
THOOM
THEN MAYBE ...!!
WHAT?
YOU GONNA COME AT ME LOOKING LIKE THAT?!
FWP
HADO 33!
SOKATSUI!!
SMASH

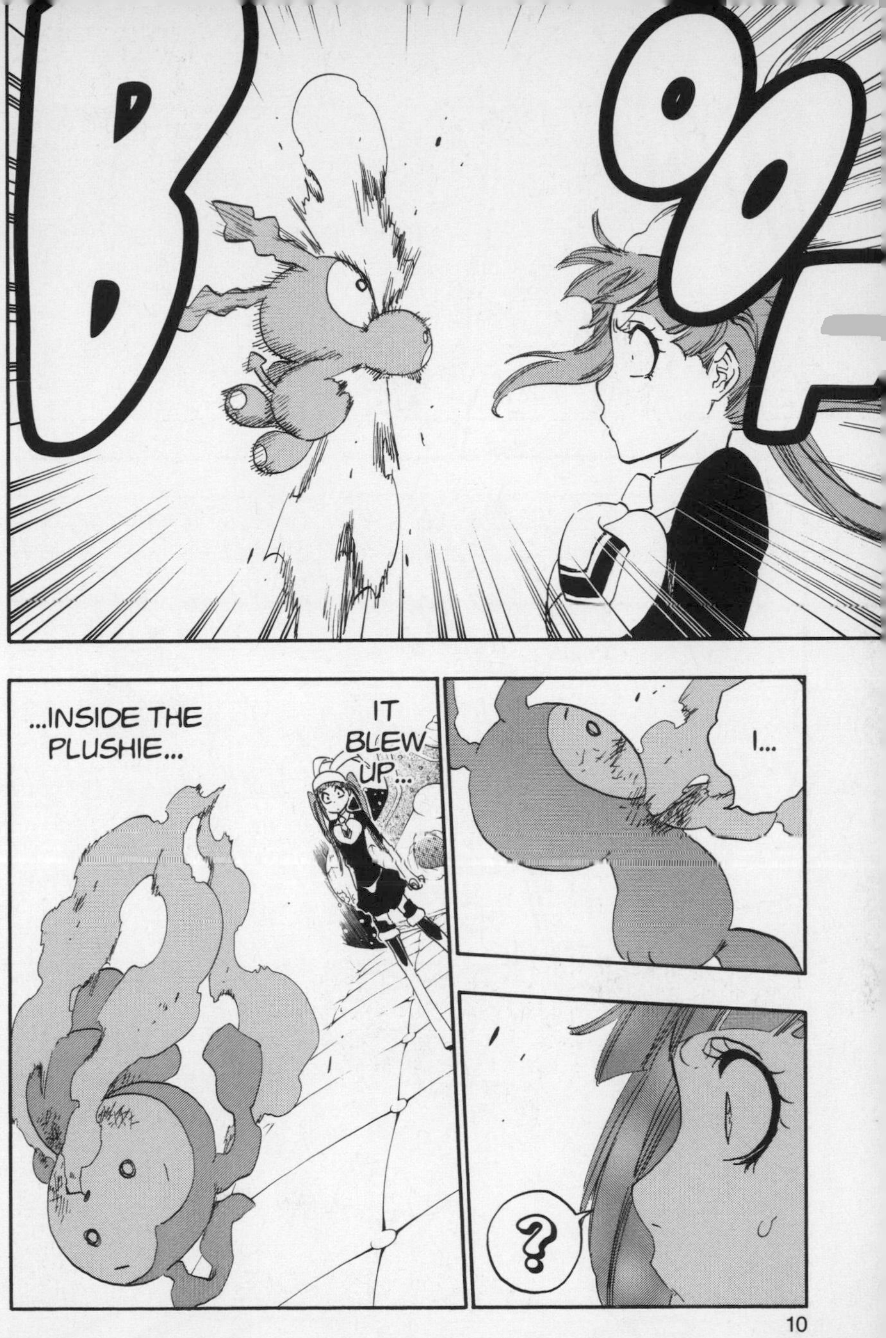
I...
?
IT BLEW UP...
...INSIDE THE PLUSHIE...

IDIOT!

I... I DON'T KNOW WHAT JUST HAPPENED, BUT...

THUD

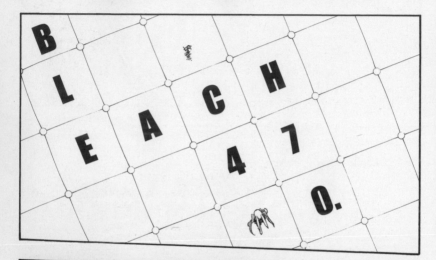

BLEACH 470.

Pray for Predators

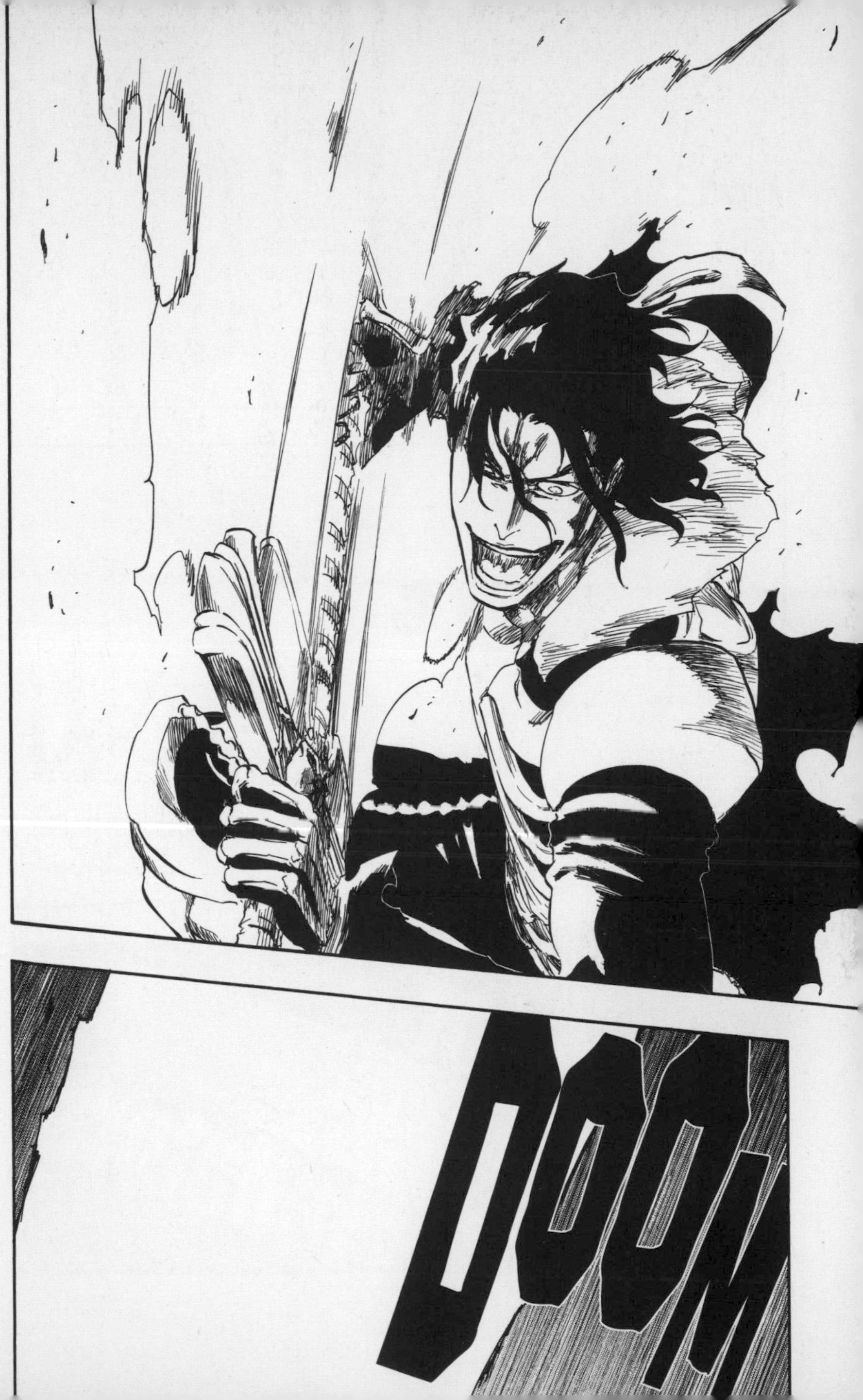
DOOM

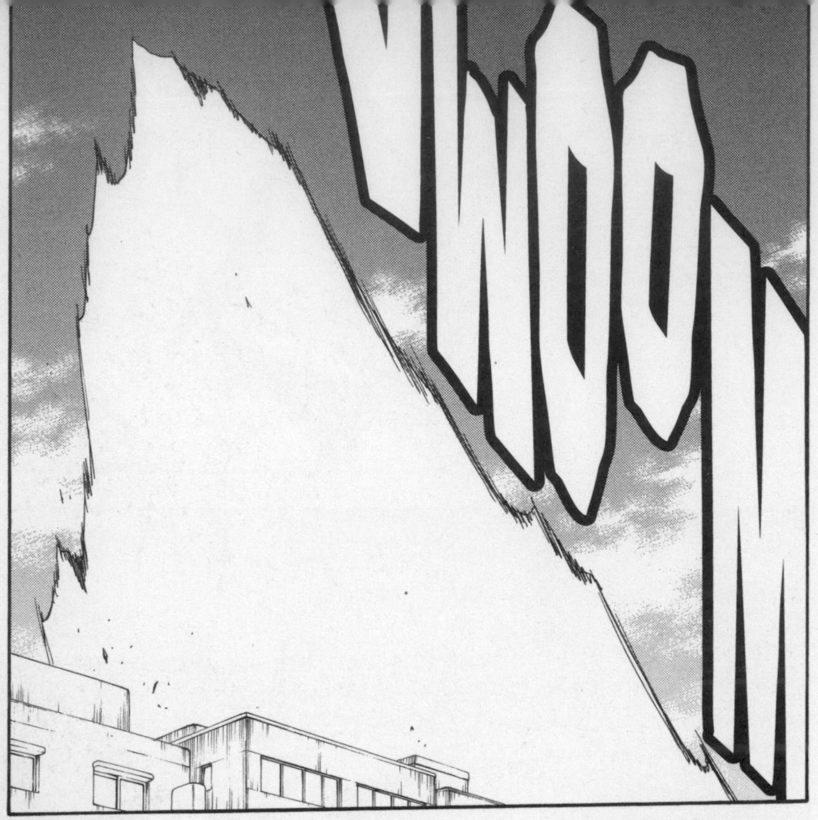

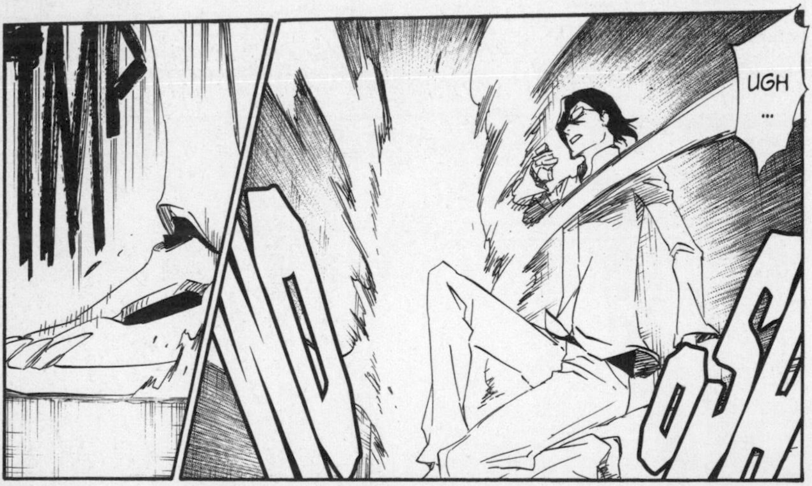
UGH ...

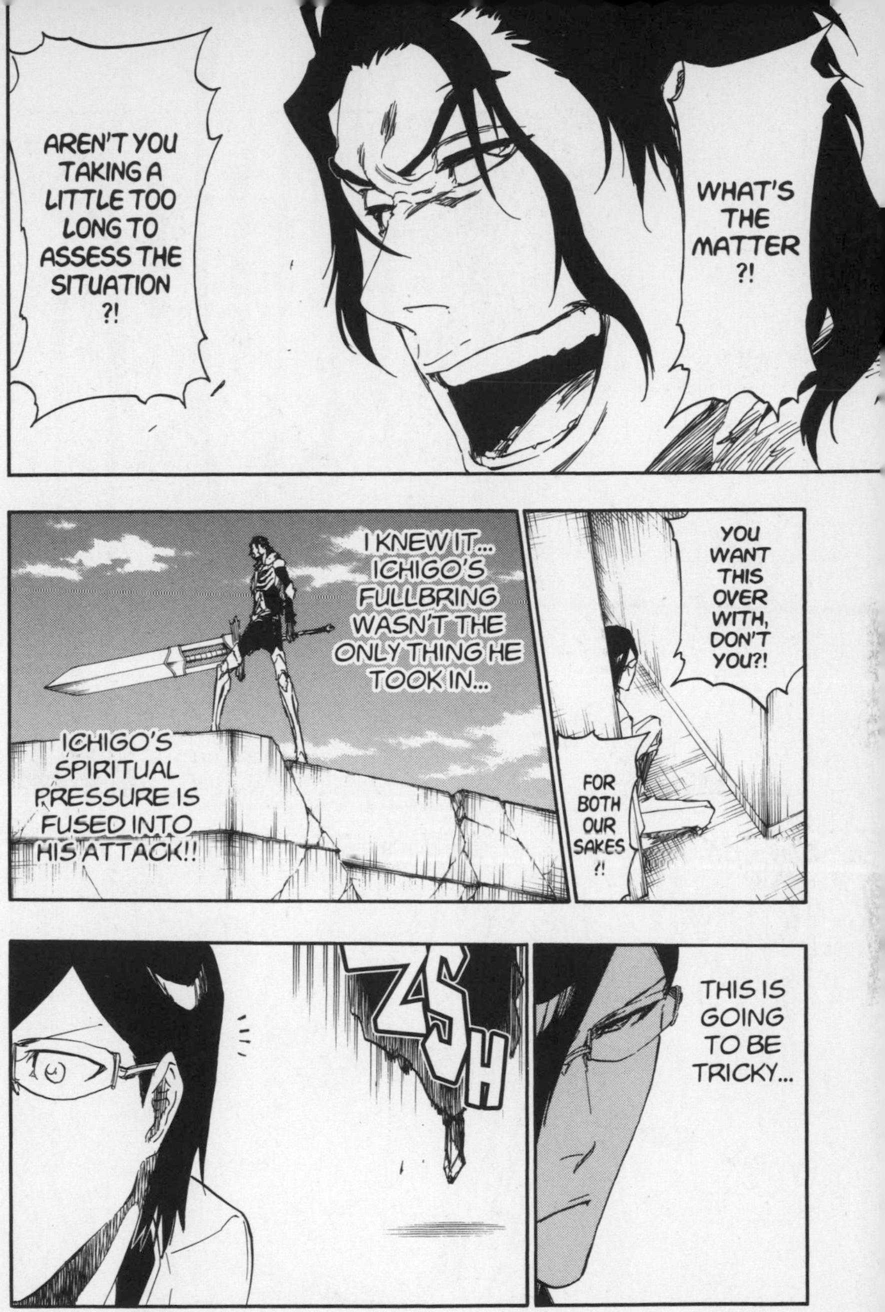
WHAT'S THE MATTER ?!
AREN'T YOU TAKING A LITTLE TOO LONG TO ASSESS THE SITUATION ?!
YOU WANT THIS OVER WITH, DON'T YOU?!
FOR BOTH OUR SAKES ?!
I KNEW IT... ICHIGO'S FULLBRING WASN'T THE ONLY THING HE TOOK IN...
ICHIGO'S SPIRITUAL PRESSURE IS FUSED INTO HIS ATTACK!!
THIS IS GOING TO BE TRICKY...
ZSH

READ THIS WAY

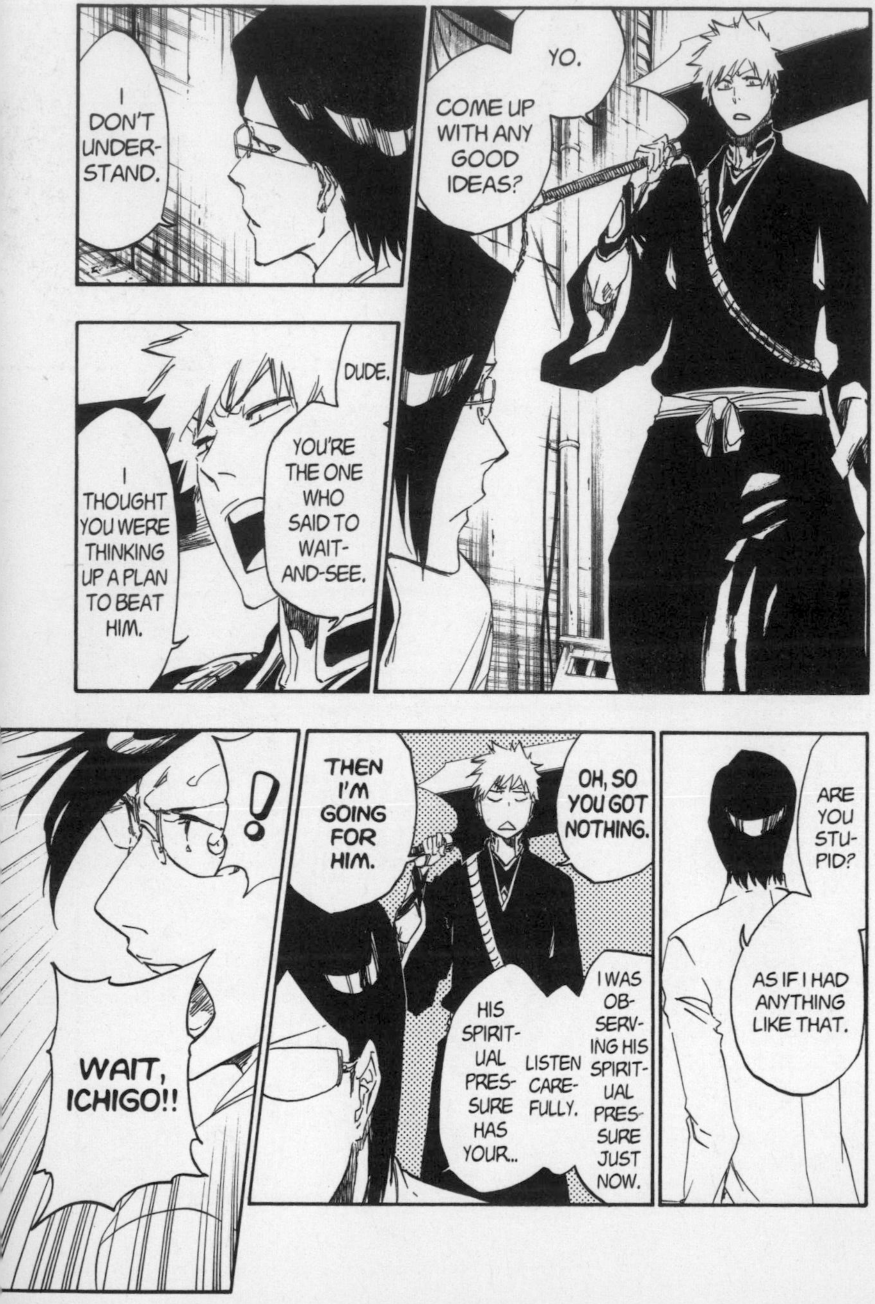
YO.
COME UP WITH ANY GOOD IDEAS?
I DON'T UNDERSTAND.
DUDE.
YOU'RE THE ONE WHO SAID TO WAIT-AND-SEE.
I THOUGHT YOU WERE THINKING UP A PLAN TO BEAT HIM.
ARE YOU STUPID?
AS IF I HAD ANYTHING LIKE THAT.
OH, SO YOU GOT NOTHING.
THEN I'M GOING FOR HIM.
I WAS OBSERVING HIS SPIRITUAL PRESSURE JUST NOW.
LISTEN CAREFULLY.
HIS SPIRITUAL PRESSURE HAS YOUR..
!
WAIT, ICHIGO!!

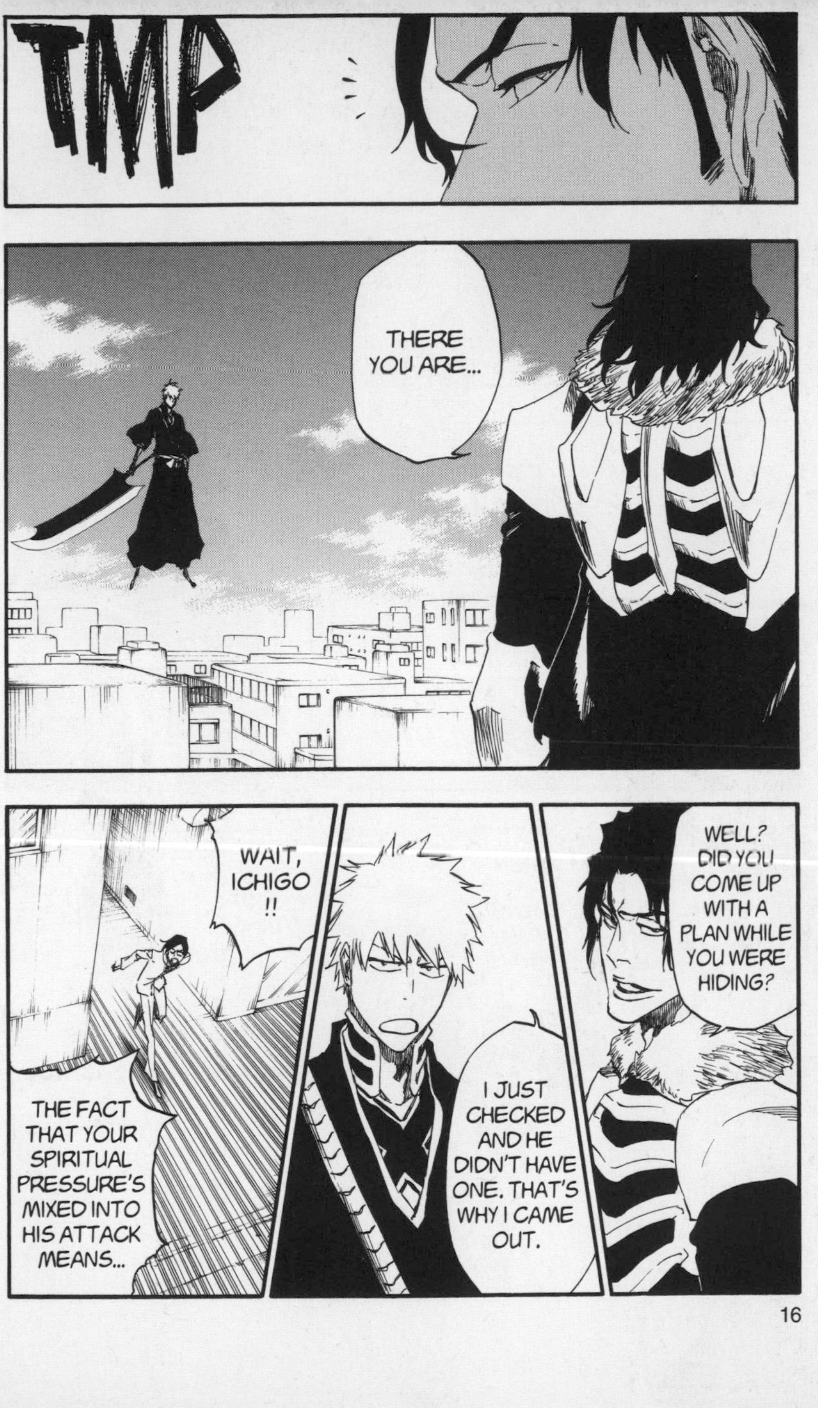
TMP
THERE YOU ARE...
WELL? DID YOU COME UP WITH A PLAN WHILE YOU WERE HIDING?
I JUST CHECKED AND HE DIDN'T HAVE ONE. THAT'S WHY I CAME OUT.
WAIT, ICHIGO!!
THE FACT THAT YOUR SPIRITUAL PRESSURE'S MIXED INTO HIS ATTACK MEANS...

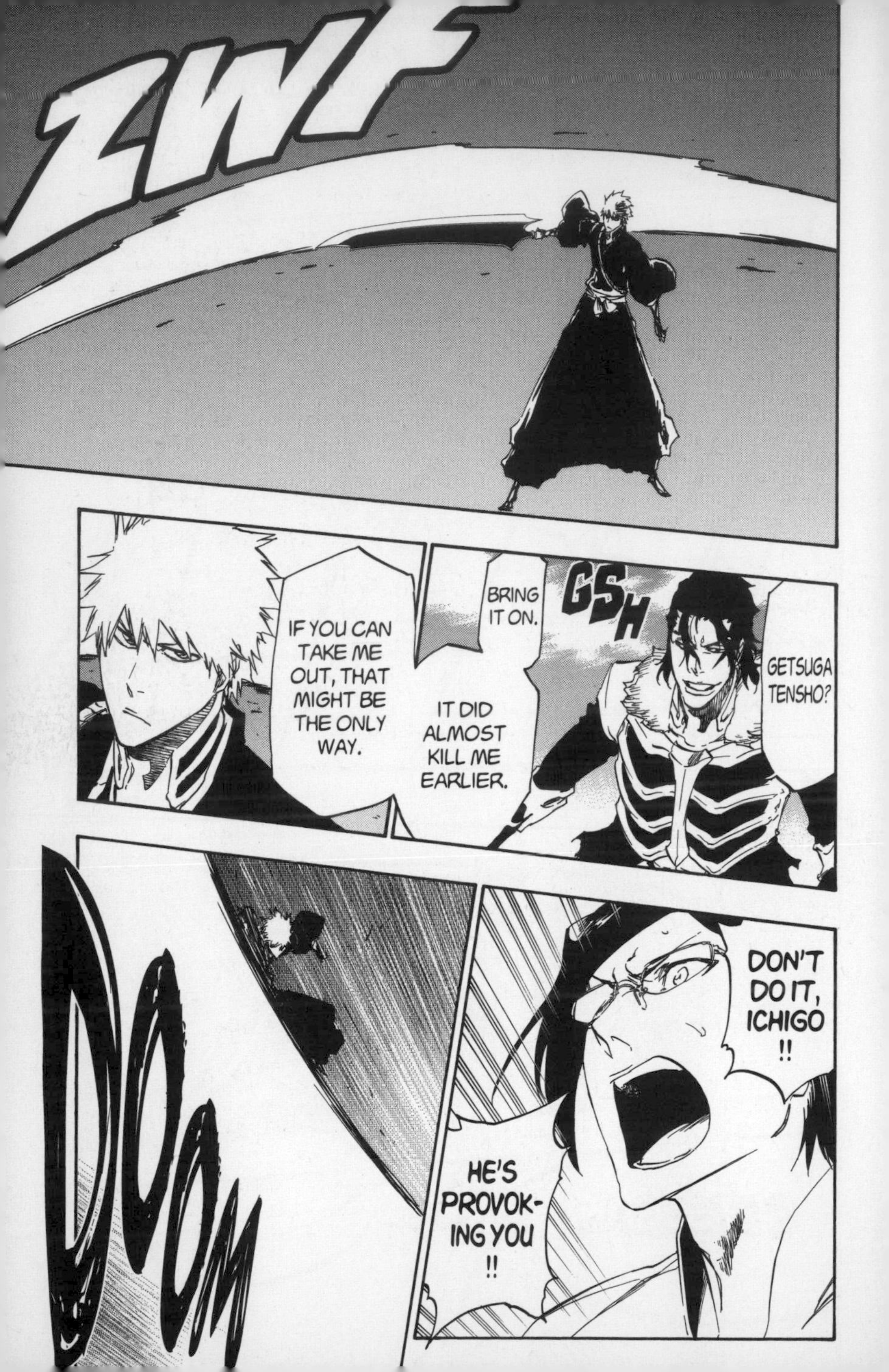
ZWF
GETSUGA TENSHO?
GSH
BRING IT ON.
IT DID ALMOST KILL ME EARLIER.
IF YOU CAN TAKE ME OUT, THAT MIGHT BE THE ONLY WAY.
DON'T DO IT, ICHIGO!!
HE'S PROVOK-ING YOU!!
DOOM

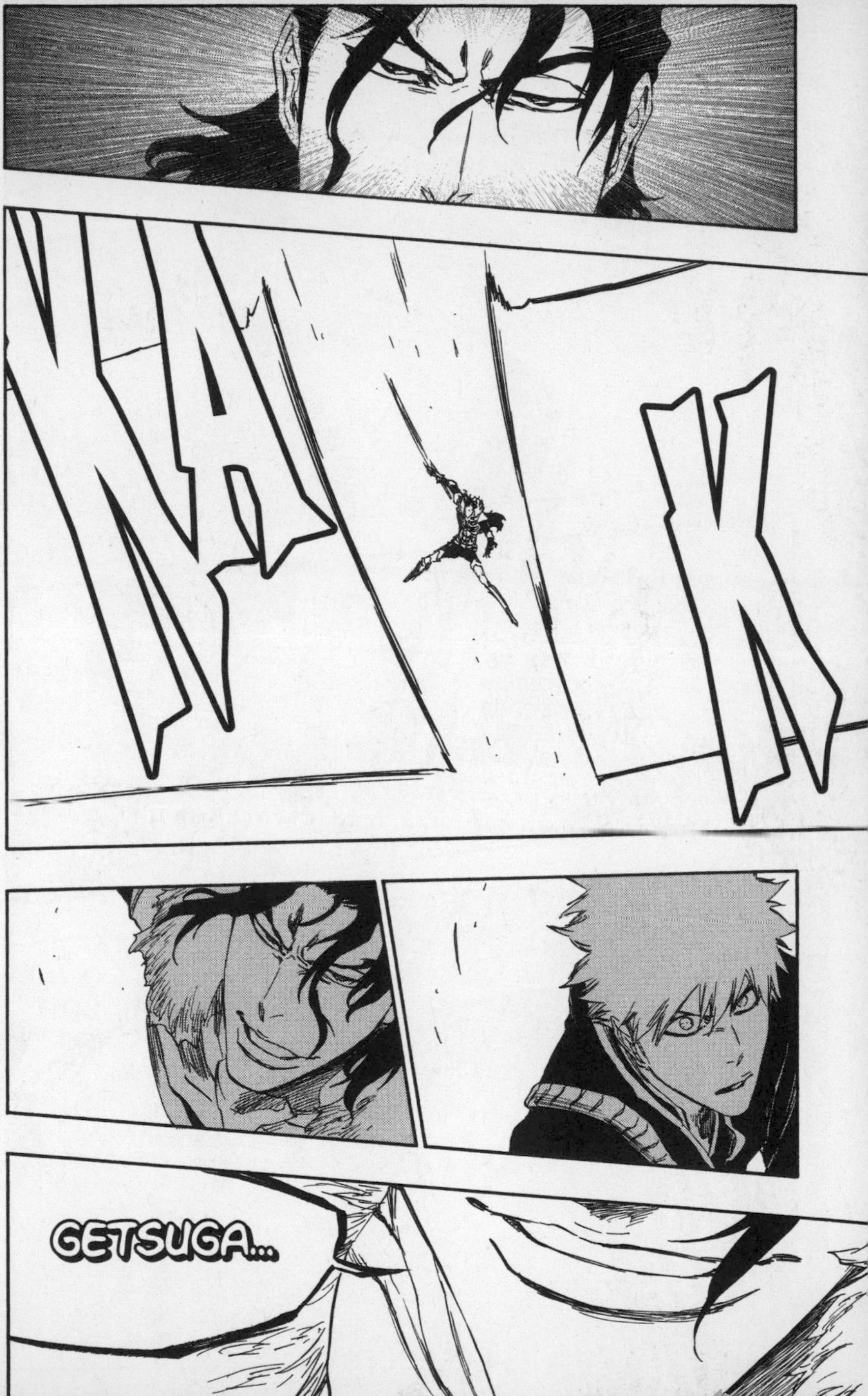
GETSUGA...

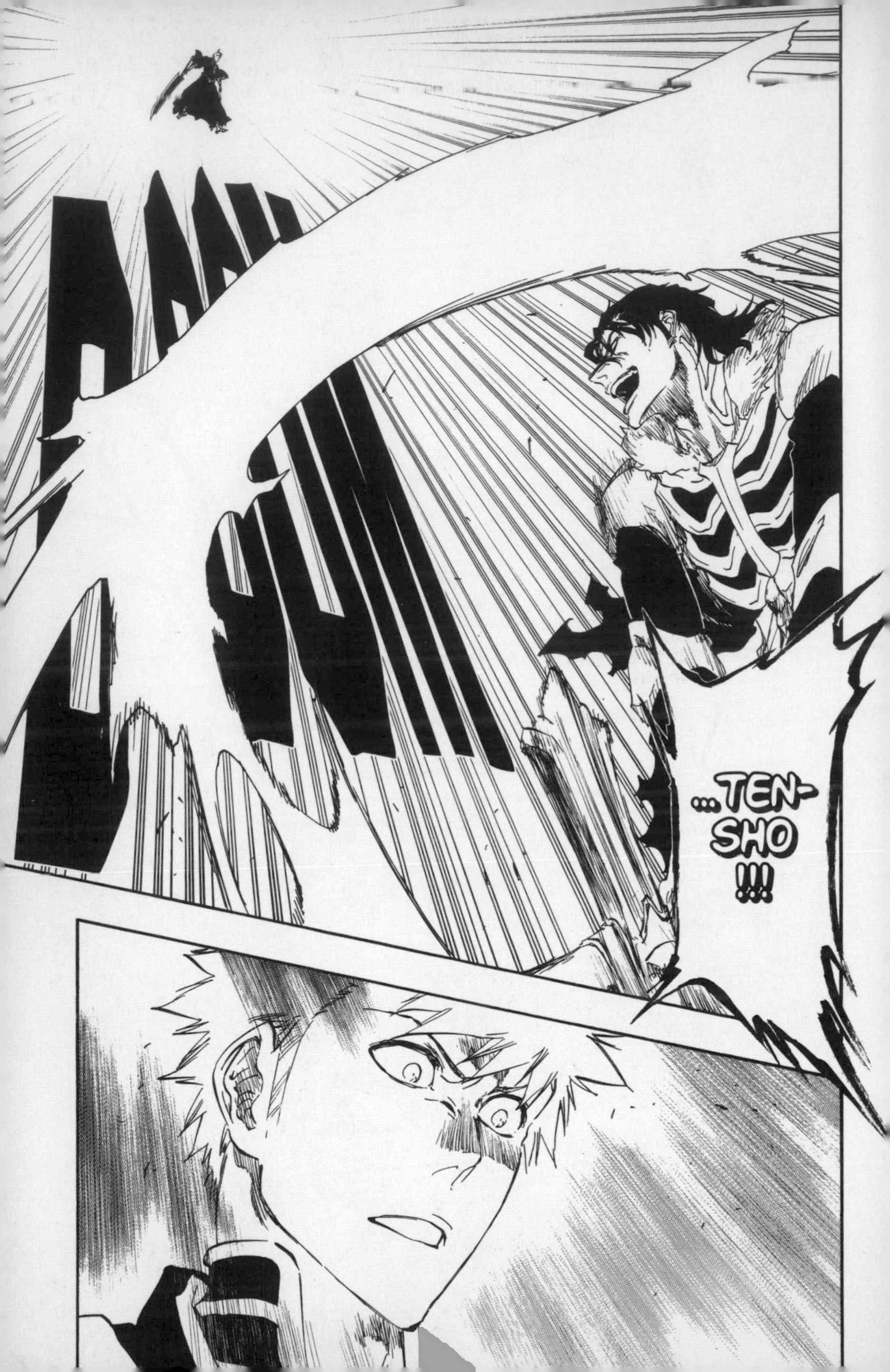
...TEN-SHO !!!

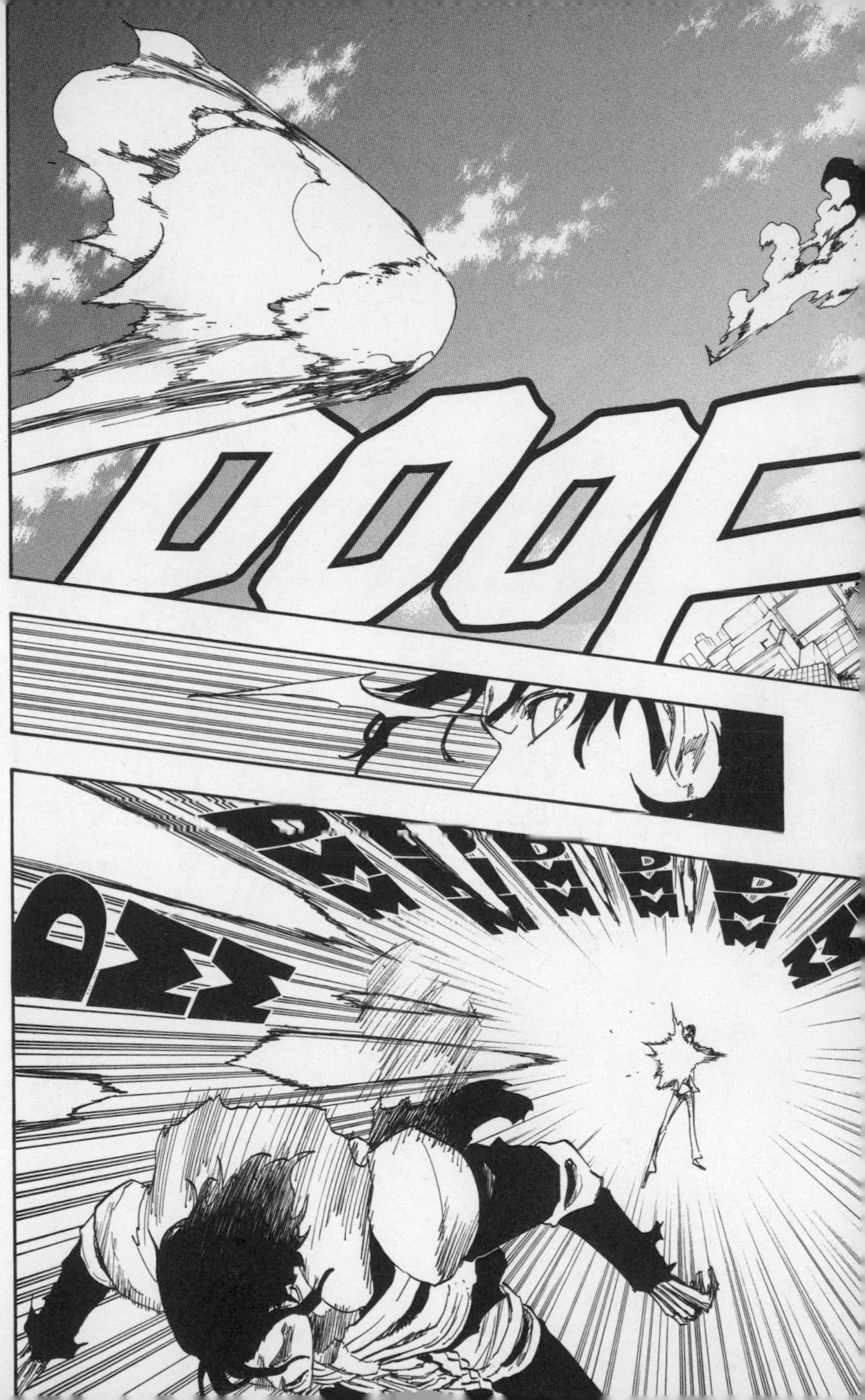
DOOF

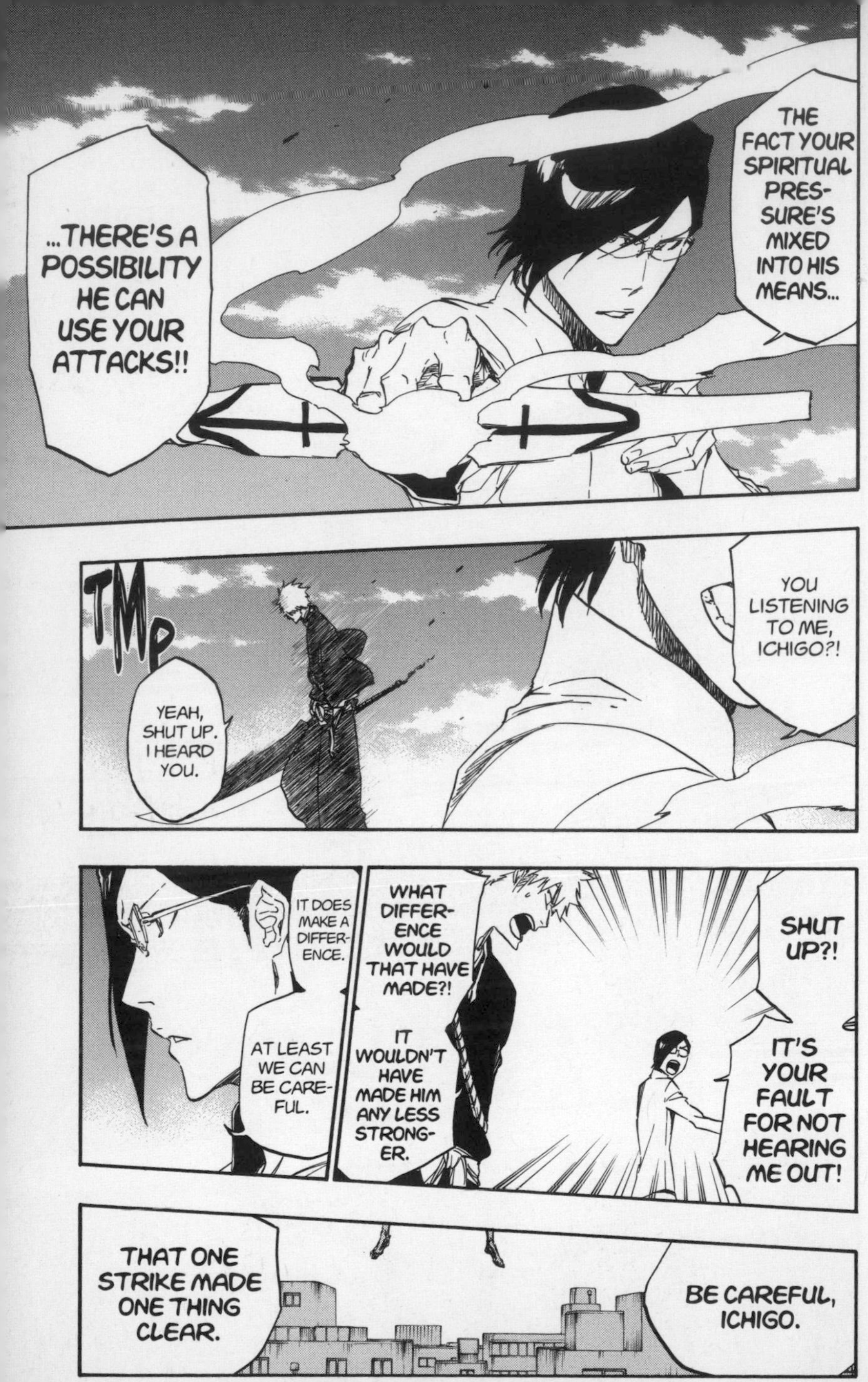
THE FACT YOUR SPIRITUAL PRES-SURE'S MIXED INTO HIS MEANS...
...THERE'S A POSSIBILITY HE CAN USE YOUR ATTACKS!!
YOU LISTENING TO ME, ICHIGO?!
TMP
YEAH, SHUT UP. I HEARD YOU.
SHUT UP?!
IT'S YOUR FAULT FOR NOT HEARING ME OUT!
WHAT DIFFER-ENCE WOULD THAT HAVE MADE?!
IT WOULDN'T HAVE MADE HIM ANY LESS STRONG-ER.
IT DOES MAKE A DIFFER-ENCE.
AT LEAST WE CAN BE CARE-FUL.
BE CAREFUL, ICHIGO.
THAT ONE STRIKE MADE ONE THING CLEAR.

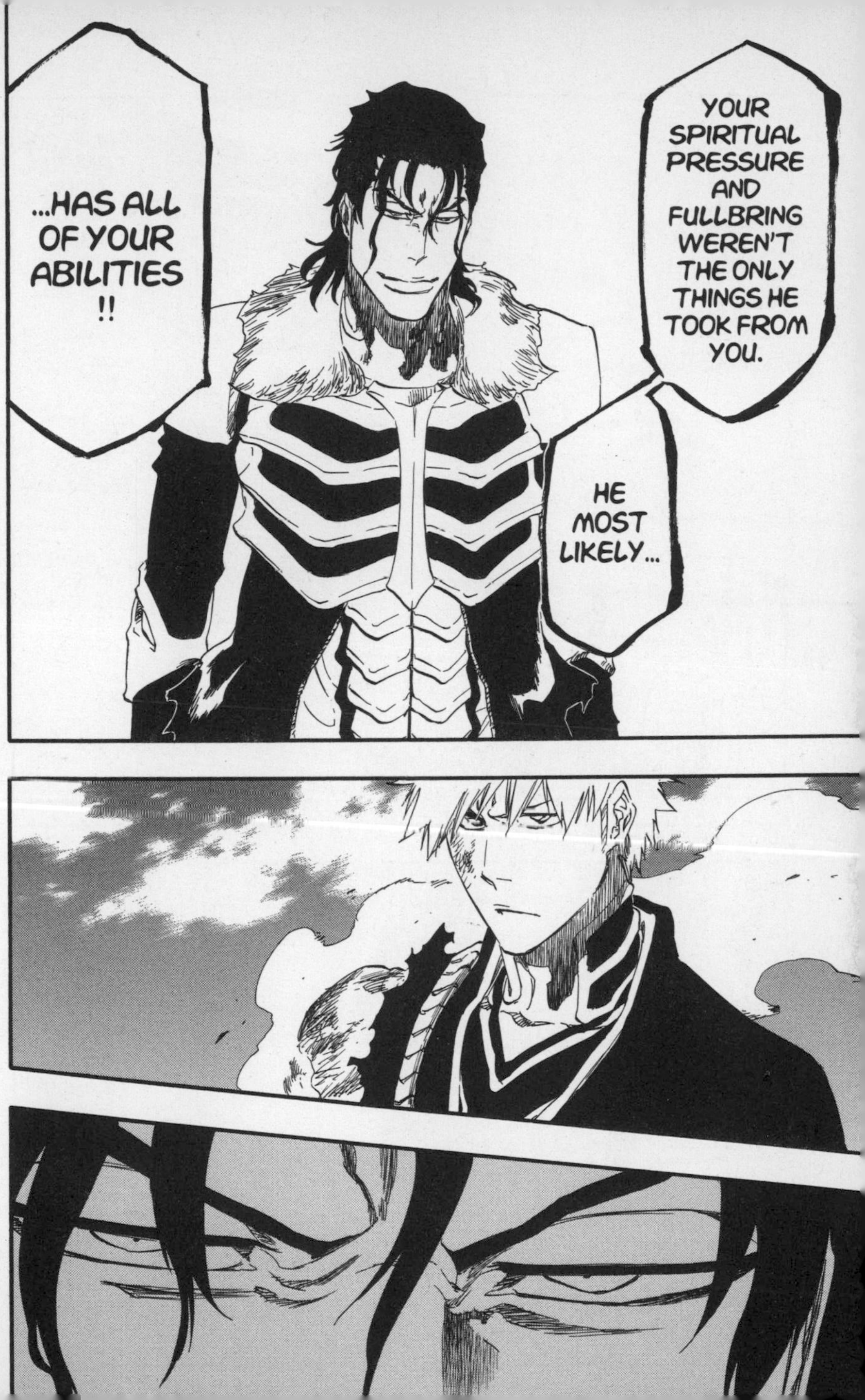
YOUR SPIRITUAL PRESSURE AND FULLBRING WEREN'T THE ONLY THINGS HE TOOK FROM YOU.
HE MOST LIKELY...
...HAS ALL OF YOUR ABILITIES !!

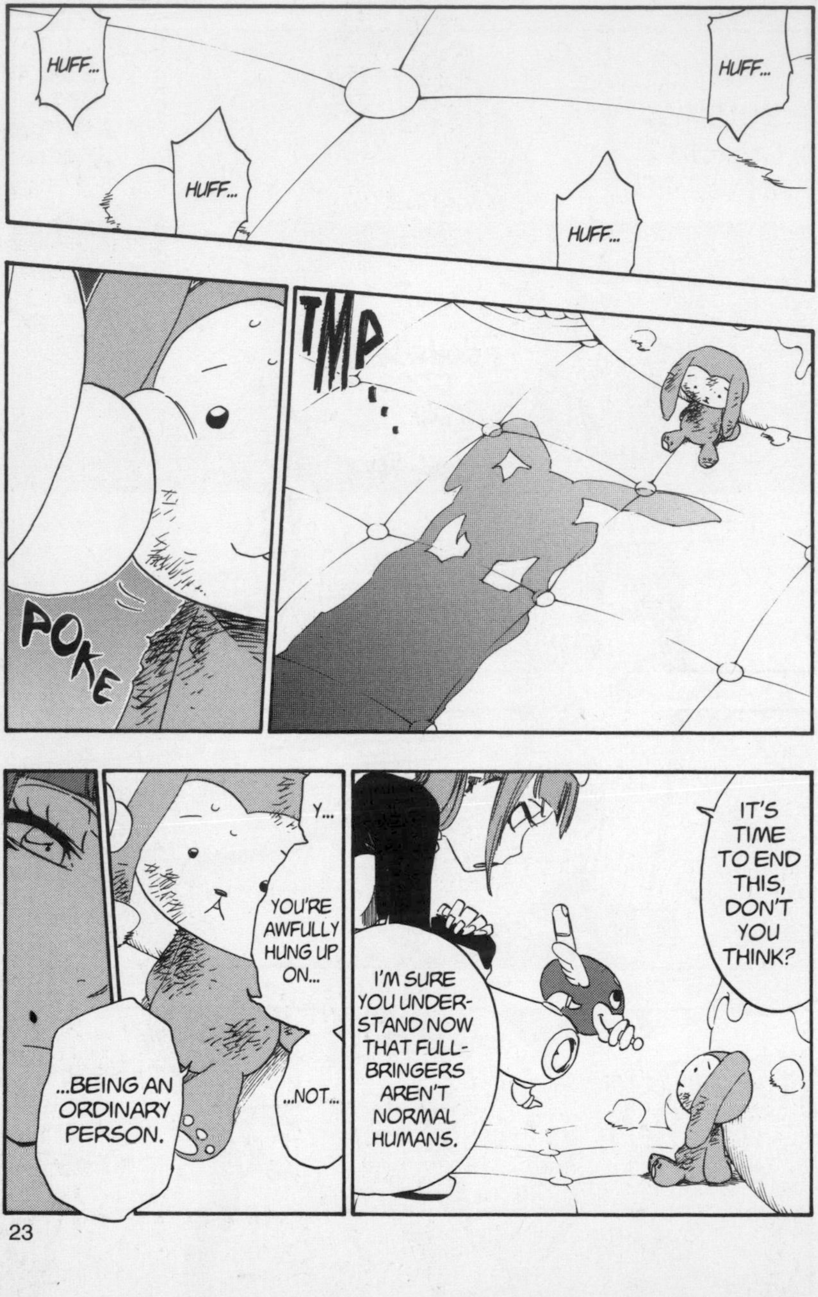

HUFF...
HUFF...
HUFF...
HUFF...
TMP
POKE
IT'S TIME TO END THIS, DON'T YOU THINK?
I'M SURE YOU UNDERSTAND NOW THAT FULLBRINGERS AREN'T NORMAL HUMANS.
Y...
YOU'RE AWFULLY HUNG UP ON...
...NOT...
...BEING AN ORDINARY PERSON.

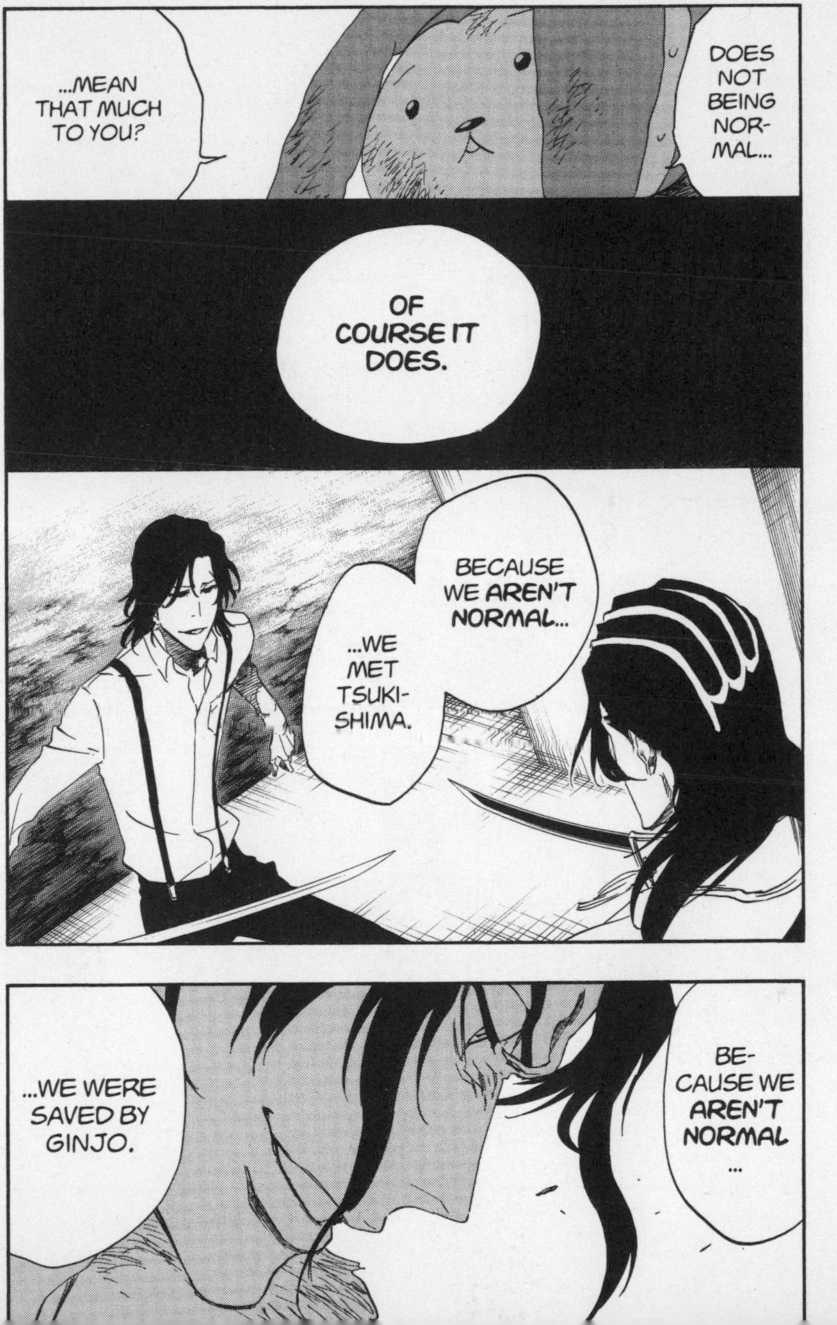
DOES NOT BEING NOR-MAL...
...MEAN THAT MUCH TO YOU?
OF COURSE IT DOES.
BECAUSE WE AREN'T NORMAL...
...WE MET TSUKI-SHIMA.
BE-CAUSE WE AREN'T NORMAL ...
...WE WERE SAVED BY GINJO.

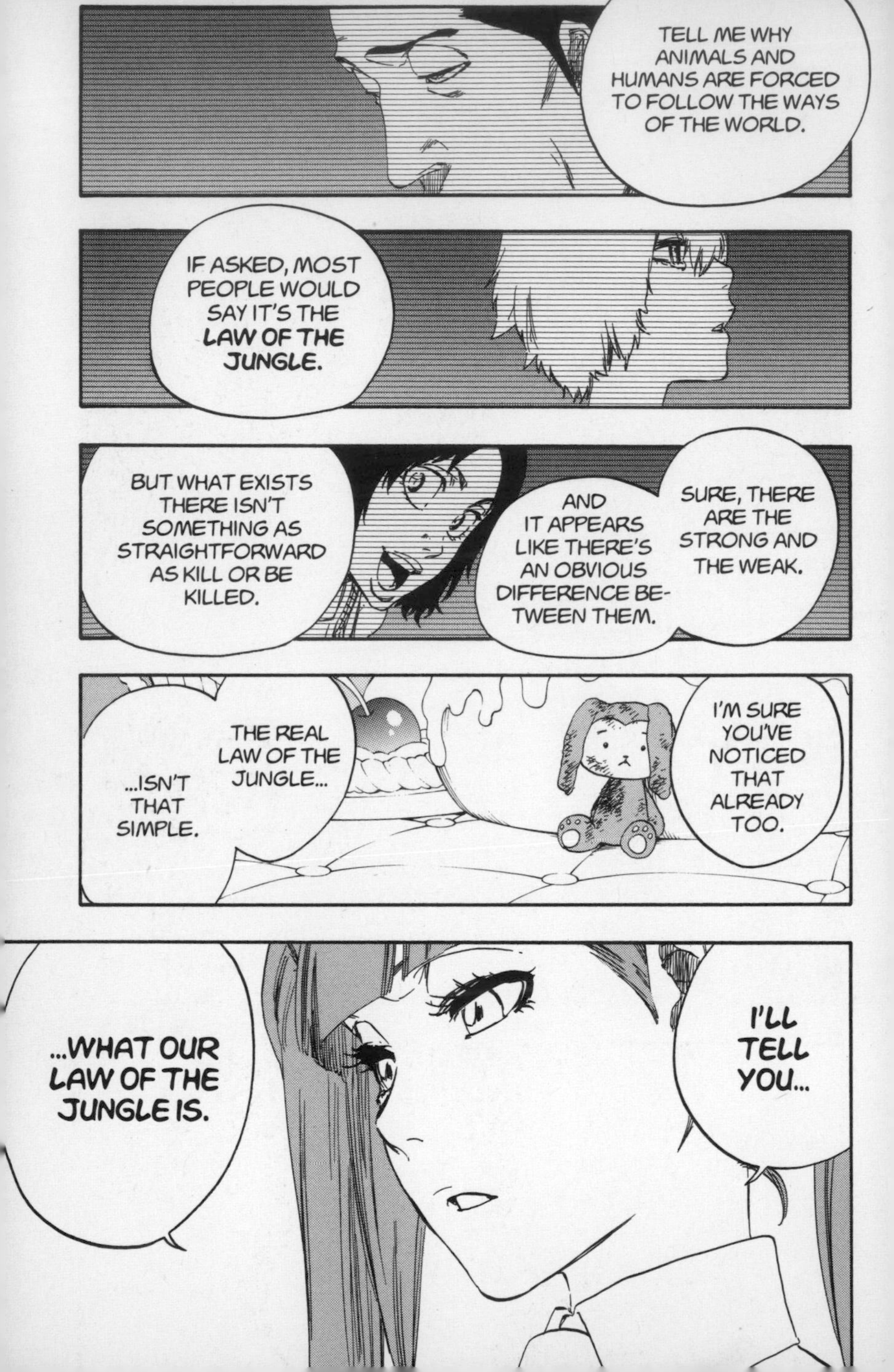
TELL ME WHY ANIMALS AND HUMANS ARE FORCED TO FOLLOW THE WAYS OF THE WORLD.
IF ASKED, MOST PEOPLE WOULD SAY IT'S THE **LAW OF THE JUNGLE.**
SURE, THERE ARE THE STRONG AND THE WEAK.
AND IT APPEARS LIKE THERE'S AN OBVIOUS DIFFERENCE BETWEEN THEM.
BUT WHAT EXISTS THERE ISN'T SOMETHING AS STRAIGHTFORWARD AS KILL OR BE KILLED.
I'M SURE YOU'VE NOTICED THAT ALREADY TOO.
THE REAL LAW OF THE JUNGLE...
...ISN'T THAT SIMPLE.
I'LL TELL YOU...
...WHAT OUR LAW OF THE JUNGLE IS.

We wanna be
predators.

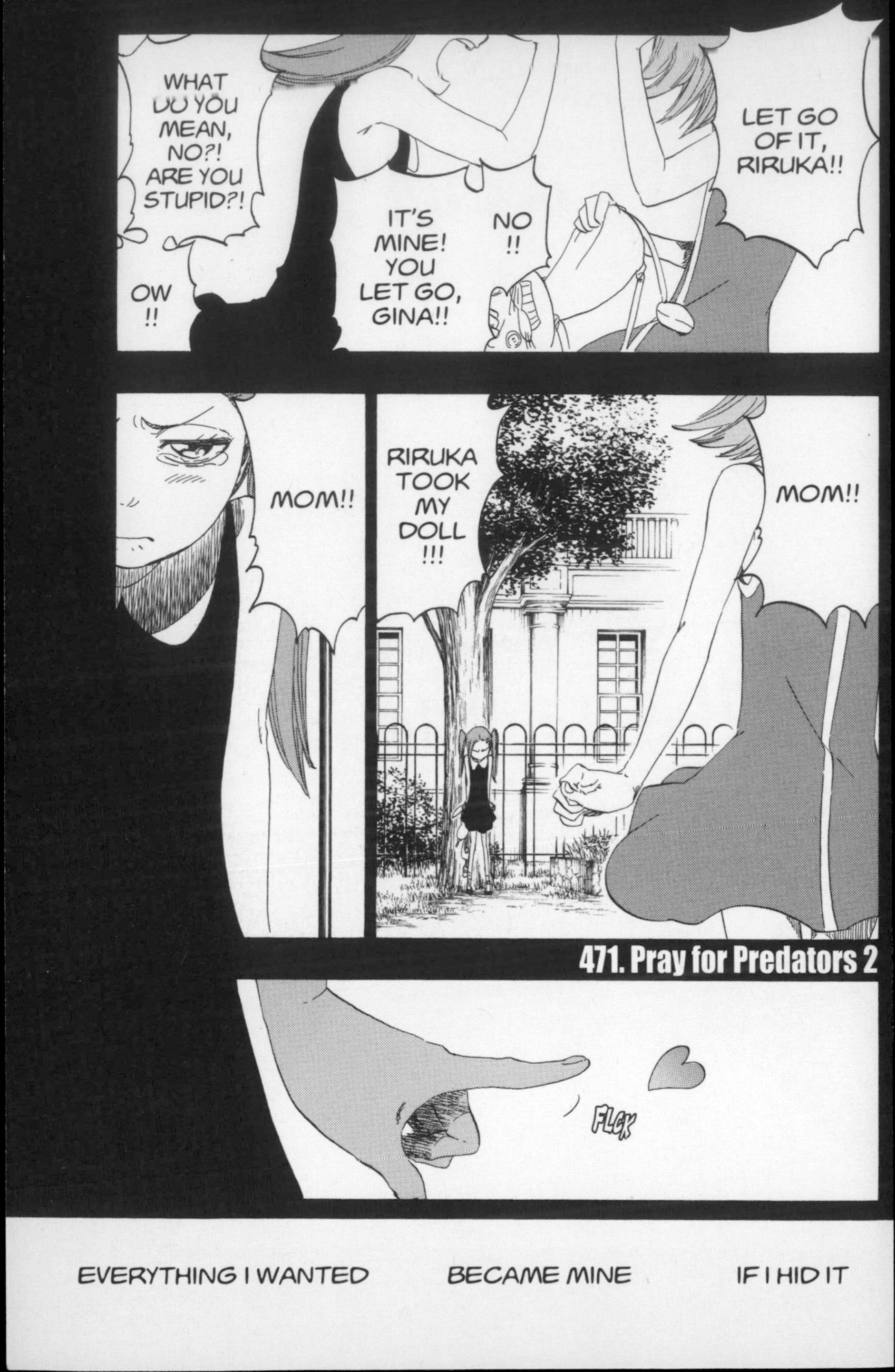
LET GO OF IT, RIRUKA!!
NO !!
IT'S MINE! YOU LET GO, GINA!!
WHAT DO YOU MEAN, NO?! ARE YOU STUPID?!
OW !!
MOM!!
RIRUKA TOOK MY DOLL !!!
MOM!!
471. Pray for Predators 2
FLCK
EVERYTHING I WANTED
BECAME MINE
IF I HID IT

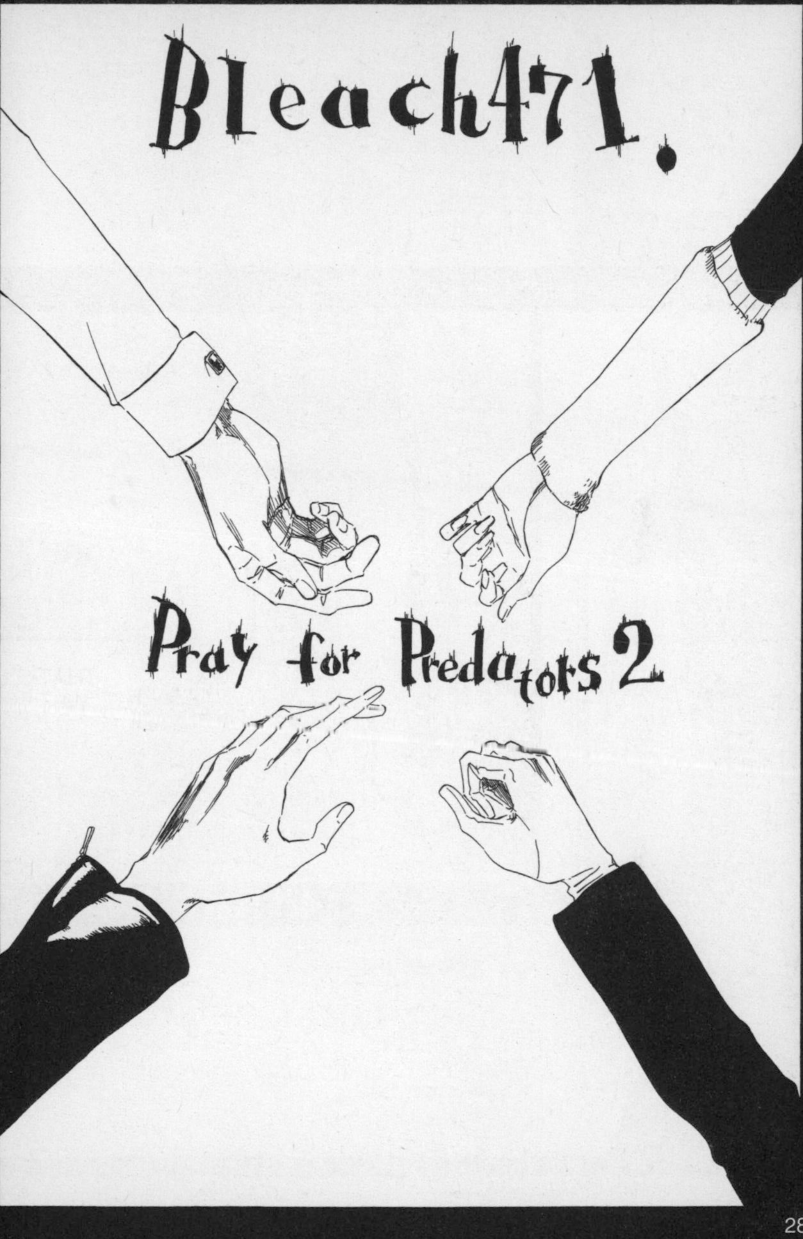
Bleach471.
Pray for Predators 2

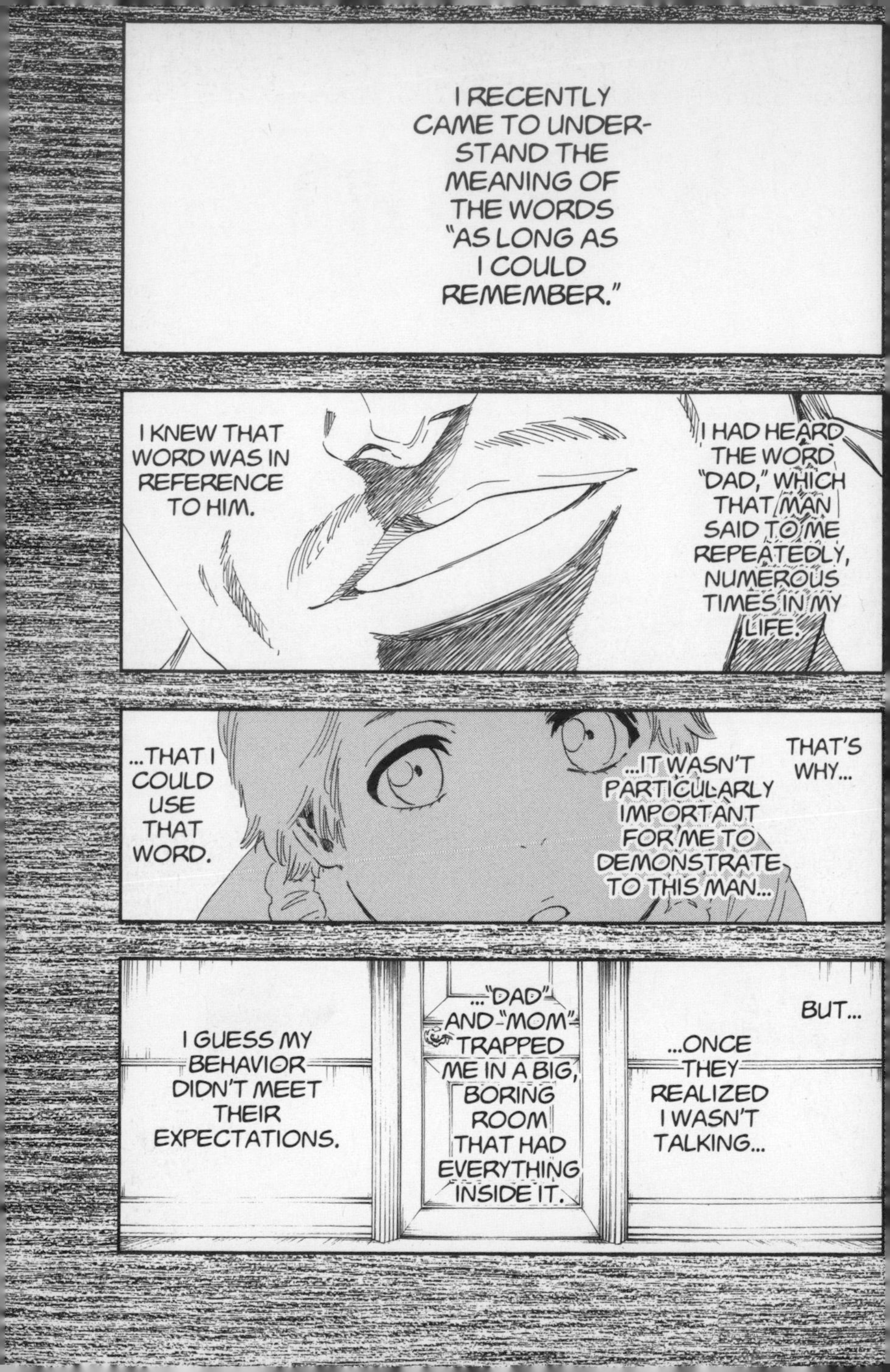
I RECENTLY CAME TO UNDER-STAND THE MEANING OF THE WORDS "AS LONG AS I COULD REMEMBER."
I HAD HEARD THE WORD "DAD," WHICH THAT MAN SAID TO ME REPEATEDLY, NUMEROUS TIMES IN MY LIFE.
I KNEW THAT WORD WAS IN REFERENCE TO HIM.
THAT'S WHY...
...IT WASN'T PARTICULARLY IMPORTANT FOR ME TO DEMONSTRATE TO THIS MAN...
...THAT I COULD USE THAT WORD.
BUT...
...ONCE THEY REALIZED I WASN'T TALKING...
..."DAD" AND "MOM" TRAPPED ME IN A BIG, BORING ROOM THAT HAD EVERYTHING INSIDE IT.
I GUESS MY BEHAVIOR DIDN'T MEET THEIR EXPECTATIONS.

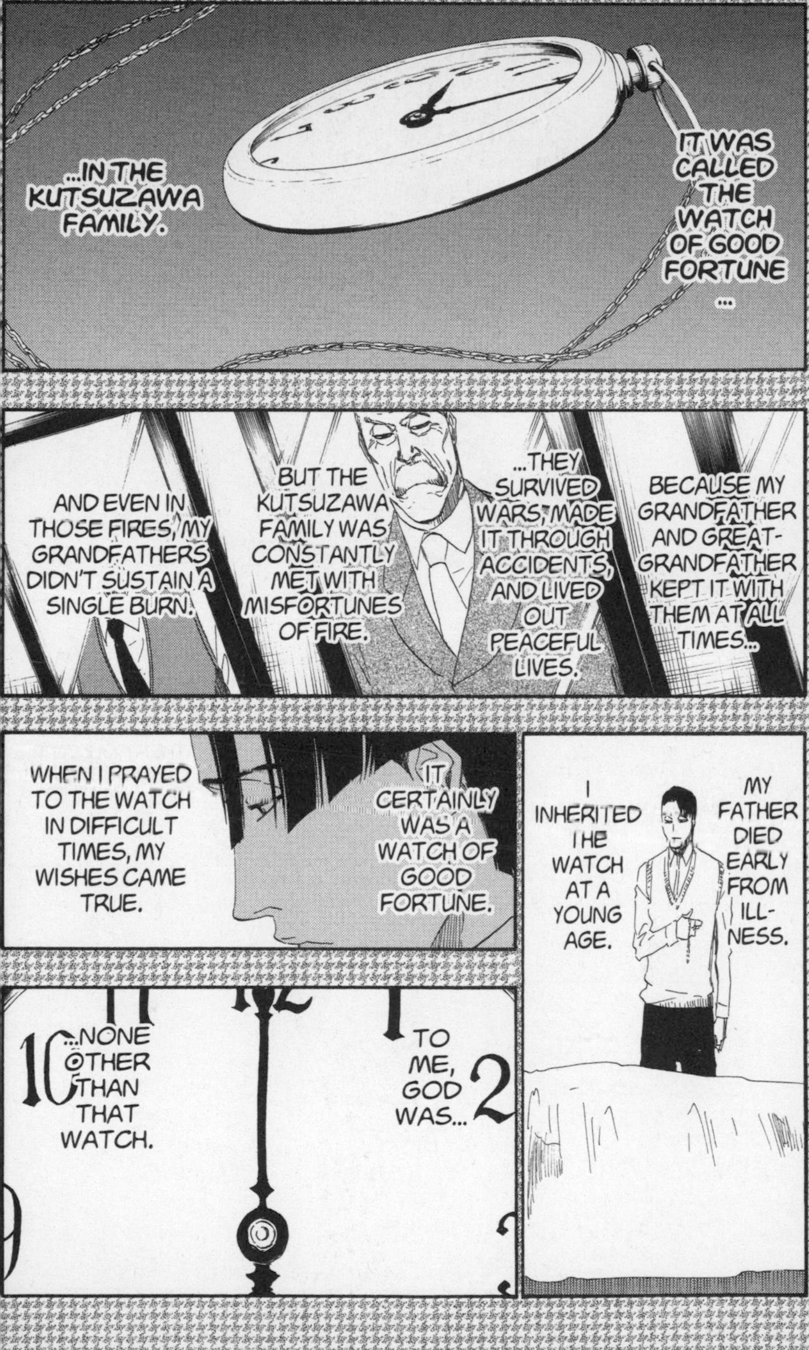
IT WAS CALLED THE WATCH OF GOOD FORTUNE...
...IN THE KUTSUZAWA FAMILY.
BECAUSE MY GRANDFATHER AND GREAT-GRANDFATHER KEPT IT WITH THEM AT ALL TIMES...
...THEY SURVIVED WARS, MADE IT THROUGH ACCIDENTS, AND LIVED OUT PEACEFUL LIVES.
BUT THE KUTSUZAWA FAMILY WAS CONSTANTLY MET WITH MISFORTUNES OF FIRE.
AND EVEN IN THOSE FIRES, MY GRANDFATHERS DIDN'T SUSTAIN A SINGLE BURN.
MY FATHER DIED EARLY FROM ILL-NESS.
I INHERITED THE WATCH AT A YOUNG AGE.
IT CERTAINLY WAS A WATCH OF GOOD FORTUNE.
WHEN I PRAYED TO THE WATCH IN DIFFICULT TIMES, MY WISHES CAME TRUE.
TO ME, GOD WAS...
...NONE OTHER THAN THAT WATCH.

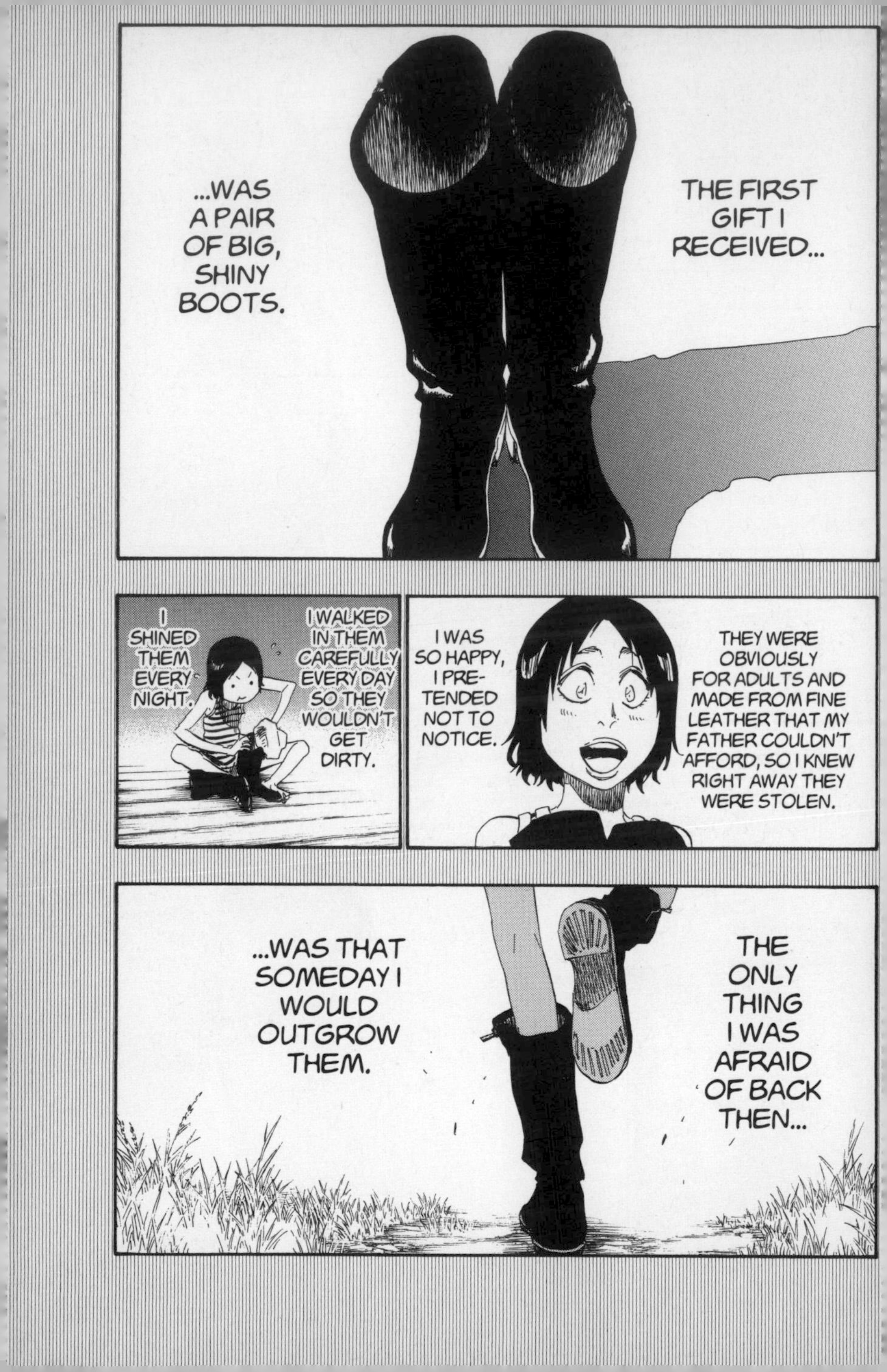
THE FIRST GIFT I RECEIVED...
...WAS A PAIR OF BIG, SHINY BOOTS.
THEY WERE OBVIOUSLY FOR ADULTS AND MADE FROM FINE LEATHER THAT MY FATHER COULDN'T AFFORD, SO I KNEW RIGHT AWAY THEY WERE STOLEN.
I WAS SO HAPPY, I PRE-TENDED NOT TO NOTICE.
I WALKED IN THEM CAREFULLY EVERY DAY SO THEY WOULDN'T GET DIRTY.
I SHINED THEM EVERY NIGHT.
THE ONLY THING I WAS AFRAID OF BACK THEN...
...WAS THAT SOMEDAY I WOULD OUTGROW THEM.

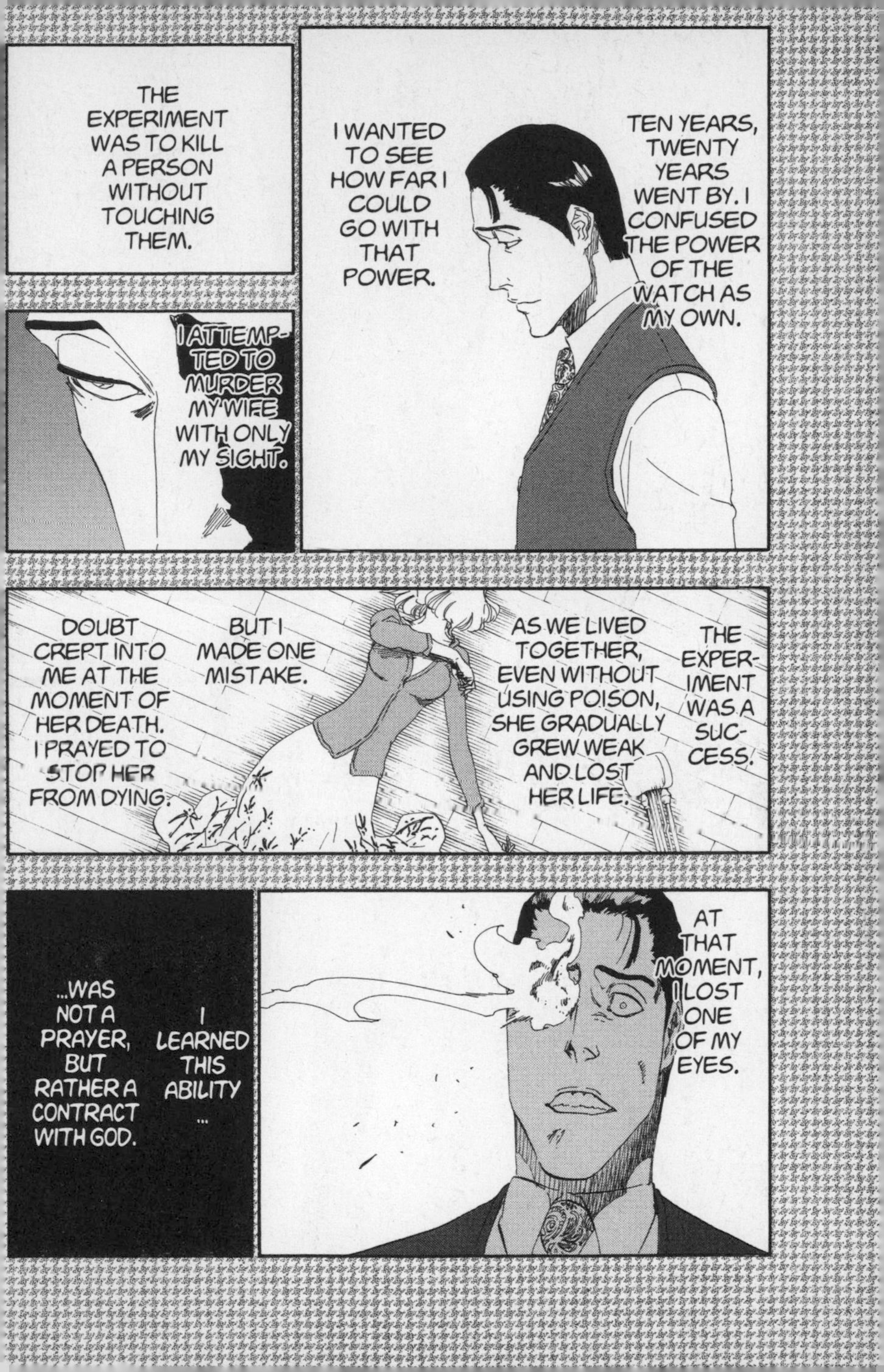
TEN YEARS, TWENTY YEARS WENT BY. I CONFUSED THE POWER OF THE WATCH AS MY OWN.
I WANTED TO SEE HOW FAR I COULD GO WITH THAT POWER.
THE EXPERIMENT WAS TO KILL A PERSON WITHOUT TOUCHING THEM.
I ATTEMPTED TO MURDER MY WIFE WITH ONLY MY SIGHT.
THE EXPERIMENT WAS A SUCCESS.
AS WE LIVED TOGETHER, EVEN WITHOUT USING POISON, SHE GRADUALLY GREW WEAK AND LOST HER LIFE.
BUT I MADE ONE MISTAKE.
DOUBT CREPT INTO ME AT THE MOMENT OF HER DEATH. I PRAYED TO STOP HER FROM DYING.
AT THAT MOMENT, I LOST ONE OF MY EYES.
I LEARNED THIS ABILITY...
...WAS NOT A PRAYER, BUT RATHER A CONTRACT WITH GOD.

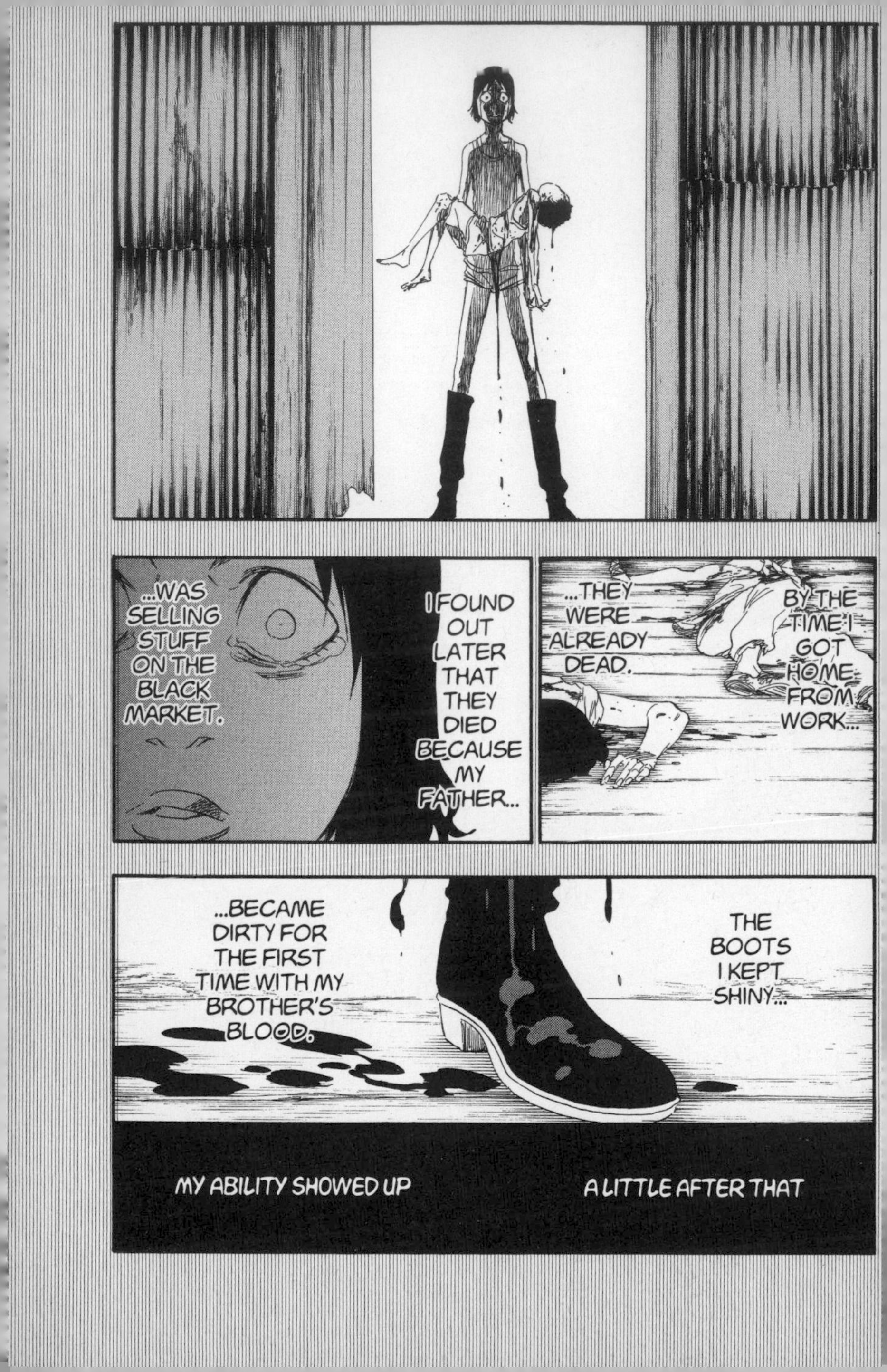
BY THE TIME I GOT HOME FROM WORK...
...THEY WERE ALREADY DEAD.
I FOUND OUT LATER THAT THEY DIED BECAUSE MY FATHER...
...WAS SELLING STUFF ON THE BLACK MARKET.
THE BOOTS I KEPT SHINY...
...BECAME DIRTY FOR THE FIRST TIME WITH MY BROTHER'S BLOOD.
MY ABILITY SHOWED UP
A LITTLE AFTER THAT

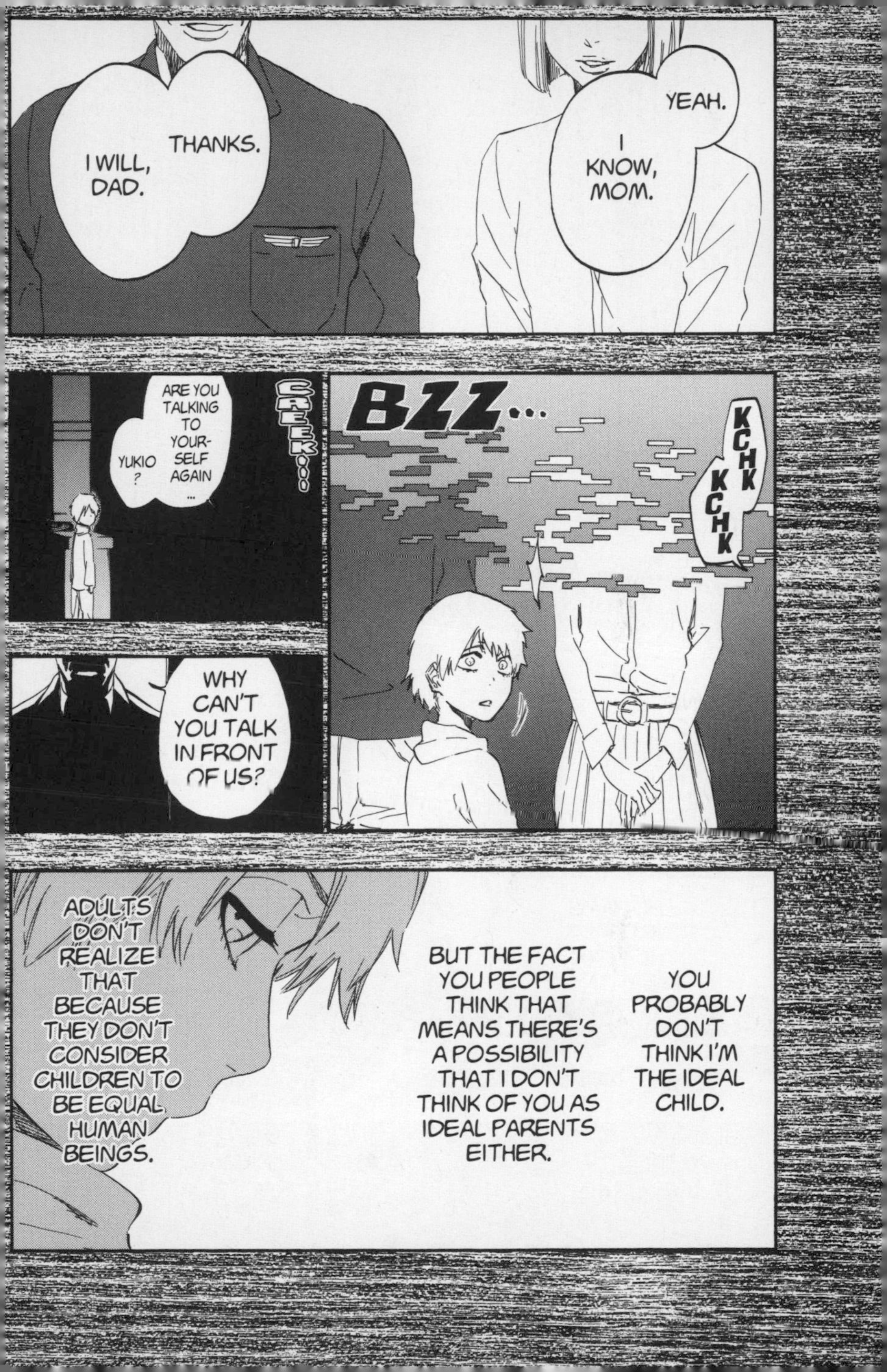
YEAH.
I KNOW, MOM.
THANKS.
I WILL, DAD.
BZZ...
KCHK KCHK
CREEK...
ARE YOU TALKING TO YOURSELF AGAIN...
YUKIO?
WHY CAN'T YOU TALK IN FRONT OF US?
YOU PROBABLY DON'T THINK I'M THE IDEAL CHILD.
BUT THE FACT YOU PEOPLE THINK THAT MEANS THERE'S A POSSIBILITY THAT I DON'T THINK OF YOU AS IDEAL PARENTS EITHER.
ADULTS DON'T REALIZE THAT BECAUSE THEY DON'T CONSIDER CHILDREN TO BE EQUAL HUMAN BEINGS.

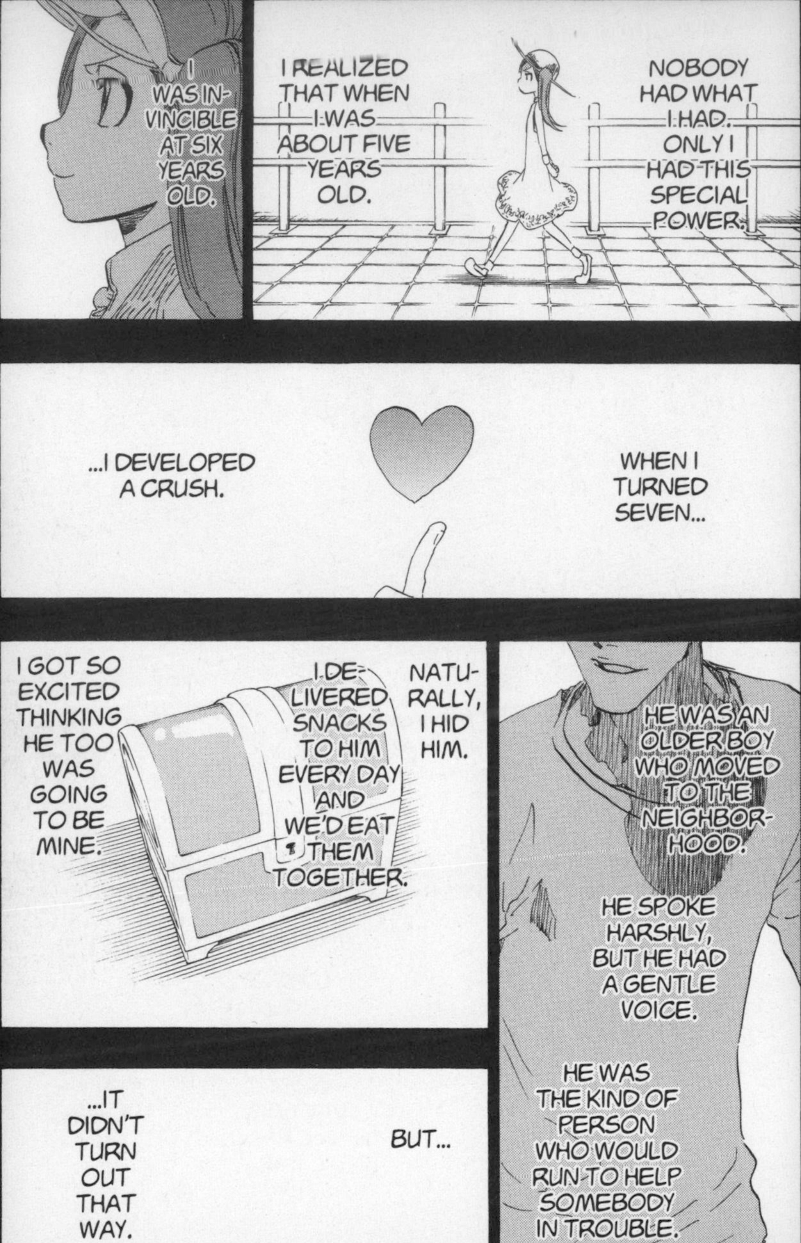
NOBODY HAD WHAT I HAD. ONLY I HAD THIS SPECIAL POWER.
I REALIZED THAT WHEN I WAS ABOUT FIVE YEARS OLD.
I WAS INVINCIBLE AT SIX YEARS OLD.
WHEN I TURNED SEVEN...
...I DEVELOPED A CRUSH.
HE WAS AN OLDER BOY WHO MOVED TO THE NEIGHBORHOOD.
HE SPOKE HARSHLY, BUT HE HAD A GENTLE VOICE.
HE WAS THE KIND OF PERSON WHO WOULD RUN TO HELP SOMEBODY IN TROUBLE.
NATURALLY, I HID HIM.
I DELIVERED SNACKS TO HIM EVERY DAY AND WE'D EAT THEM TOGETHER.
I GOT SO EXCITED THINKING HE TOO WAS GOING TO BE MINE.
BUT...
...IT DIDN'T TURN OUT THAT WAY.

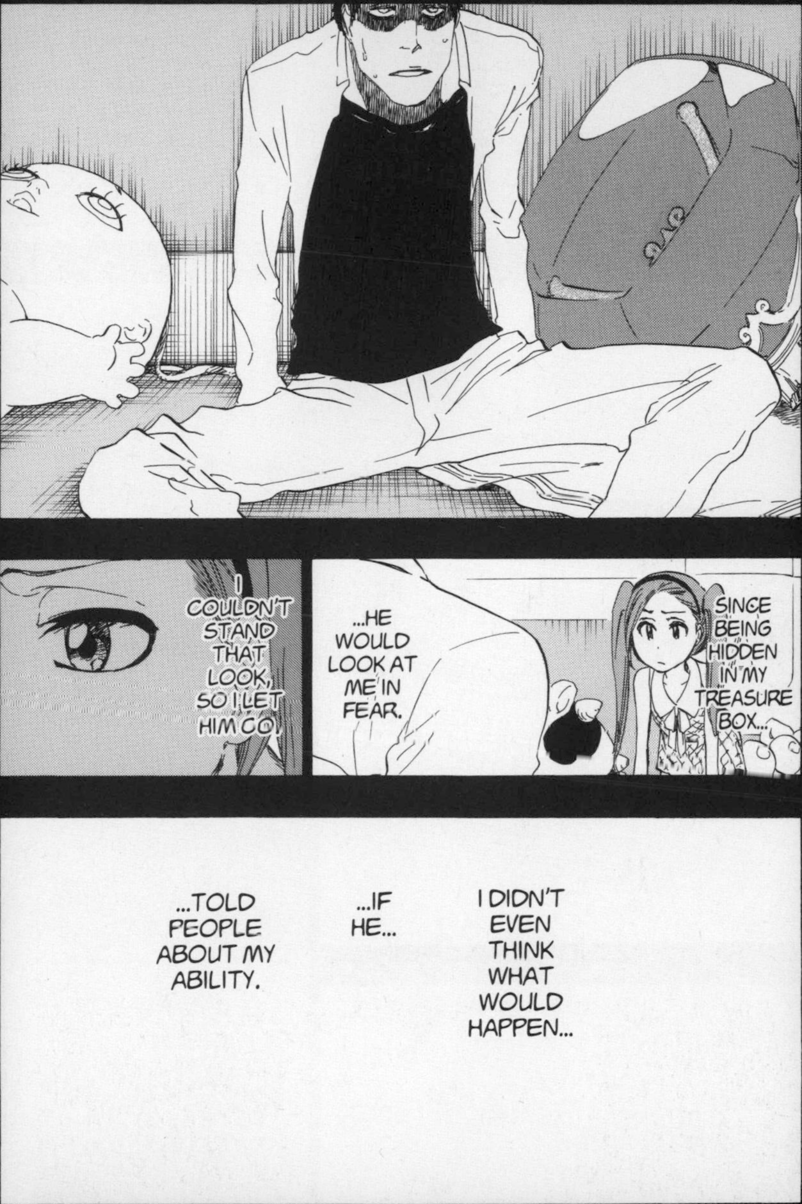
SINCE BEING HIDDEN IN MY TREASURE BOX...
...HE WOULD LOOK AT ME IN FEAR.
I COULDN'T STAND THAT LOOK, SO I LET HIM GO.
I DIDN'T EVEN THINK WHAT WOULD HAPPEN...
...IF HE...
...TOLD PEOPLE ABOUT MY ABILITY.

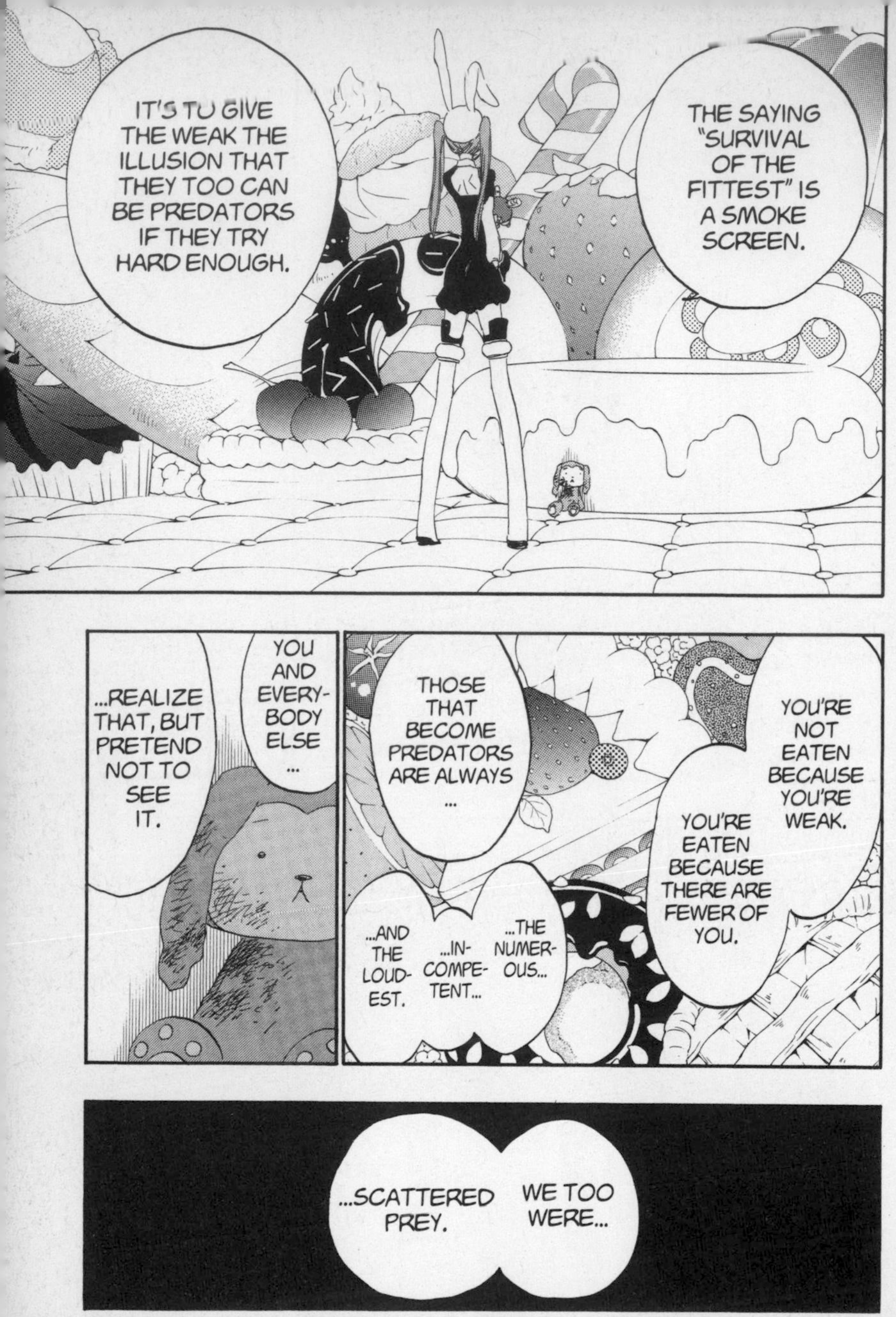
THE SAYING "SURVIVAL OF THE FITTEST" IS A SMOKE SCREEN.
IT'S TO GIVE THE WEAK THE ILLUSION THAT THEY TOO CAN BE PREDATORS IF THEY TRY HARD ENOUGH.
YOU'RE NOT EATEN BECAUSE YOU'RE WEAK.
YOU'RE EATEN BECAUSE THERE ARE FEWER OF YOU.
THOSE THAT BECOME PREDATORS ARE ALWAYS ...
...THE NUMER-OUS...
...IN-COMPE-TENT...
...AND THE LOUD-EST.
YOU AND EVERY-BODY ELSE ...
...REALIZE THAT, BUT PRETEND NOT TO SEE IT.
WE TOO WERE...
...SCATTERED PREY.

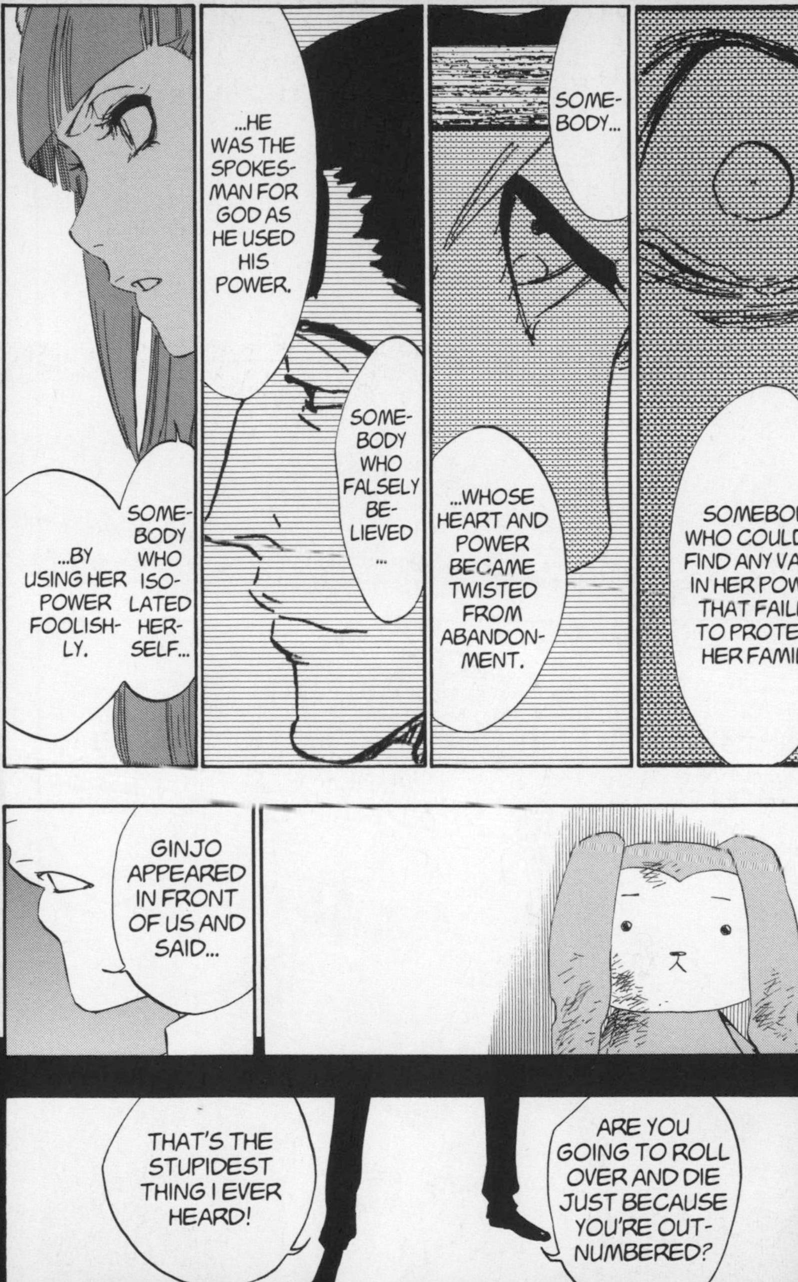
SOMEBODY WHO COULDN'T FIND ANY VALUE IN HER POWER THAT FAILED TO PROTECT HER FAMILY.
SOMEBODY...
...WHOSE HEART AND POWER BECAME TWISTED FROM ABANDONMENT.
SOMEBODY WHO FALSELY BELIEVED...
...HE WAS THE SPOKESMAN FOR GOD AS HE USED HIS POWER.
SOMEBODY WHO ISOLATED HERSELF...
...BY USING HER POWER FOOLISHLY.
GINJO APPEARED IN FRONT OF US AND SAID...
ARE YOU GOING TO ROLL OVER AND DIE JUST BECAUSE YOU'RE OUTNUMBERED?
THAT'S THE STUPIDEST THING I EVER HEARD!

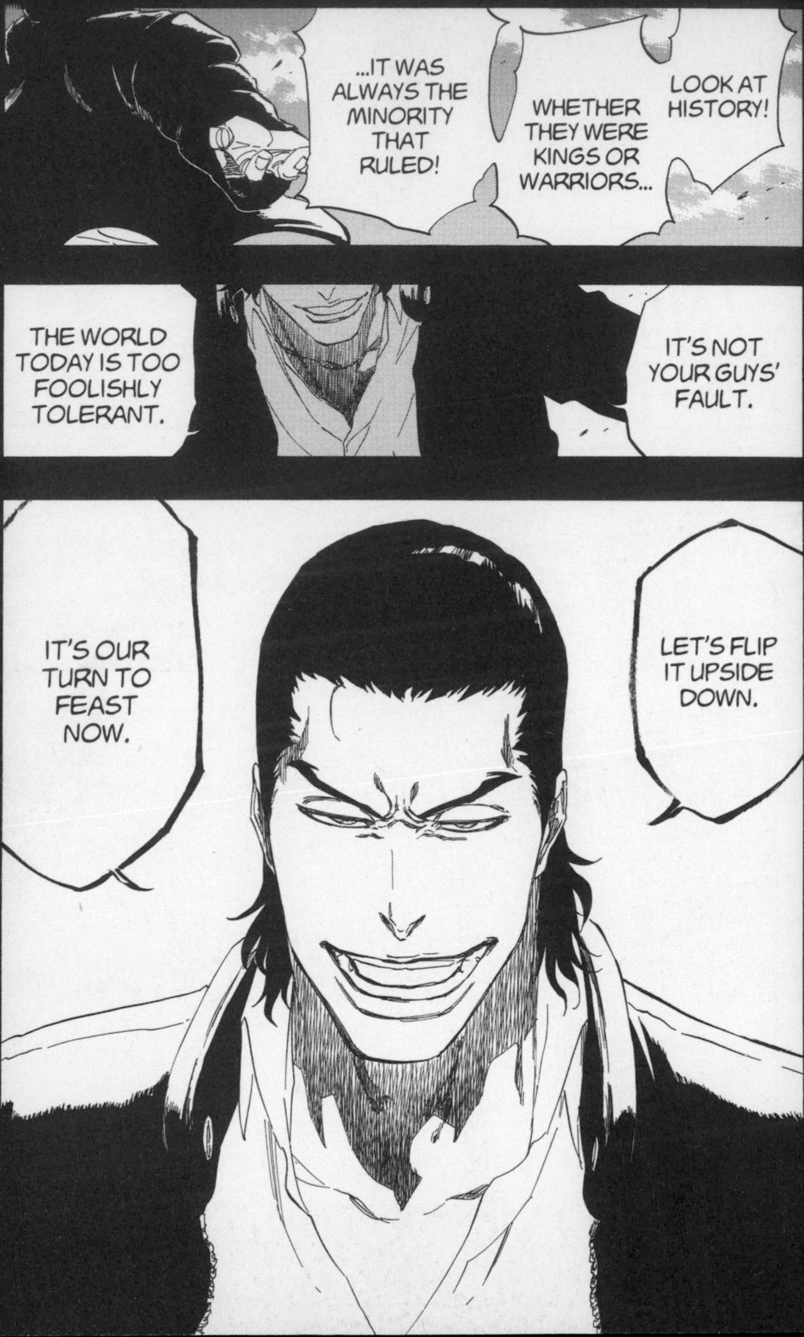
LOOK AT HISTORY!
WHETHER THEY WERE KINGS OR WARRIORS...
...IT WAS ALWAYS THE MINORITY THAT RULED!
IT'S NOT YOUR GUYS' FAULT.
THE WORLD TODAY IS TOO FOOLISHLY TOLERANT.
LET'S FLIP IT UPSIDE DOWN.
IT'S OUR TURN TO FEAST NOW.

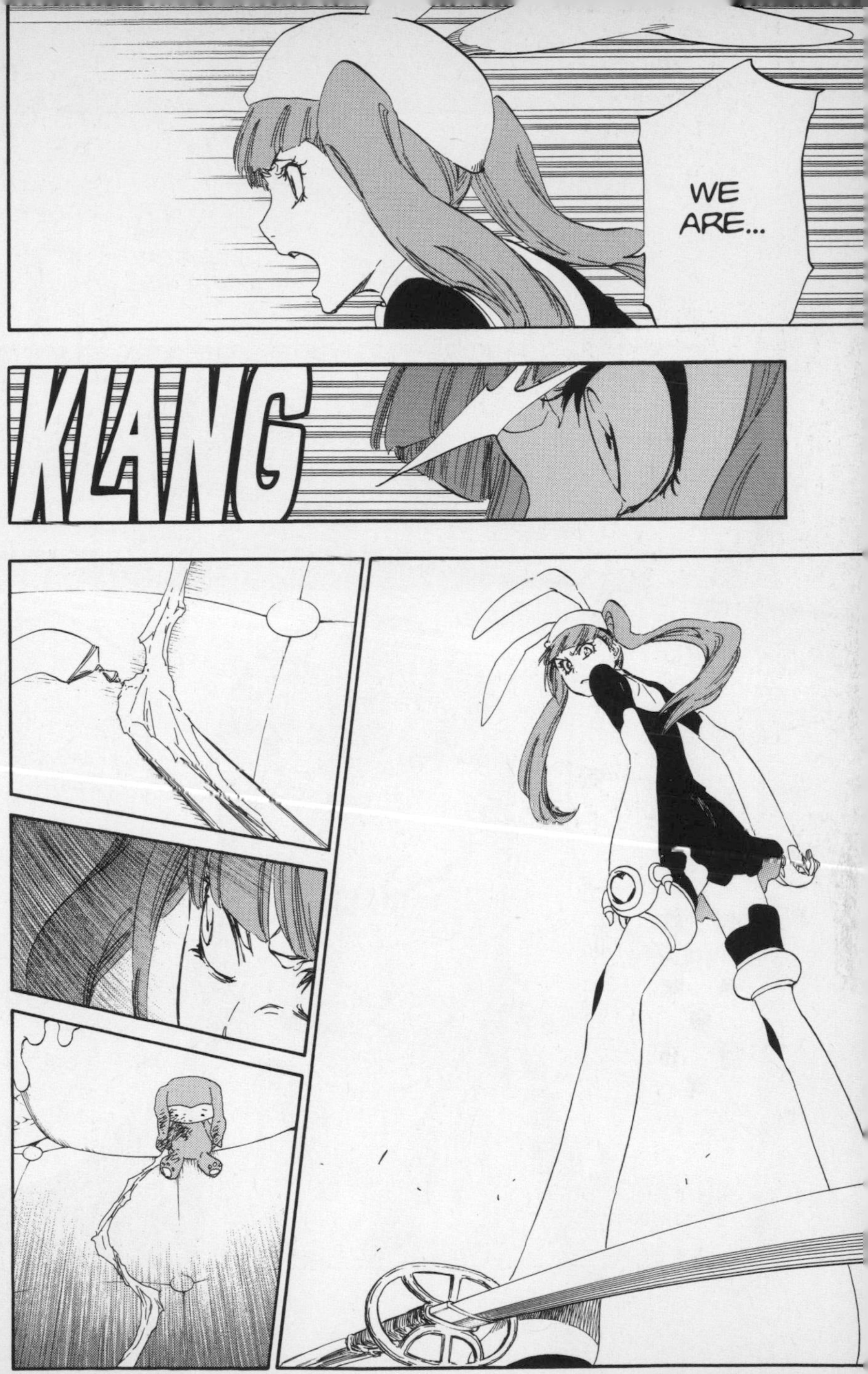
WE ARE...
KLANG

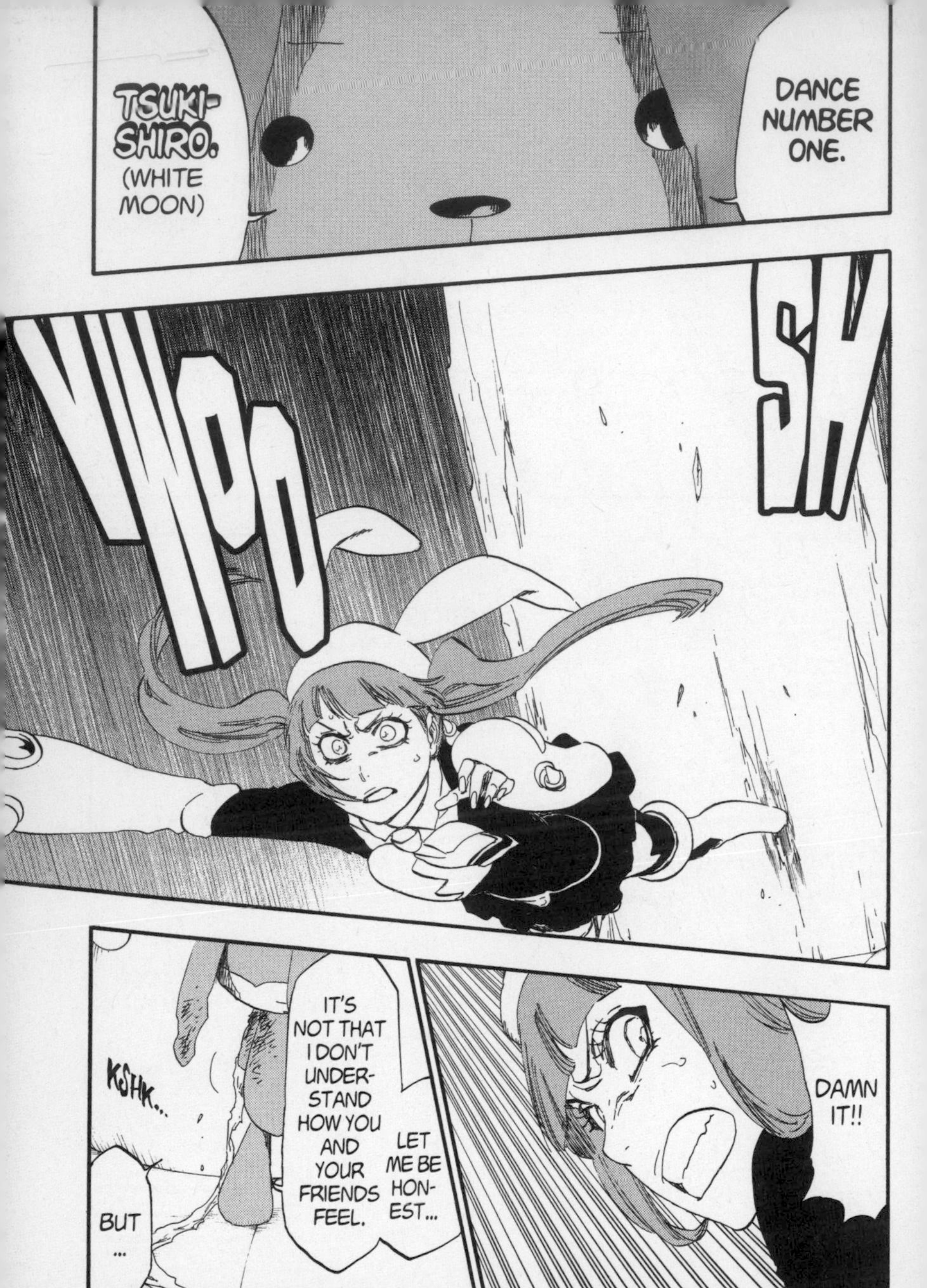
DANCE NUMBER ONE.
TSUKI-SHIRO.
(WHITE MOON)
SH
DAMN IT!!
LET ME BE HON-EST...
IT'S NOT THAT I DON'T UNDER-STAND HOW YOU AND YOUR FRIENDS FEEL.
KSHK...
BUT ...

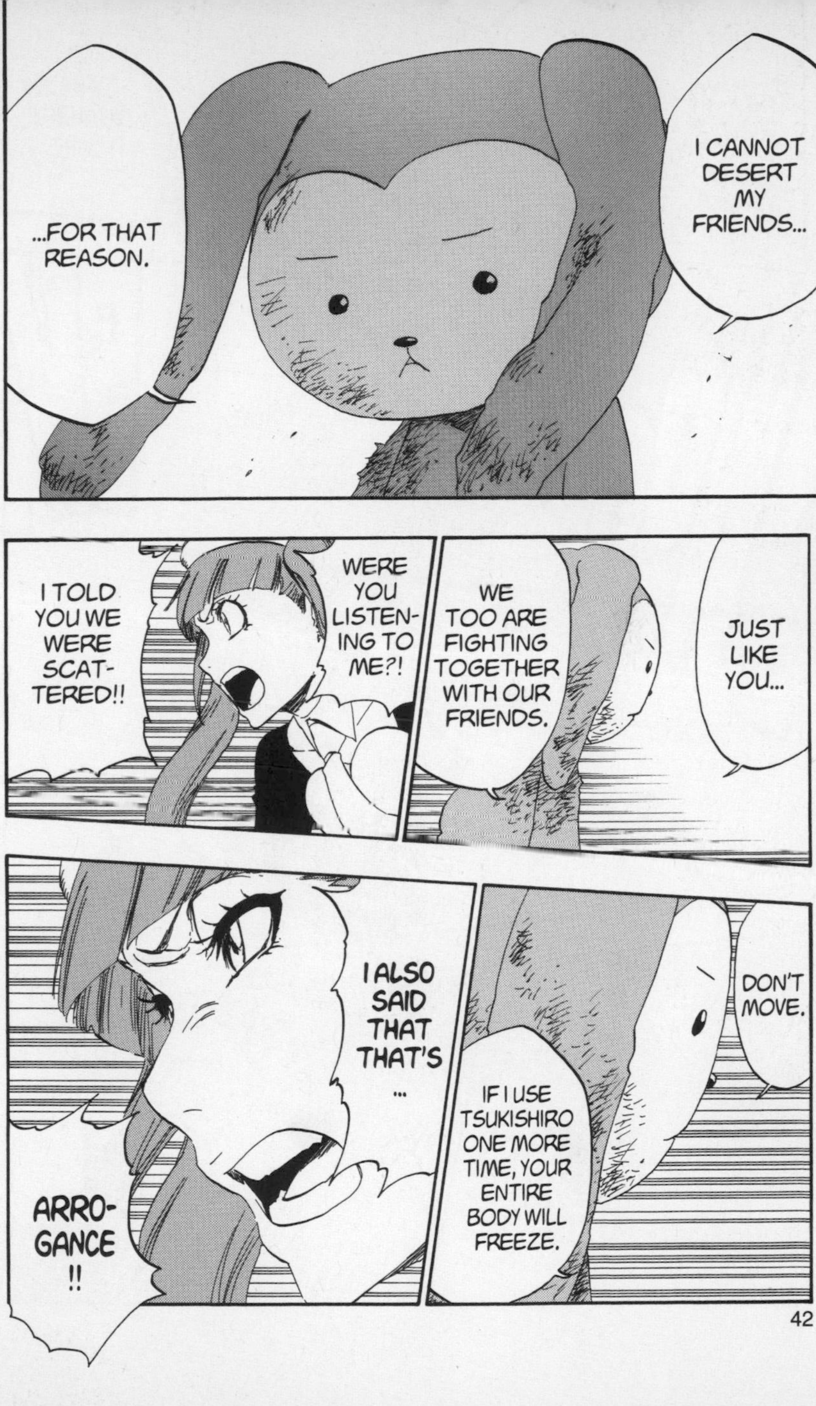
I CANNOT DESERT MY FRIENDS...
...FOR THAT REASON.
JUST LIKE YOU...
WE TOO ARE FIGHTING TOGETHER WITH OUR FRIENDS.
WERE YOU LISTENING TO ME?!
I TOLD YOU WE WERE SCATTERED!!
DON'T MOVE.
IF I USE TSUKISHIRO ONE MORE TIME, YOUR ENTIRE BODY WILL FREEZE.
I ALSO SAID THAT THAT'S ...
ARROGANCE!!

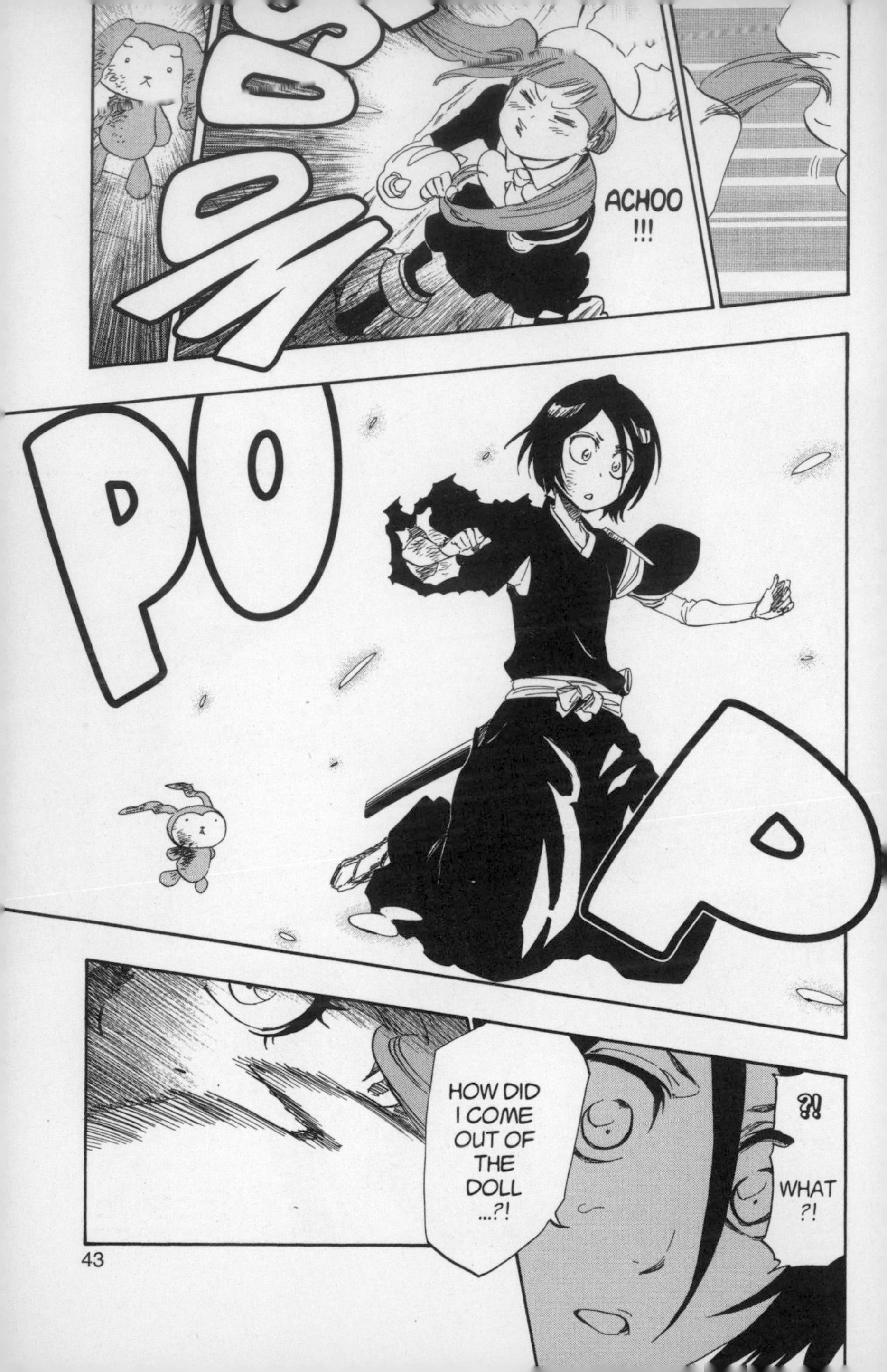
ACHOO !!!
POP
?!
WHAT ?!
HOW DID I COME OUT OF THE DOLL ...?!

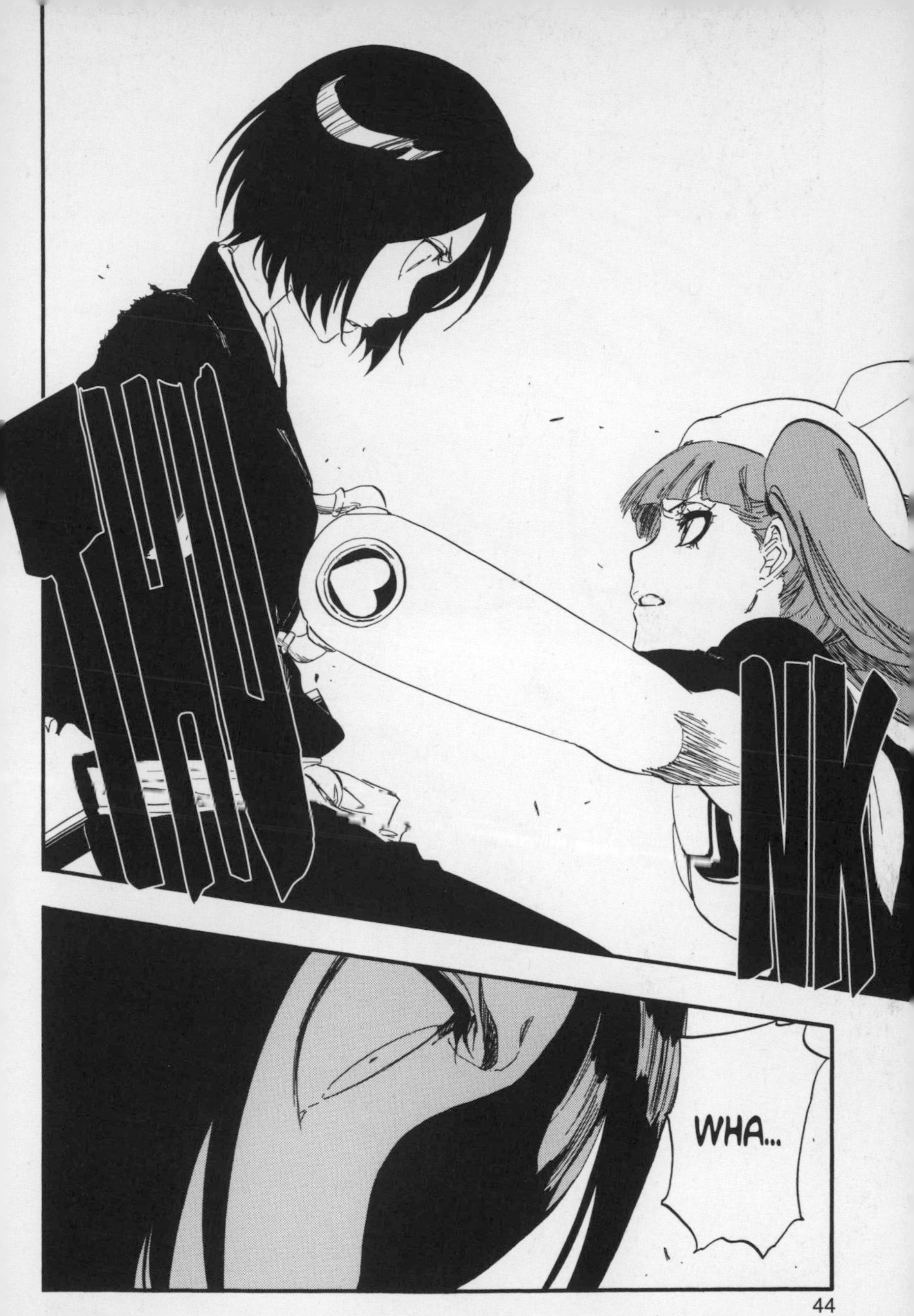
WHA...

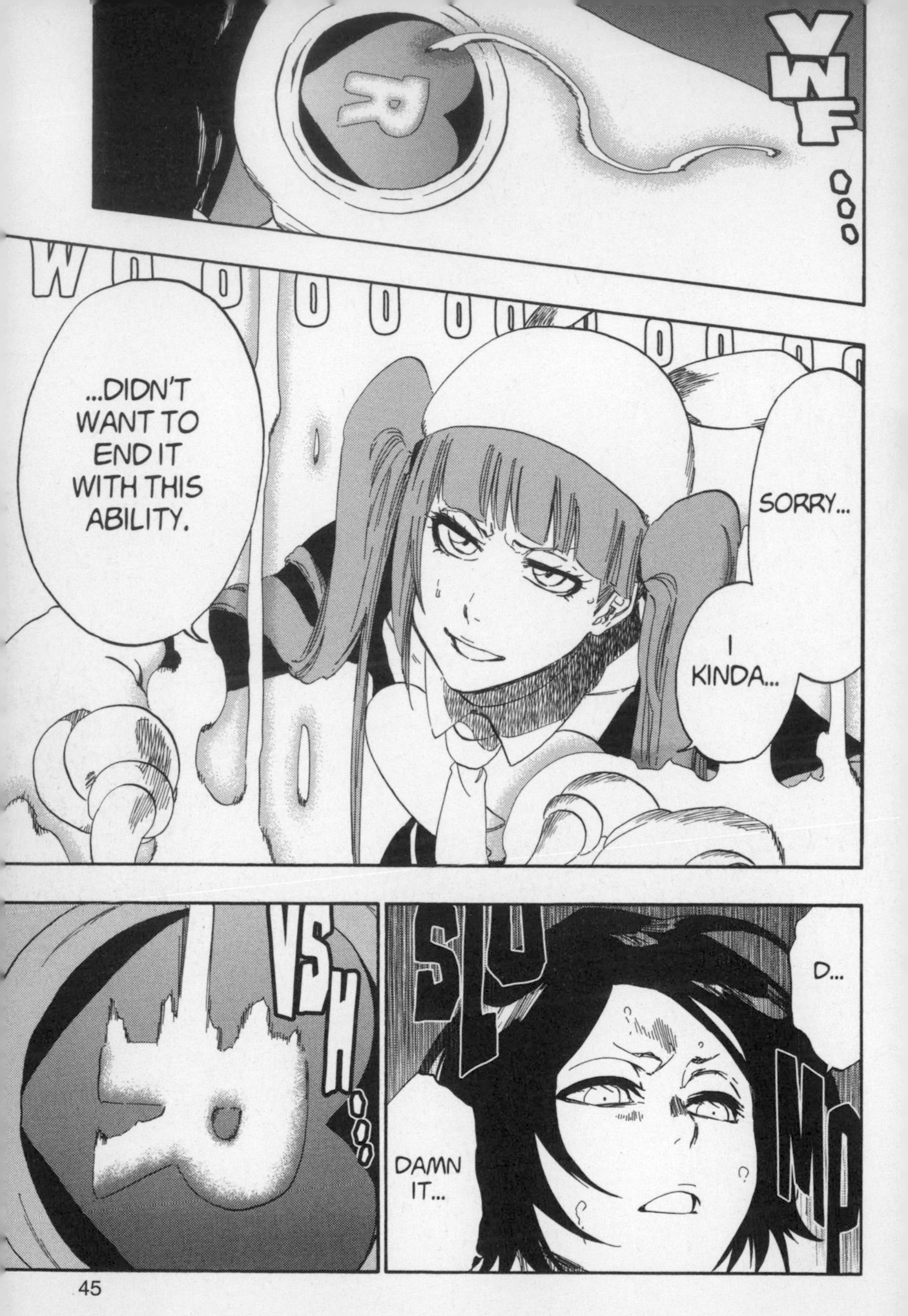
VWF
OOO
WOOOOOOOOOO
SORRY...
I KINDA...
...DIDN'T WANT TO END IT WITH THIS ABILITY.
D...
SLU
MP
DAMN IT...
VSH
OOO

please

pray for us.

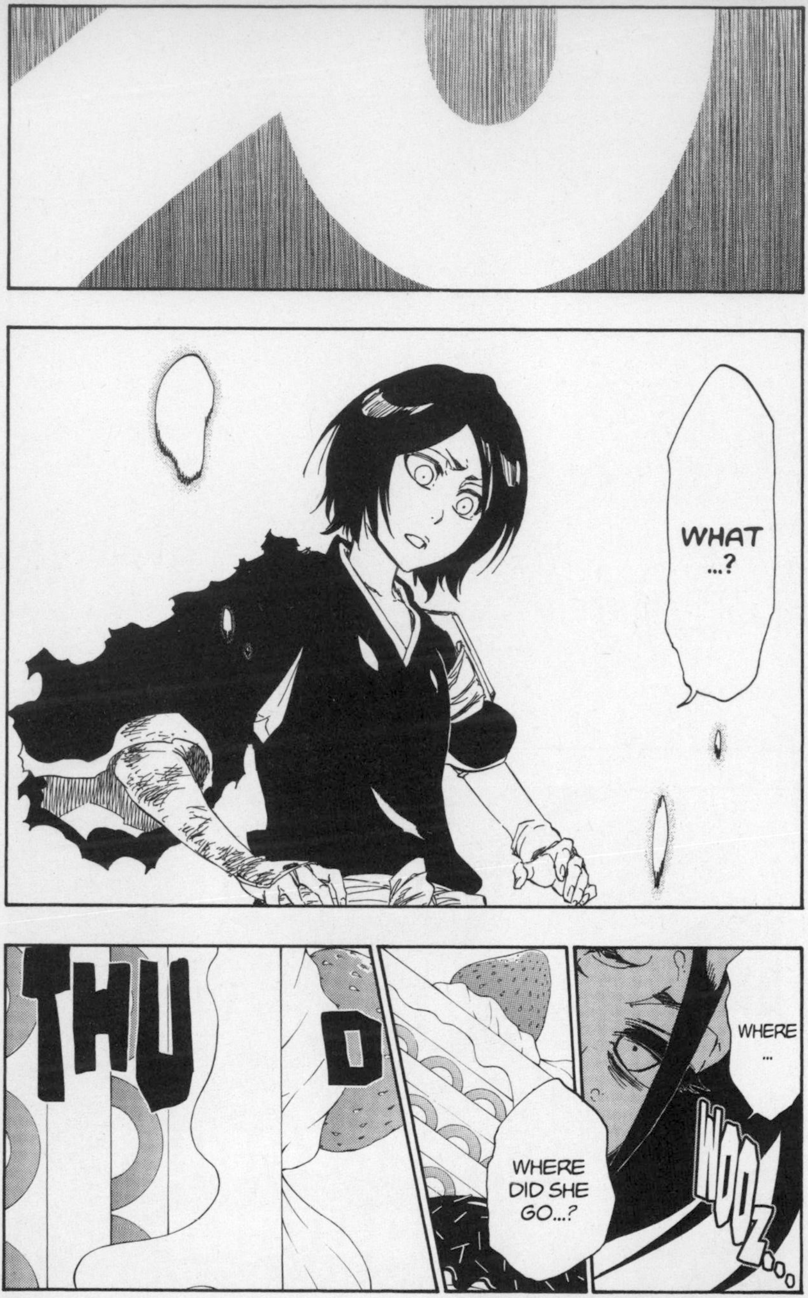
WHAT ...?
WHERE ...
WHOOZooo
WHERE DID SHE GO...?
THUD

472. Razoredge Requiem

BLEACH
472.

Razoredge requiem

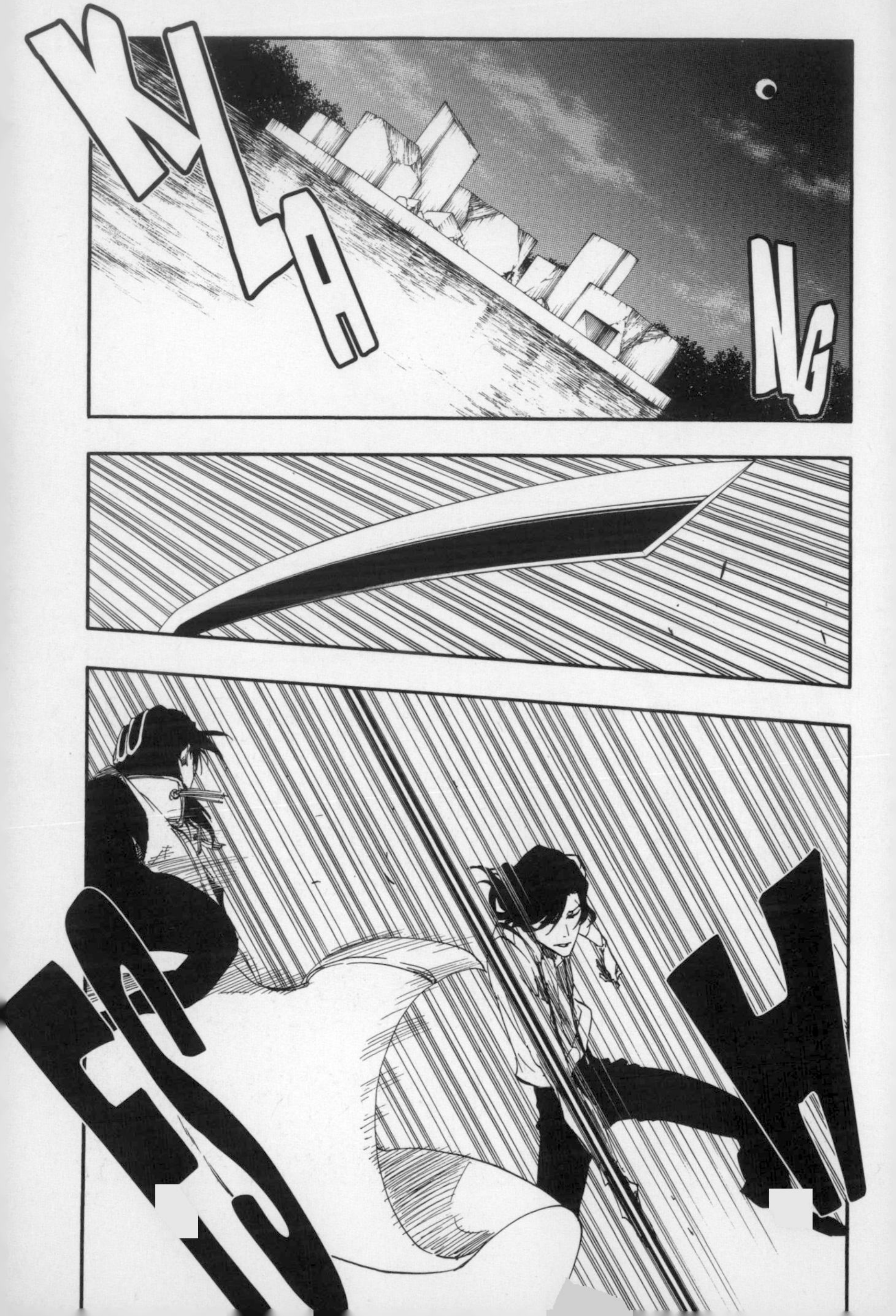
KLANG

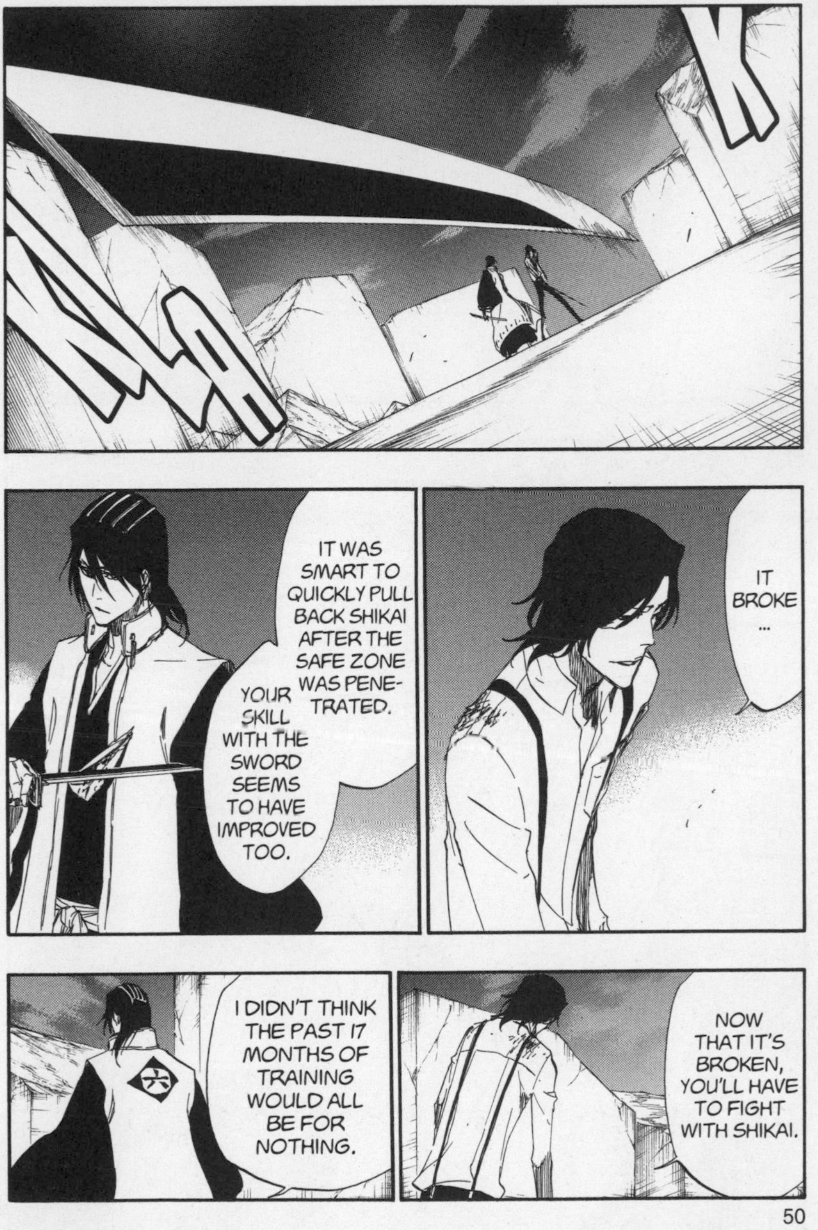
IT BROKE ...
IT WAS SMART TO QUICKLY PULL BACK SHIKAI AFTER THE SAFE ZONE WAS PENE-TRATED.
YOUR SKILL WITH THE SWORD SEEMS TO HAVE IMPROVED TOO.
NOW THAT IT'S BROKEN, YOU'LL HAVE TO FIGHT WITH SHIKAI.
I DIDN'T THINK THE PAST 17 MONTHS OF TRAINING WOULD ALL BE FOR NOTHING.

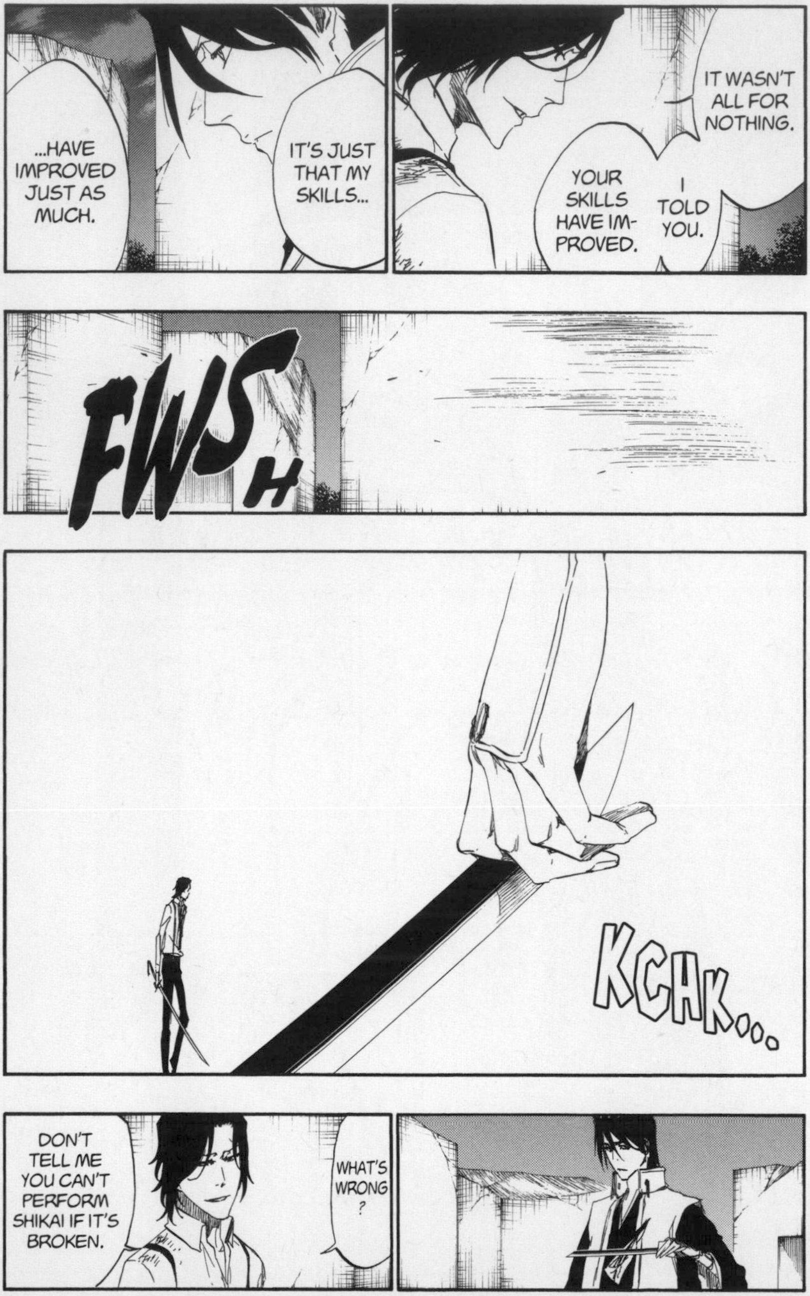
IT WASN'T ALL FOR NOTHING.
I TOLD YOU.
YOUR SKILLS HAVE IMPROVED.
IT'S JUST THAT MY SKILLS...
...HAVE IMPROVED JUST AS MUCH.
FWSH
KCHK...
WHAT'S WRONG?
DON'T TELL ME YOU CAN'T PERFORM SHIKAI IF IT'S BROKEN.

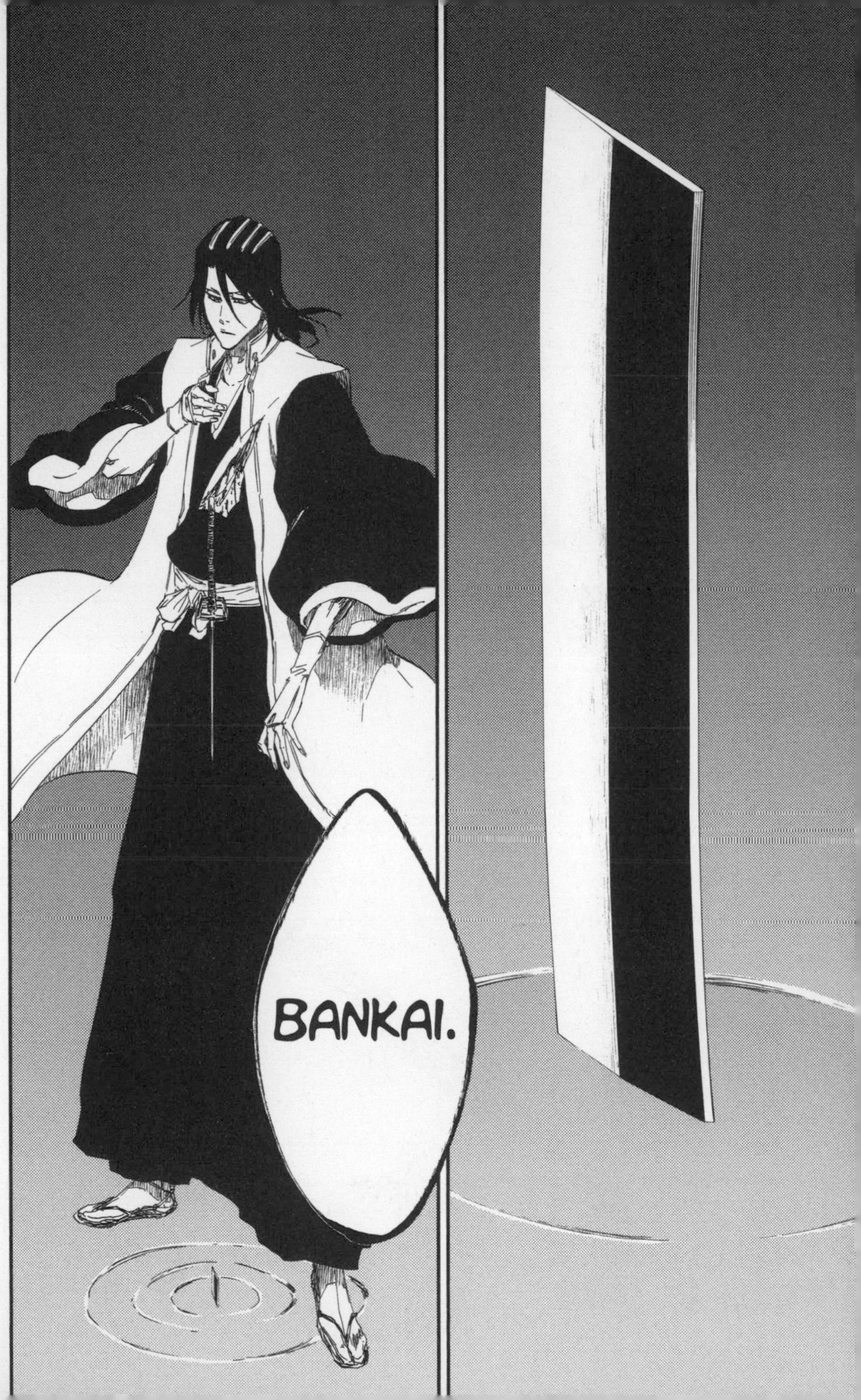
BANKAI.

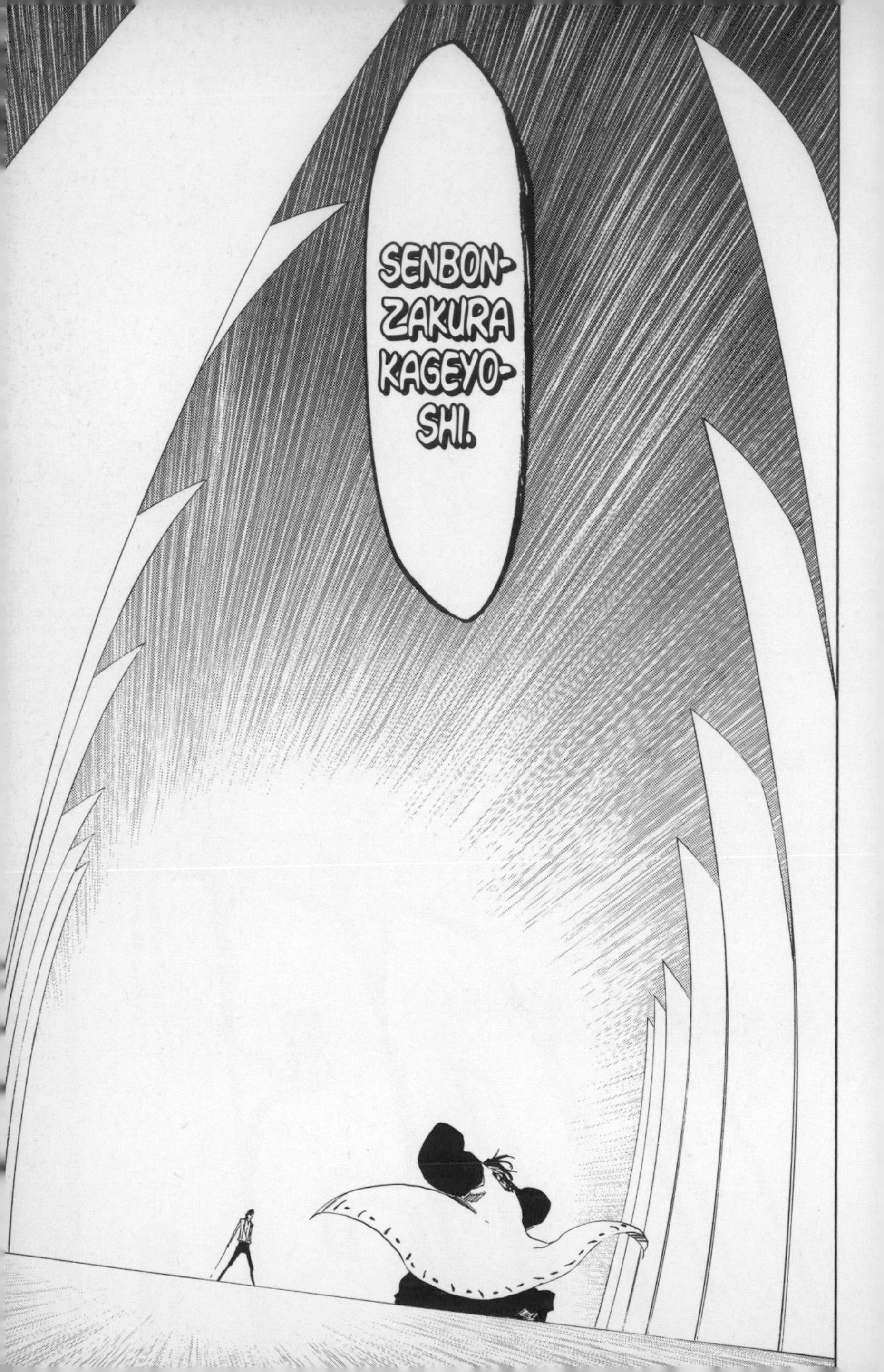
SENBON-ZAKURA KAGEYOSHI.

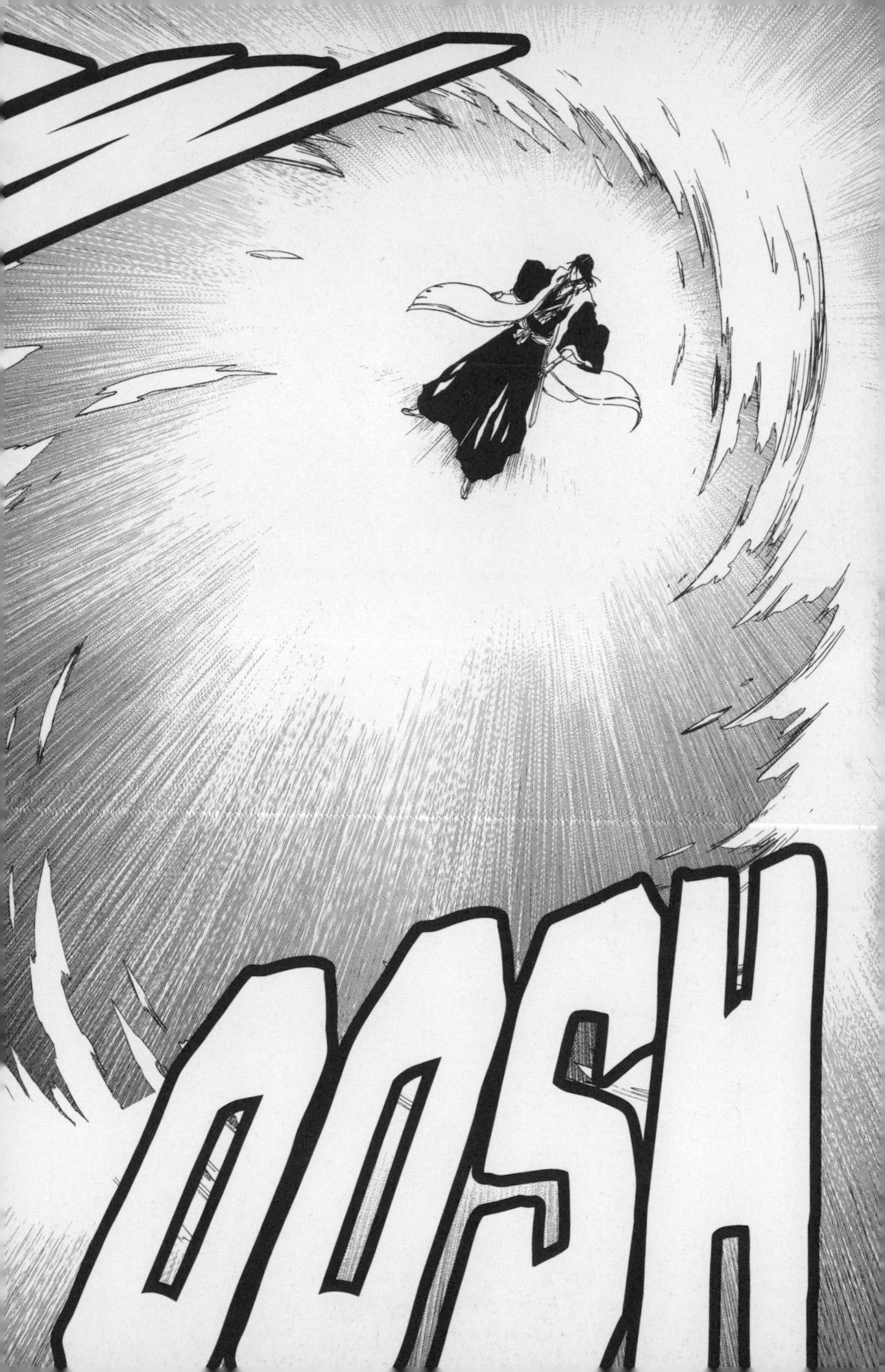
DOSH

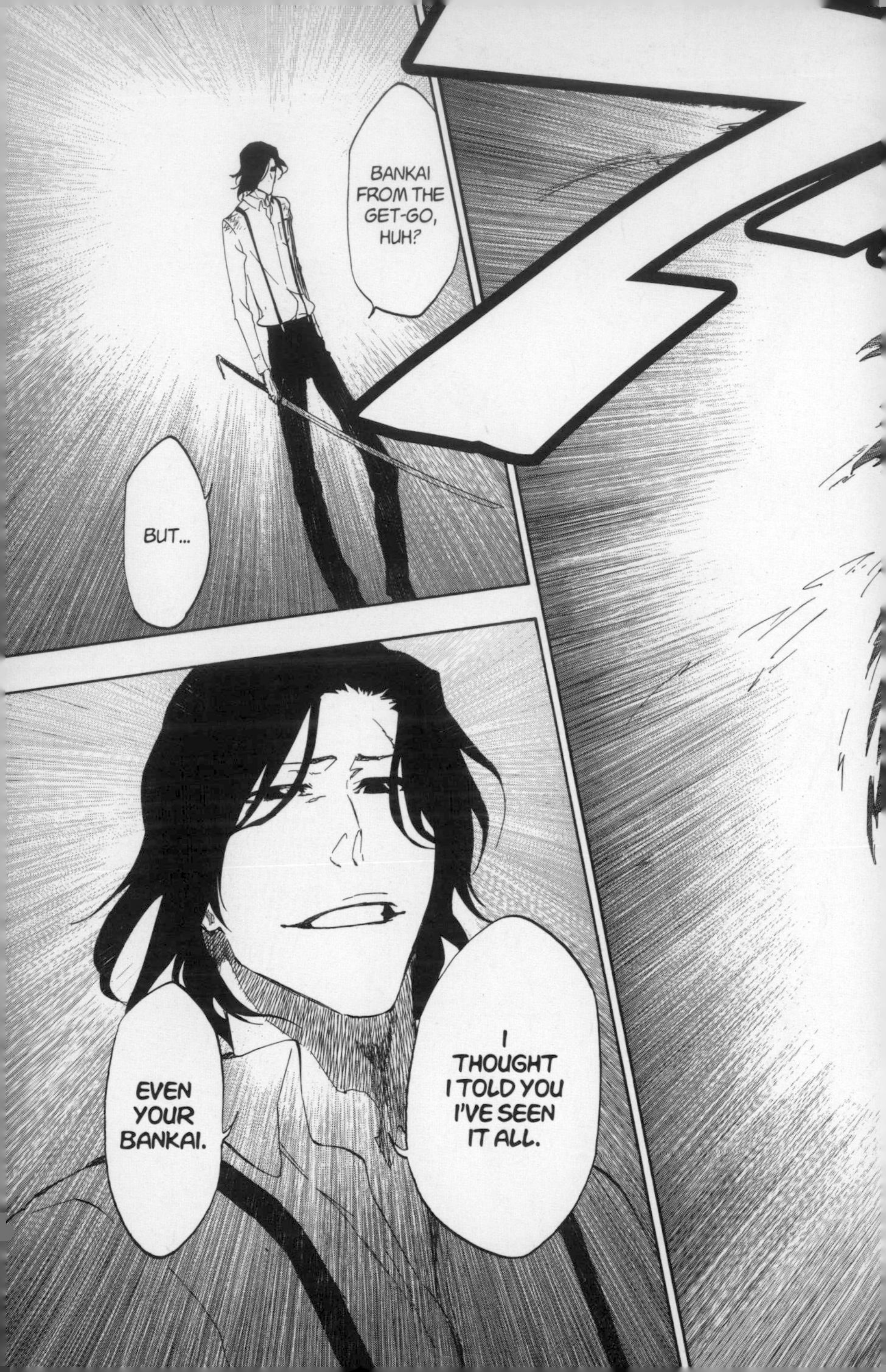
BANKAI FROM THE GET-GO, HUH?
BUT...
I THOUGHT I TOLD YOU I'VE SEEN IT ALL.
EVEN YOUR BANKAI.

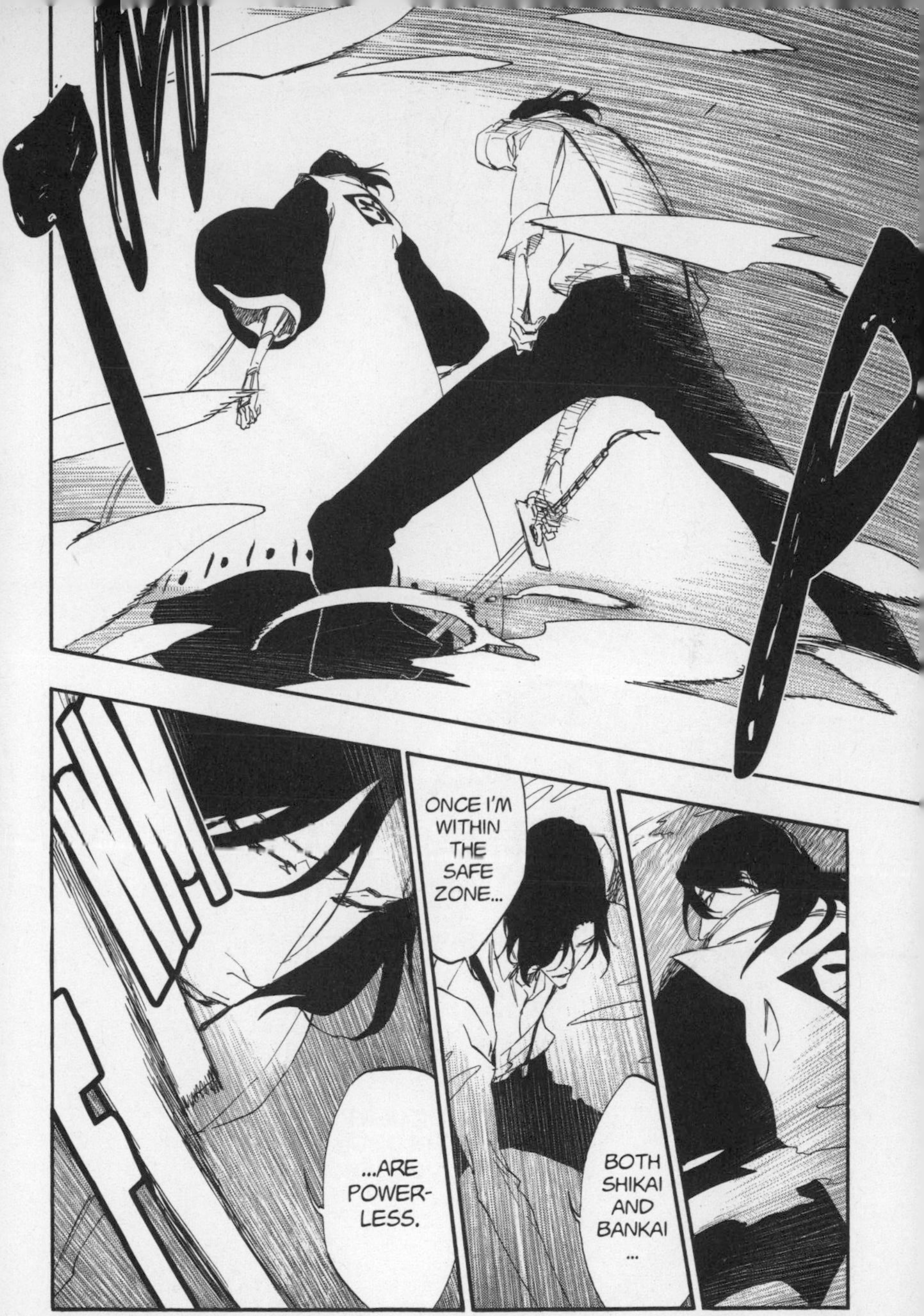
BOTH SHIKAI AND BANKAI ...
ONCE I'M WITHIN THE SAFE ZONE...
...ARE POWER-LESS.

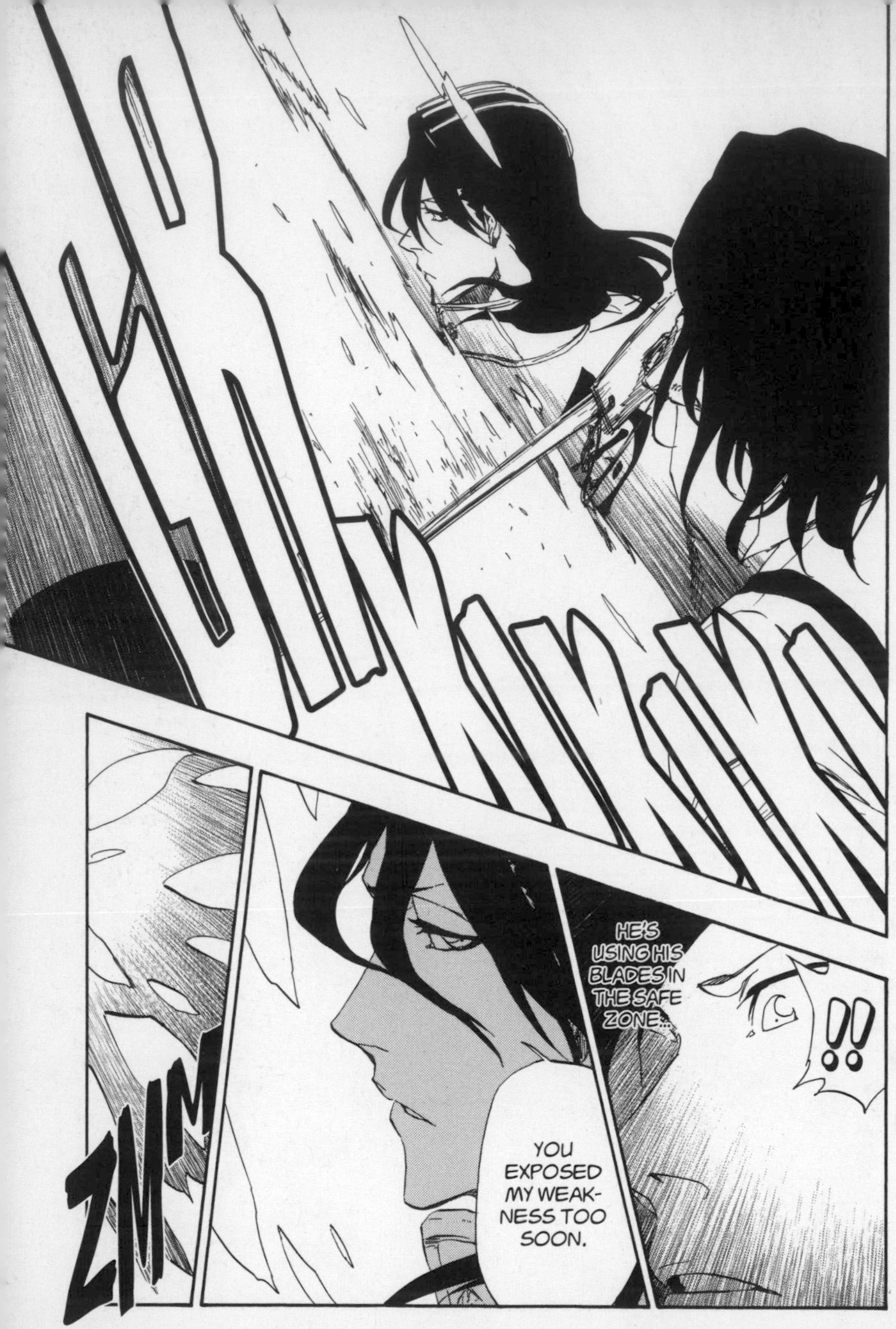
HE'S USING HIS BLADES IN THE SAFE ZONE...
!!
YOU EXPOSED MY WEAK-NESS TOO SOON.
ZMM

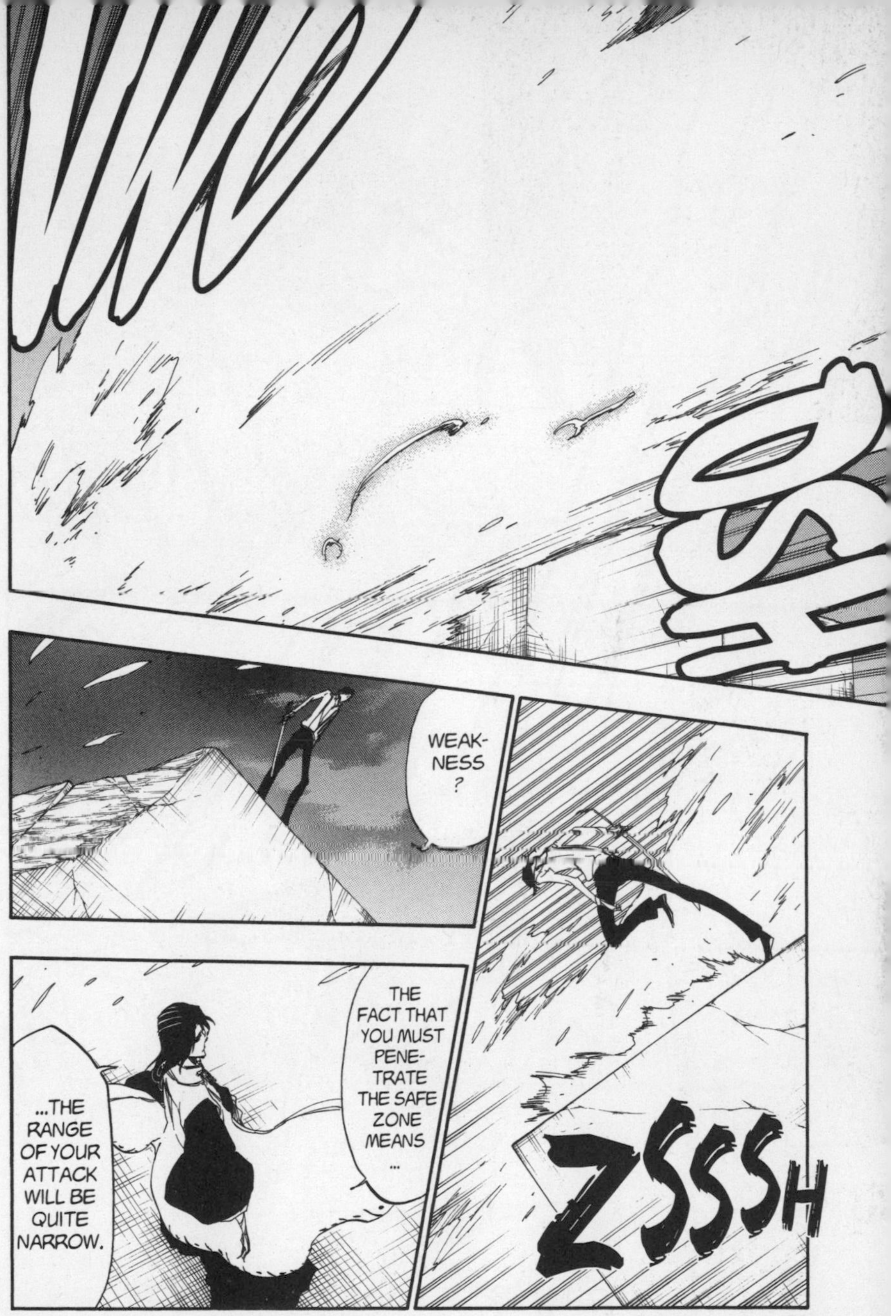
ZSSSH
WEAK-NESS?
THE FACT THAT YOU MUST PENE-TRATE THE SAFE ZONE MEANS...
...THE RANGE OF YOUR ATTACK WILL BE QUITE NARROW.

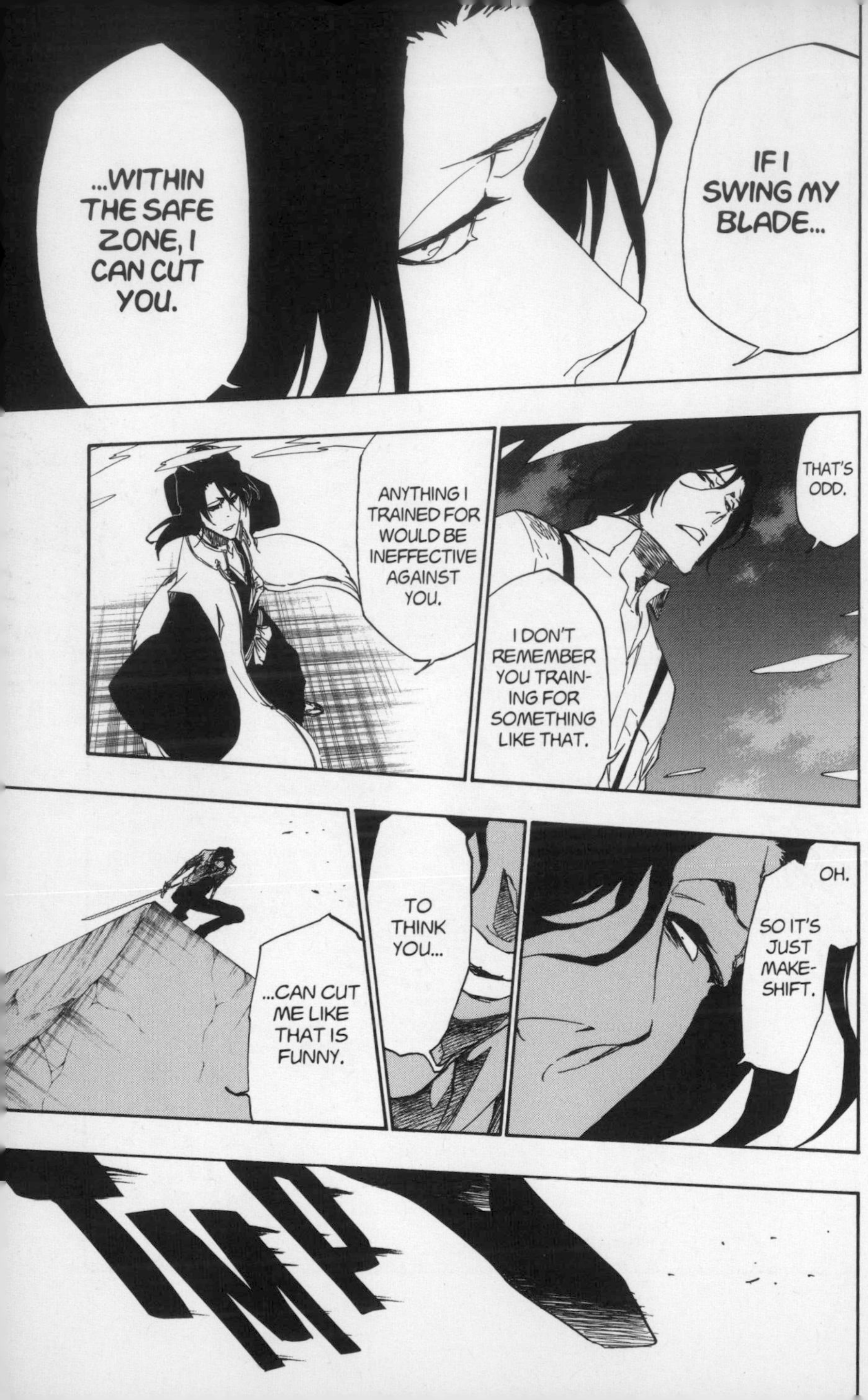
IF I SWING MY BLADE...
...WITHIN THE SAFE ZONE, I CAN CUT YOU.
THAT'S ODD.
I DON'T REMEMBER YOU TRAIN-ING FOR SOMETHING LIKE THAT.
ANYTHING I TRAINED FOR WOULD BE INEFFECTIVE AGAINST YOU.
OH.
SO IT'S JUST MAKE-SHIFT.
TO THINK YOU...
...CAN CUT ME LIKE THAT IS FUNNY.

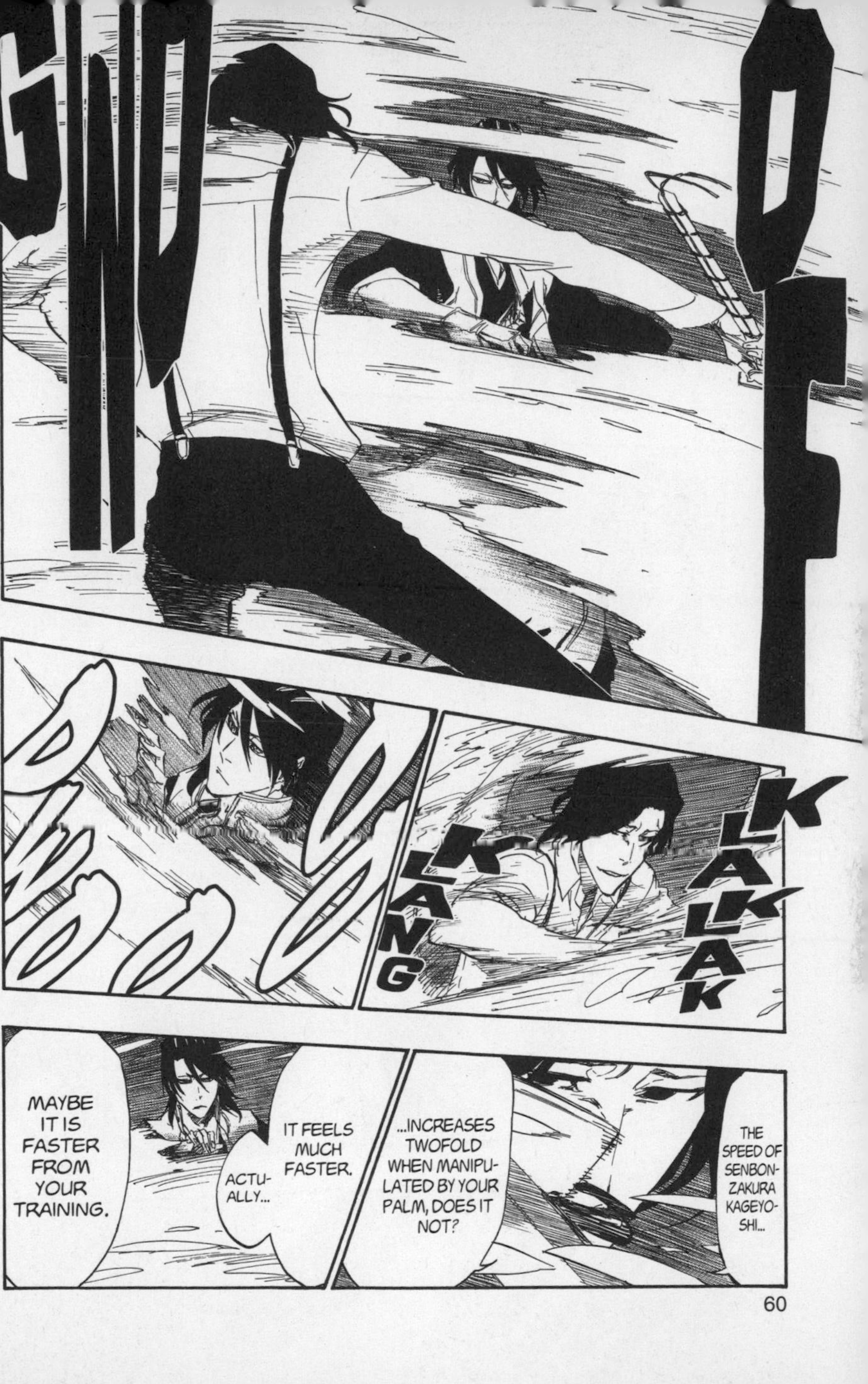
KLAK KLAK
KLANG
THE SPEED OF SENBON-ZAKURA KAGEYO-SHI...
...INCREASES TWOFOLD WHEN MANIPU-LATED BY YOUR PALM, DOES IT NOT?
ACTU-ALLY...
IT FEELS MUCH FASTER.
MAYBE IT IS FASTER FROM YOUR TRAINING.

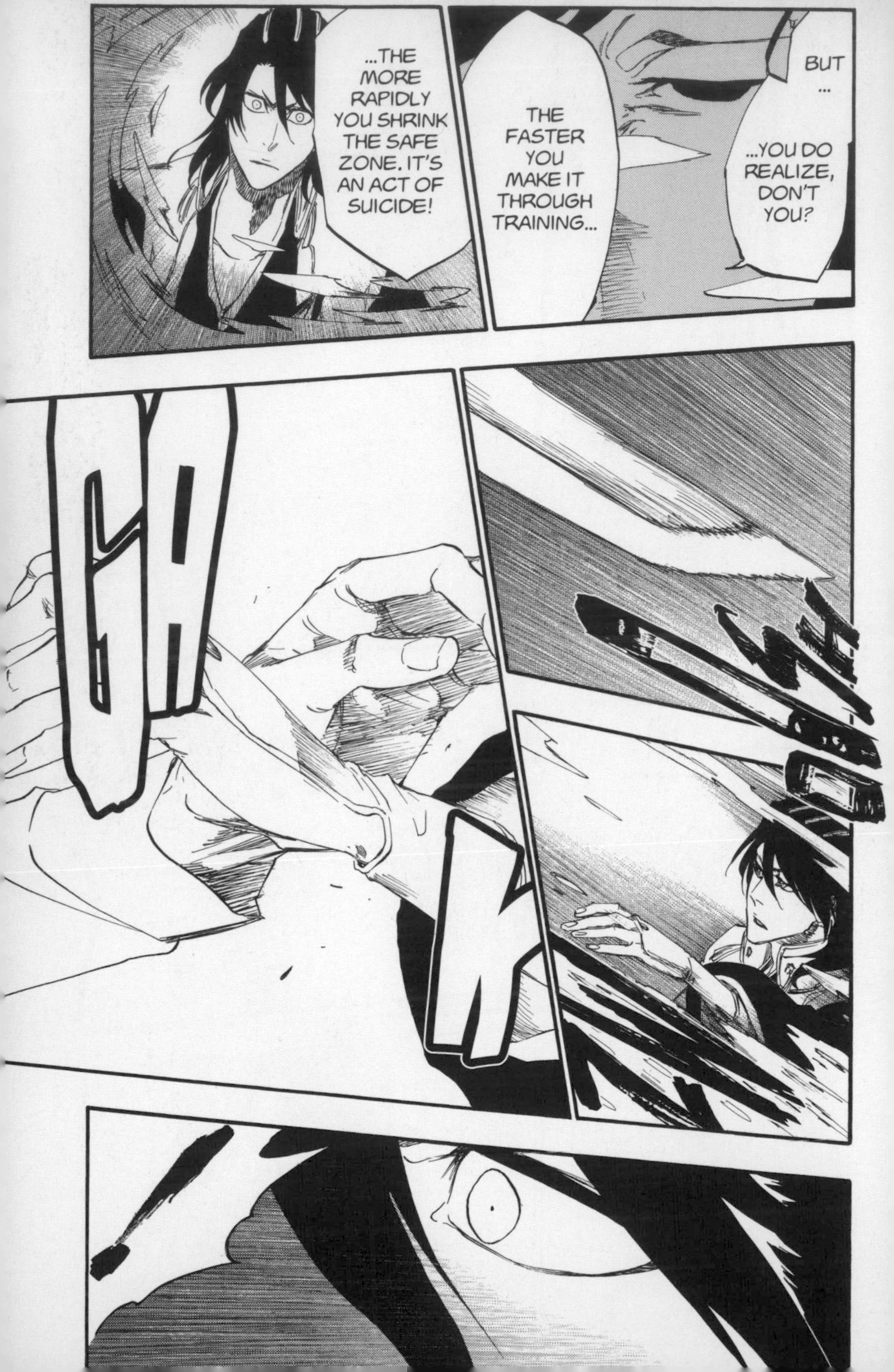
BUT ...
...YOU DO REALIZE, DON'T YOU?
THE FASTER YOU MAKE IT THROUGH TRAINING...
...THE MORE RAPIDLY YOU SHRINK THE SAFE ZONE. IT'S AN ACT OF SUICIDE!

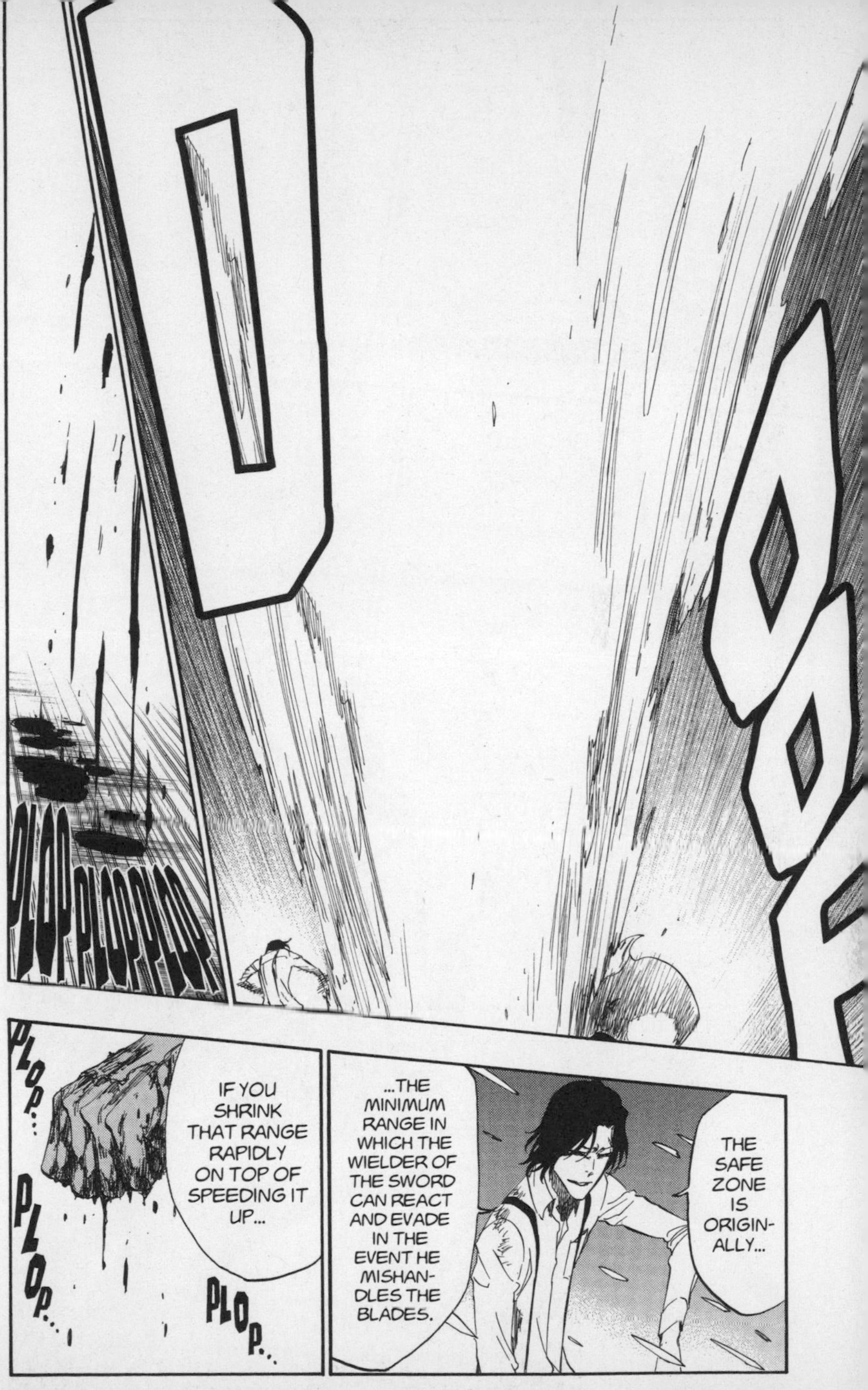
PLOP PLOPPLOP
THE SAFE ZONE IS ORIGINALLY...
...THE MINIMUM RANGE IN WHICH THE WIELDER OF THE SWORD CAN REACT AND EVADE IN THE EVENT HE MISHANDLES THE BLADES.
IF YOU SHRINK THAT RANGE RAPIDLY ON TOP OF SPEEDING IT UP...
PLOP...
PLOP...
PLOP...
PLOP...

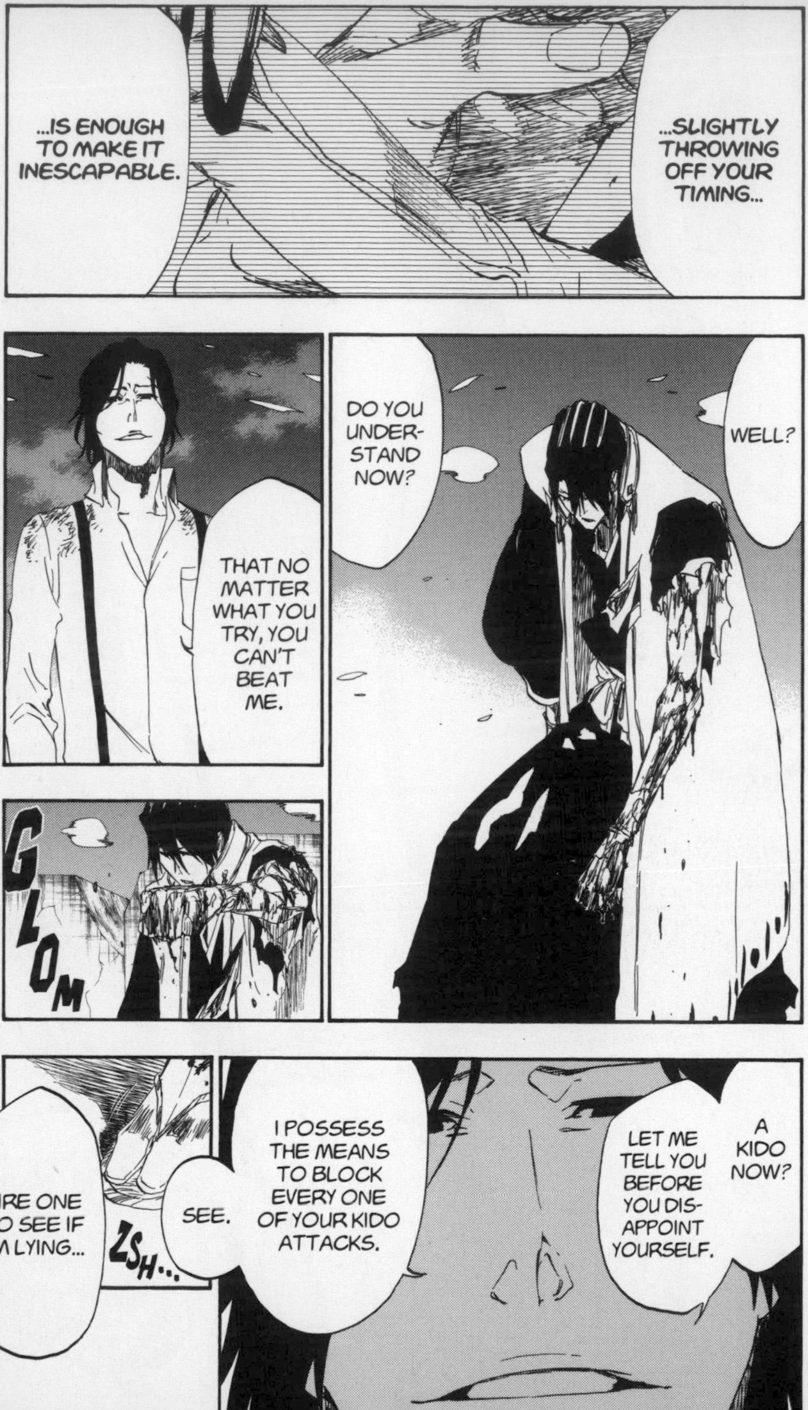
...SLIGHTLY THROWING OFF YOUR TIMING...
...IS ENOUGH TO MAKE IT INESCAPABLE.
WELL?
DO YOU UNDERSTAND NOW?
THAT NO MATTER WHAT YOU TRY, YOU CAN'T BEAT ME.
GLOM
A KIDO NOW?
LET ME TELL YOU BEFORE YOU DISAPPOINT YOURSELF.
I POSSESS THE MEANS TO BLOCK EVERY ONE OF YOUR KIDO ATTACKS.
SEE.
FIRE ONE TO SEE IF I'M LYING...
ZSH...

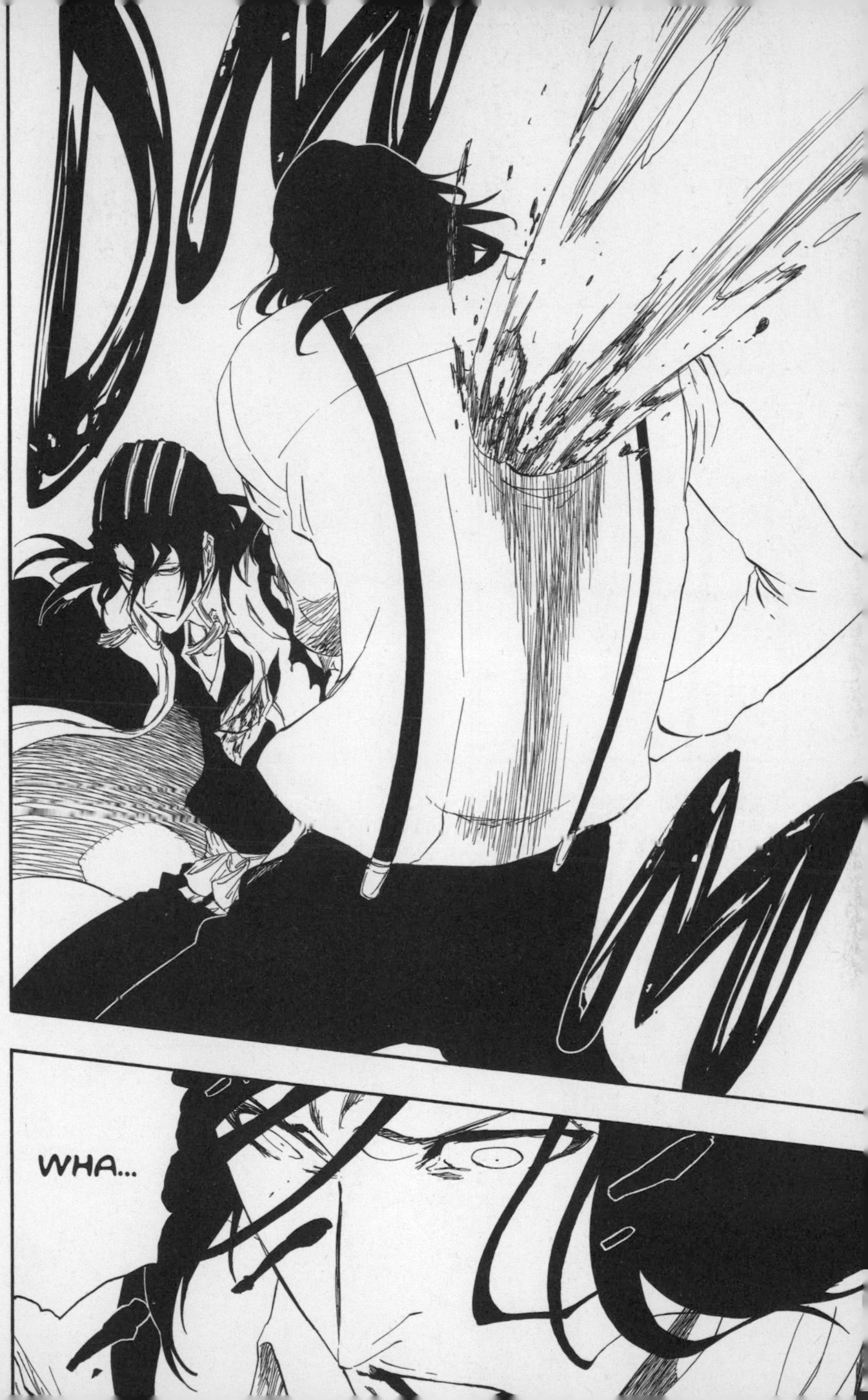
DOM
WHA...

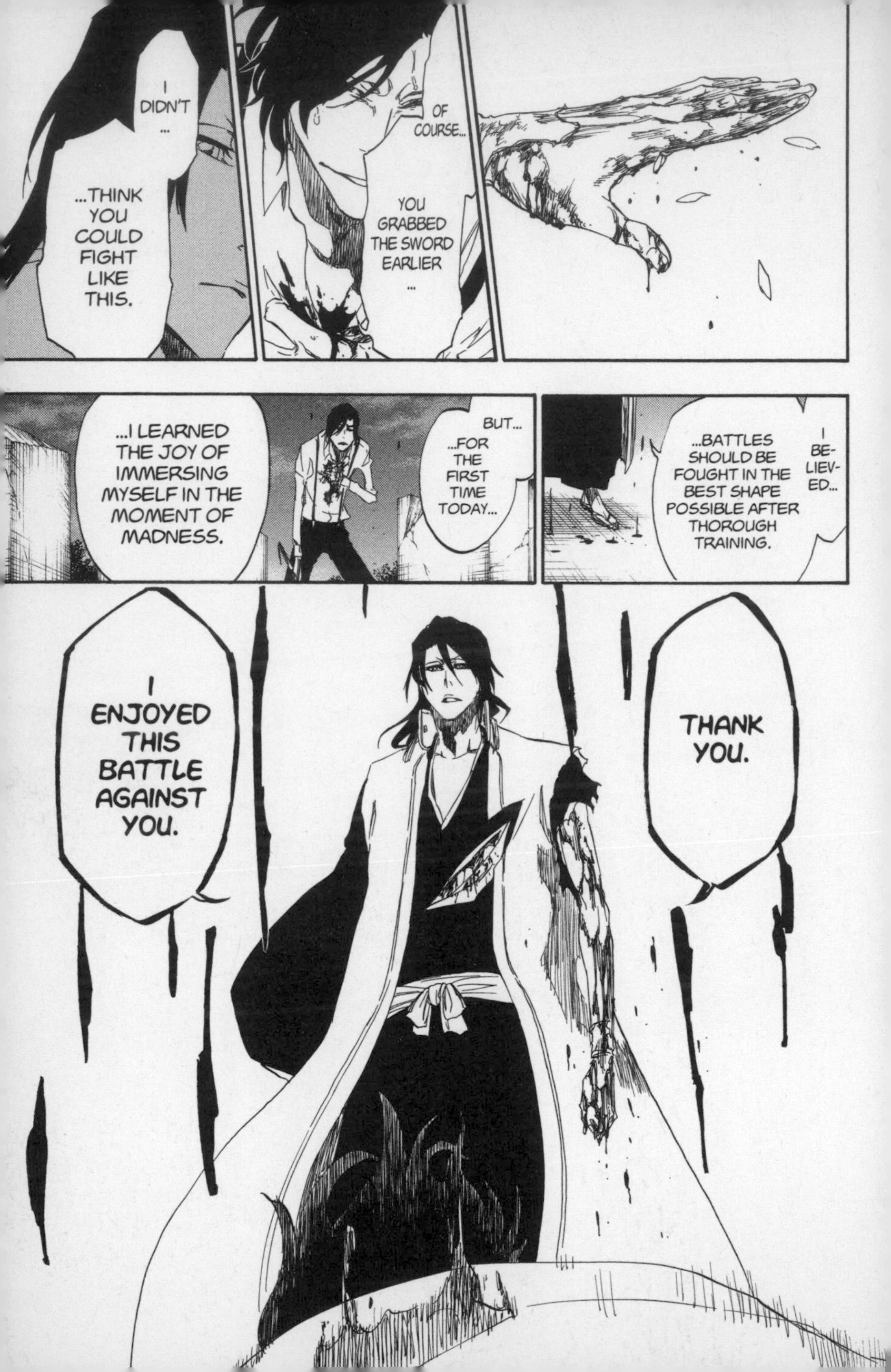
OF COURSE...
YOU GRABBED THE SWORD EARLIER ...
I DIDN'T ...
...THINK YOU COULD FIGHT LIKE THIS.
I BE-LIEV-ED...
...BATTLES SHOULD BE FOUGHT IN THE BEST SHAPE POSSIBLE AFTER THOROUGH TRAINING.
BUT... ...FOR THE FIRST TIME TODAY...
...I LEARNED THE JOY OF IMMERSING MYSELF IN THE MOMENT OF MADNESS.
THANK YOU.
I ENJOYED THIS BATTLE AGAINST YOU.

held thing is edge.
lost thing is safe.

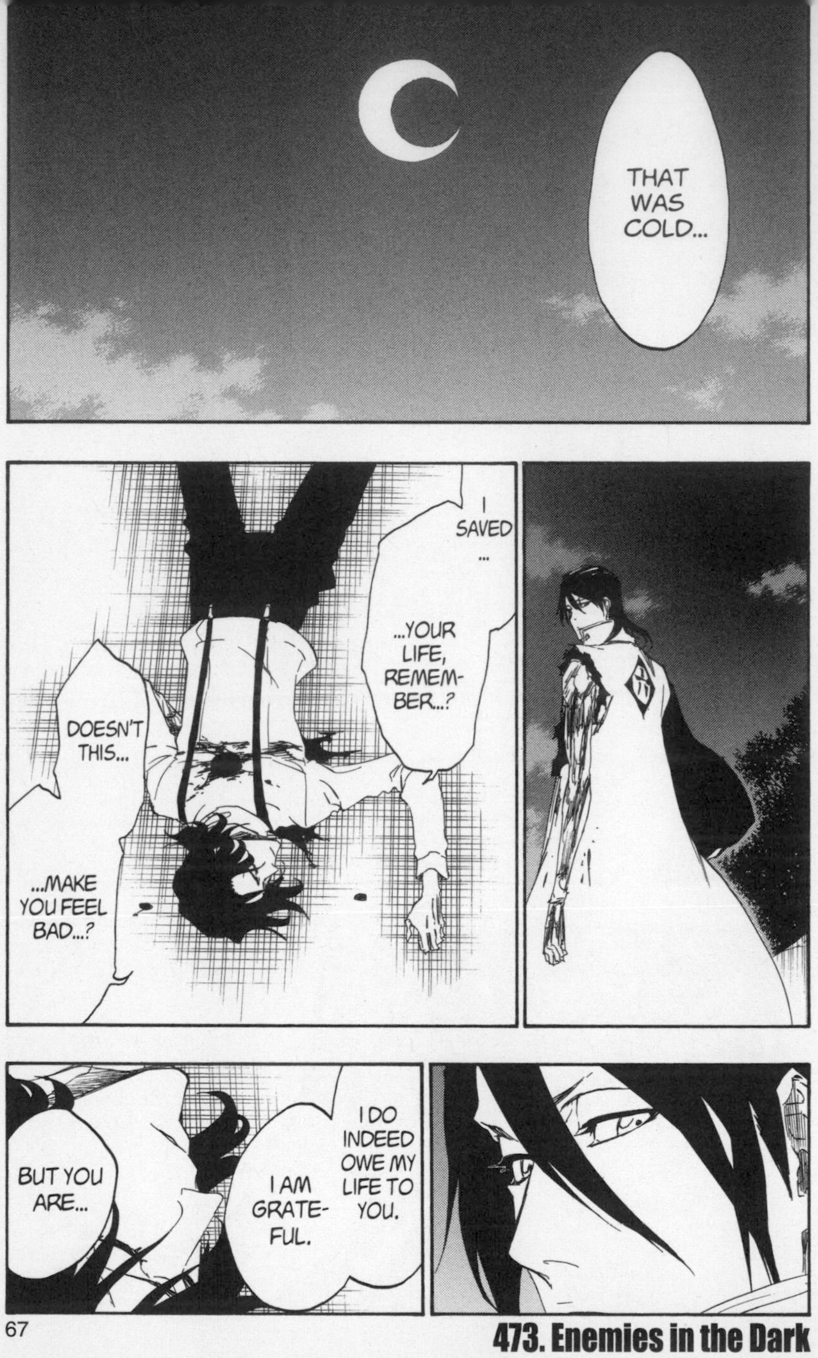
THAT WAS COLD...
I SAVED ...
...YOUR LIFE, REMEMBER...?
DOESN'T THIS...
...MAKE YOU FEEL BAD...?
I DO INDEED OWE MY LIFE TO YOU.
I AM GRATEFUL.
BUT YOU ARE...

473. Enemies in the Dark

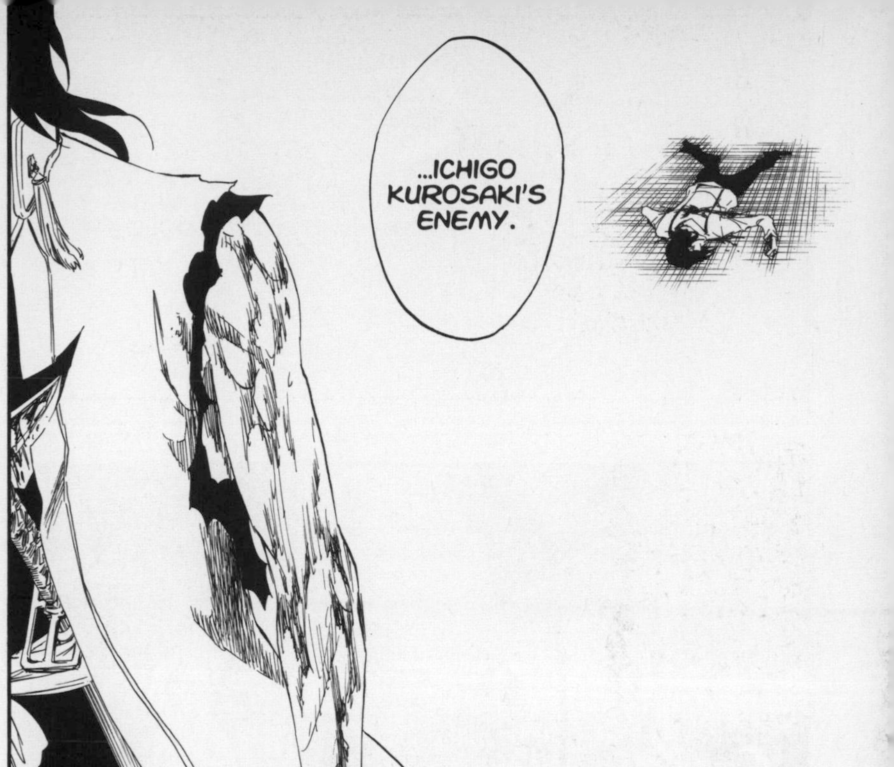
...ICHIGO
KUROSAKI'S
ENEMY.
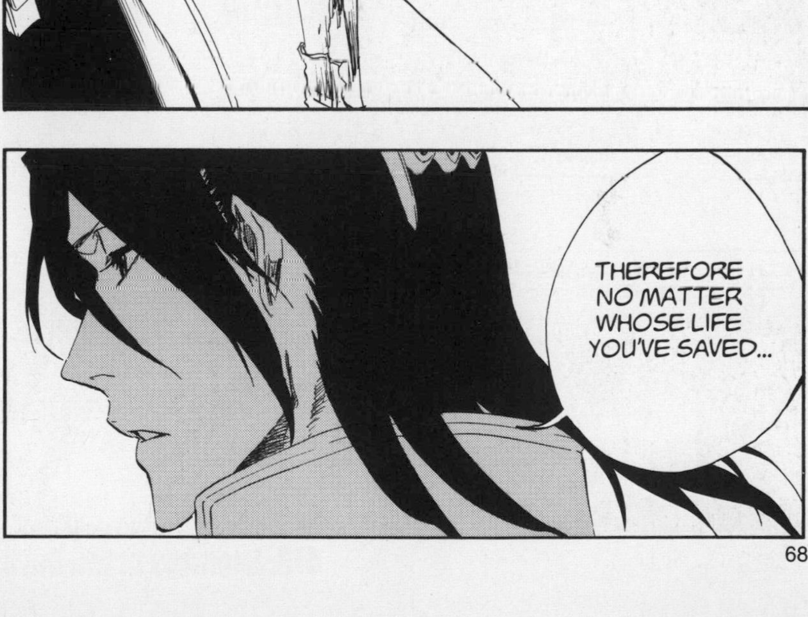
THEREFORE
NO MATTER
WHOSE LIFE
YOU'VE SAVED...

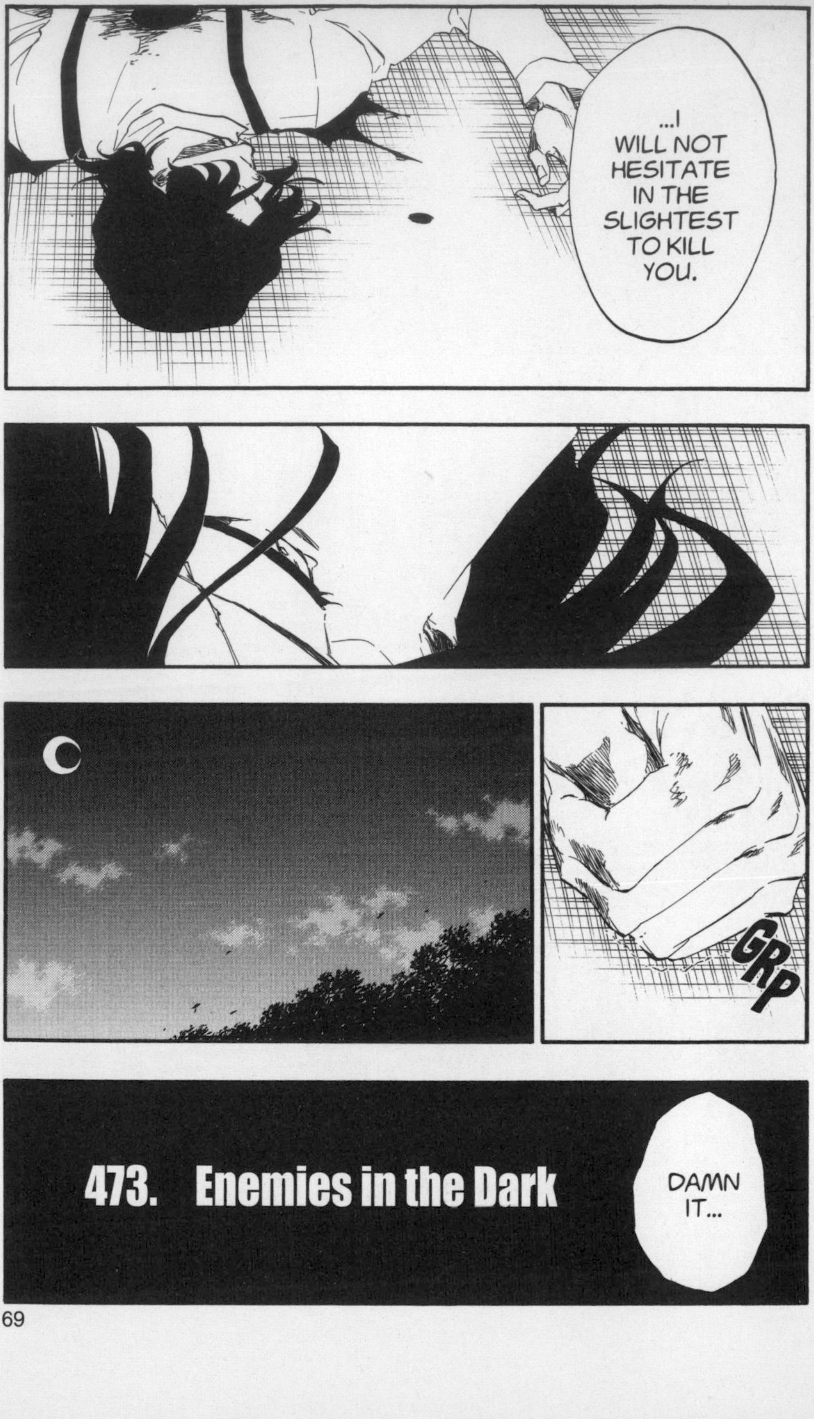
...I WILL NOT HESITATE IN THE SLIGHTEST TO KILL YOU.
GRP
DAMN IT...
473. Enemies in the Dark

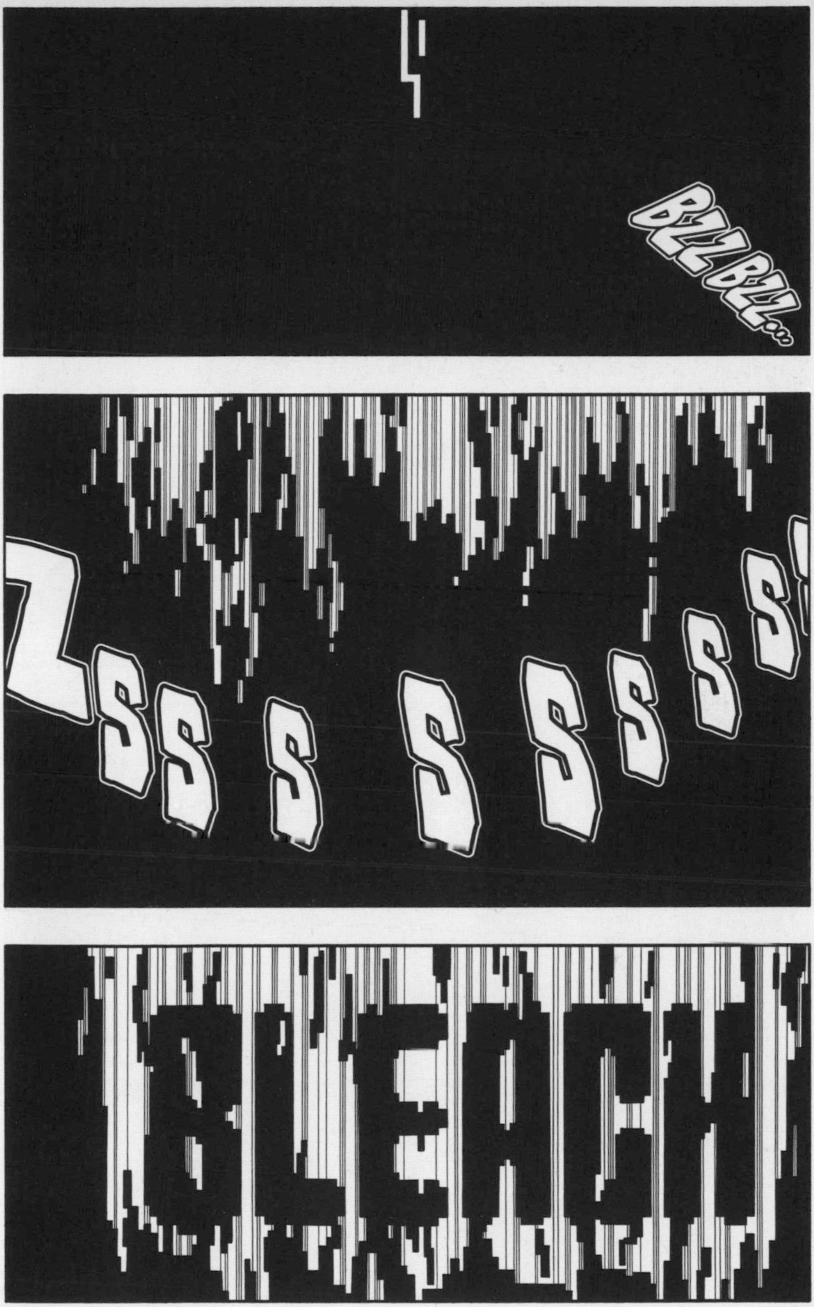
BZZ BZZ...
ZSSSSSSSS!
BLEACH

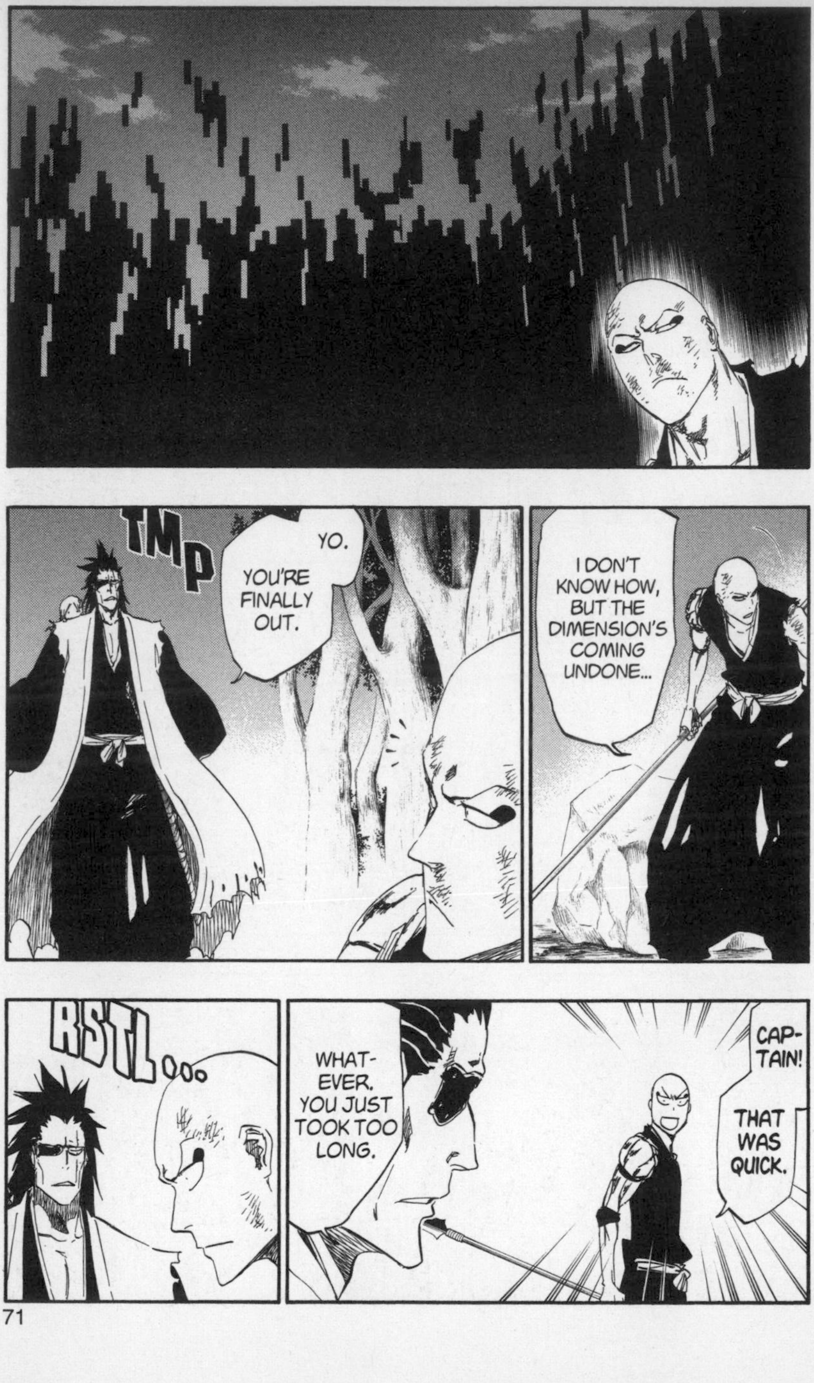
I DON'T KNOW HOW, BUT THE DIMENSION'S COMING UNDONE...
YO.
YOU'RE FINALLY OUT.
TMP
CAP-TAIN!
THAT WAS QUICK.
WHAT-EVER. YOU JUST TOOK TOO LONG.
RSTL...

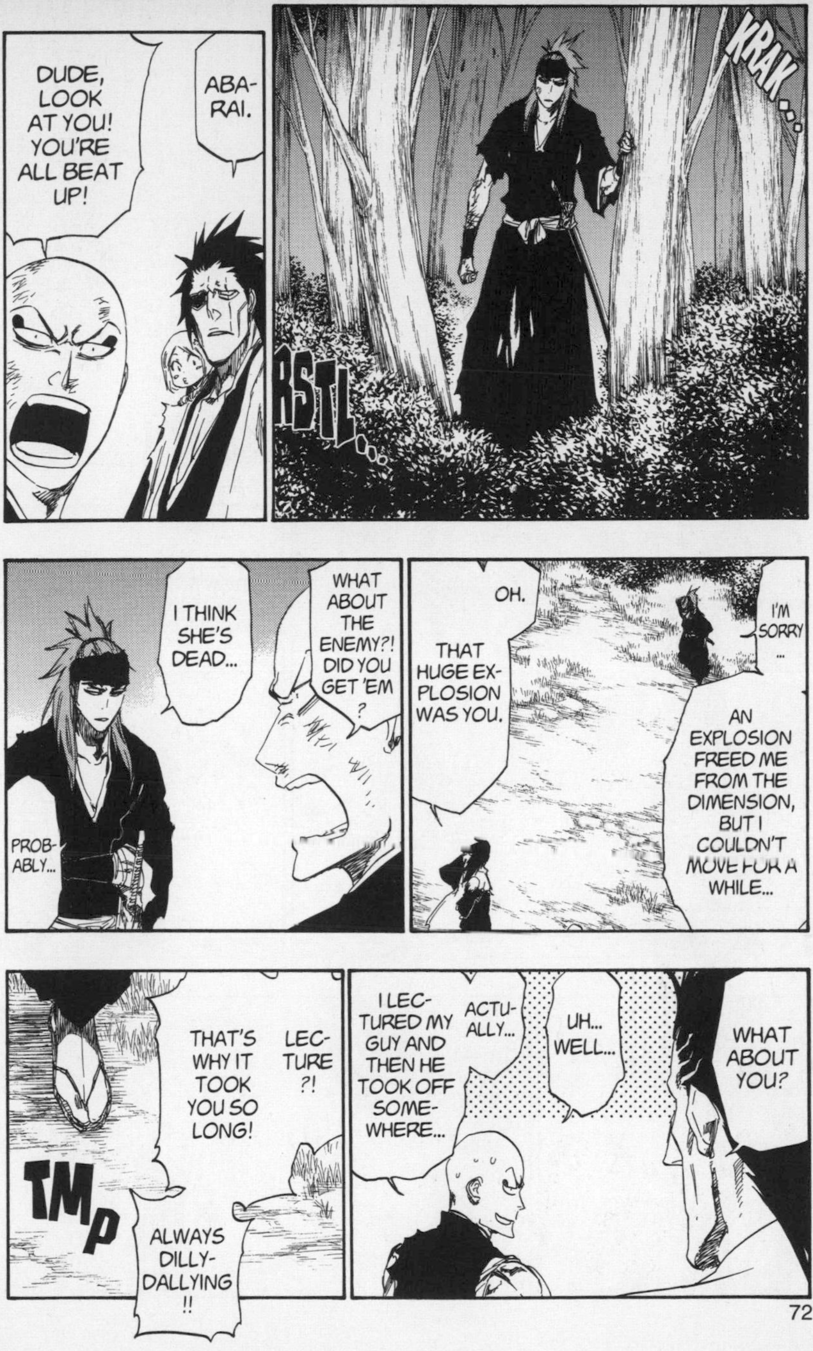
KRAK...
RSTL...
ABA-RAI.
DUDE, LOOK AT YOU! YOU'RE ALL BEAT UP!
I'M SORRY...
AN EXPLOSION FREED ME FROM THE DIMENSION, BUT I COULDN'T MOVE FOR A WHILE...
OH.
THAT HUGE EXPLOSION WAS YOU.
WHAT ABOUT THE ENEMY?! DID YOU GET 'EM ?
I THINK SHE'S DEAD...
PROBABLY...
WHAT ABOUT YOU?
UH... WELL...
ACTUALLY...
I LECTURED MY GUY AND THEN HE TOOK OFF SOMEWHERE...
LECTURE?!
THAT'S WHY IT TOOK YOU SO LONG!
ALWAYS DILLY-DALLYING !!
TMP

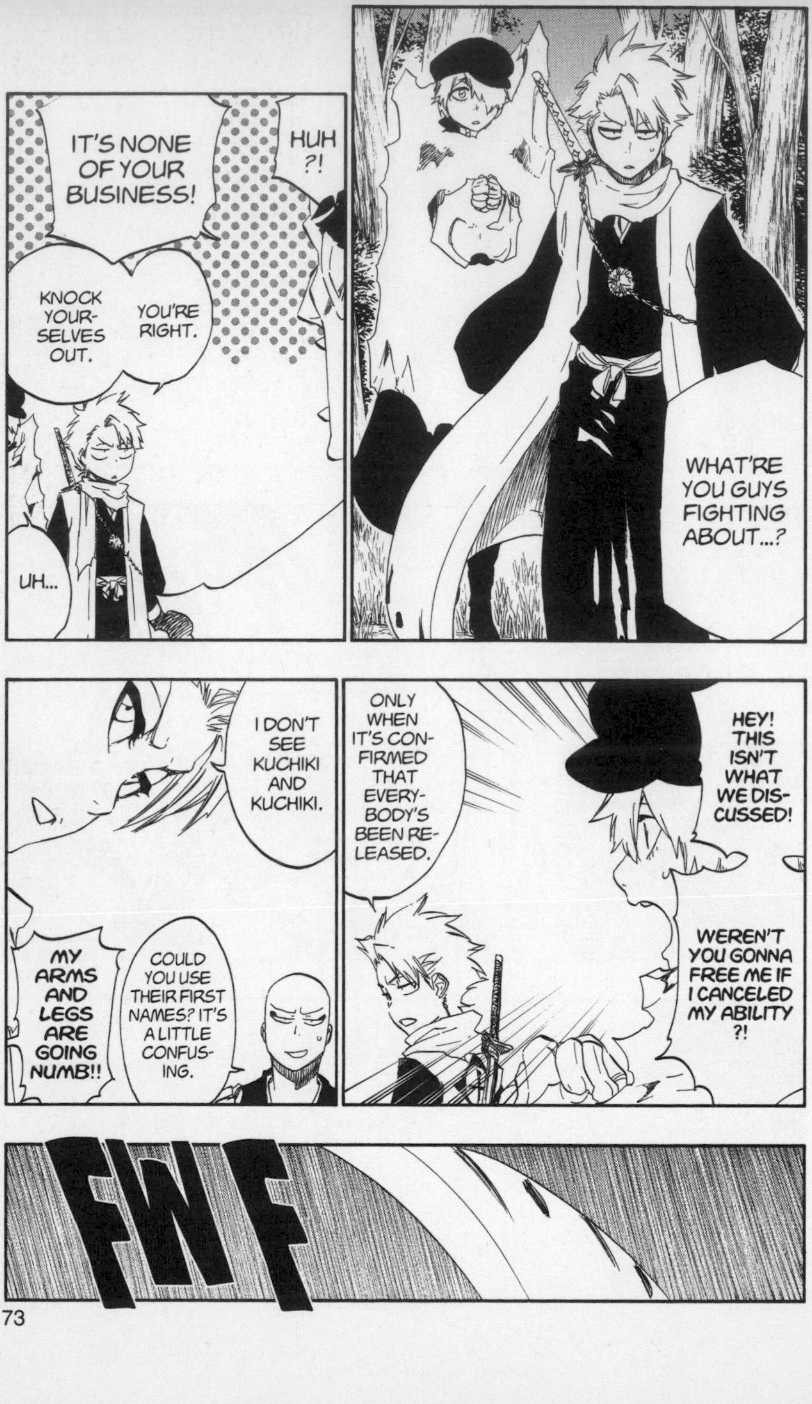
WHAT'RE YOU GUYS FIGHTING ABOUT...?
HUH?!
IT'S NONE OF YOUR BUSINESS!
YOU'RE RIGHT.
KNOCK YOURSELVES OUT.
UH...
HEY! THIS ISN'T WHAT WE DISCUSSED!
WEREN'T YOU GONNA FREE ME IF I CANCELED MY ABILITY?!
ONLY WHEN IT'S CONFIRMED THAT EVERYBODY'S BEEN RELEASED.
I DON'T SEE KUCHIKI AND KUCHIKI.
COULD YOU USE THEIR FIRST NAMES? IT'S A LITTLE CONFUSING.
MY ARMS AND LEGS ARE GOING NUMB!!
FWF

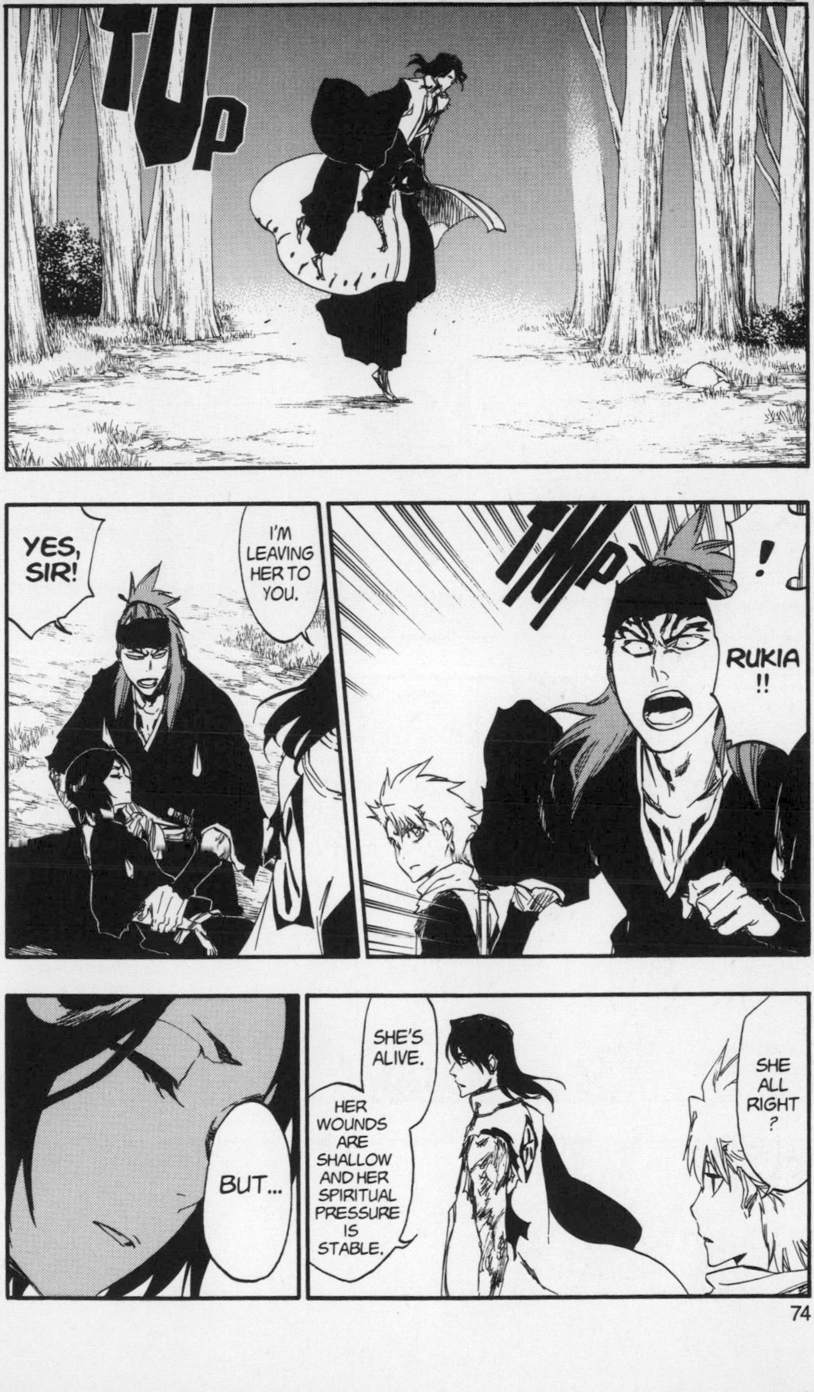
TUP
TMP
!
RUKIA!!
I'M LEAVING HER TO YOU.
YES, SIR!
SHE ALL RIGHT?
SHE'S ALIVE.
HER WOUNDS ARE SHALLOW AND HER SPIRITUAL PRESSURE IS STABLE.
BUT...

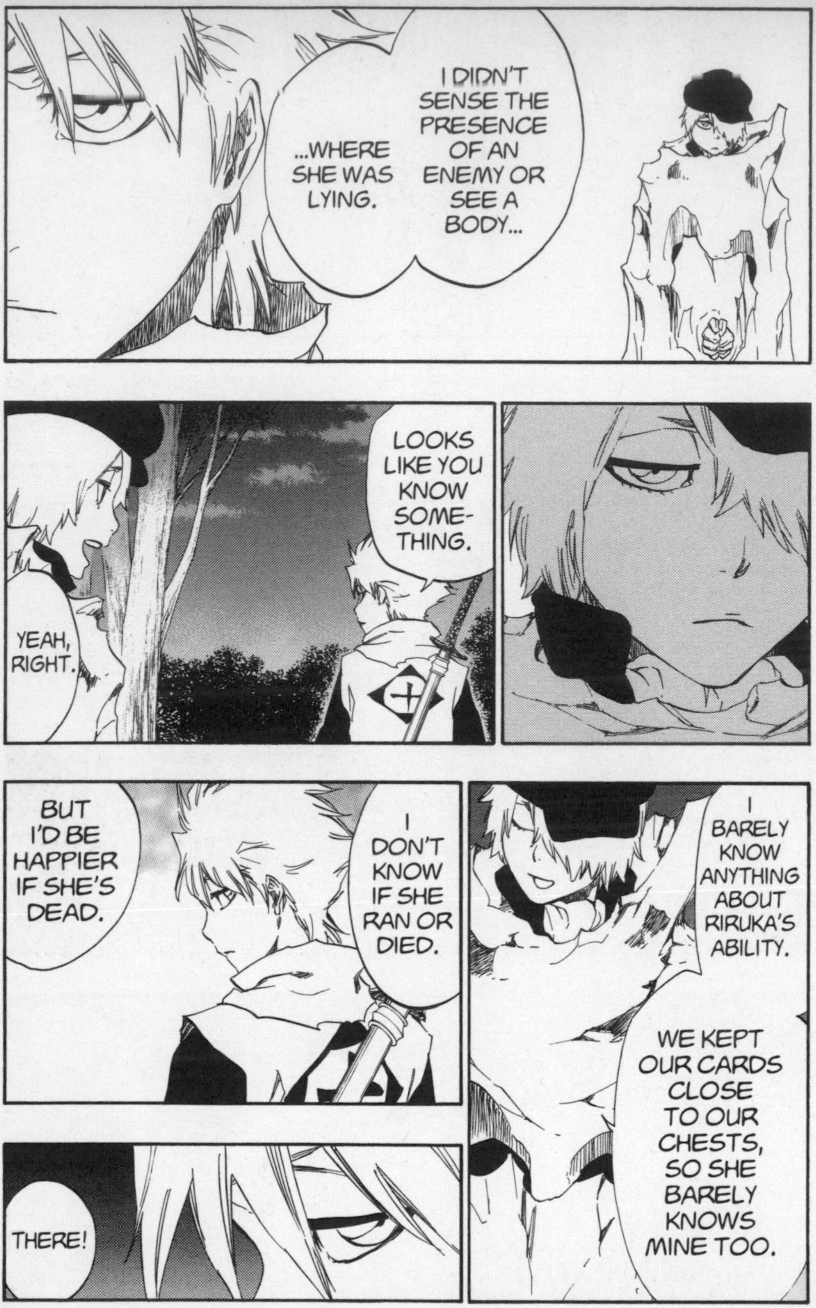
I DIDN'T SENSE THE PRESENCE OF AN ENEMY OR SEE A BODY...
...WHERE SHE WAS LYING.
LOOKS LIKE YOU KNOW SOME-THING.
YEAH, RIGHT.
I BARELY KNOW ANYTHING ABOUT RIRUKA'S ABILITY.
WE KEPT OUR CARDS CLOSE TO OUR CHESTS, SO SHE BARELY KNOWS MINE TOO.
I DON'T KNOW IF SHE RAN OR DIED.
BUT I'D BE HAPPIER IF SHE'S DEAD.
THERE!

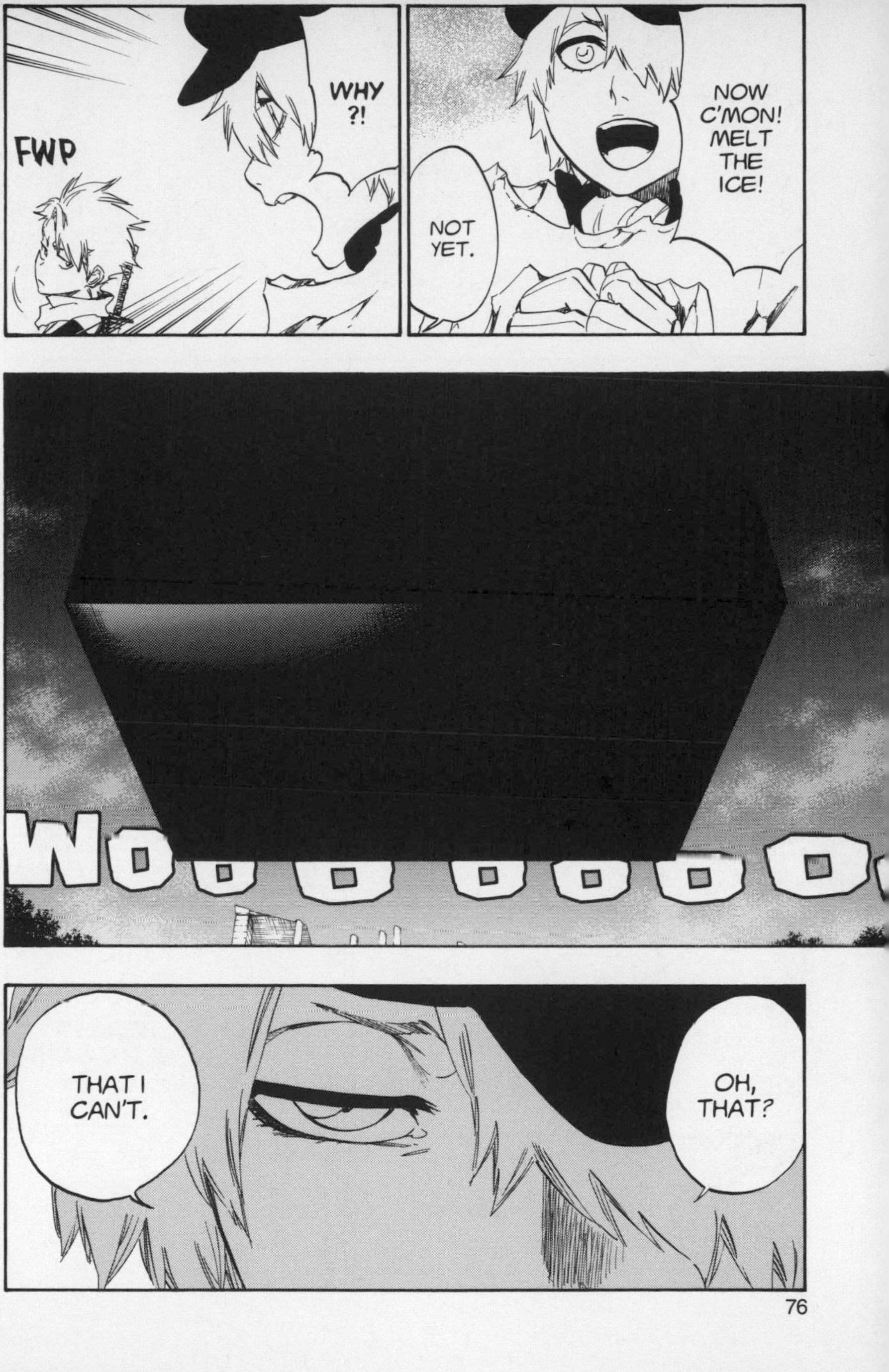
NOW C'MON! MELT THE ICE!
NOT YET.
WHY ?!
FWP
WOOOOOOO
OH, THAT?
THAT I CAN'T.

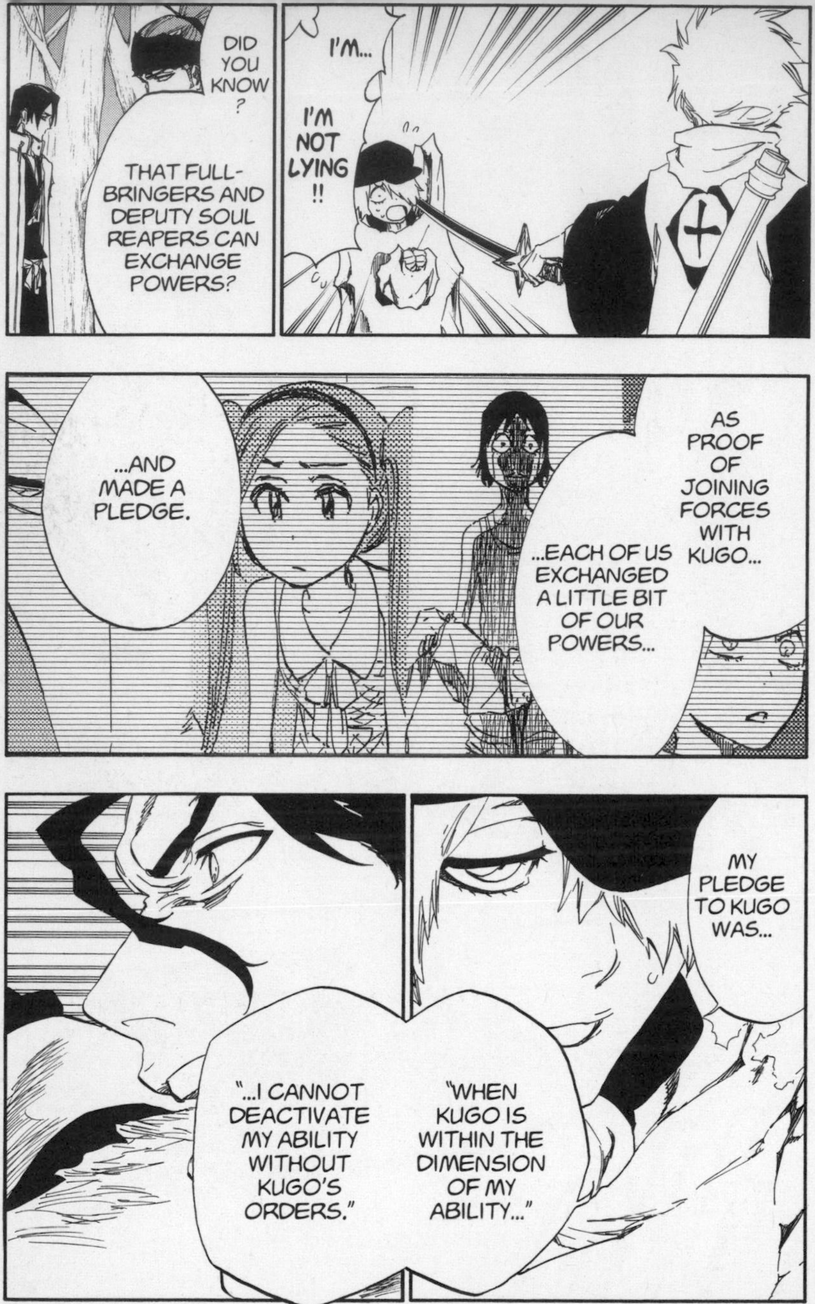
I'M...
I'M NOT LYING !!
DID YOU KNOW ?
THAT FULL-BRINGERS AND DEPUTY SOUL REAPERS CAN EXCHANGE POWERS?
AS PROOF OF JOINING FORCES WITH KUGO...
...EACH OF US EXCHANGED A LITTLE BIT OF OUR POWERS...
...AND MADE A PLEDGE.
MY PLEDGE TO KUGO WAS...
"WHEN KUGO IS WITHIN THE DIMENSION OF MY ABILITY..."
"...I CANNOT DEACTIVATE MY ABILITY WITHOUT KUGO'S ORDERS."

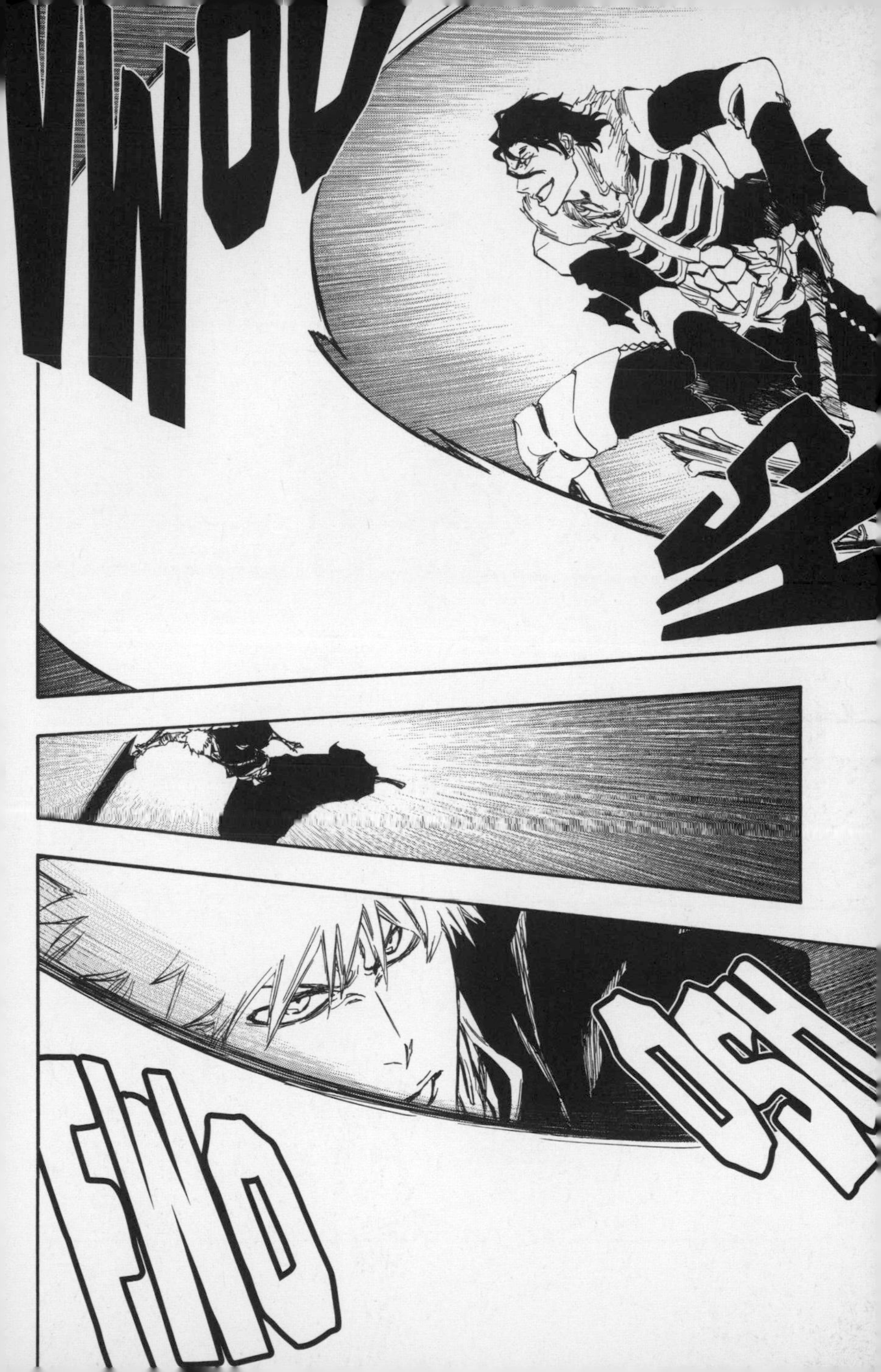
FWOOSH

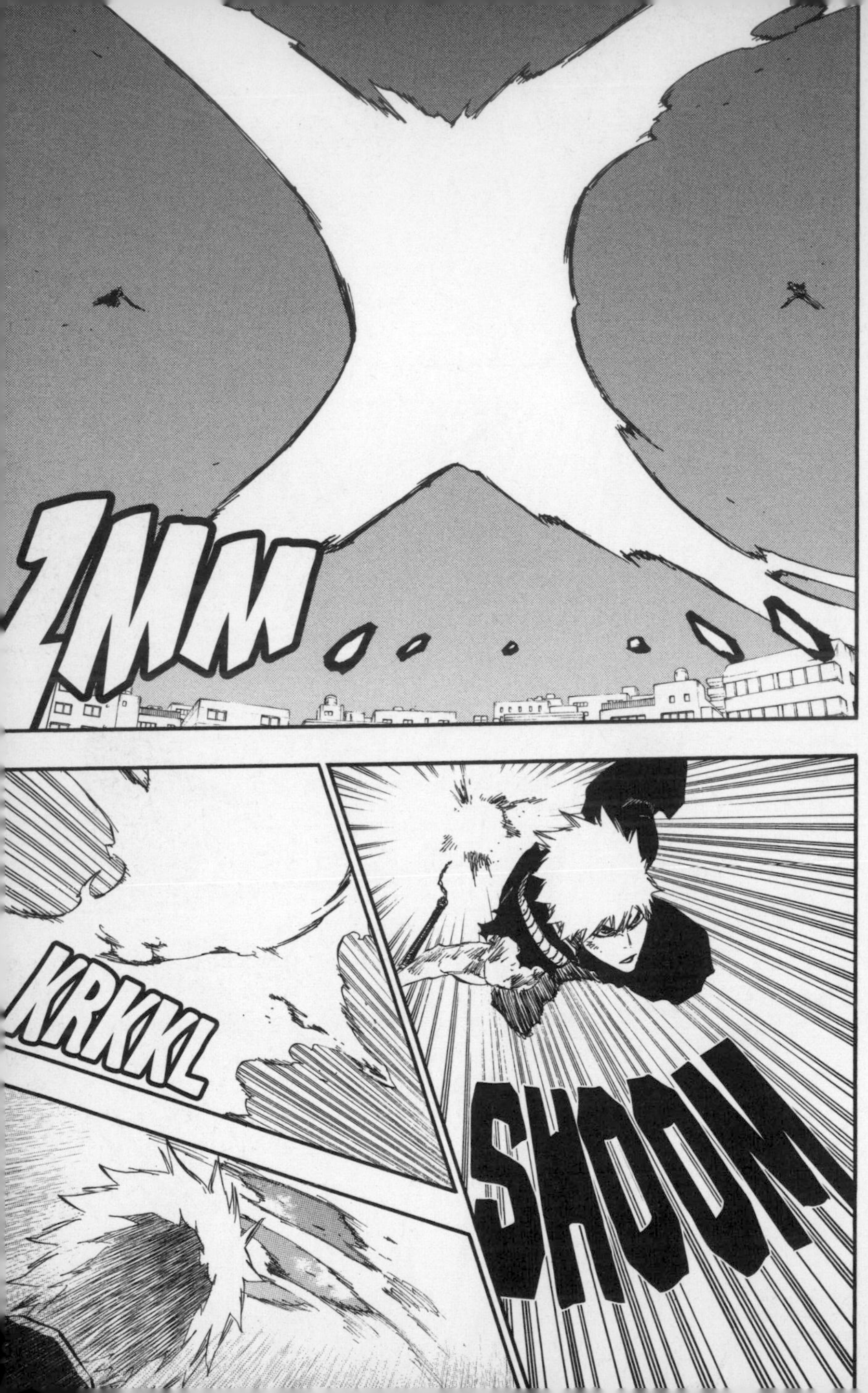
ZMM...
SHOOM
KRKKL

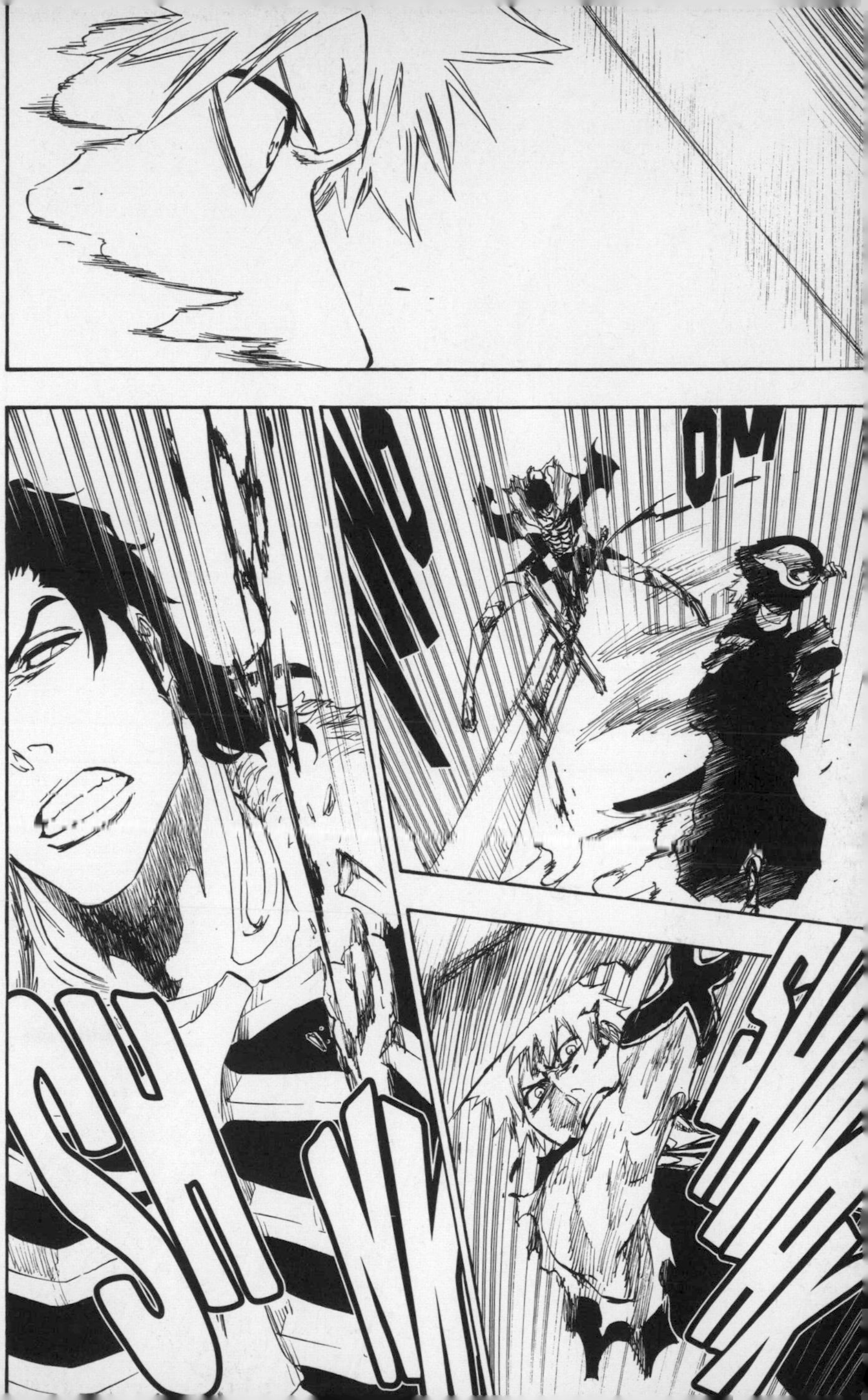

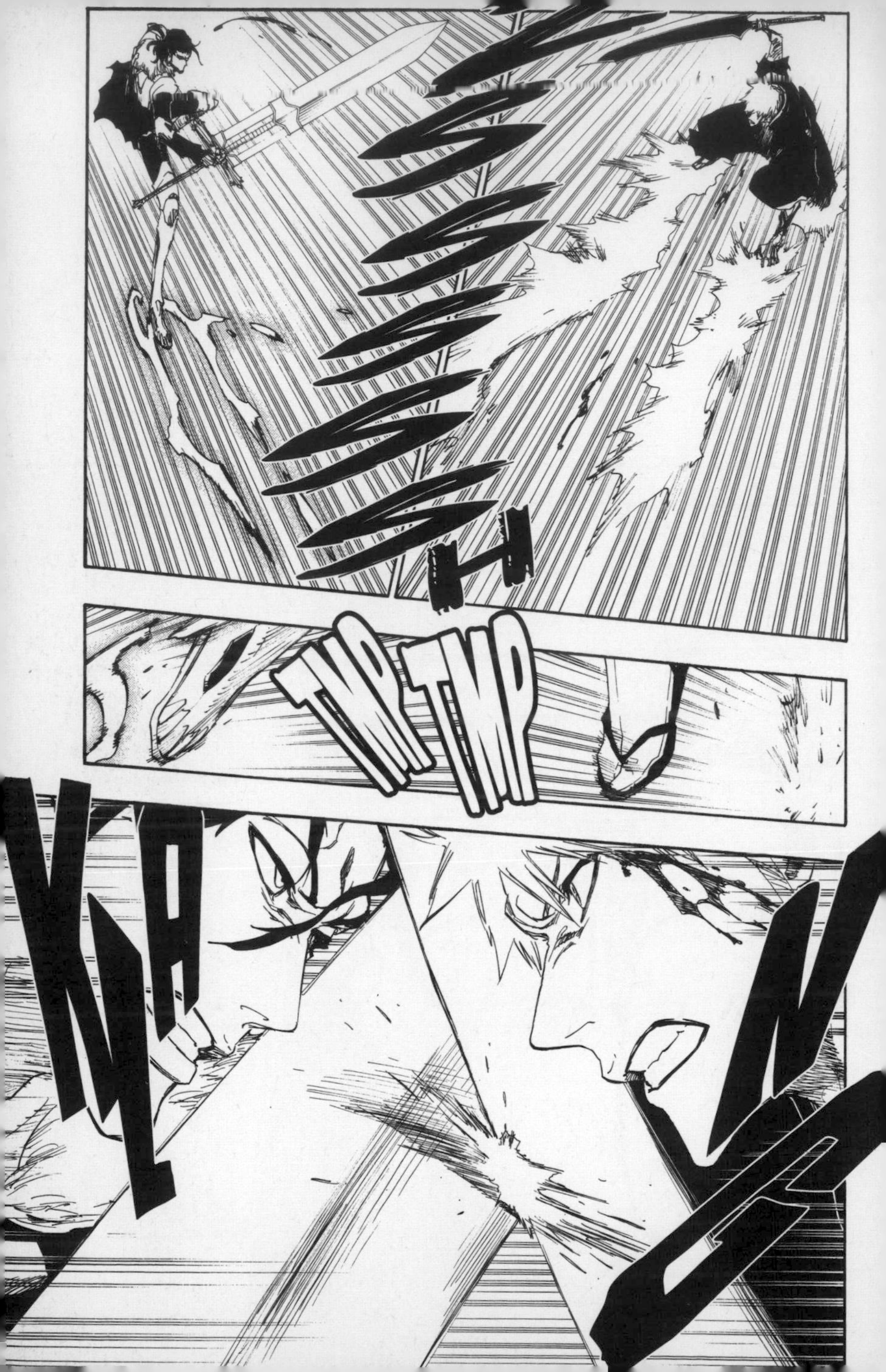
TMP TMP

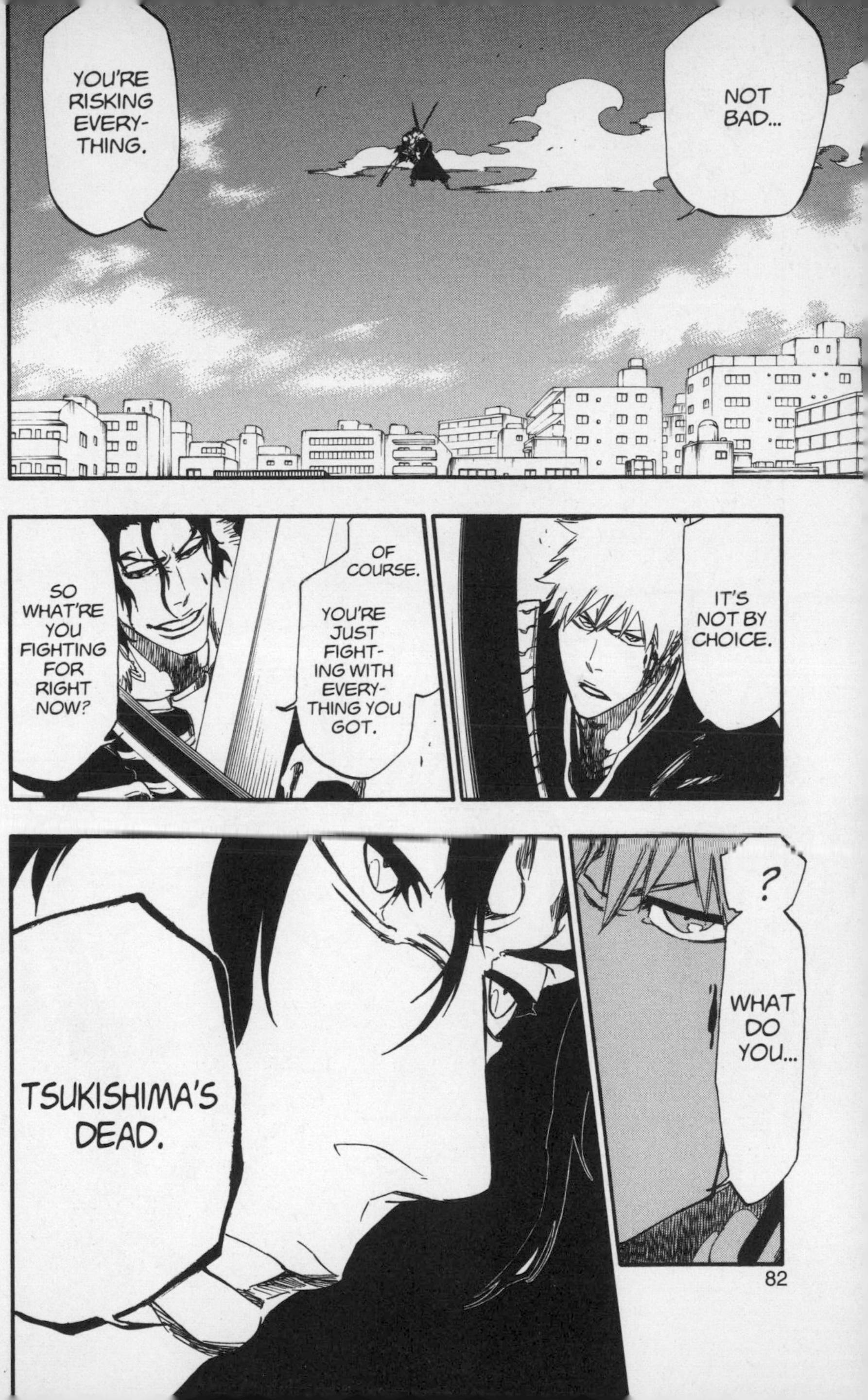
NOT BAD...
YOU'RE RISKING EVERY-THING.
IT'S NOT BY CHOICE.
OF COURSE.
YOU'RE JUST FIGHT-ING WITH EVERY-THING YOU GOT.
SO WHAT'RE YOU FIGHTING FOR RIGHT NOW?
?
WHAT DO YOU...
TSUKISHIMA'S DEAD.

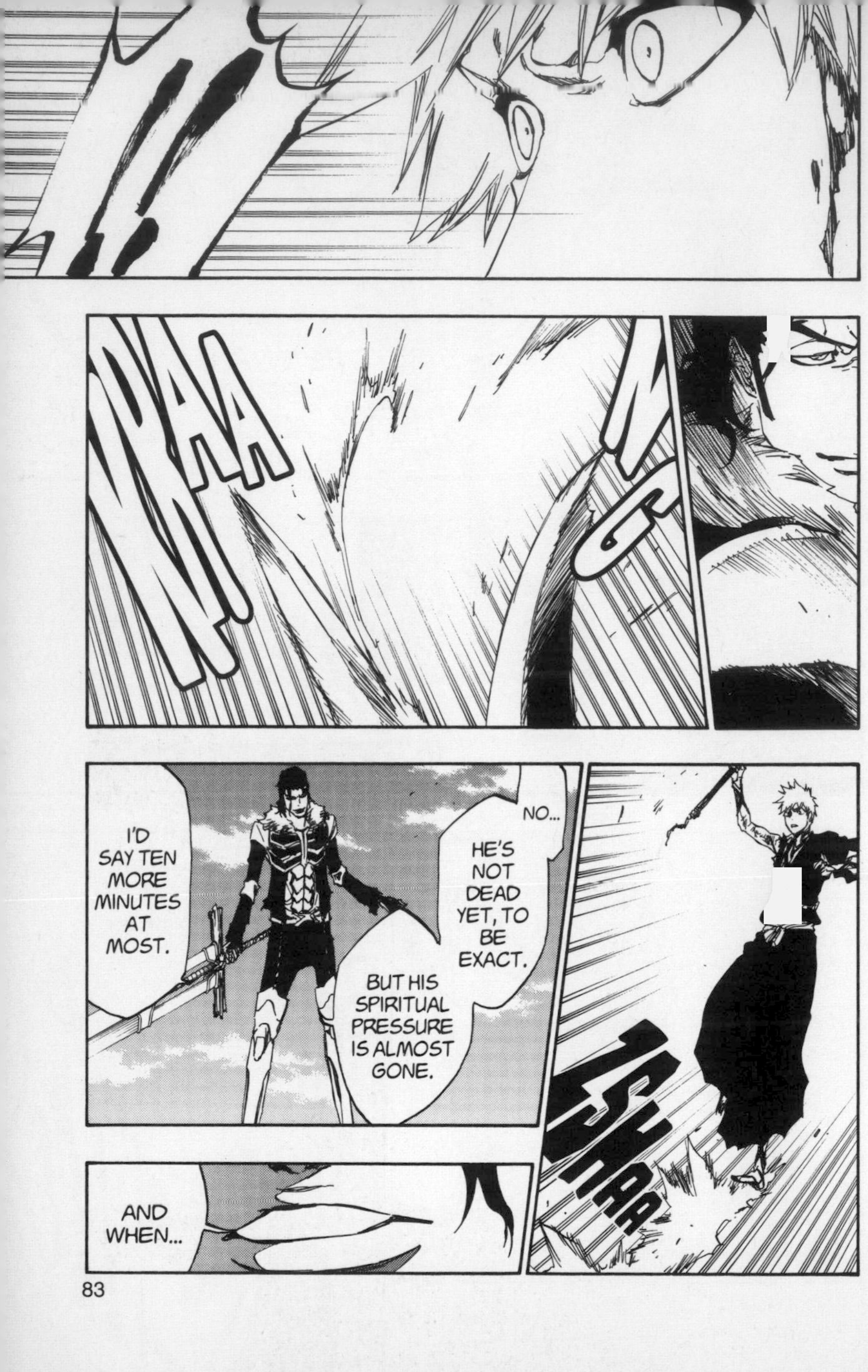
TSHAA
NO...
HE'S NOT DEAD YET, TO BE EXACT.
BUT HIS SPIRITUAL PRESSURE IS ALMOST GONE.
I'D SAY TEN MORE MINUTES AT MOST.
AND WHEN...

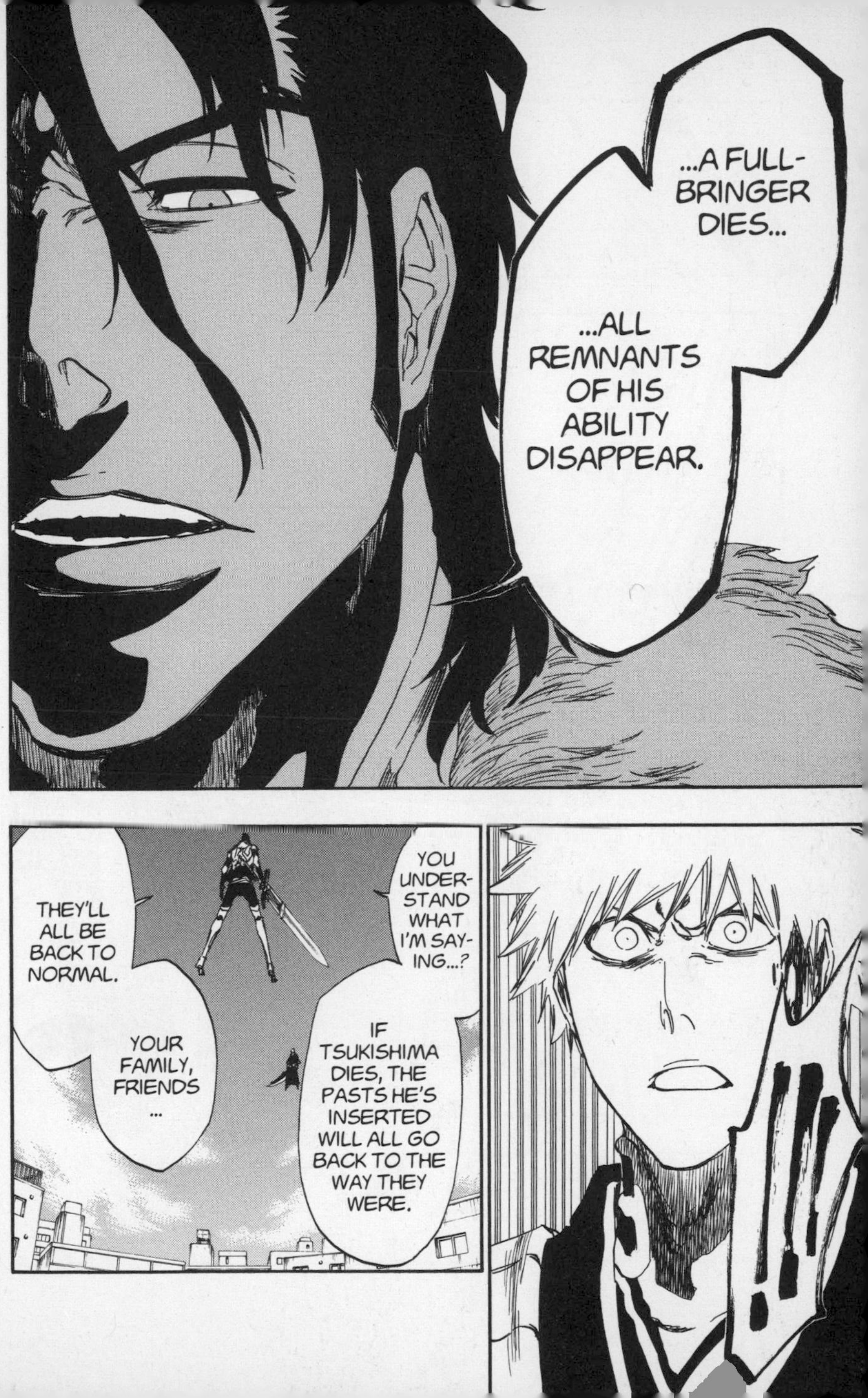
...A FULL-BRINGER DIES...
...ALL REMNANTS OF HIS ABILITY DISAPPEAR.
!!
YOU UNDERSTAND WHAT I'M SAYING...?
IF TSUKISHIMA DIES, THE PASTS HE'S INSERTED WILL ALL GO BACK TO THE WAY THEY WERE.
THEY'LL ALL BE BACK TO NORMAL.
YOUR FAMILY, FRIENDS ...

READ THIS WAY

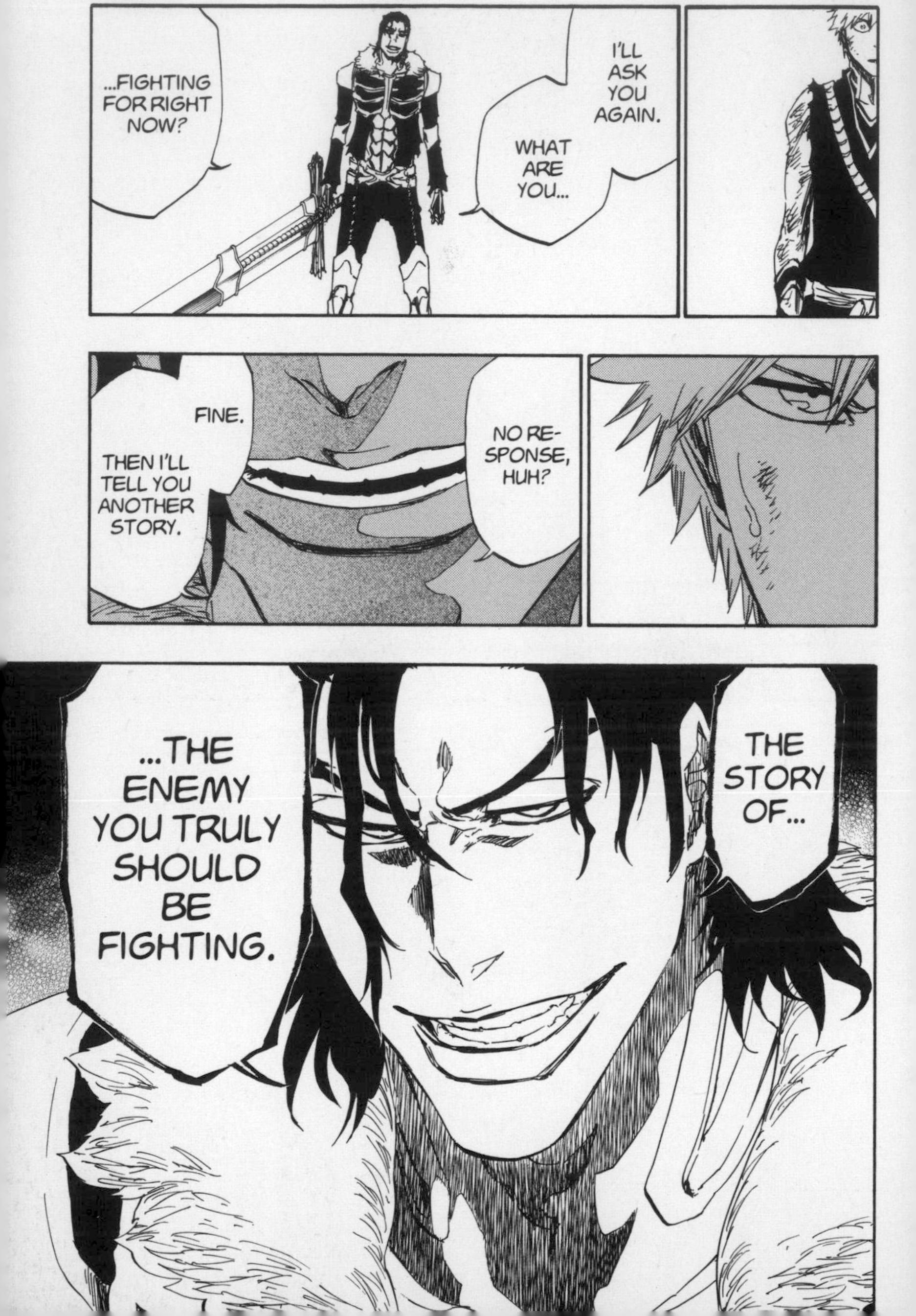
I'LL ASK YOU AGAIN.
WHAT ARE YOU...
...FIGHTING FOR RIGHT NOW?
NO RE-SPONSE, HUH?
FINE.
THEN I'LL TELL YOU ANOTHER STORY.
THE STORY OF...
...THE ENEMY YOU TRULY SHOULD BE FIGHTING.

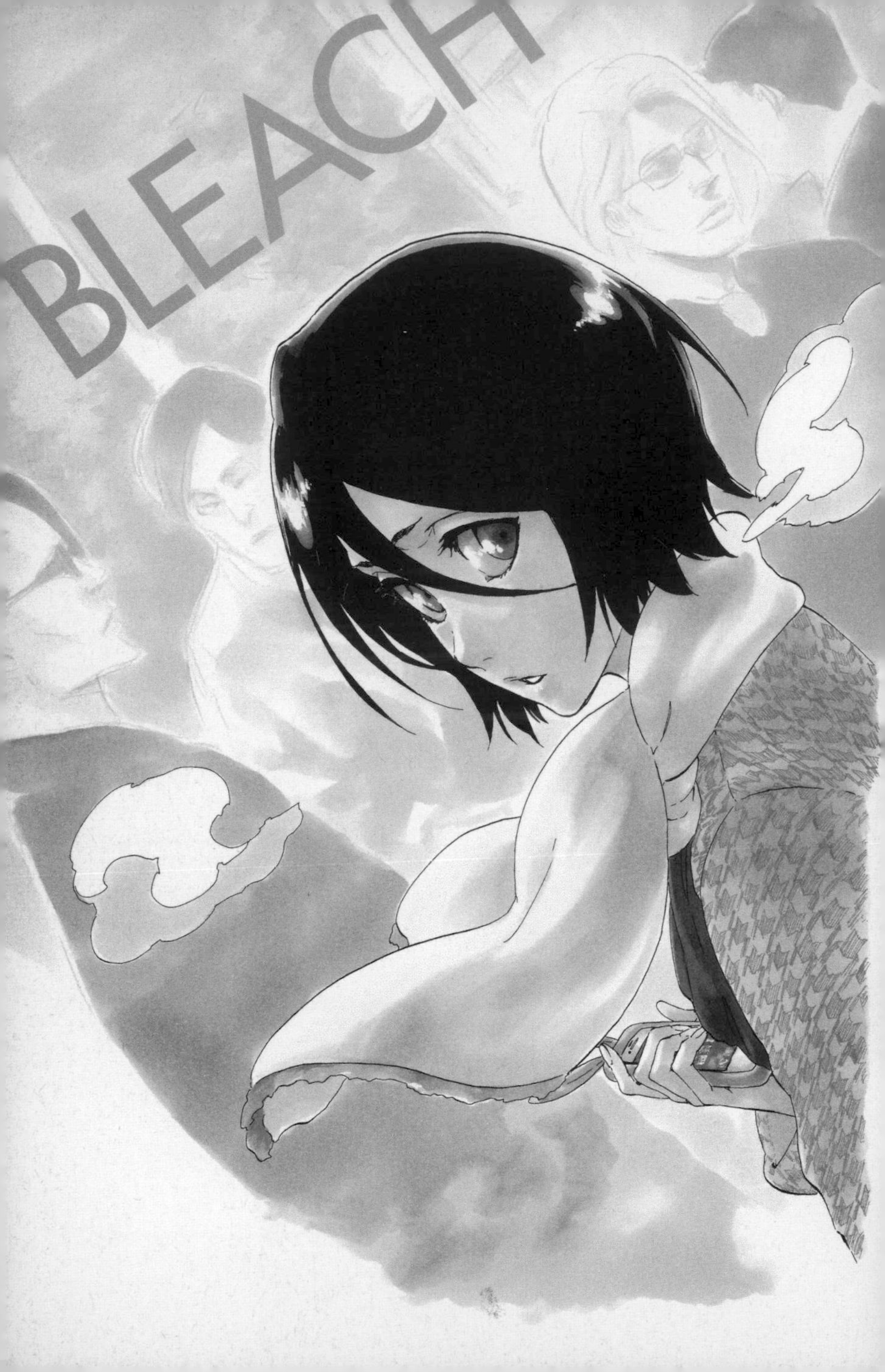
BLEACH

BLEACH
ブリーチ

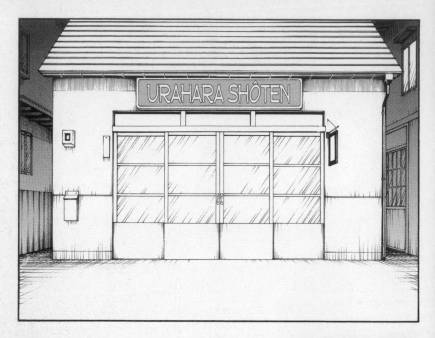

YEAH.

THEY'RE BEGINNING TO STABILIZE...

TESSAI...

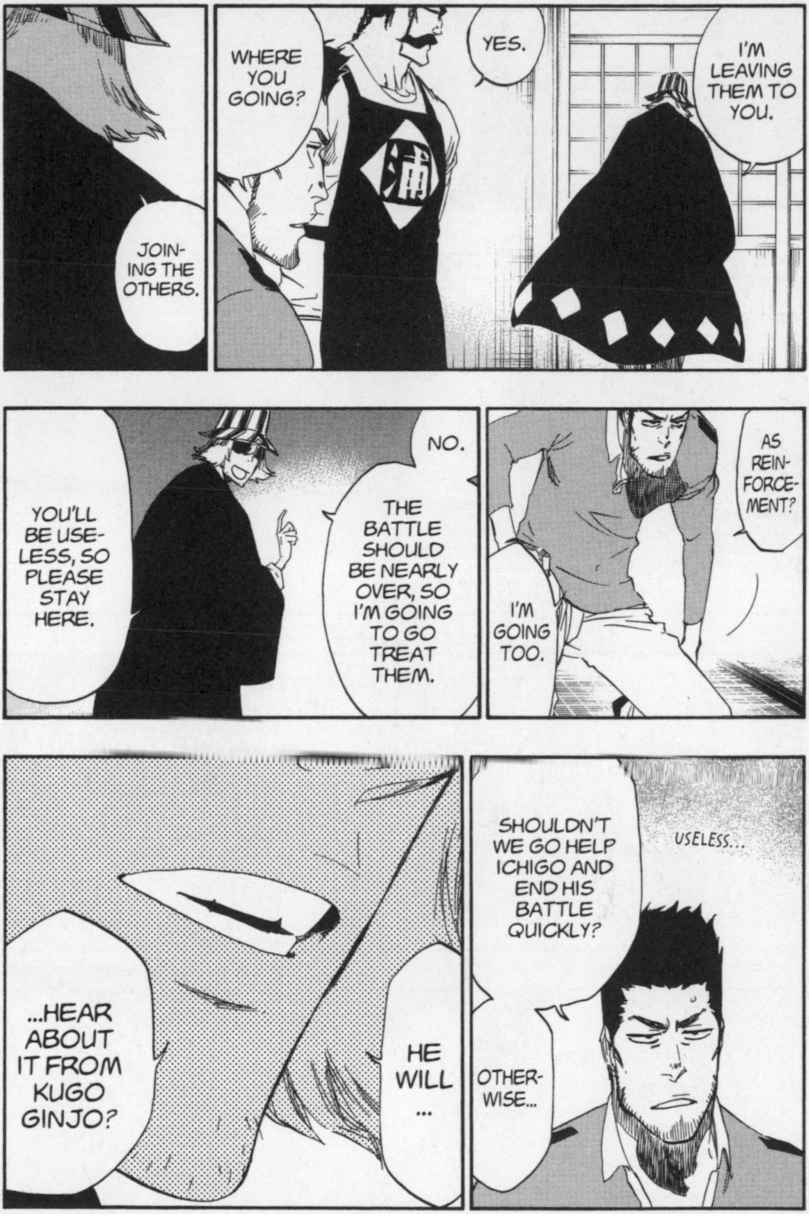
I'M LEAVING THEM TO YOU.
YES.
WHERE YOU GOING?
JOINING THE OTHERS.
AS REINFORCEMENT?
I'M GOING TOO.
NO.
THE BATTLE SHOULD BE NEARLY OVER, SO I'M GOING TO GO TREAT THEM.
YOU'LL BE USELESS, SO PLEASE STAY HERE.
USELESS...
SHOULDN'T WE GO HELP ICHIGO AND END HIS BATTLE QUICKLY?
OTHERWISE...
HE WILL ...
...HEAR ABOUT IT FROM KUGO GINJO?

READ THIS WAY

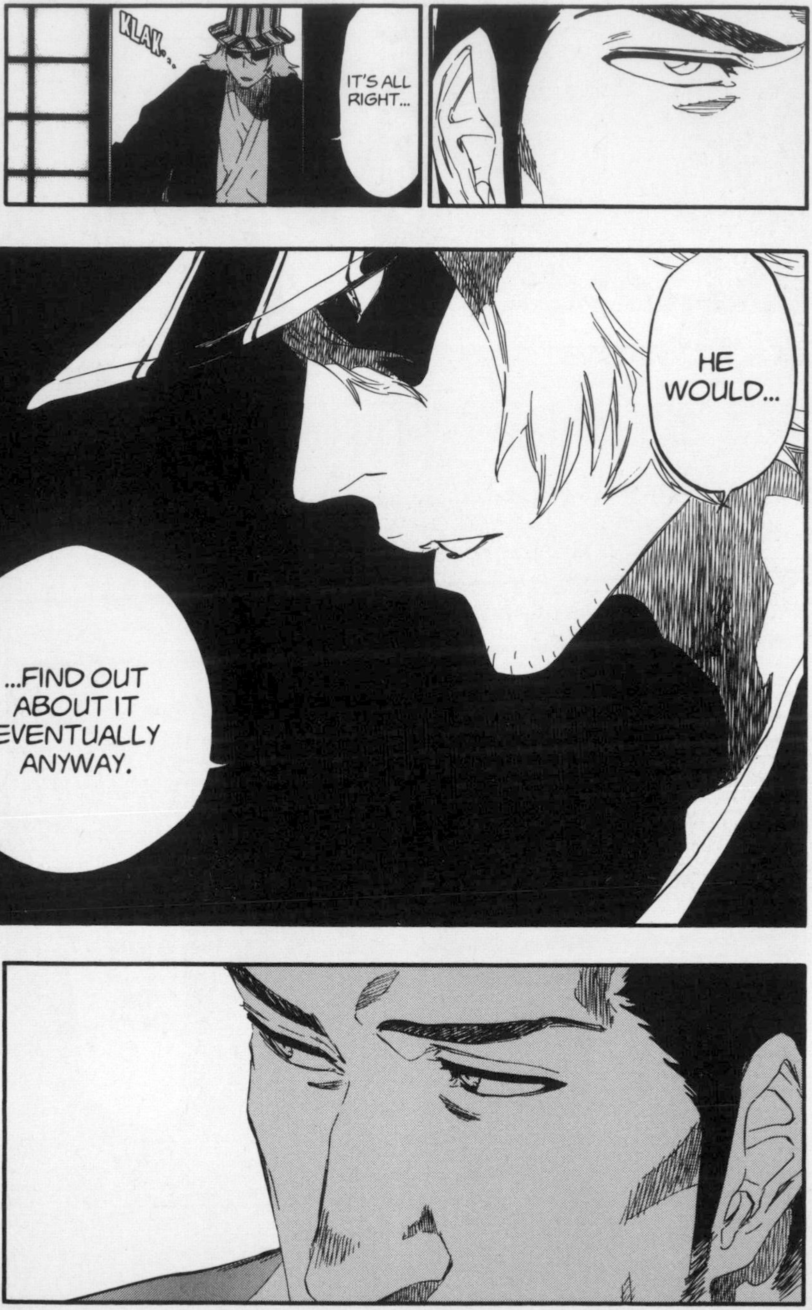

IT'S ALL RIGHT...
KLAK...
HE WOULD...
...FIND OUT ABOUT IT EVENTUALLY ANYWAY.

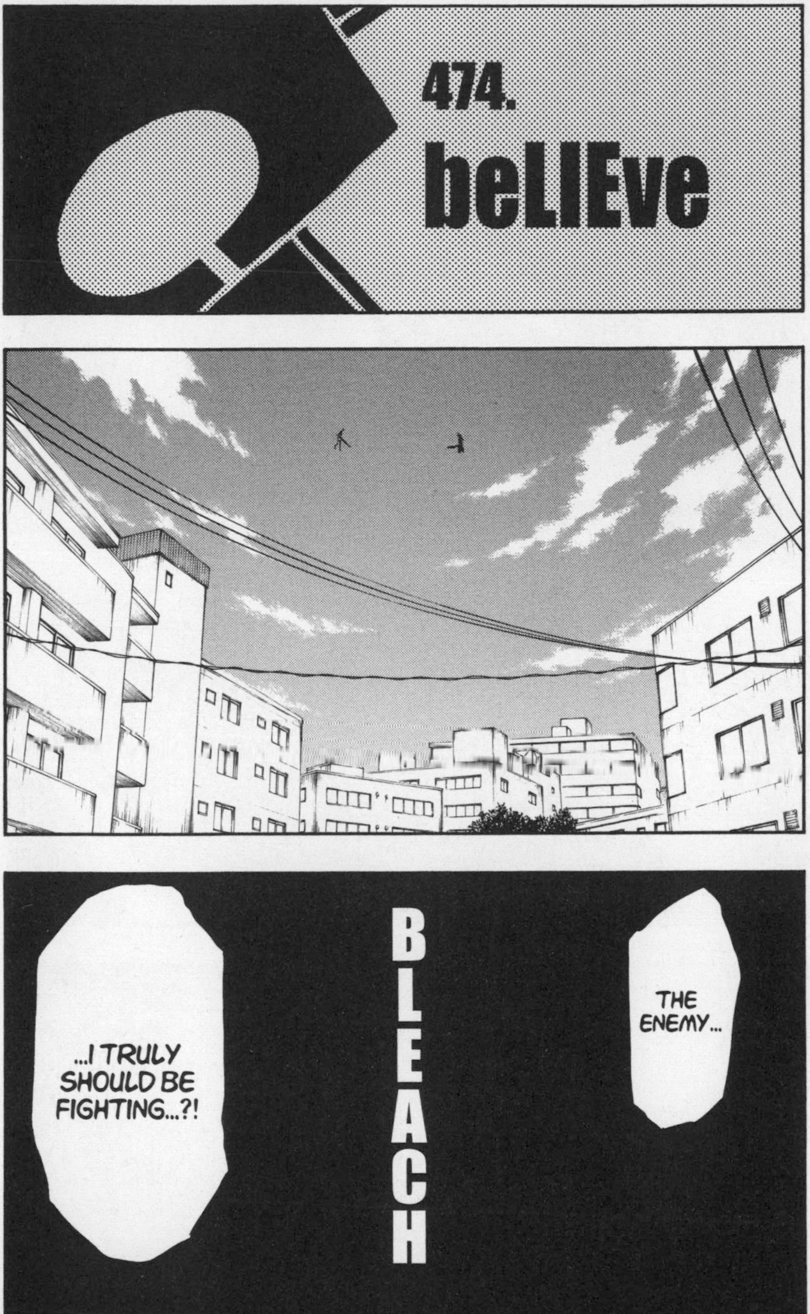
474.
beLIEve
THE ENEMY...
BLEACH
...I TRULY SHOULD BE FIGHTING...?!

READ THIS WAY

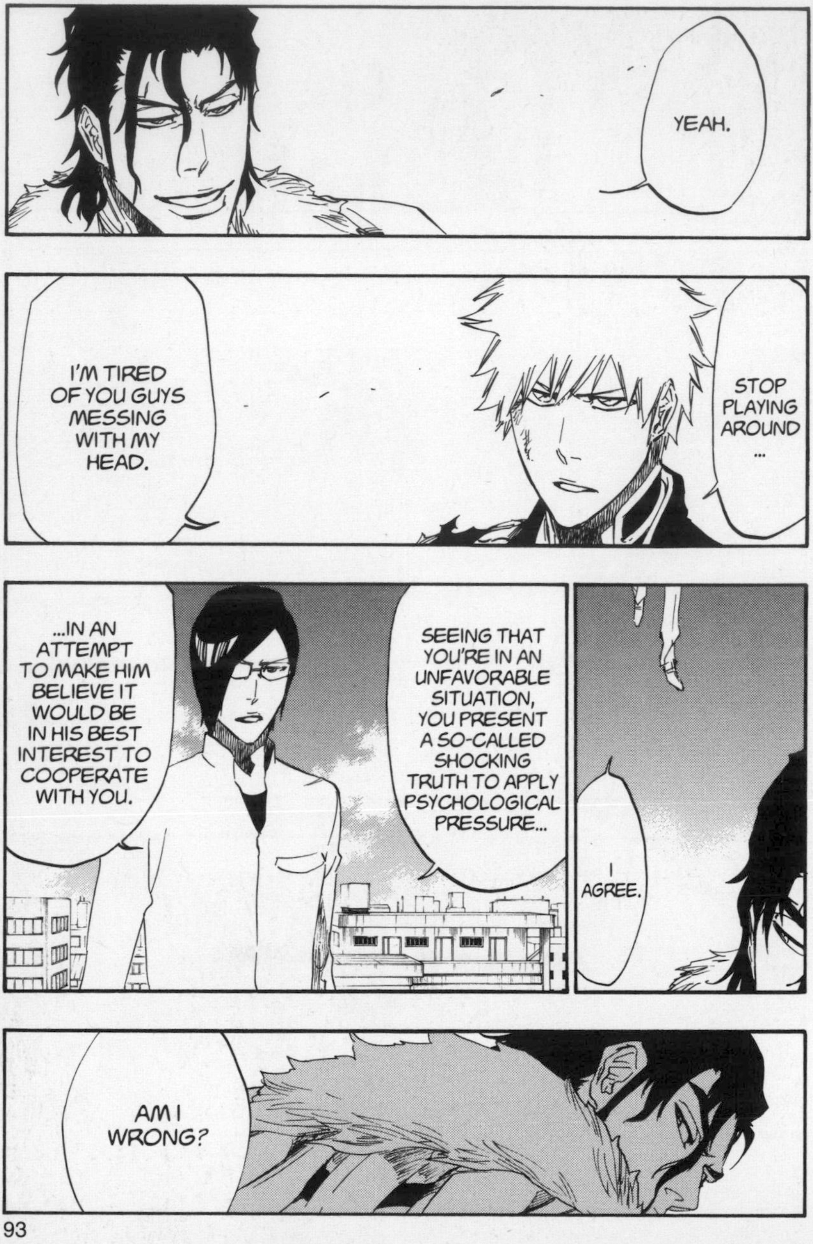

YEAH.
STOP PLAYING AROUND ...
I'M TIRED OF YOU GUYS MESSING WITH MY HEAD.
I AGREE.
SEEING THAT YOU'RE IN AN UNFAVORABLE SITUATION, YOU PRESENT A SO-CALLED SHOCKING TRUTH TO APPLY PSYCHOLOGICAL PRESSURE...
...IN AN ATTEMPT TO MAKE HIM BELIEVE IT WOULD BE IN HIS BEST INTEREST TO COOPERATE WITH YOU.
AM I WRONG?

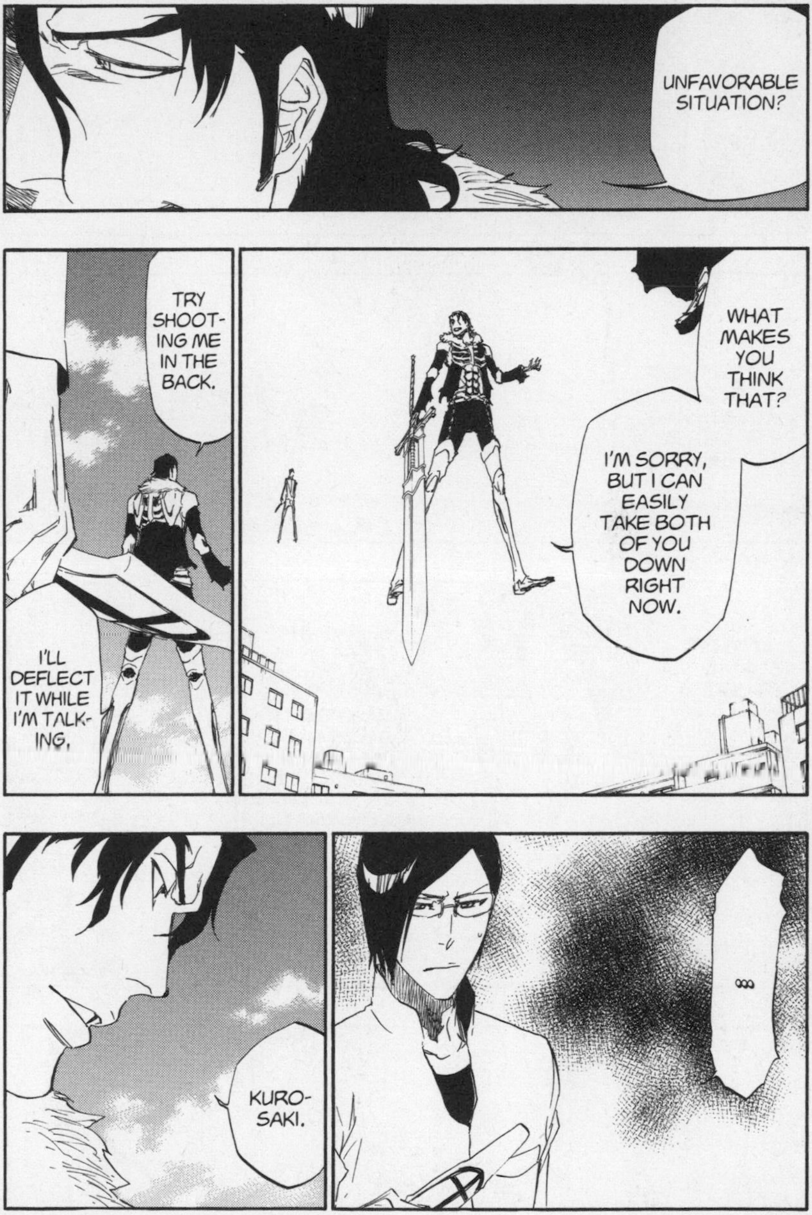
UNFAVORABLE SITUATION?
WHAT MAKES YOU THINK THAT?
I'M SORRY, BUT I CAN EASILY TAKE BOTH OF YOU DOWN RIGHT NOW.
TRY SHOOTING ME IN THE BACK.
I'LL DEFLECT IT WHILE I'M TALKING.
...
KURO-SAKI.

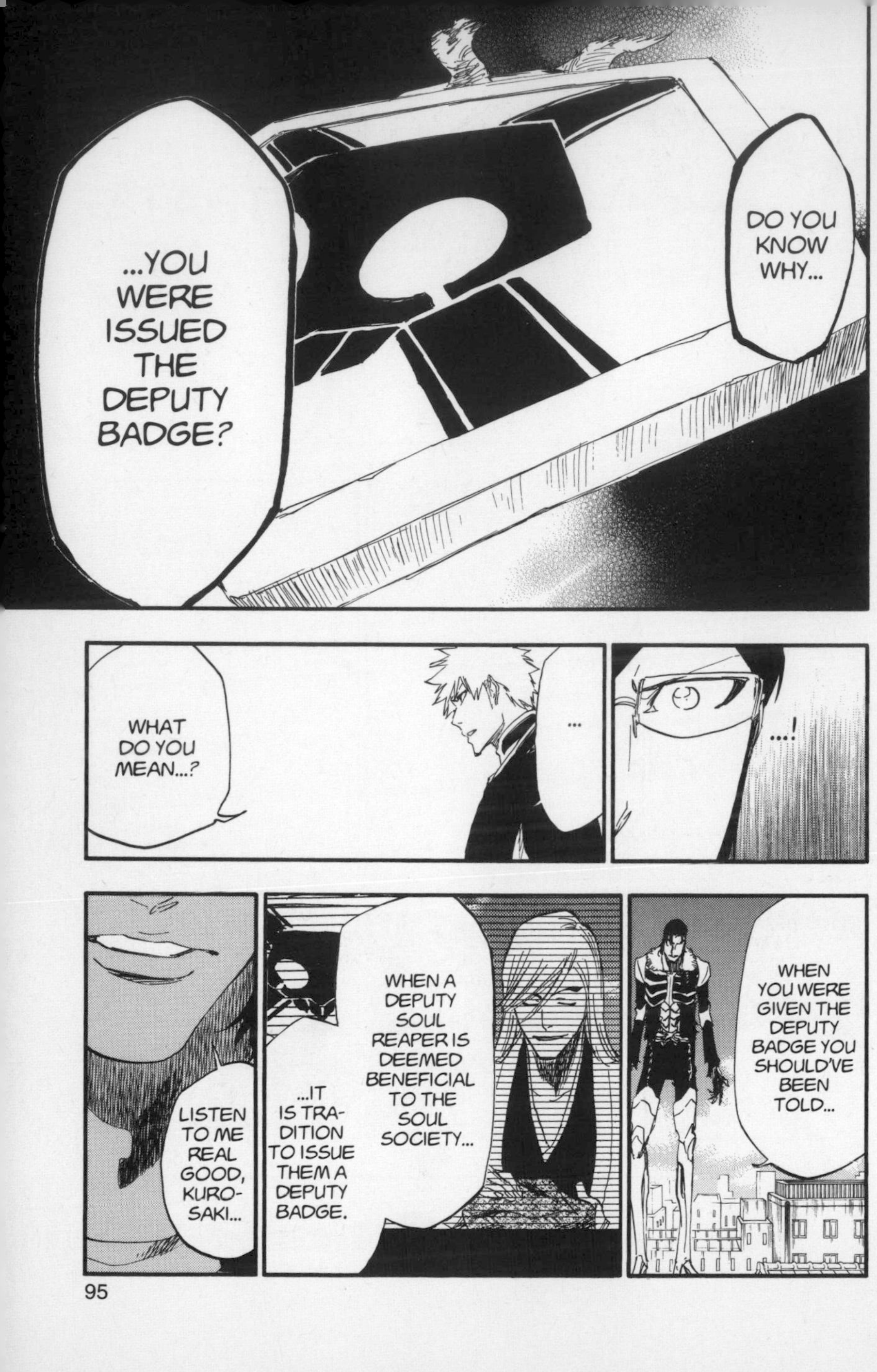
DO YOU KNOW WHY...
...YOU WERE ISSUED THE DEPUTY BADGE?
...!
...
WHAT DO YOU MEAN...?
WHEN YOU WERE GIVEN THE DEPUTY BADGE YOU SHOULD'VE BEEN TOLD...
WHEN A DEPUTY SOUL REAPER IS DEEMED BENEFICIAL TO THE SOUL SOCIETY...
...IT IS TRADITION TO ISSUE THEM A DEPUTY BADGE.
LISTEN TO ME REAL GOOD, KUROSAKI...

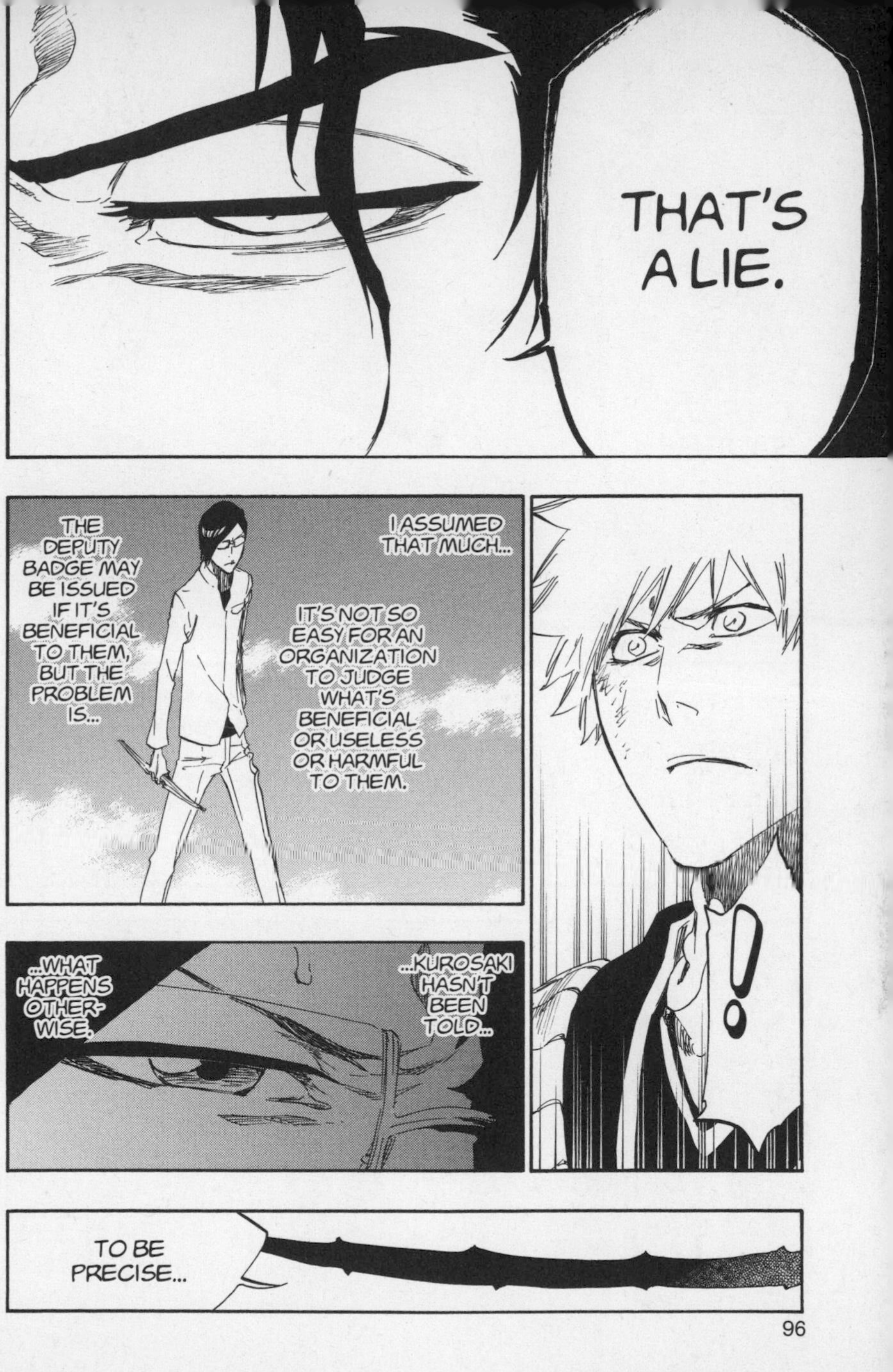
THAT'S A LIE.
I ASSUMED THAT MUCH...
THE DEPUTY BADGE MAY BE ISSUED IF IT'S BENEFICIAL TO THEM, BUT THE PROBLEM IS...
IT'S NOT SO EASY FOR AN ORGANIZATION TO JUDGE WHAT'S BENEFICIAL OR USELESS OR HARMFUL TO THEM.
...KUROSAKI HASN'T BEEN TOLD...
...WHAT HAPPENS OTHER-WISE.
!
TO BE PRECISE...

READ THIS WAY

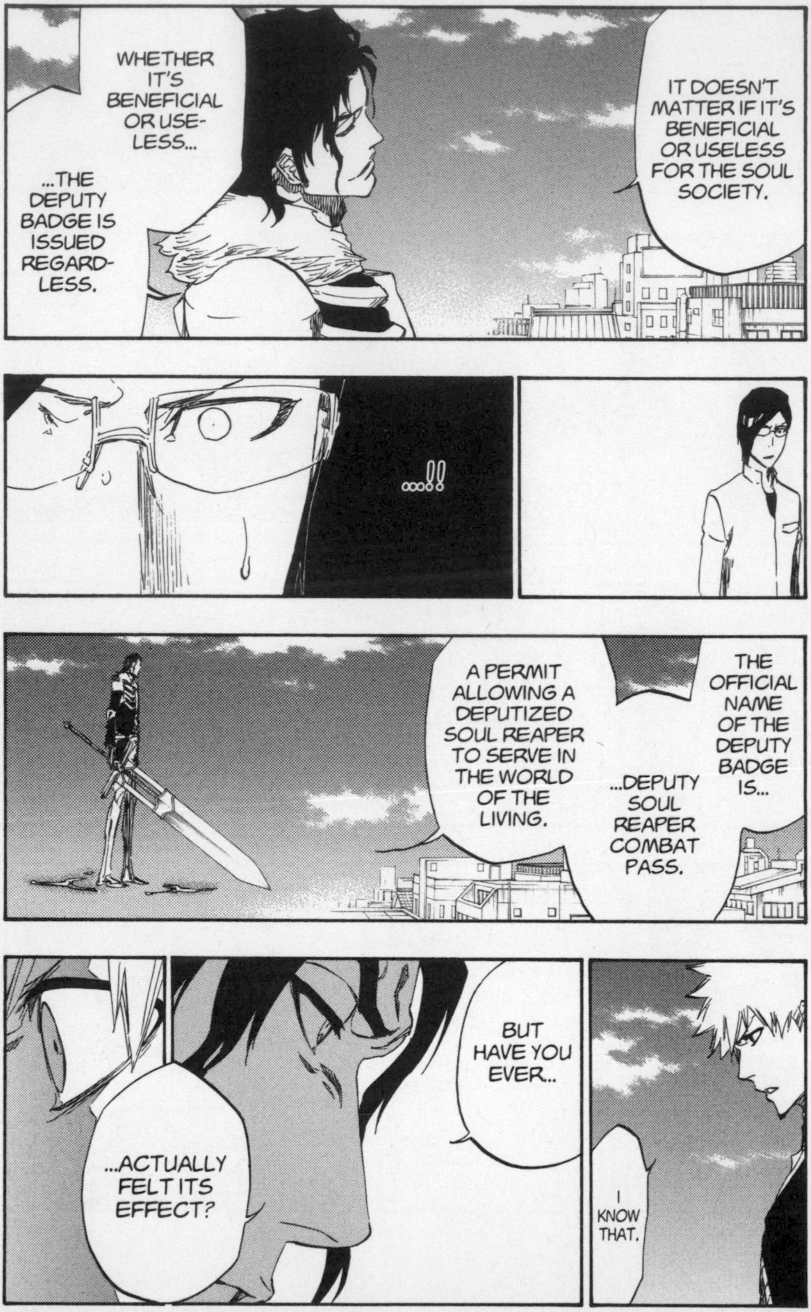
IT DOESN'T MATTER IF IT'S BENEFICIAL OR USELESS FOR THE SOUL SOCIETY.
WHETHER IT'S BENEFICIAL OR USE-LESS...
...THE DEPUTY BADGE IS ISSUED REGARD-LESS.
...!!
THE OFFICIAL NAME OF THE DEPUTY BADGE IS...
...DEPUTY SOUL REAPER COMBAT PASS.
A PERMIT ALLOWING A DEPUTIZED SOUL REAPER TO SERVE IN THE WORLD OF THE LIVING.
I KNOW THAT.
BUT HAVE YOU EVER...
...ACTUALLY FELT ITS EFFECT?

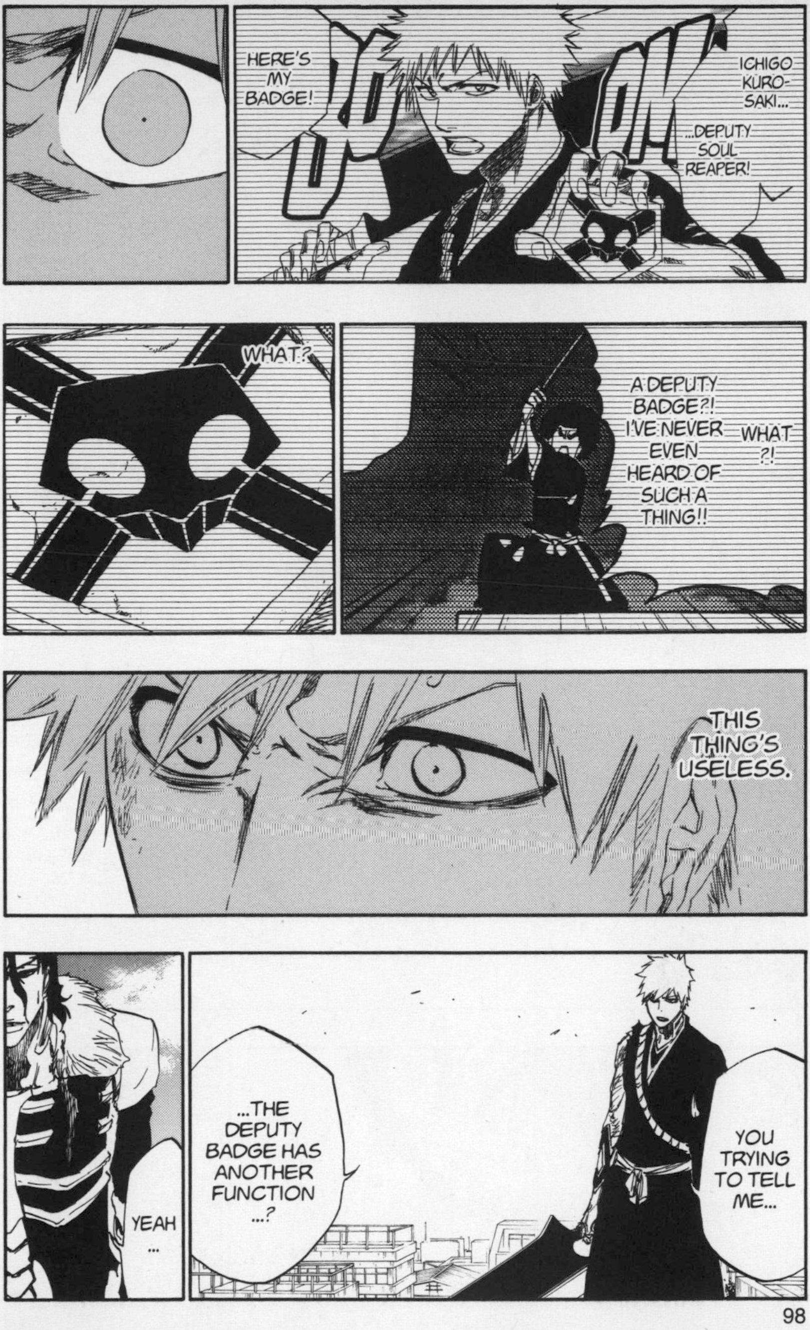
ICHIGO KUROSAKI...
...DEPUTY SOUL REAPER!
HERE'S MY BADGE!
WHAT?!
A DEPUTY BADGE?! I'VE NEVER EVEN HEARD OF SUCH A THING!!
WHAT?
THIS THING'S USELESS.
YOU TRYING TO TELL ME...
...THE DEPUTY BADGE HAS ANOTHER FUNCTION ...?
YEAH ...

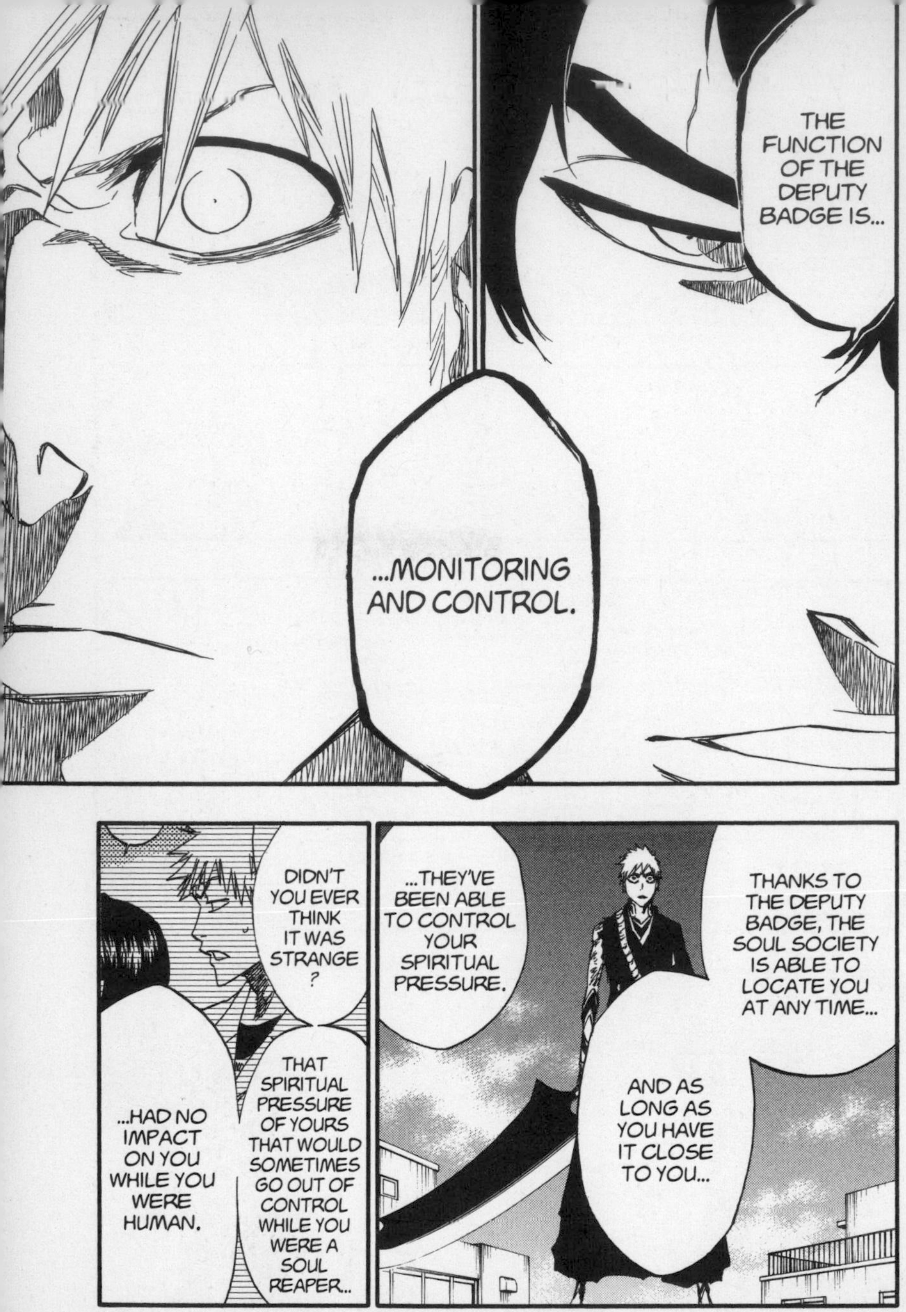
THE FUNCTION OF THE DEPUTY BADGE IS...
...MONITORING AND CONTROL.
THANKS TO THE DEPUTY BADGE, THE SOUL SOCIETY IS ABLE TO LOCATE YOU AT ANY TIME...
AND AS LONG AS YOU HAVE IT CLOSE TO YOU...
...THEY'VE BEEN ABLE TO CONTROL YOUR SPIRITUAL PRESSURE.
DIDN'T YOU EVER THINK IT WAS STRANGE?
THAT SPIRITUAL PRESSURE OF YOURS THAT WOULD SOMETIMES GO OUT OF CONTROL WHILE YOU WERE A SOUL REAPER...
...HAD NO IMPACT ON YOU WHILE YOU WERE HUMAN.

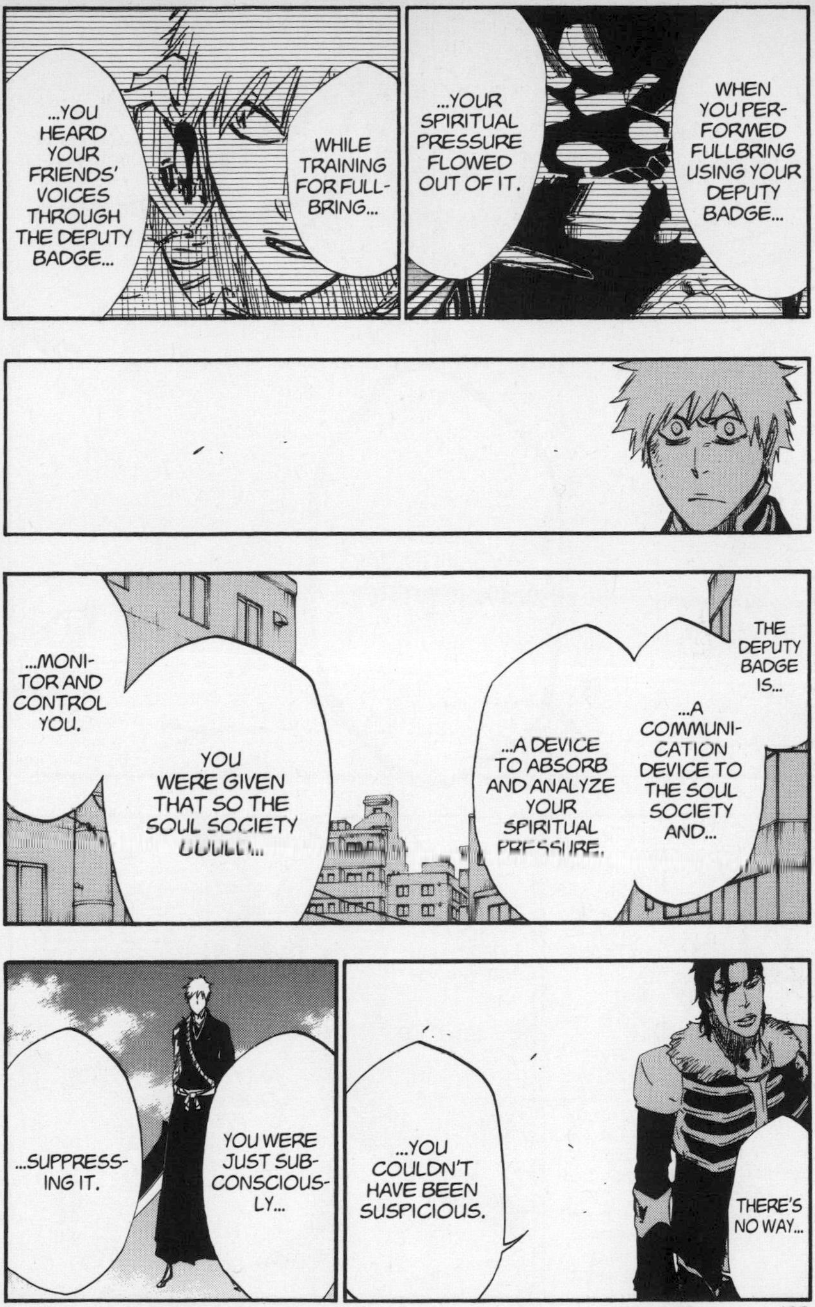

WHEN YOU PERFORMED FULLBRING USING YOUR DEPUTY BADGE...
...YOUR SPIRITUAL PRESSURE FLOWED OUT OF IT.
WHILE TRAINING FOR FULLBRING...
...YOU HEARD YOUR FRIENDS' VOICES THROUGH THE DEPUTY BADGE...
THE DEPUTY BADGE IS...
...A COMMUNICATION DEVICE TO THE SOUL SOCIETY AND...
...A DEVICE TO ABSORB AND ANALYZE YOUR SPIRITUAL PRESSURE.
YOU WERE GIVEN THAT SO THE SOUL SOCIETY COULD...
...MONITOR AND CONTROL YOU.
THERE'S NO WAY...
...YOU COULDN'T HAVE BEEN SUSPICIOUS.
YOU WERE JUST SUBCONSCIOUSLY...
...SUPPRESSING IT.

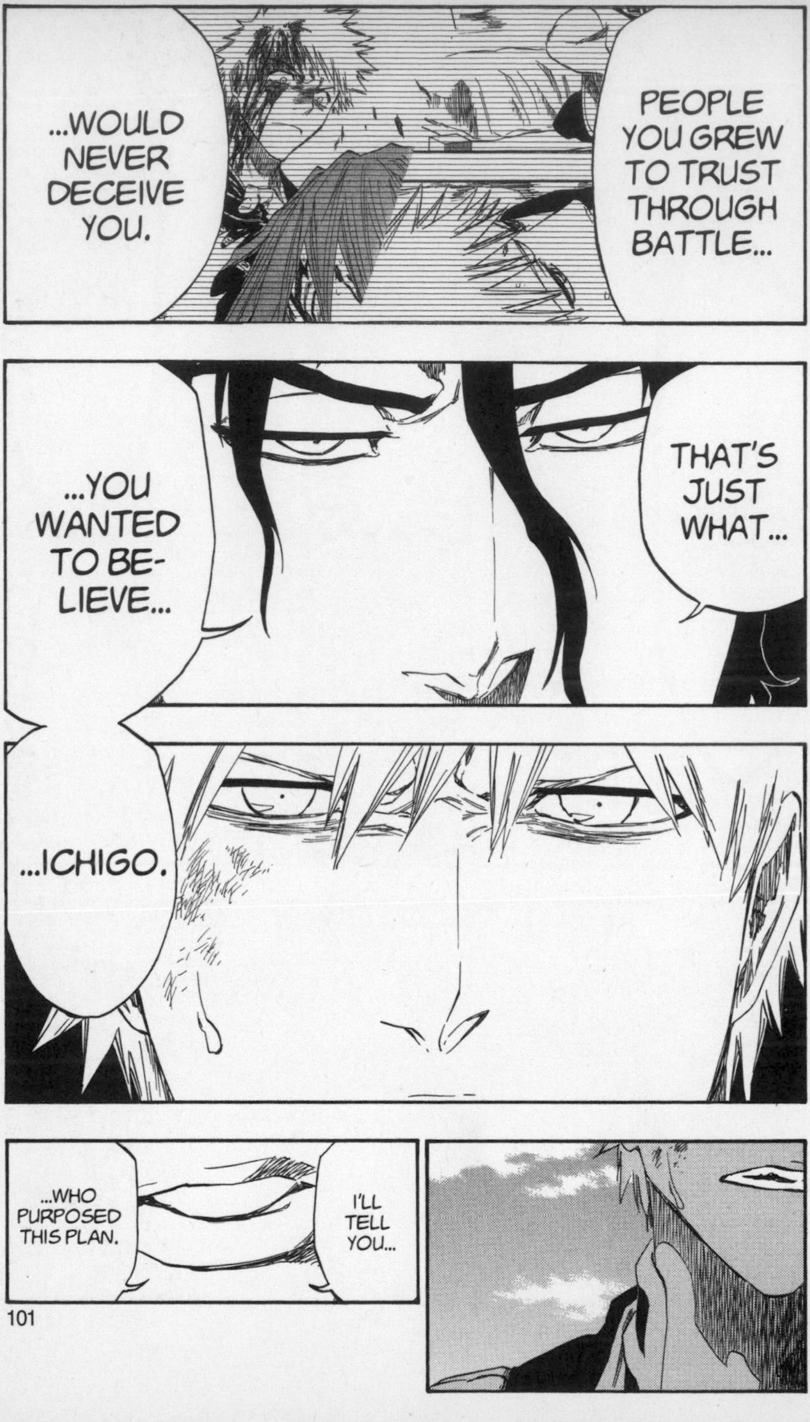
PEOPLE YOU GREW TO TRUST THROUGH BATTLE...
...WOULD NEVER DECEIVE YOU.
THAT'S JUST WHAT...
...YOU WANTED TO BE-LIEVE...
...ICHIGO.
I'LL TELL YOU...
...WHO PURPOSED THIS PLAN.

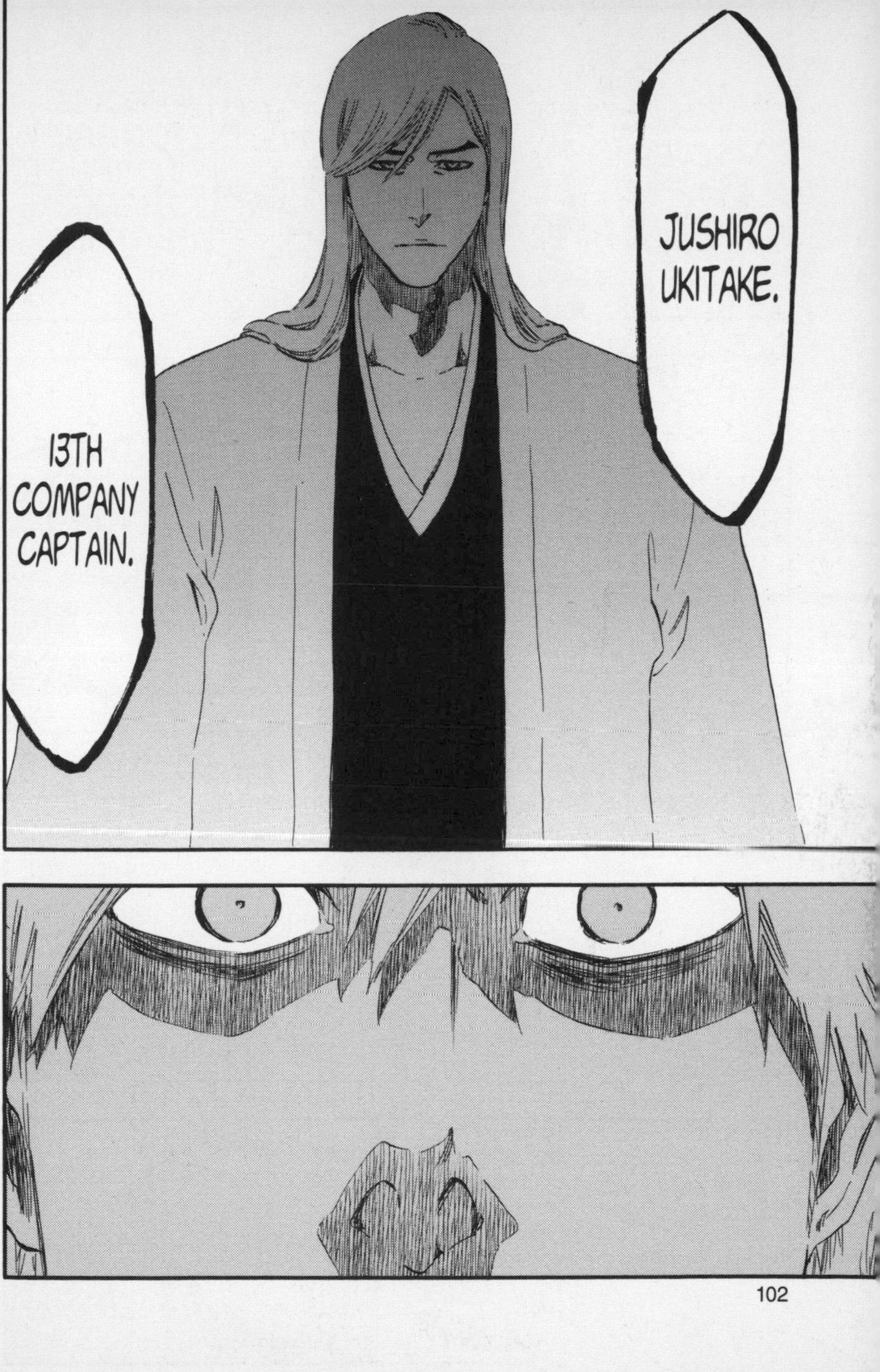
JUSHIRO UKITAKE.
13TH COMPANY CAPTAIN.

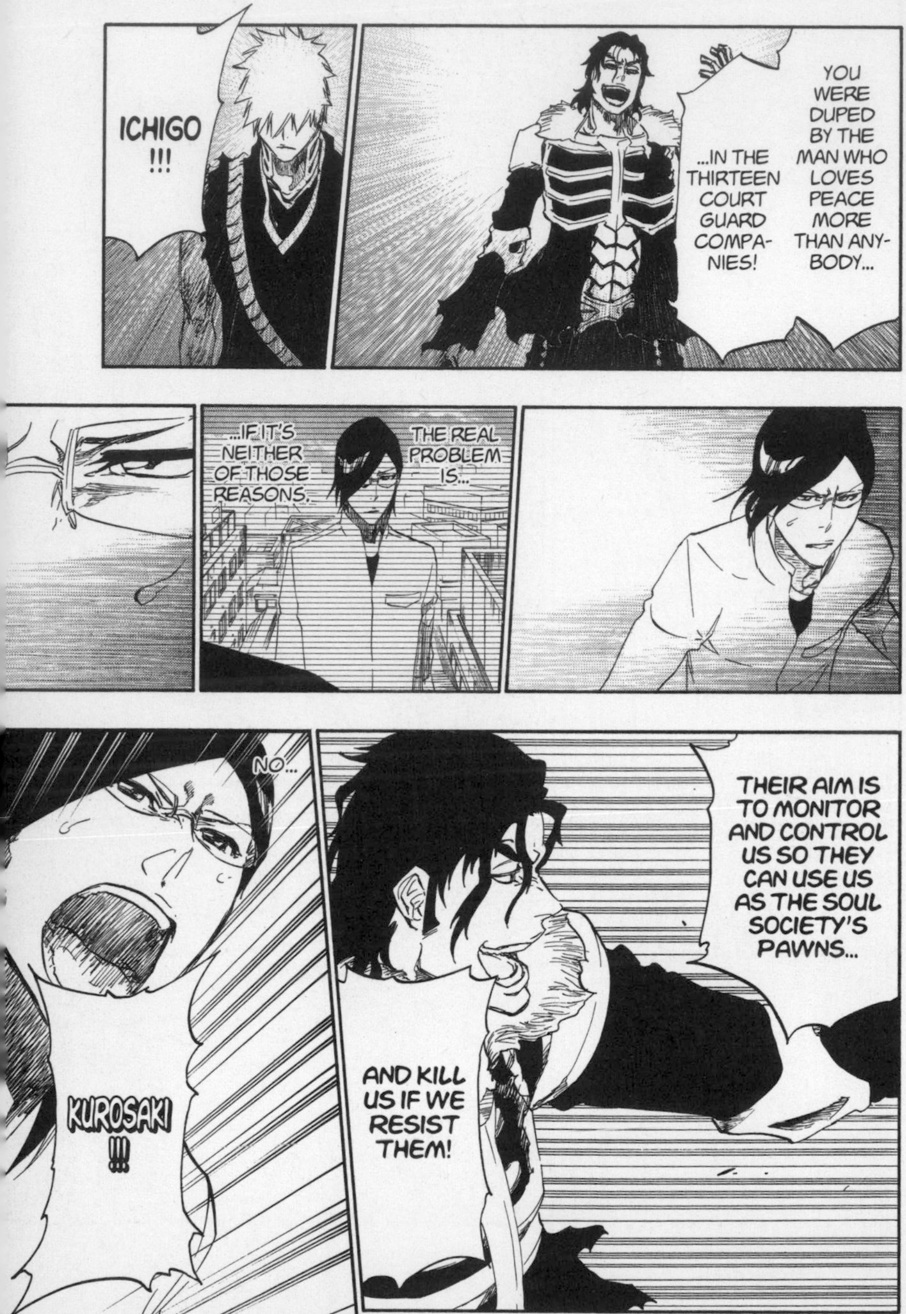
YOU WERE DUPED BY THE MAN WHO LOVES PEACE MORE THAN ANYBODY...
...IN THE THIRTEEN COURT GUARD COMPANIES!
ICHIGO !!!
THE REAL PROBLEM IS...
...IF IT'S NEITHER OF THOSE REASONS.
THEIR AIM IS TO MONITOR AND CONTROL US SO THEY CAN USE US AS THE SOUL SOCIETY'S PAWNS...
AND KILL US IF WE RESIST THEM!
NO...
KUROSAKI !!!

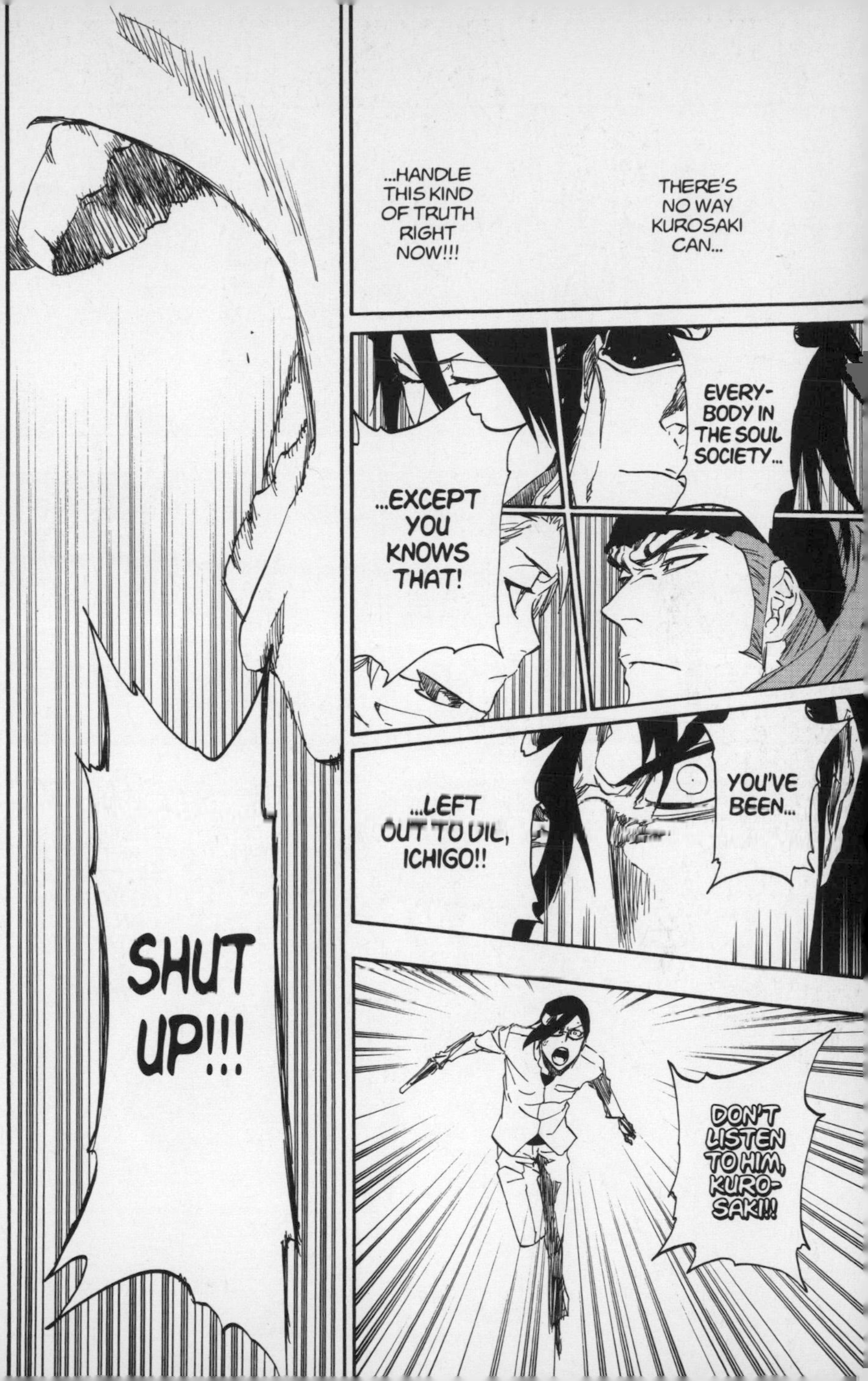
THERE'S NO WAY KUROSAKI CAN...
...HANDLE THIS KIND OF TRUTH RIGHT NOW!!!
EVERYBODY IN THE SOUL SOCIETY...
...EXCEPT YOU KNOWS THAT!
YOU'VE BEEN...
...LEFT OUT TO DIE, ICHIGO!!
DON'T LISTEN TO HIM, KUROSAKI!!
SHUT UP!!!

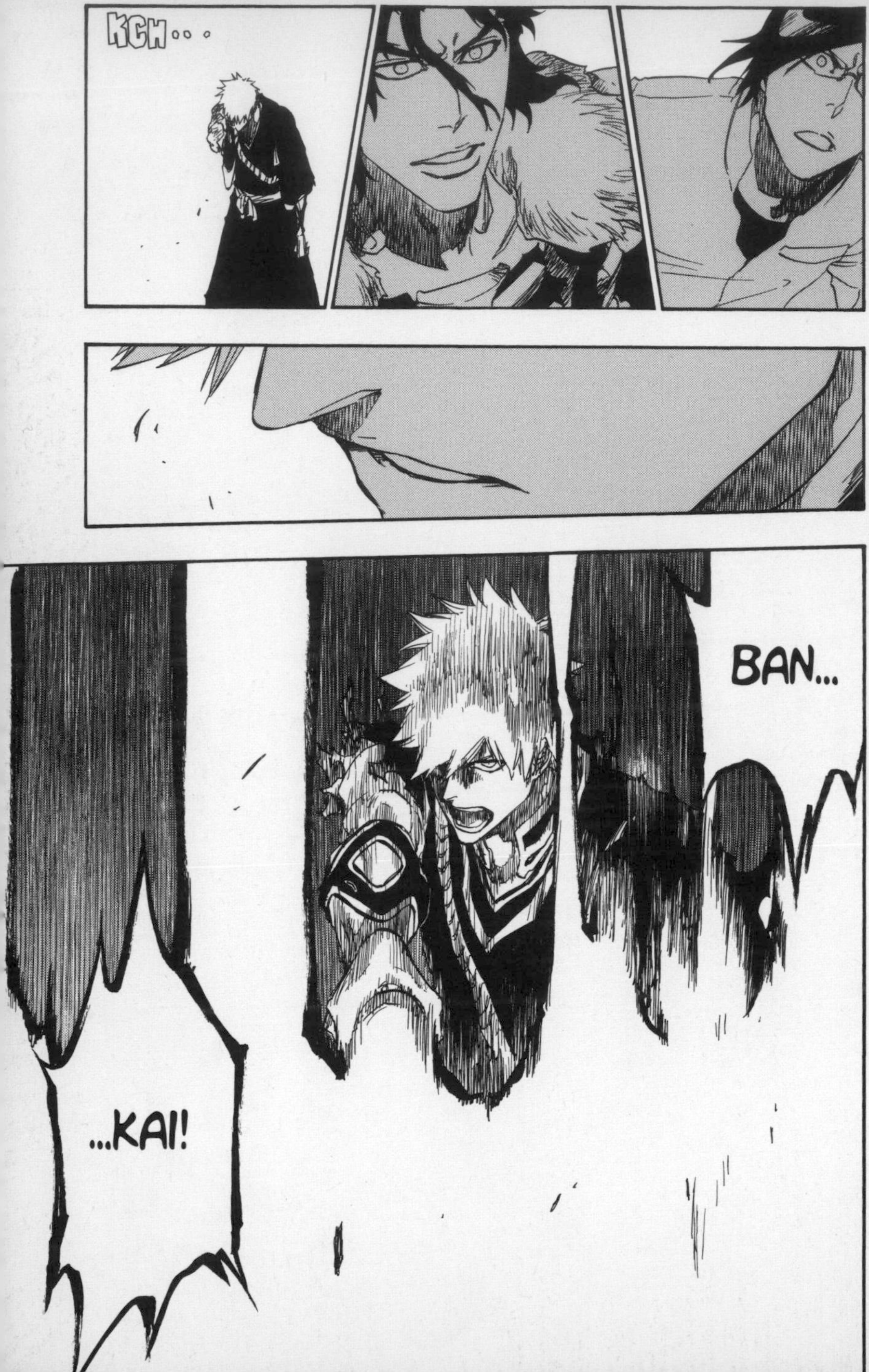

KCH...
BAN...
...KAI!

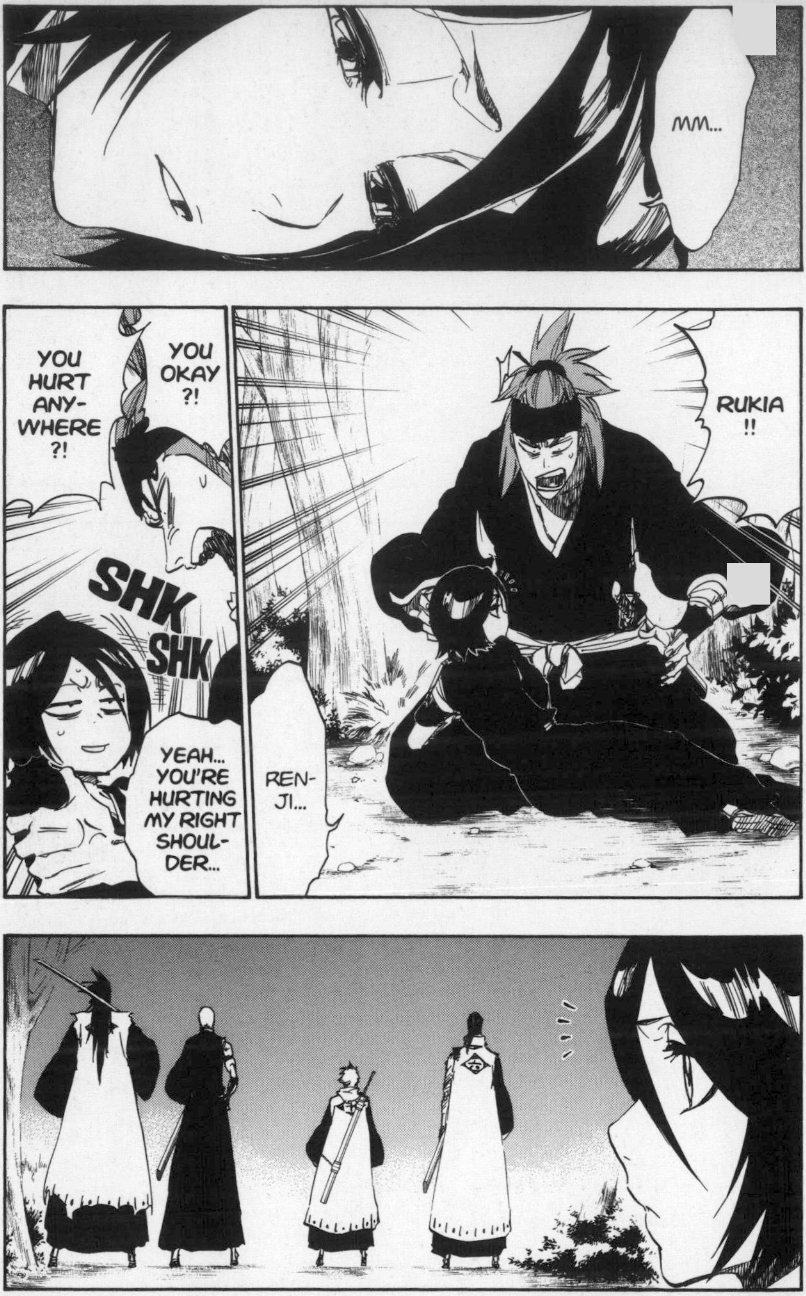
MM...
RUKIA !!
REN- JI...
YOU OKAY ?!
YOU HURT ANY- WHERE ?!
SHK SHK
YEAH... YOU'RE HURTING MY RIGHT SHOUL- DER...

475. Shades of the Bond

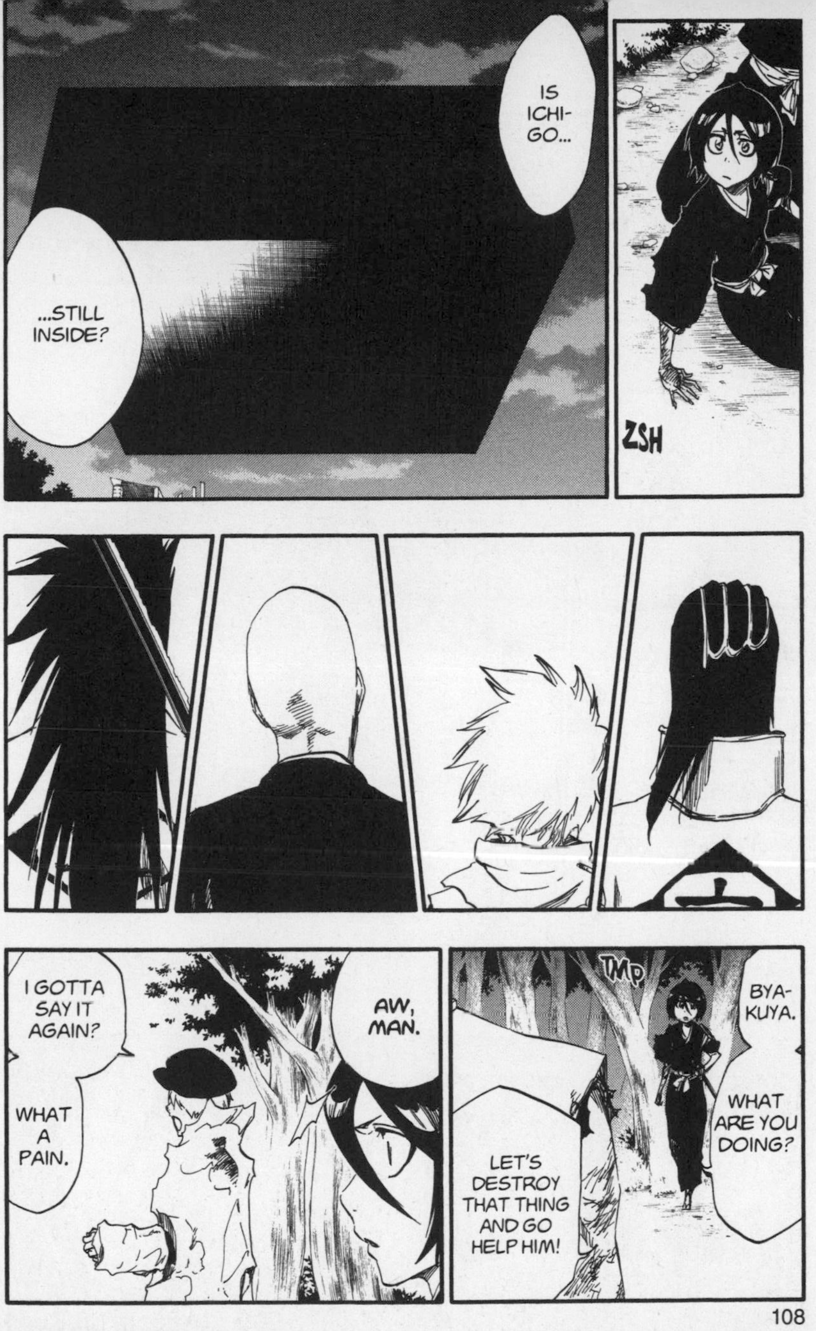
ZSH
IS ICHI-GO...
...STILL INSIDE?
TMP
BYA-KUYA.
WHAT ARE YOU DOING?
LET'S DESTROY THAT THING AND GO HELP HIM!
AW, MAN.
I GOTTA SAY IT AGAIN?
WHAT A PAIN.

READ THIS WAY

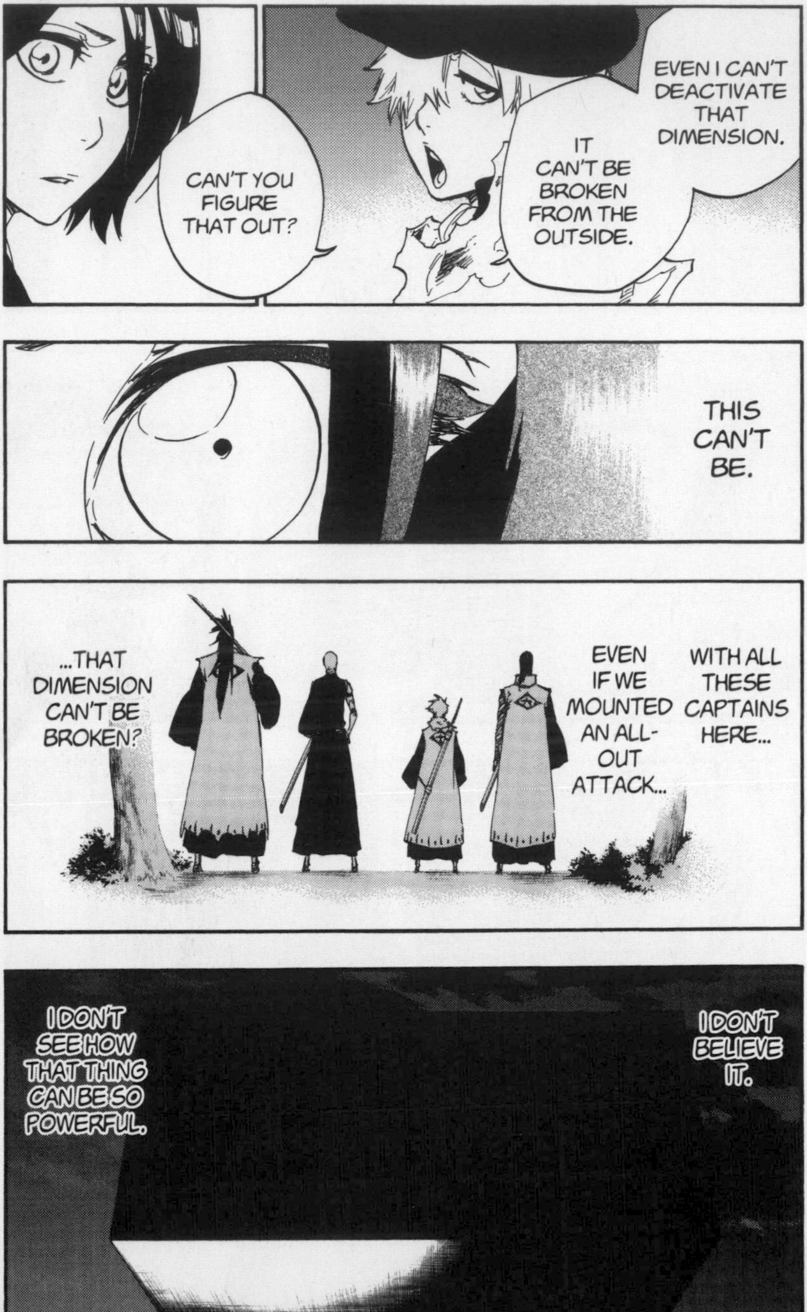
EVEN I CAN'T DEACTIVATE THAT DIMENSION.
IT CAN'T BE BROKEN FROM THE OUTSIDE.
CAN'T YOU FIGURE THAT OUT?
THIS CAN'T BE.
WITH ALL THESE CAPTAINS HERE...
EVEN IF WE MOUNTED AN ALL-OUT ATTACK...
...THAT DIMENSION CAN'T BE BROKEN?
I DON'T BELIEVE IT.
I DON'T SEE HOW THAT THING CAN BE SO POWERFUL.

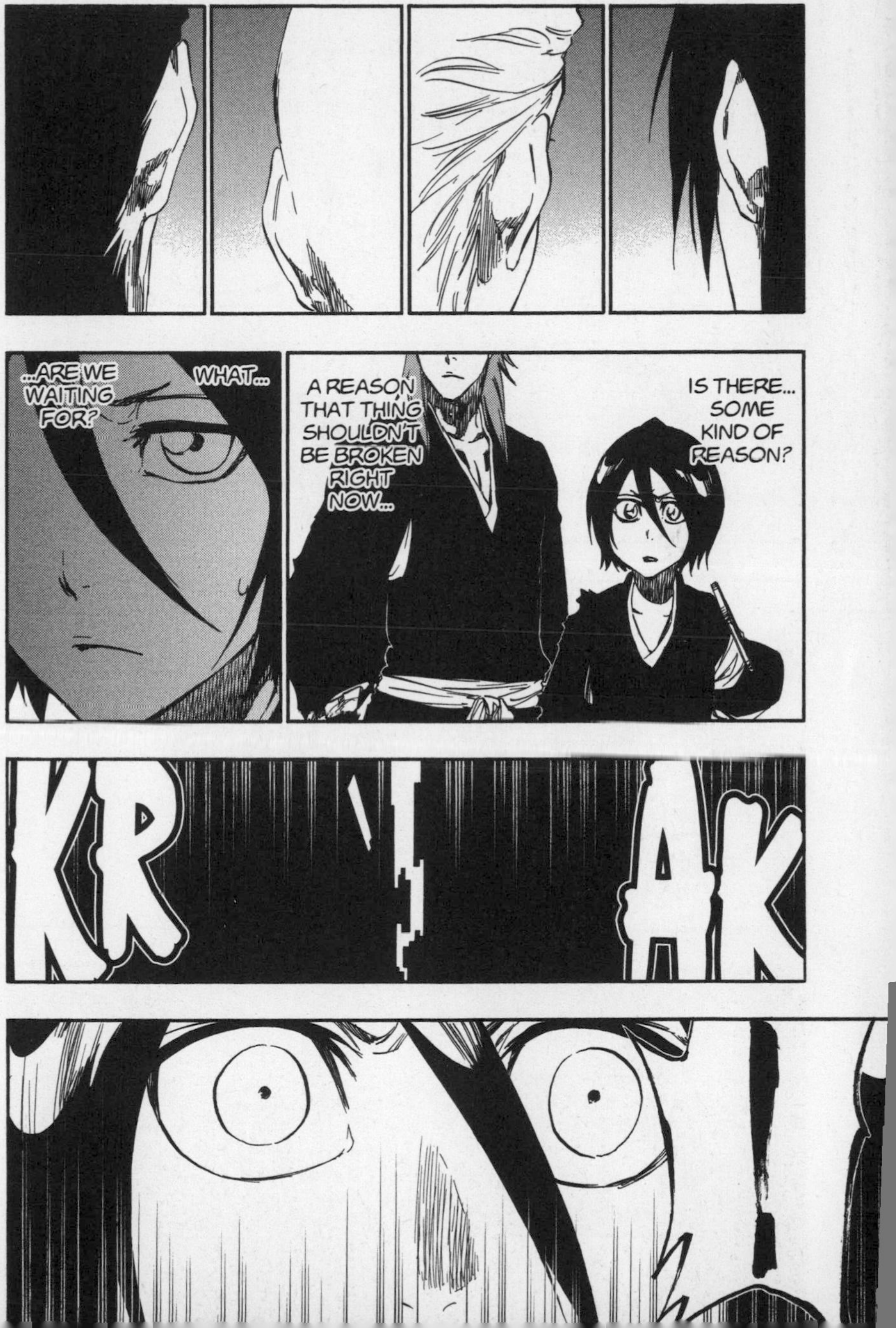
IS THERE... SOME KIND OF REASON?
A REASON THAT THING SHOULDN'T BE BROKEN RIGHT NOW...
WHAT...
...ARE WE WAITING FOR?
KR AK

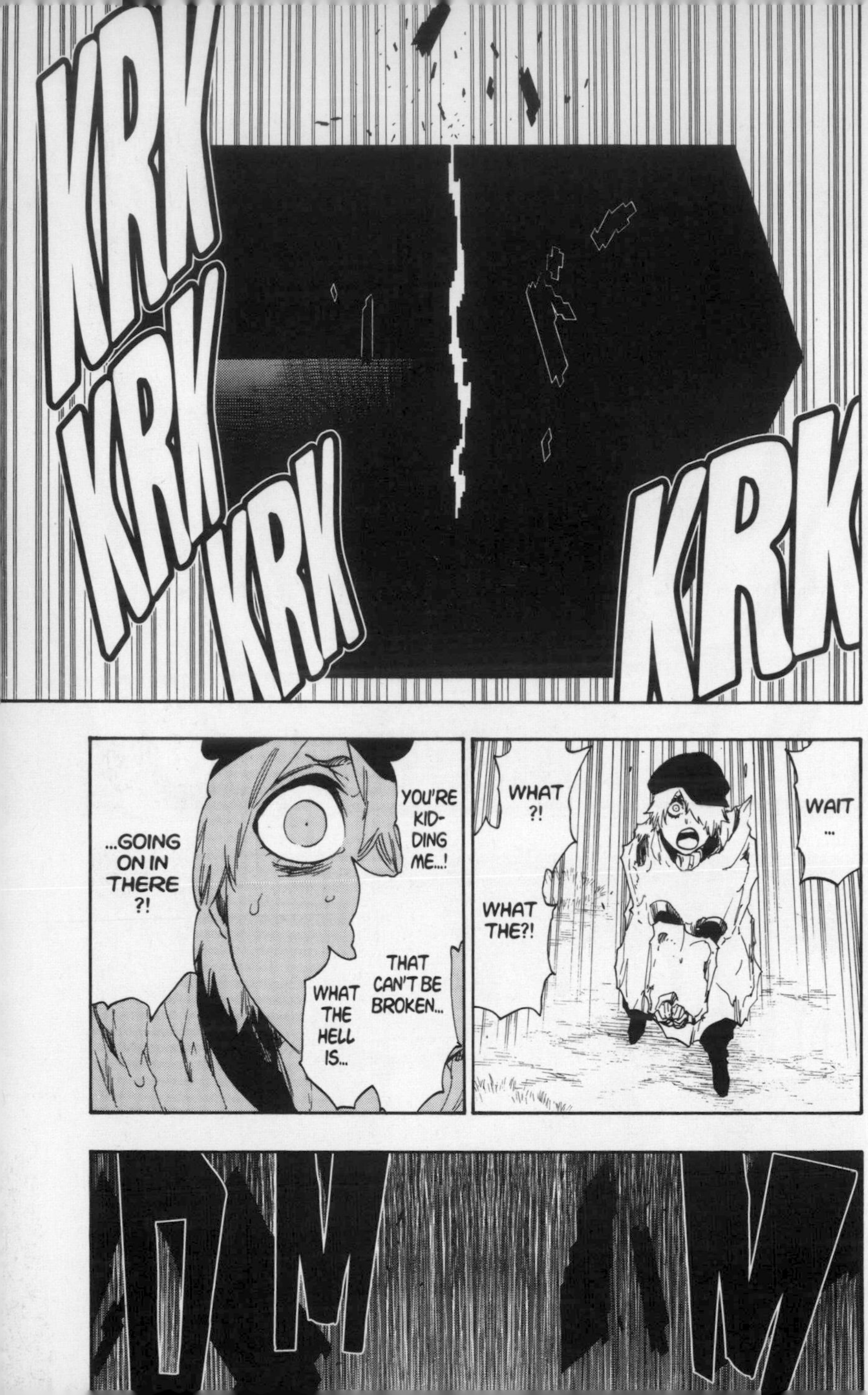
KRK
KRK
KRK
KRK
WAIT ...
WHAT ?!
WHAT THE?!
YOU'RE KID- DING ME...!
THAT CAN'T BE BROKEN...
WHAT THE HELL IS...
...GOING ON IN THERE ?!

BLEACH 475.

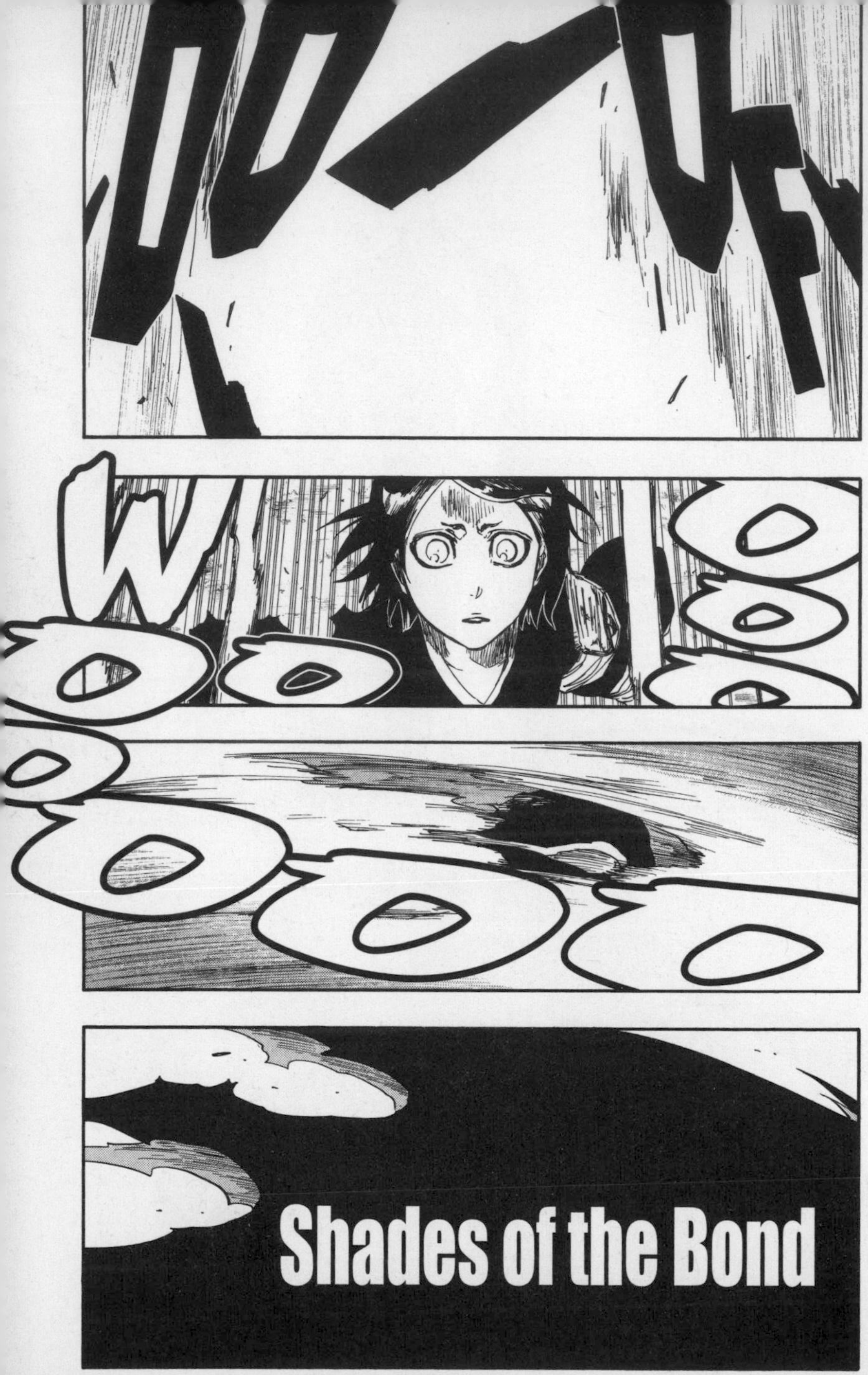
Shades of the Bond

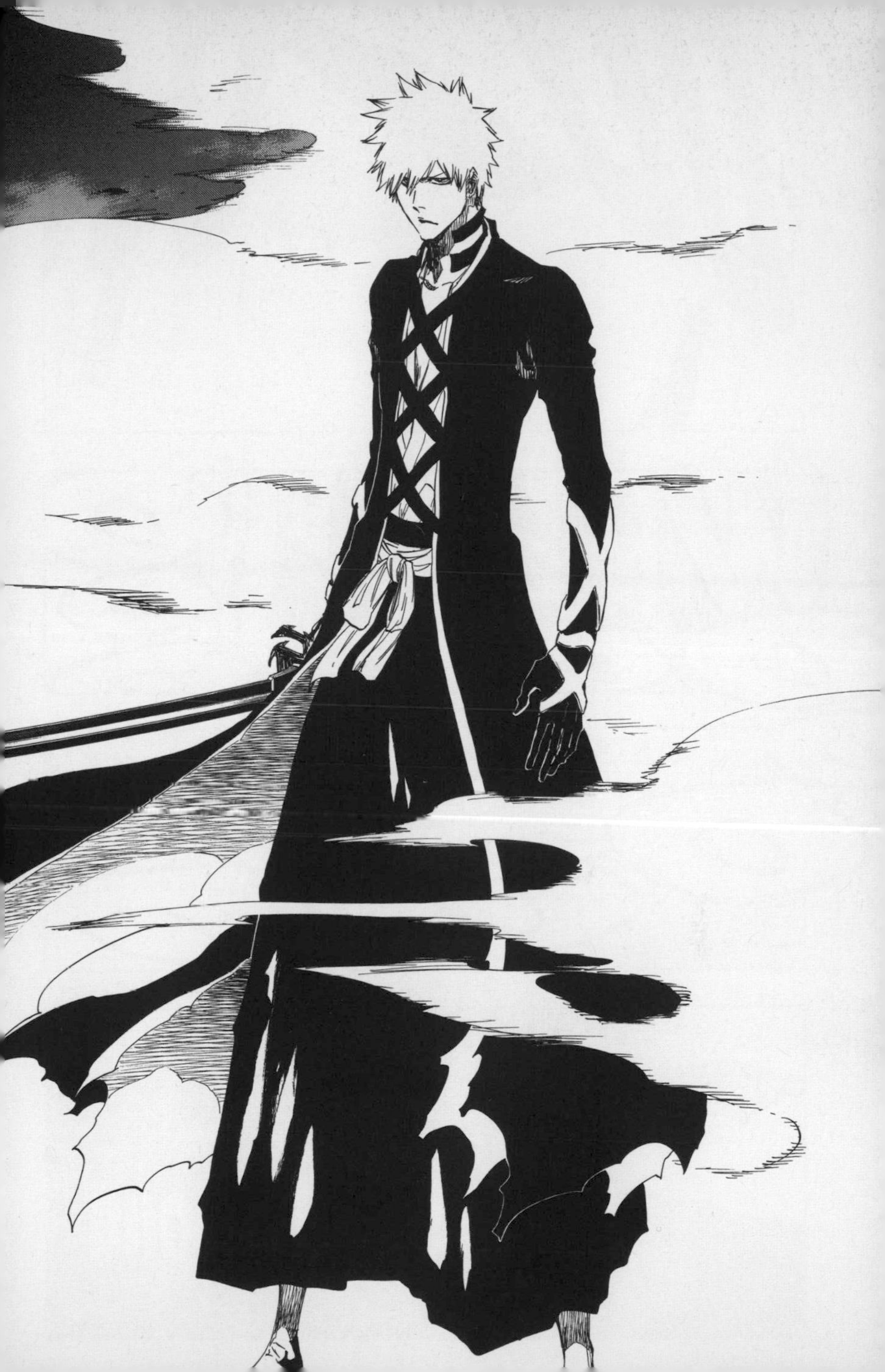

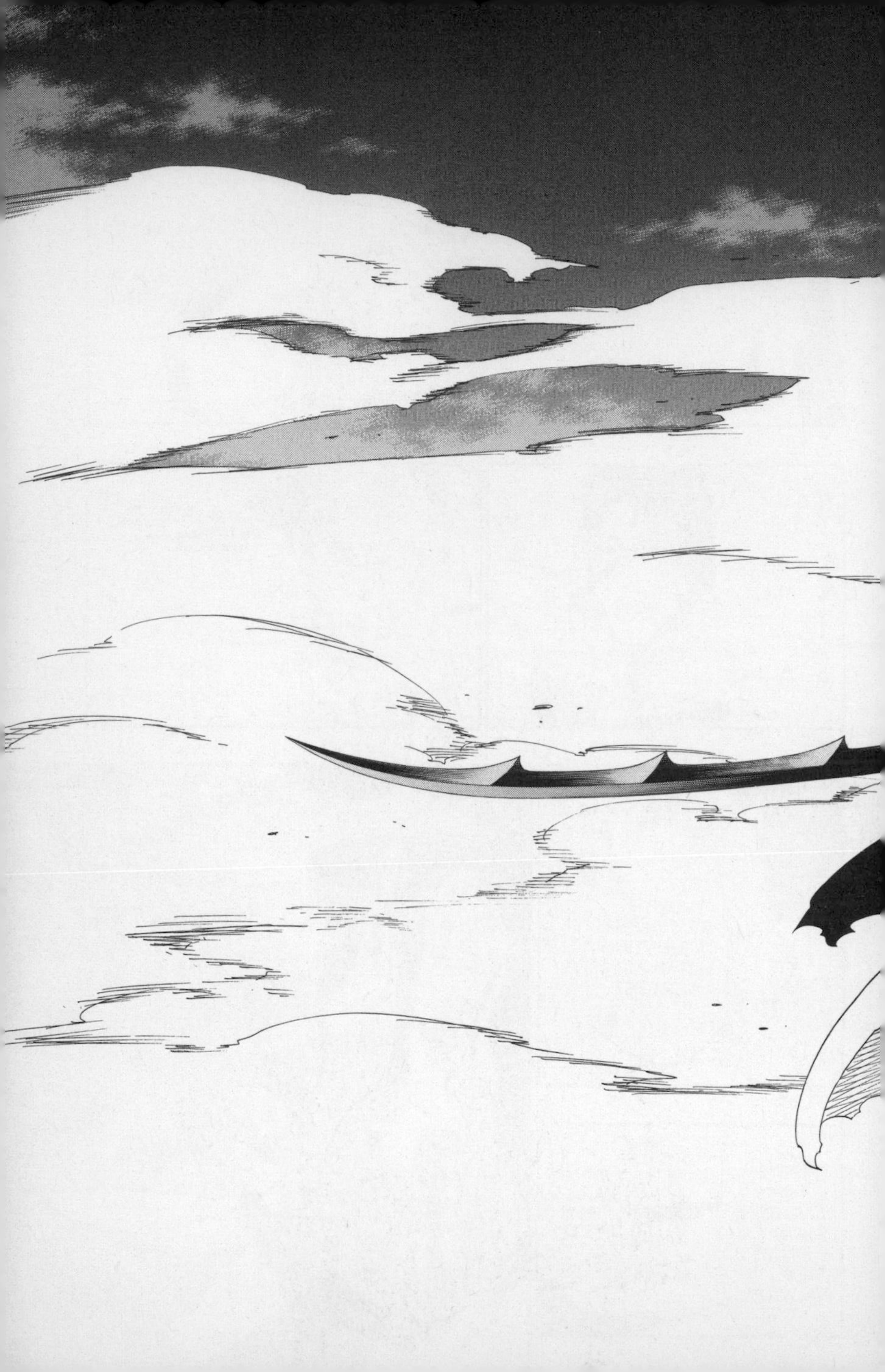

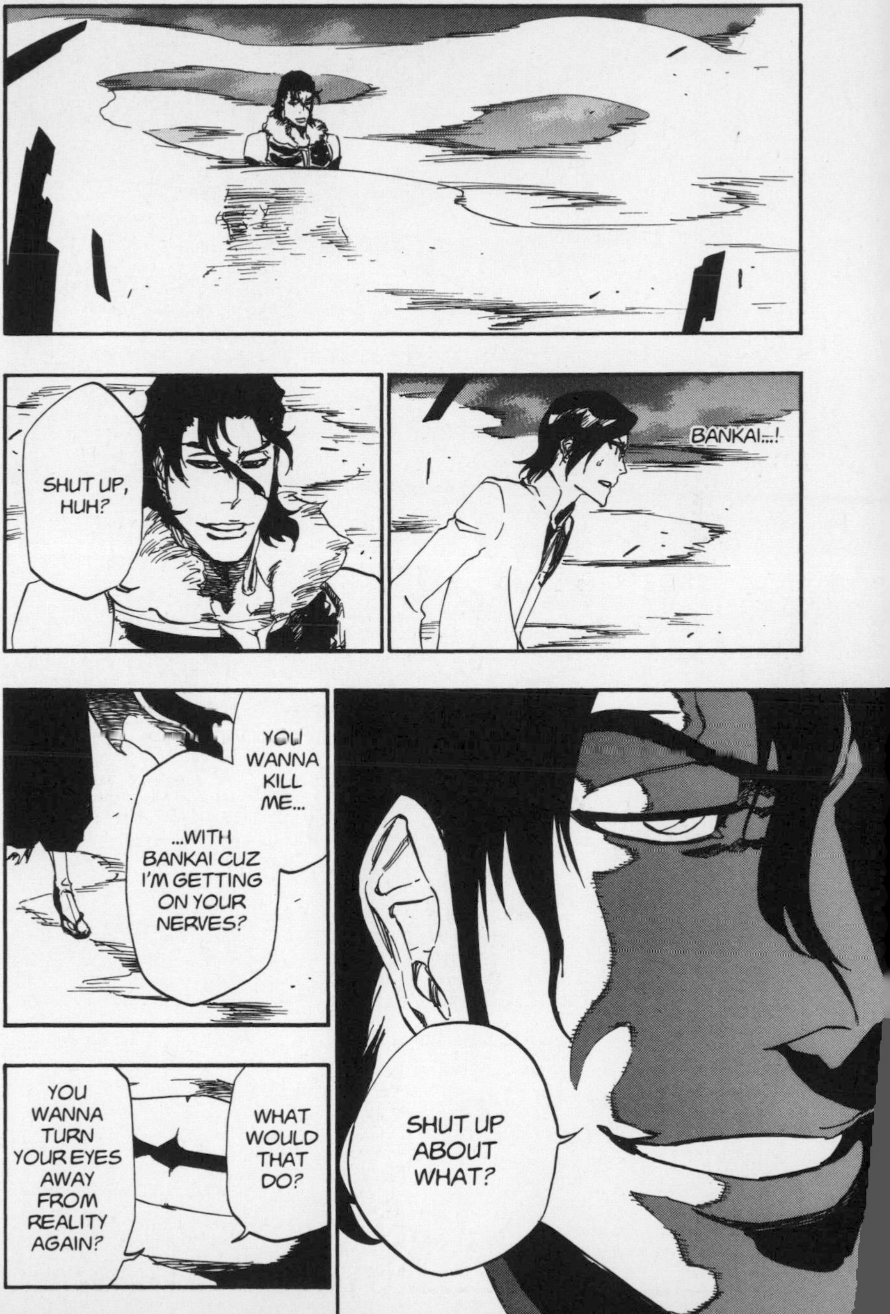
BANKAI...!
SHUT UP, HUH?
SHUT UP ABOUT WHAT?
YOU WANNA KILL ME...
...WITH BANKAI CUZ I'M GETTING ON YOUR NERVES?
WHAT WOULD THAT DO?
YOU WANNA TURN YOUR EYES AWAY FROM REALITY AGAIN?

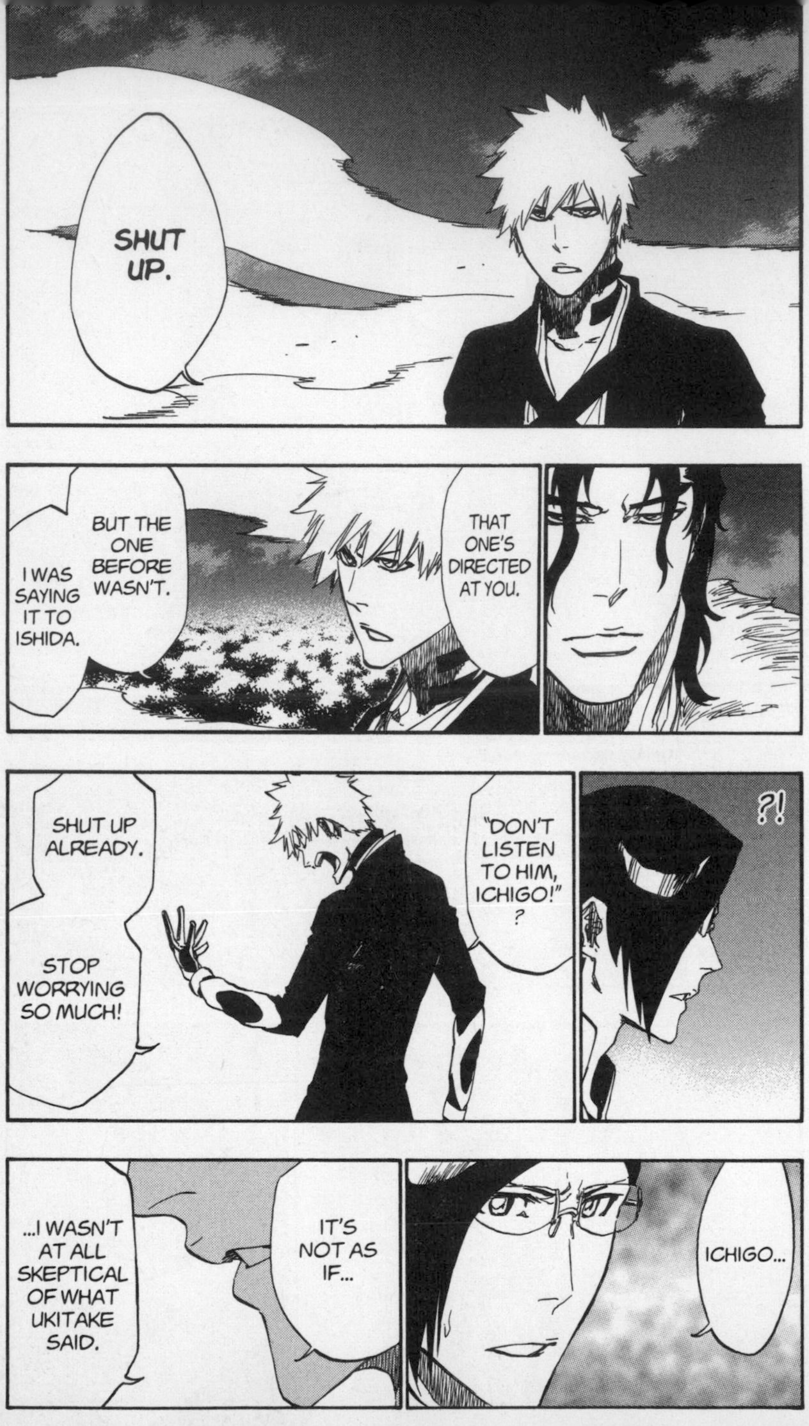
SHUT UP.
THAT ONE'S DIRECTED AT YOU.
BUT THE ONE BEFORE WASN'T.
I WAS SAYING IT TO ISHIDA.
?!
"DON'T LISTEN TO HIM, ICHIGO!" ?
SHUT UP ALREADY.
STOP WORRYING SO MUCH!
ICHIGO...
IT'S NOT AS IF...
...I WASN'T AT ALL SKEPTICAL OF WHAT UKITAKE SAID.

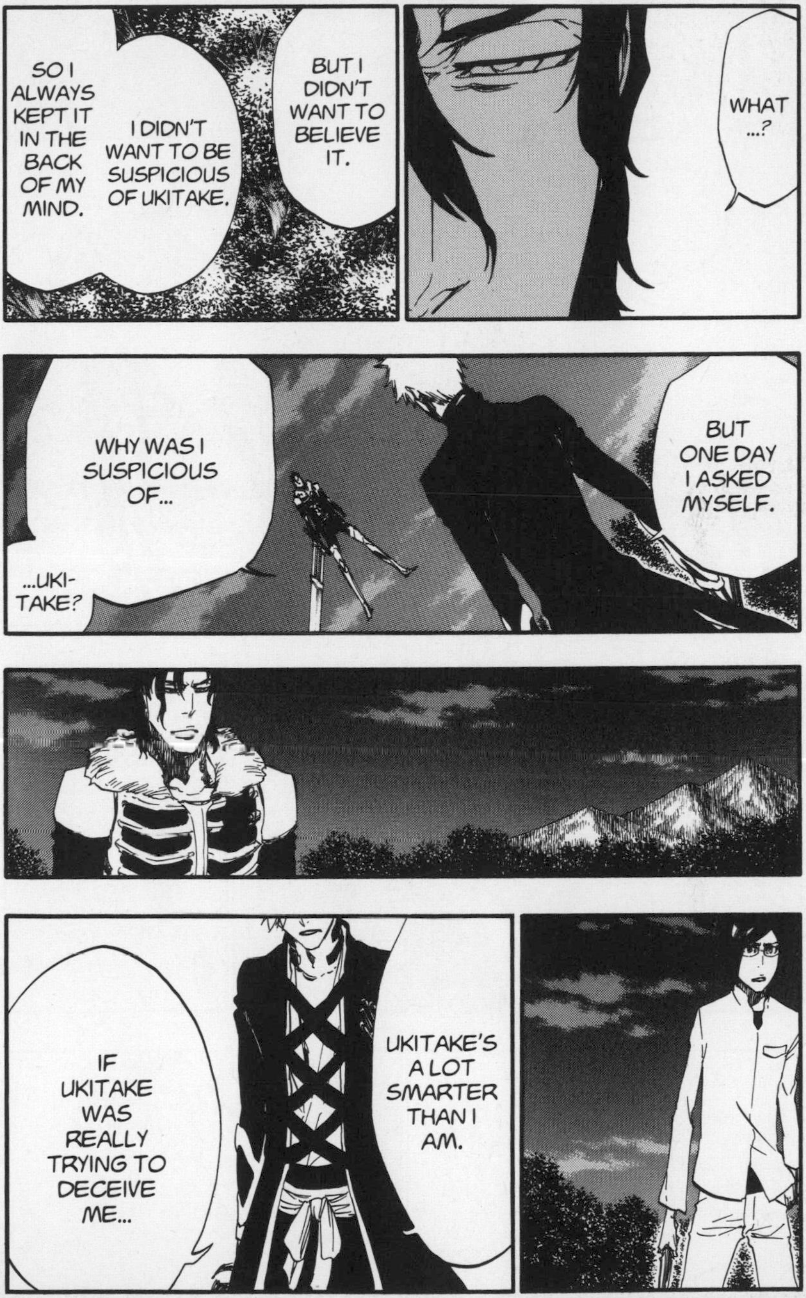
WHAT ...?
BUT I DIDN'T WANT TO BELIEVE IT.
I DIDN'T WANT TO BE SUSPICIOUS OF UKITAKE.
SO I ALWAYS KEPT IT IN THE BACK OF MY MIND.
BUT ONE DAY I ASKED MYSELF.
WHY WAS I SUSPICIOUS OF...
...UKI-TAKE?
UKITAKE'S A LOT SMARTER THAN I AM.
IF UKITAKE WAS REALLY TRYING TO DECEIVE ME...

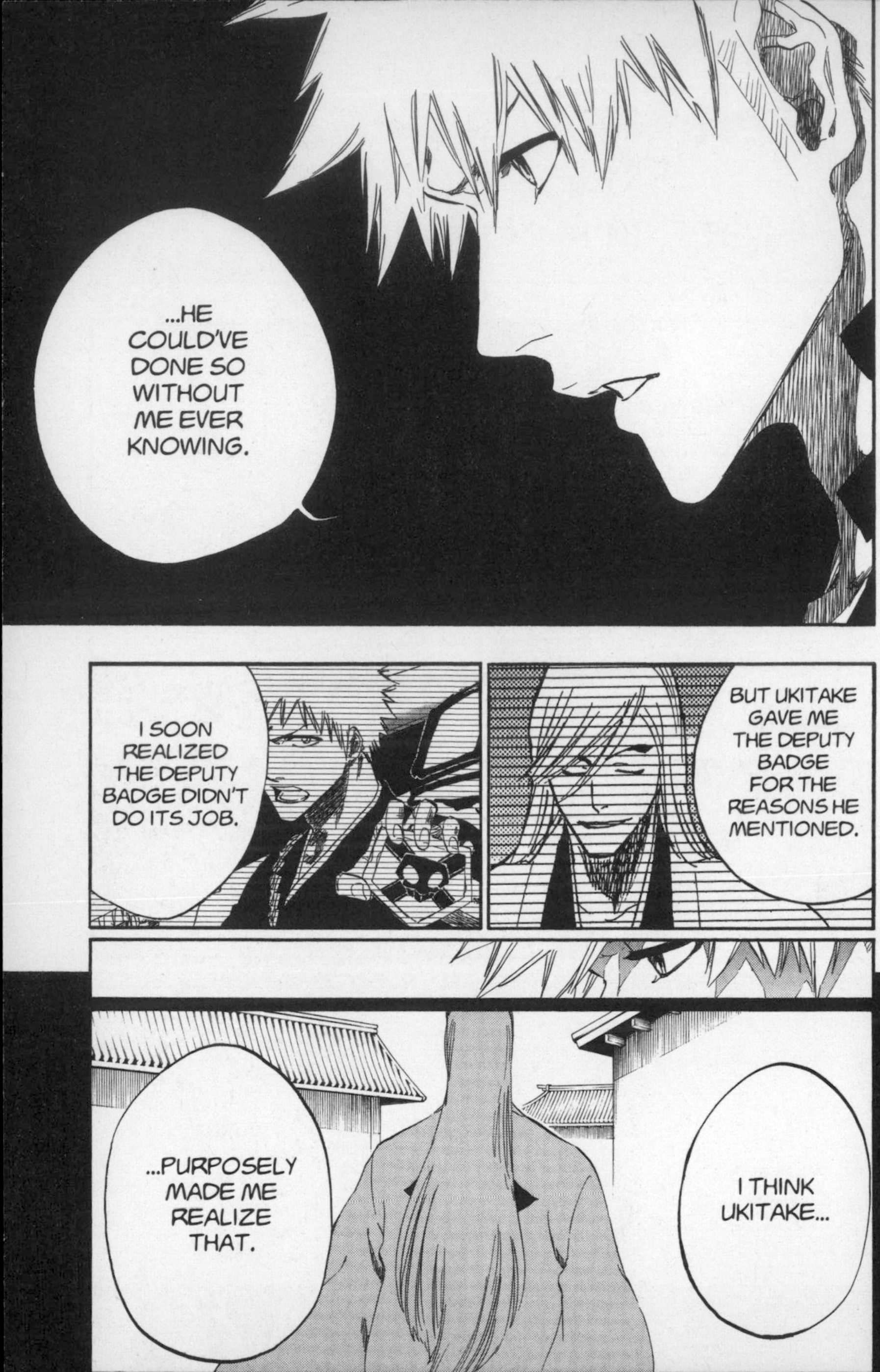
...HE COULD'VE DONE SO WITHOUT ME EVER KNOWING.
BUT UKITAKE GAVE ME THE DEPUTY BADGE FOR THE REASONS HE MENTIONED.
I SOON REALIZED THE DEPUTY BADGE DIDN'T DO ITS JOB.
I THINK UKITAKE...
...PURPOSELY MADE ME REALIZE THAT.

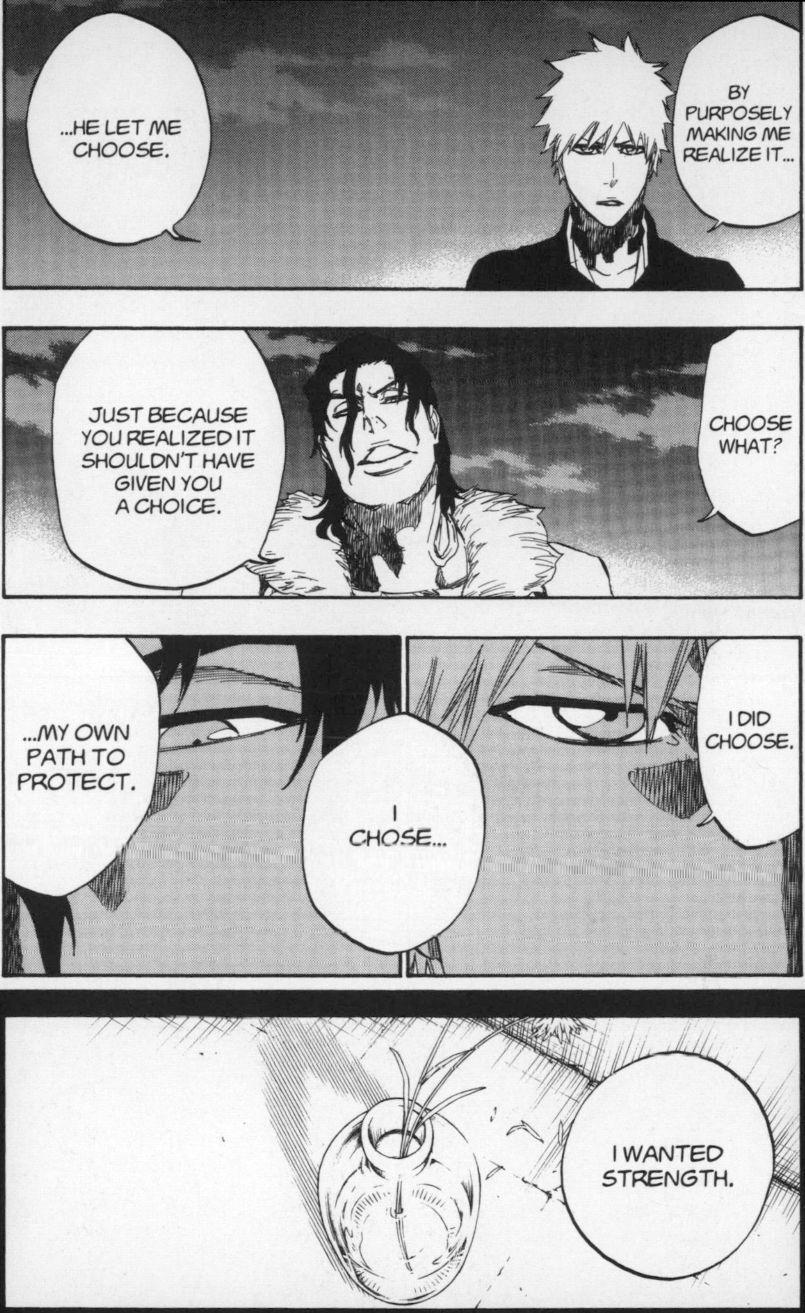
BY PURPOSELY MAKING ME REALIZE IT...
...HE LET ME CHOOSE.
CHOOSE WHAT?
JUST BECAUSE YOU REALIZED IT SHOULDN'T HAVE GIVEN YOU A CHOICE.
I DID CHOOSE.
I CHOSE...
...MY OWN PATH TO PROTECT.
I WANTED STRENGTH.

READ THIS WAY

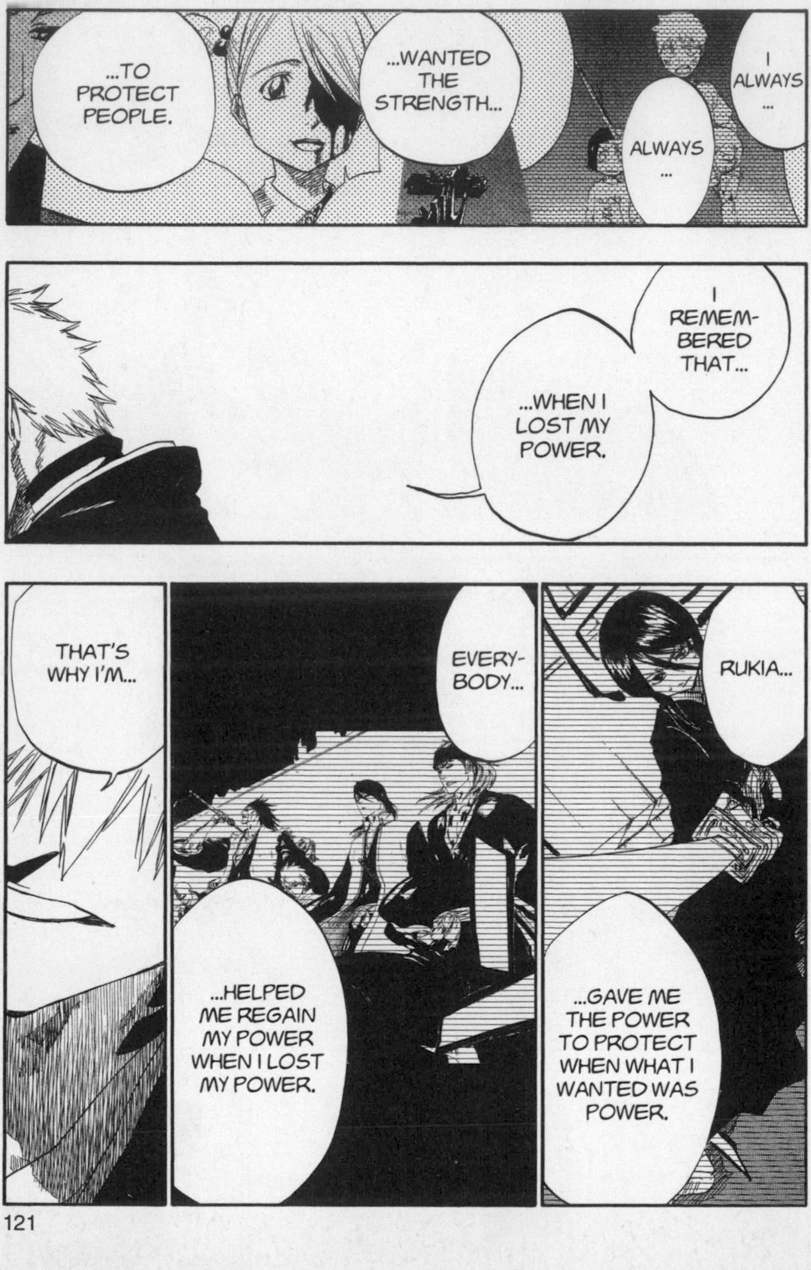
I ALWAYS ...
ALWAYS ...
...WANTED THE STRENGTH...
...TO PROTECT PEOPLE.
I REMEMBERED THAT...
...WHEN I LOST MY POWER.
RUKIA...
...GAVE ME THE POWER TO PROTECT WHEN WHAT I WANTED WAS POWER.
EVERYBODY...
...HELPED ME REGAIN MY POWER WHEN I LOST MY POWER.
THAT'S WHY I'M...

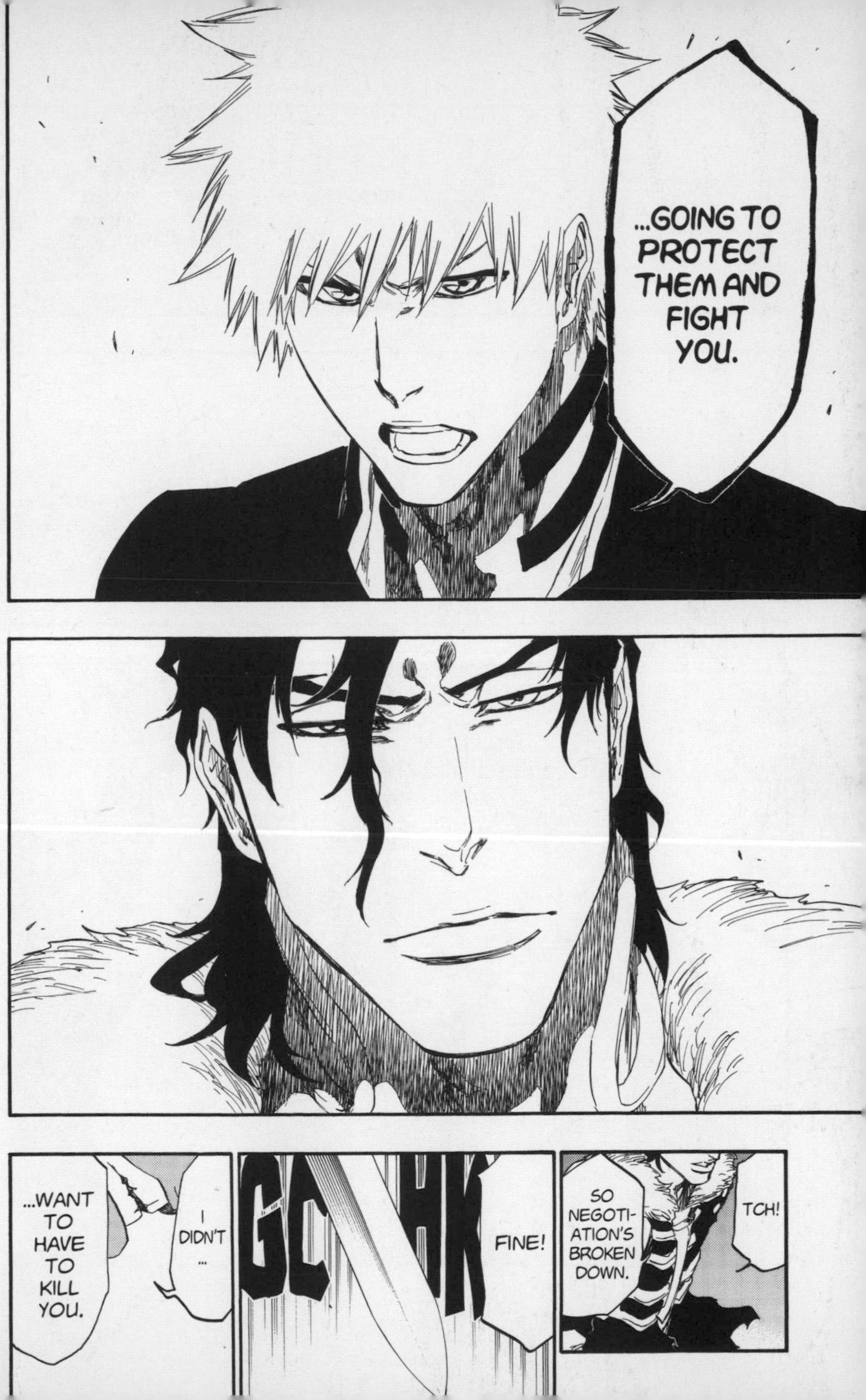
...GOING TO PROTECT THEM AND FIGHT YOU.
TCH!
SO NEGOTIATION'S BROKEN DOWN.
FINE!
GCHK
I DIDN'T ...
...WANT TO HAVE TO KILL YOU.

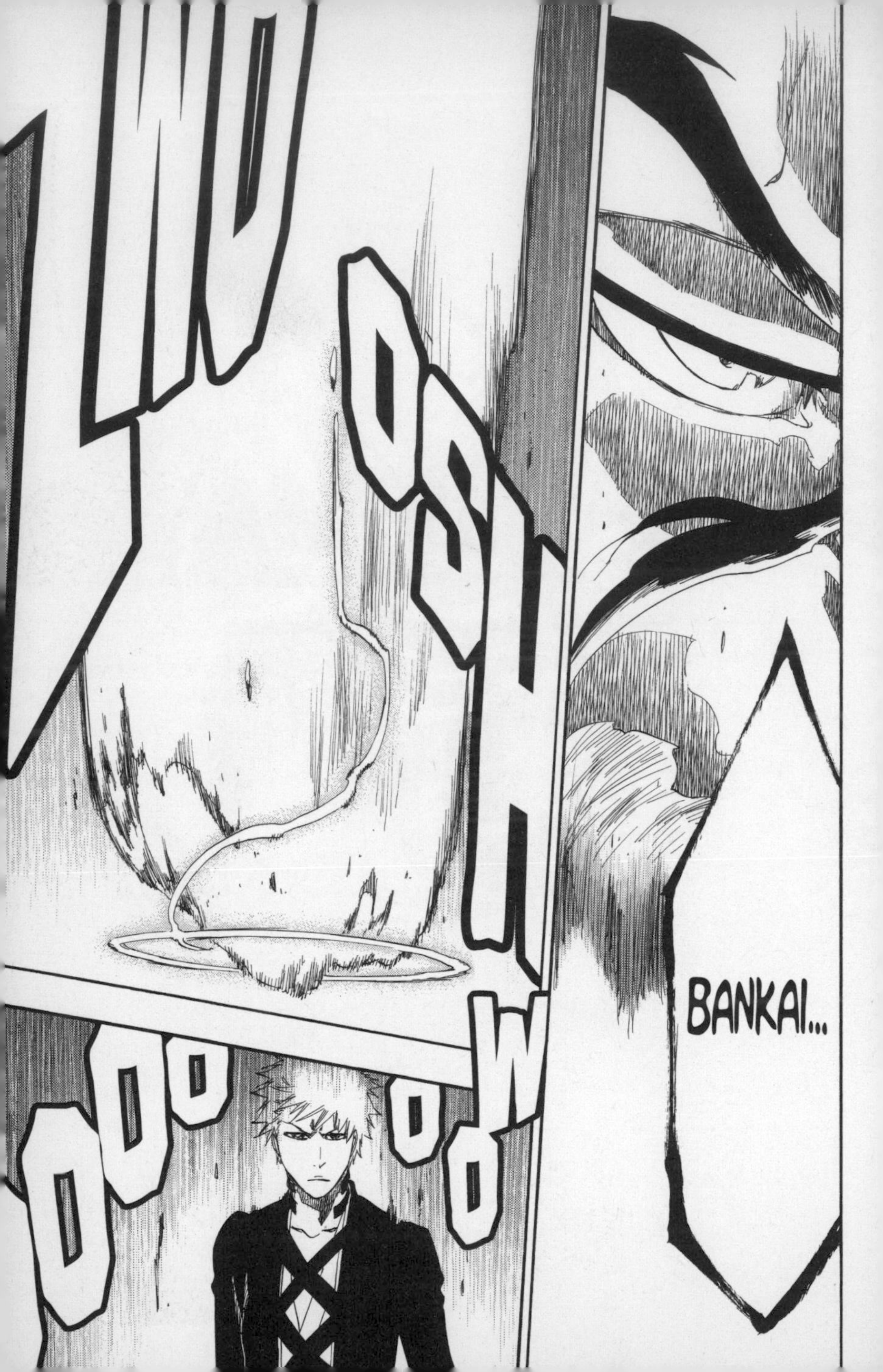
BANKAI...

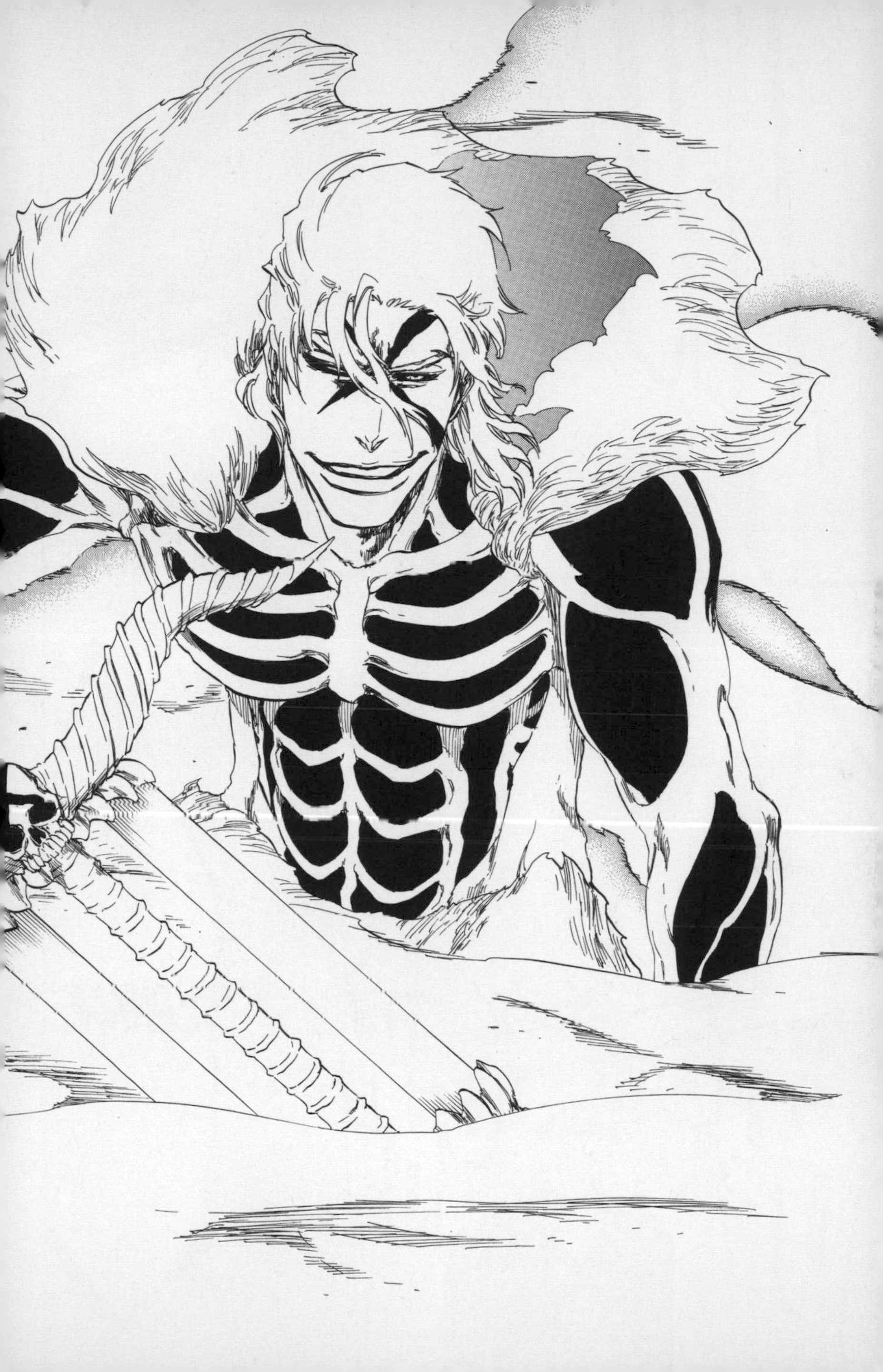

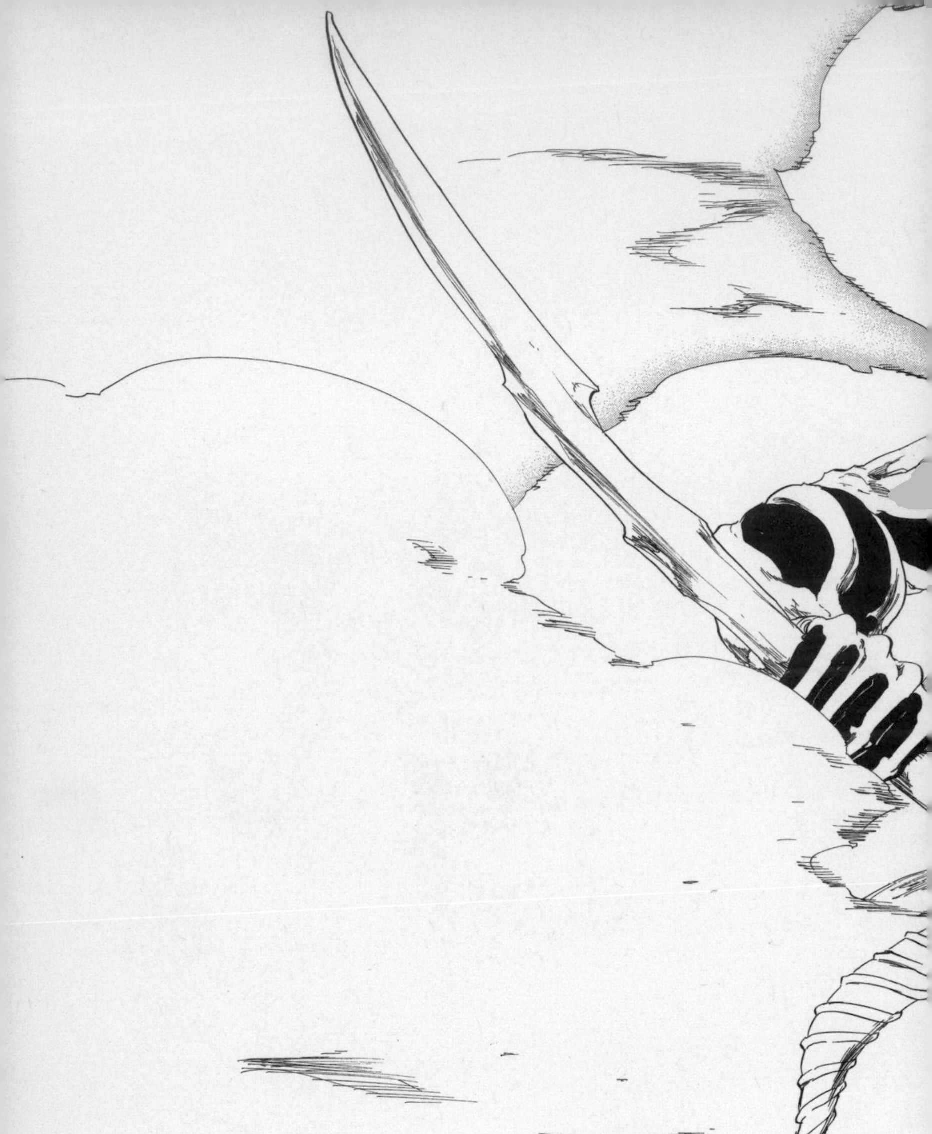

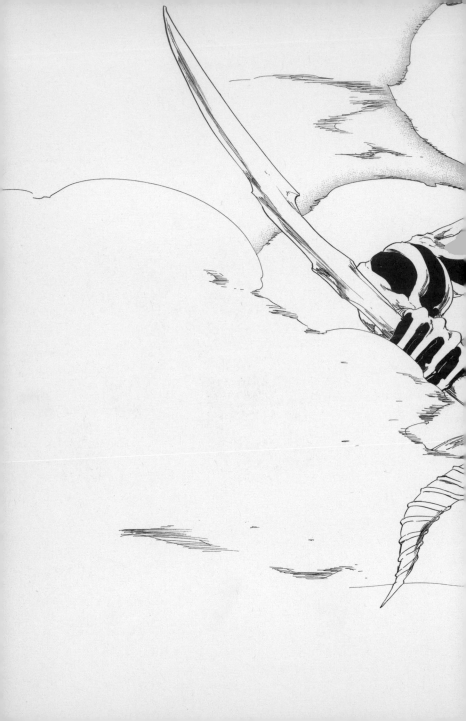

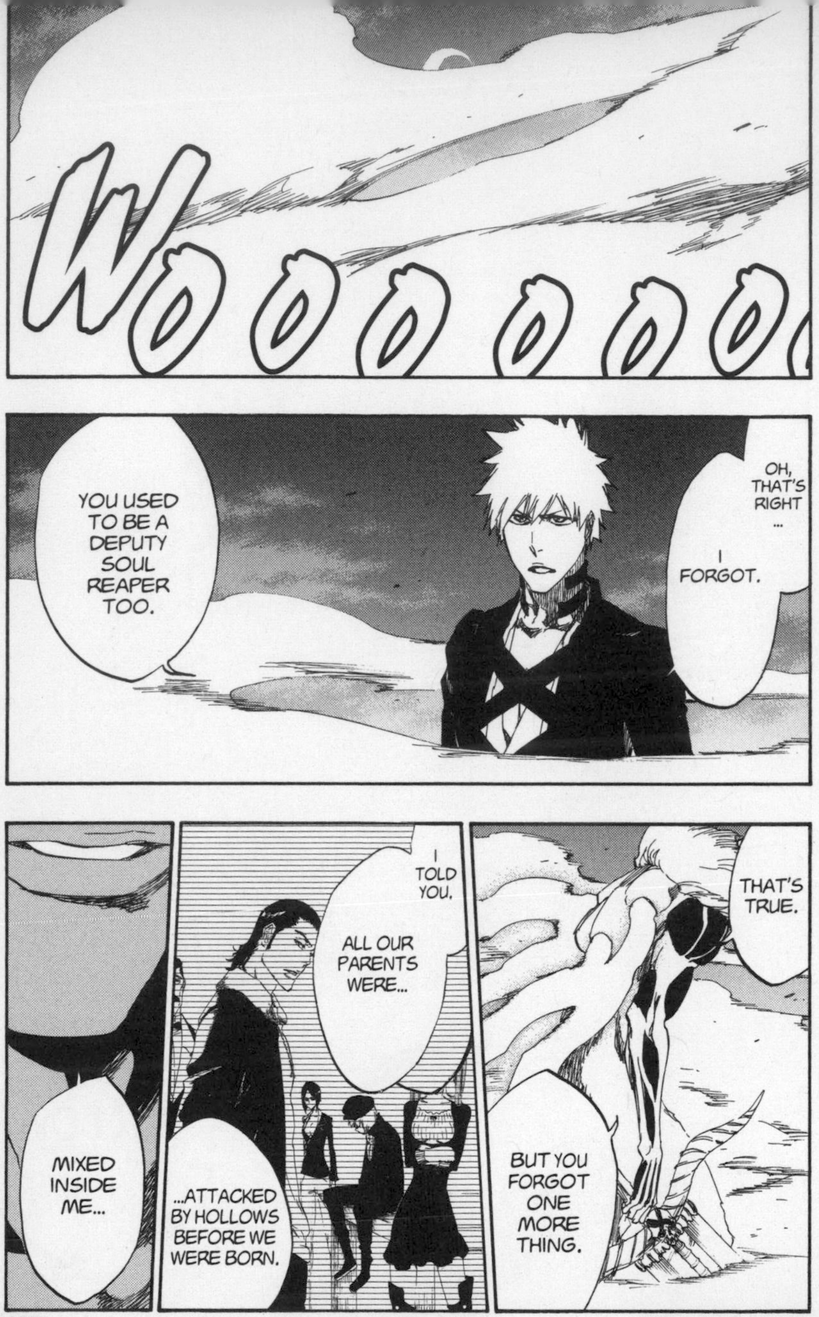
WOOOOOOO
OH, THAT'S RIGHT... I FORGOT.
YOU USED TO BE A DEPUTY SOUL REAPER TOO.
THAT'S TRUE.
BUT YOU FORGOT ONE MORE THING.
I TOLD YOU.
ALL OUR PARENTS WERE...
...ATTACKED BY HOLLOWS BEFORE WE WERE BORN.
MIXED INSIDE ME...

476. THE LOST

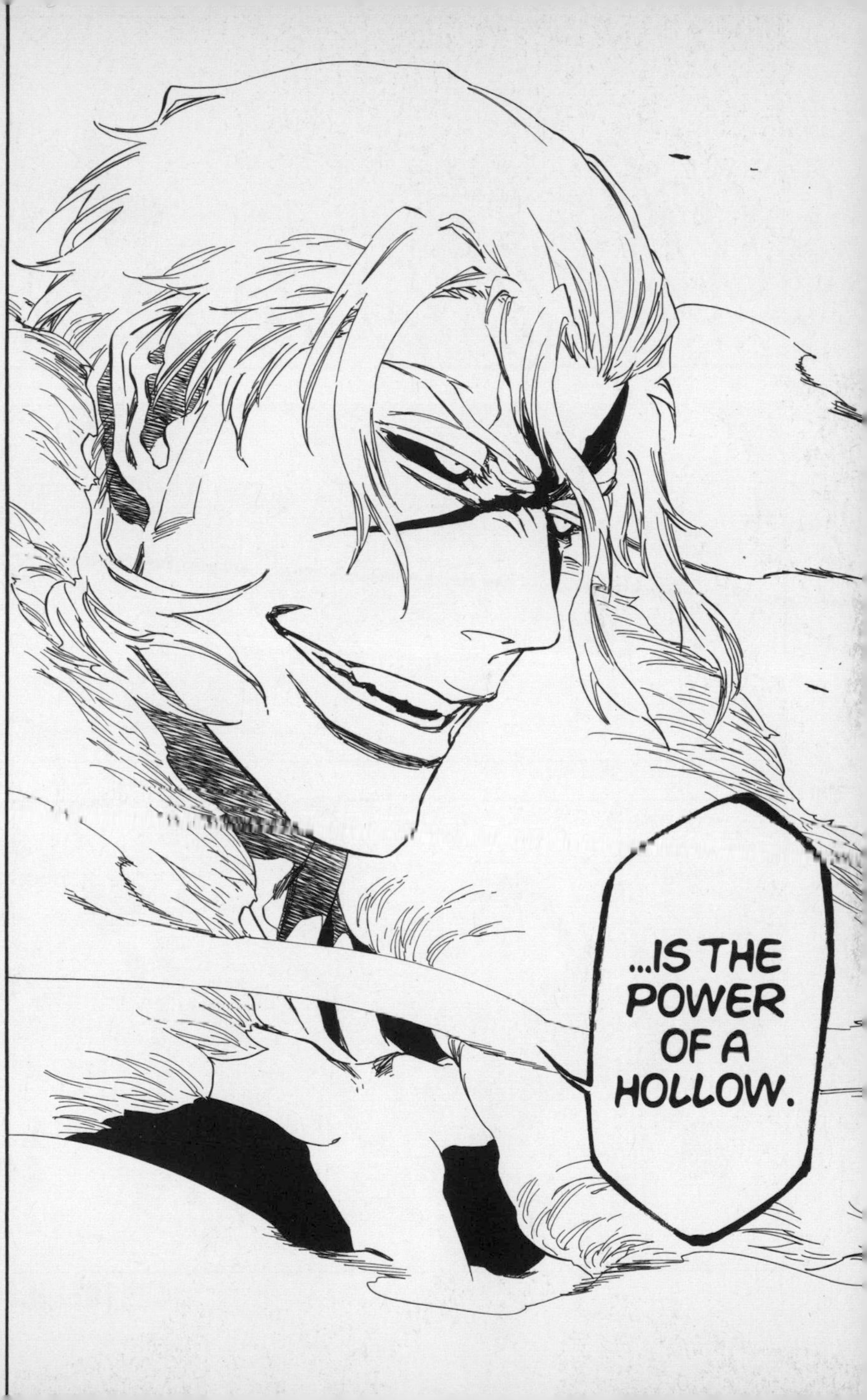
...IS THE POWER OF A HOLLOW.

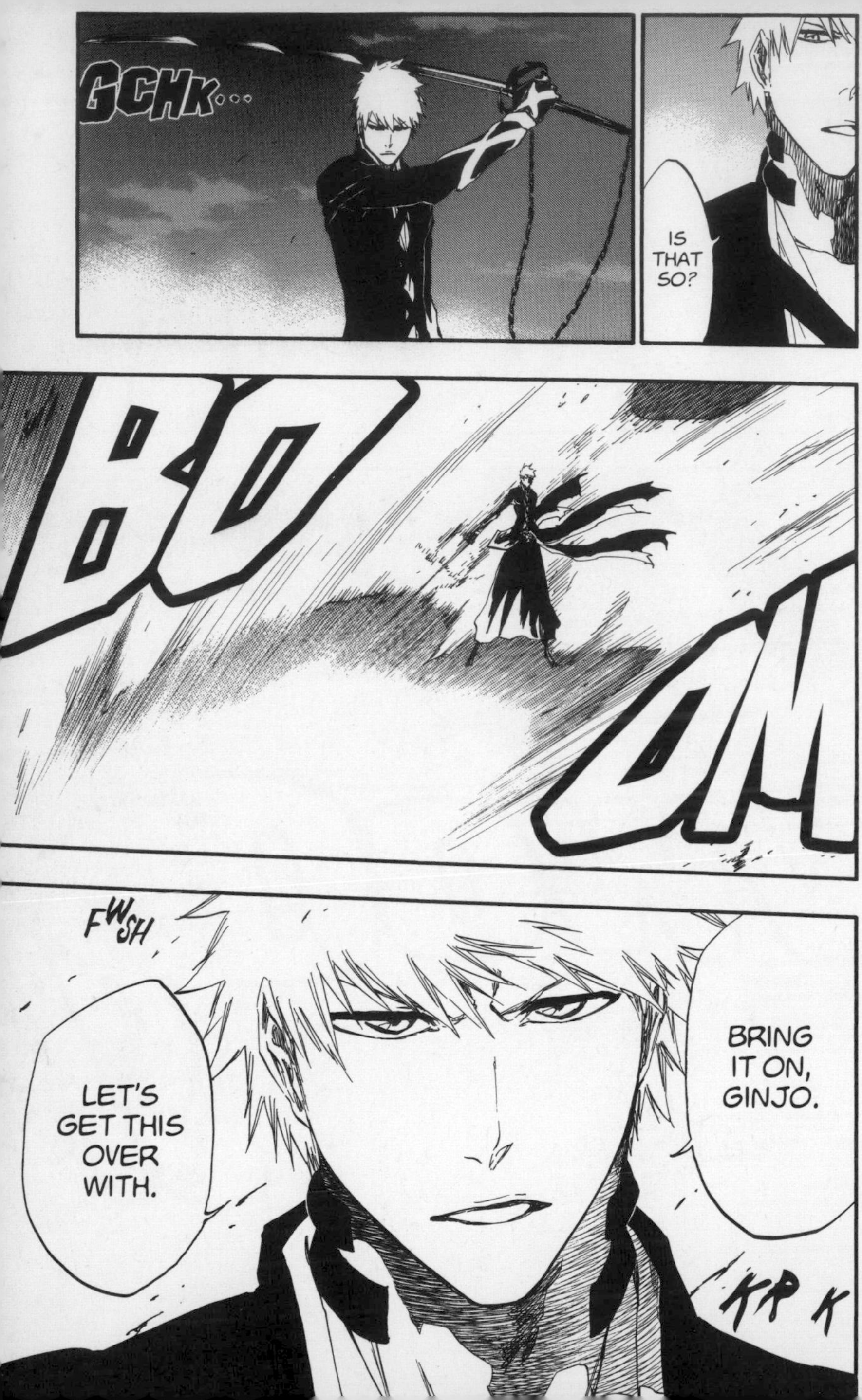
IS THAT SO?
GCHK...
BOOM
BRING IT ON, GINJO.
FWSH
LET'S GET THIS OVER WITH.
KRK

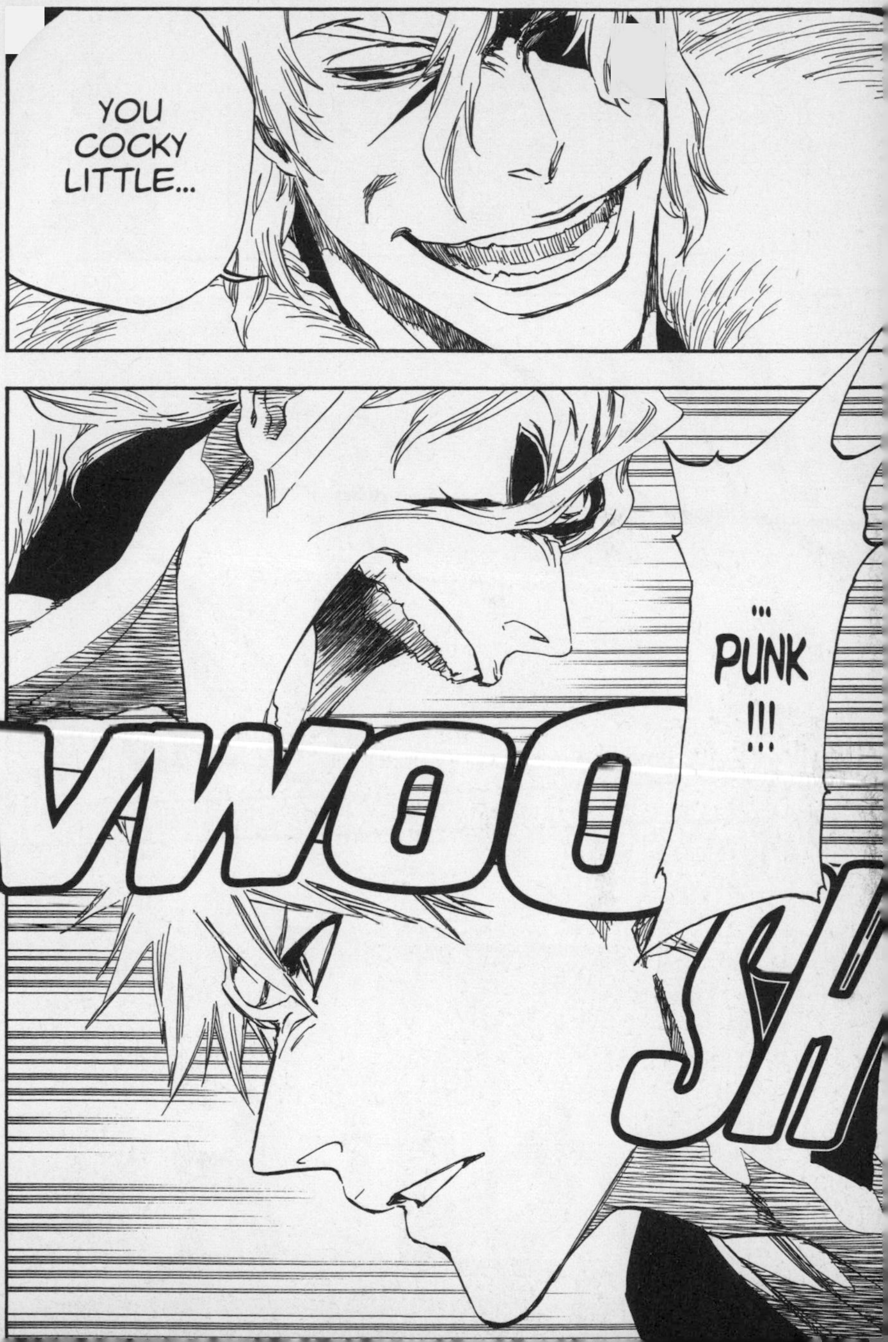
YOU COCKY LITTLE...
...PUNK!!!
VWOOSH

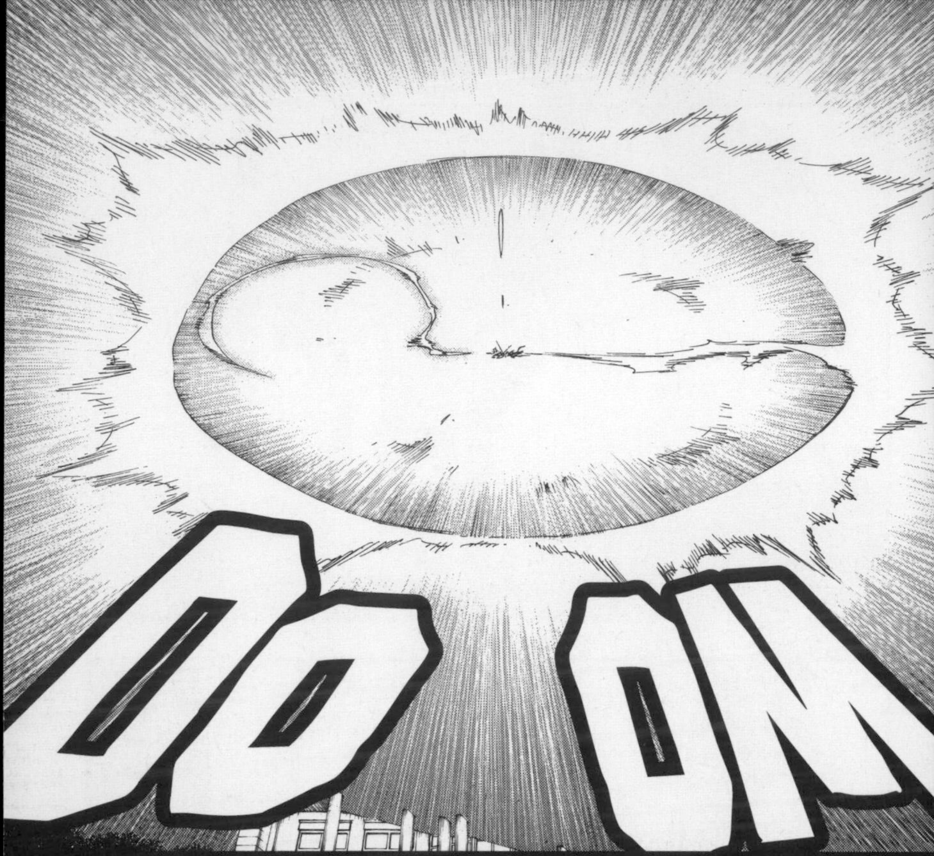
DOOM

BLEACH

476.

THE LOST

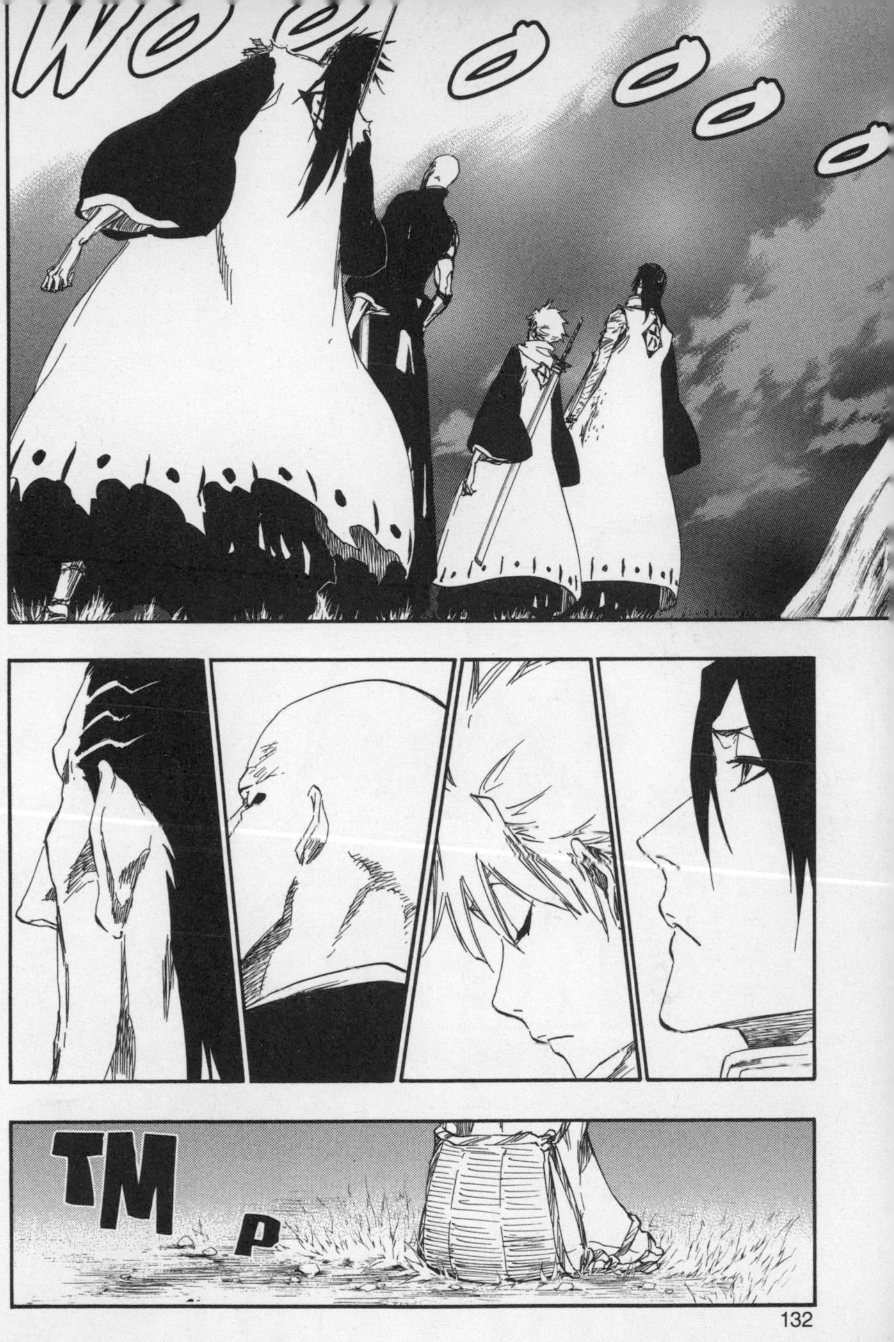
Weeeeeee
TMP

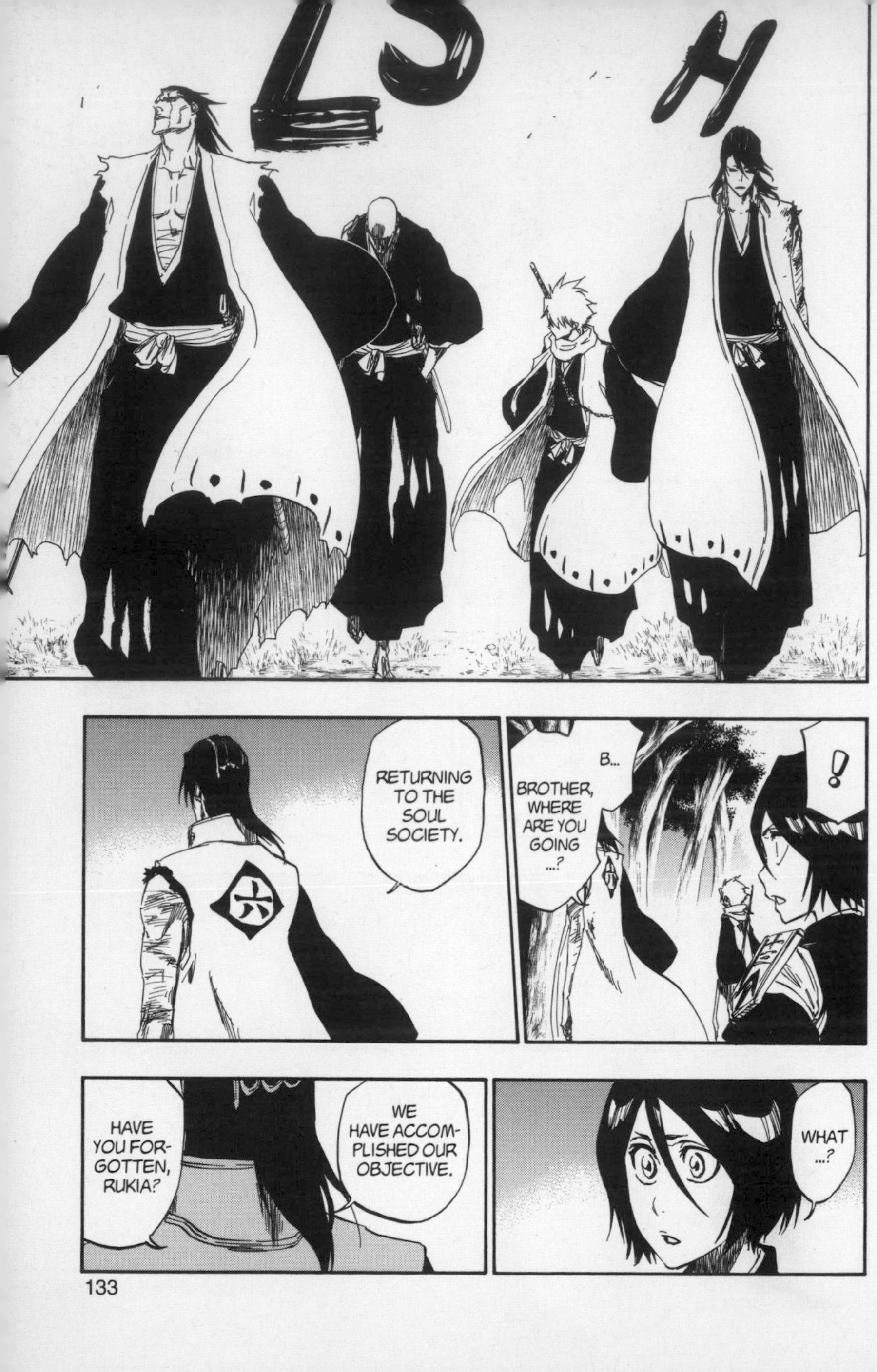
!
B...
BROTHER, WHERE ARE YOU GOING ...?
RETURNING TO THE SOUL SOCIETY.
WHAT ...?
WE HAVE ACCOM-PLISHED OUR OBJECTIVE.
HAVE YOU FOR-GOTTEN, RUKIA?

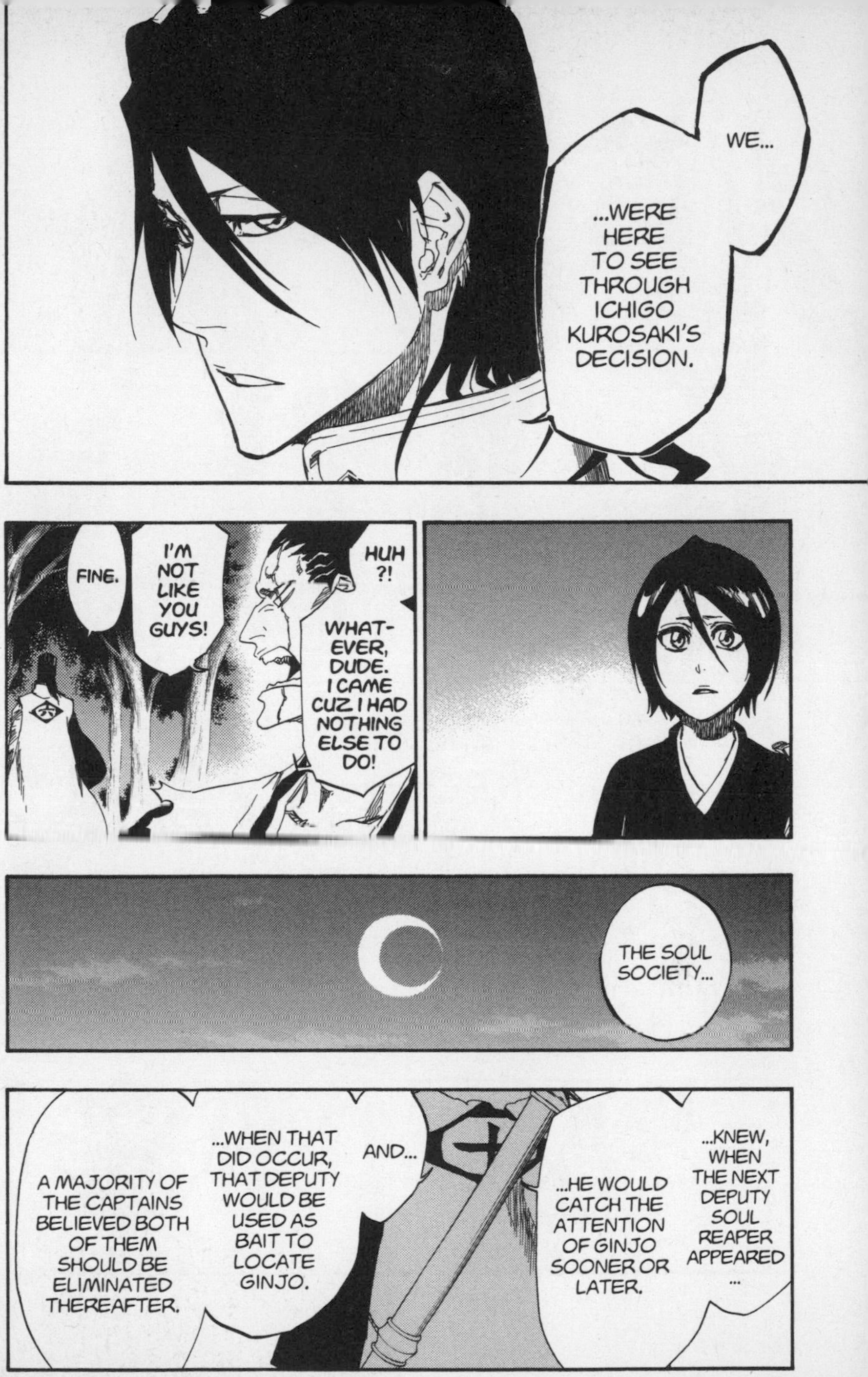
WE...
...WERE HERE TO SEE THROUGH ICHIGO KUROSAKI'S DECISION.
HUH ?!
WHAT-EVER, DUDE. I CAME CUZ I HAD NOTHING ELSE TO DO!
I'M NOT LIKE YOU GUYS!
FINE.
THE SOUL SOCIETY...
...KNEW, WHEN THE NEXT DEPUTY SOUL REAPER APPEARED ...
...HE WOULD CATCH THE ATTENTION OF GINJO SOONER OR LATER.
AND...
...WHEN THAT DID OCCUR, THAT DEPUTY WOULD BE USED AS BAIT TO LOCATE GINJO.
A MAJORITY OF THE CAPTAINS BELIEVED BOTH OF THEM SHOULD BE ELIMINATED THEREAFTER.

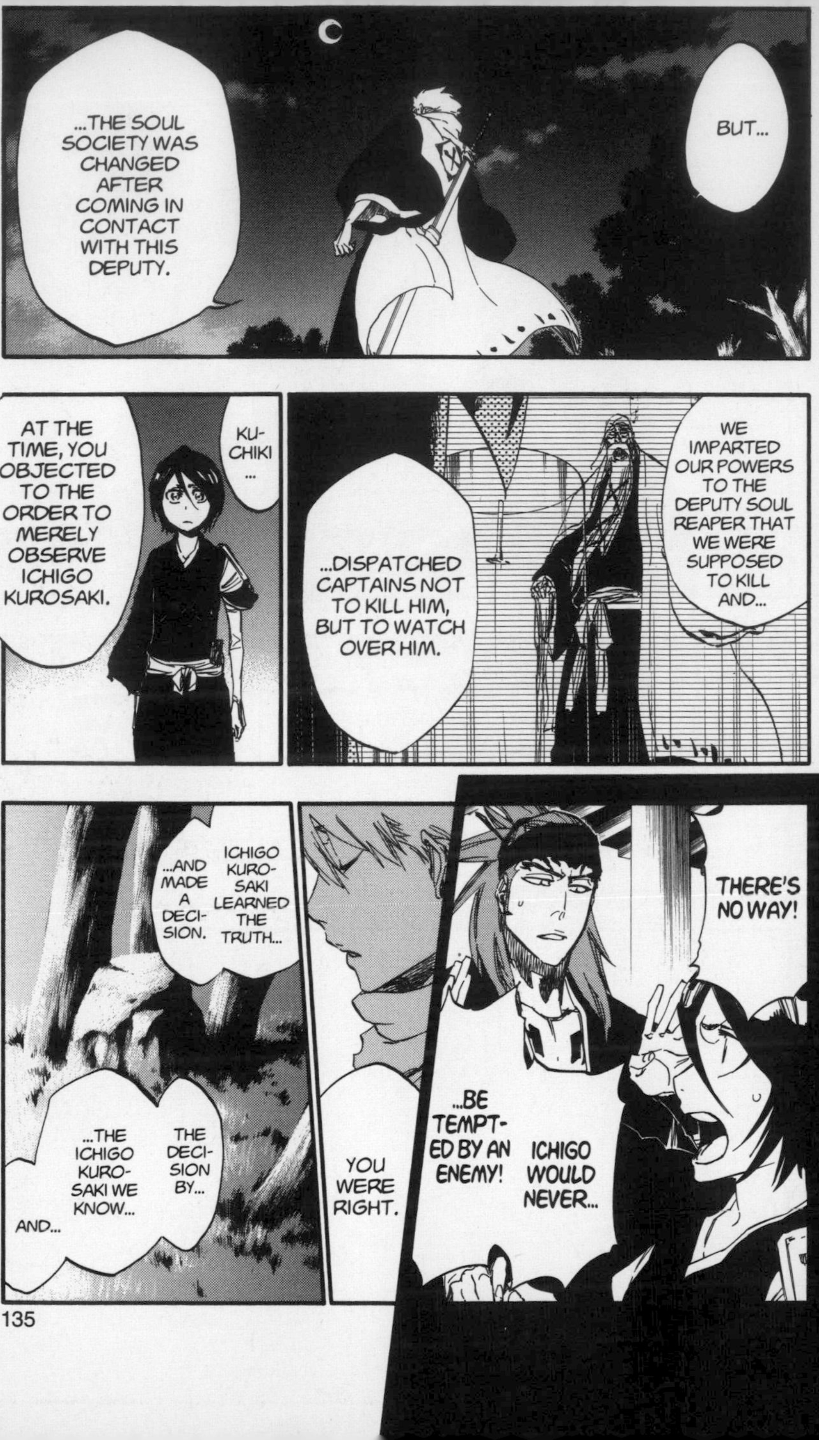
BUT...
...THE SOUL SOCIETY WAS CHANGED AFTER COMING IN CONTACT WITH THIS DEPUTY.
WE IMPARTED OUR POWERS TO THE DEPUTY SOUL REAPER THAT WE WERE SUPPOSED TO KILL AND...
...DISPATCHED CAPTAINS NOT TO KILL HIM, BUT TO WATCH OVER HIM.
KU-CHIKI...
AT THE TIME, YOU OBJECTED TO THE ORDER TO MERELY OBSERVE ICHIGO KUROSAKI.
THERE'S NO WAY!
ICHIGO WOULD NEVER...
...BE TEMPT-ED BY AN ENEMY!
YOU WERE RIGHT.
ICHIGO KURO-SAKI LEARNED THE TRUTH...
...AND MADE A DECI-SION.
THE DECI-SION BY...
...THE ICHIGO KURO-SAKI WE KNOW...
AND...

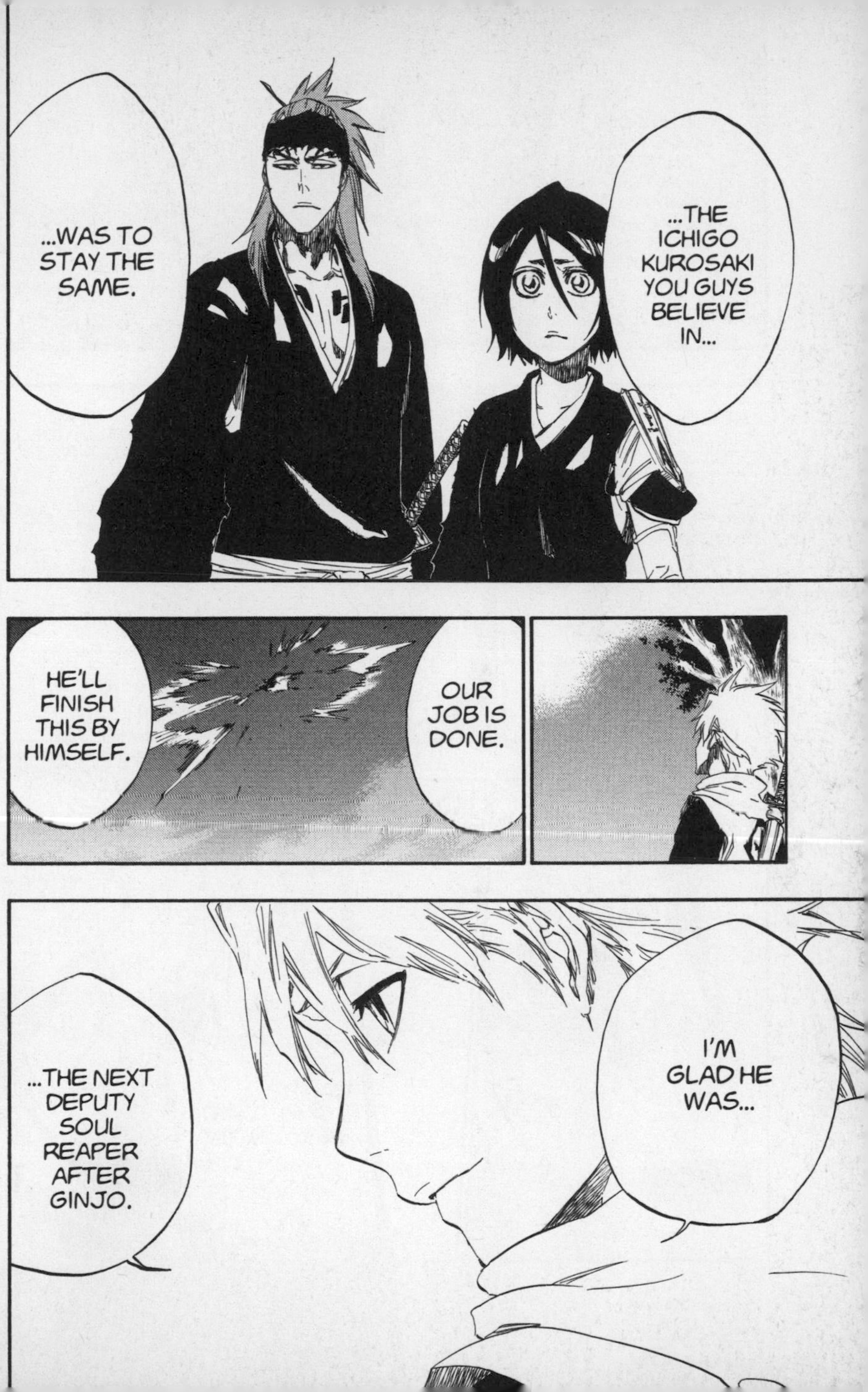
...THE ICHIGO KUROSAKI YOU GUYS BELIEVE IN...
...WAS TO STAY THE SAME.
OUR JOB IS DONE.
HE'LL FINISH THIS BY HIMSELF.
I'M GLAD HE WAS...
...THE NEXT DEPUTY SOUL REAPER AFTER GINJO.

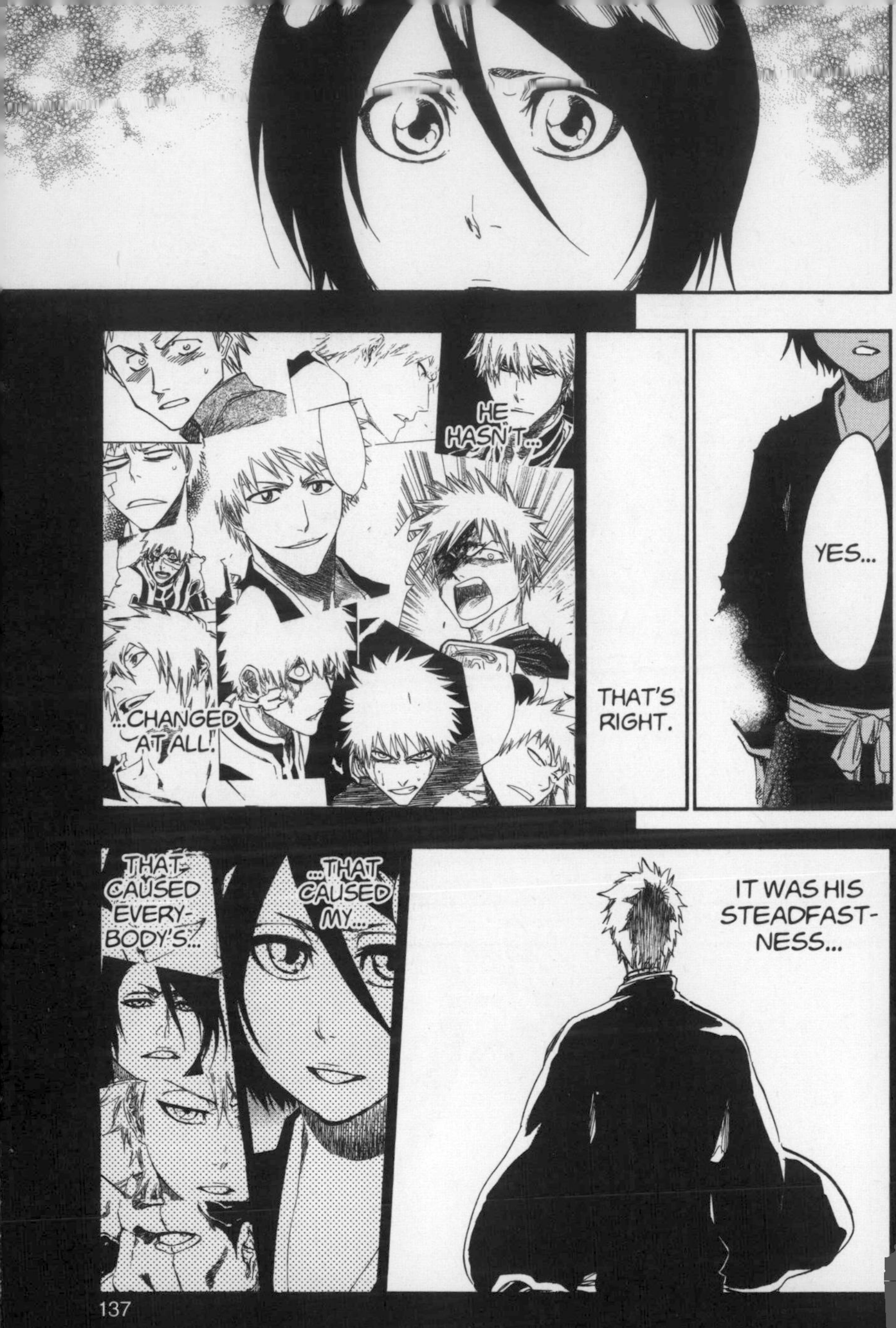
YES...
THAT'S RIGHT.
HE HASN'T...
...CHANGED AT ALL!
IT WAS HIS STEADFAST-NESS...
...THAT CAUSED MY...
THAT CAUSED EVERY-BODY'S...

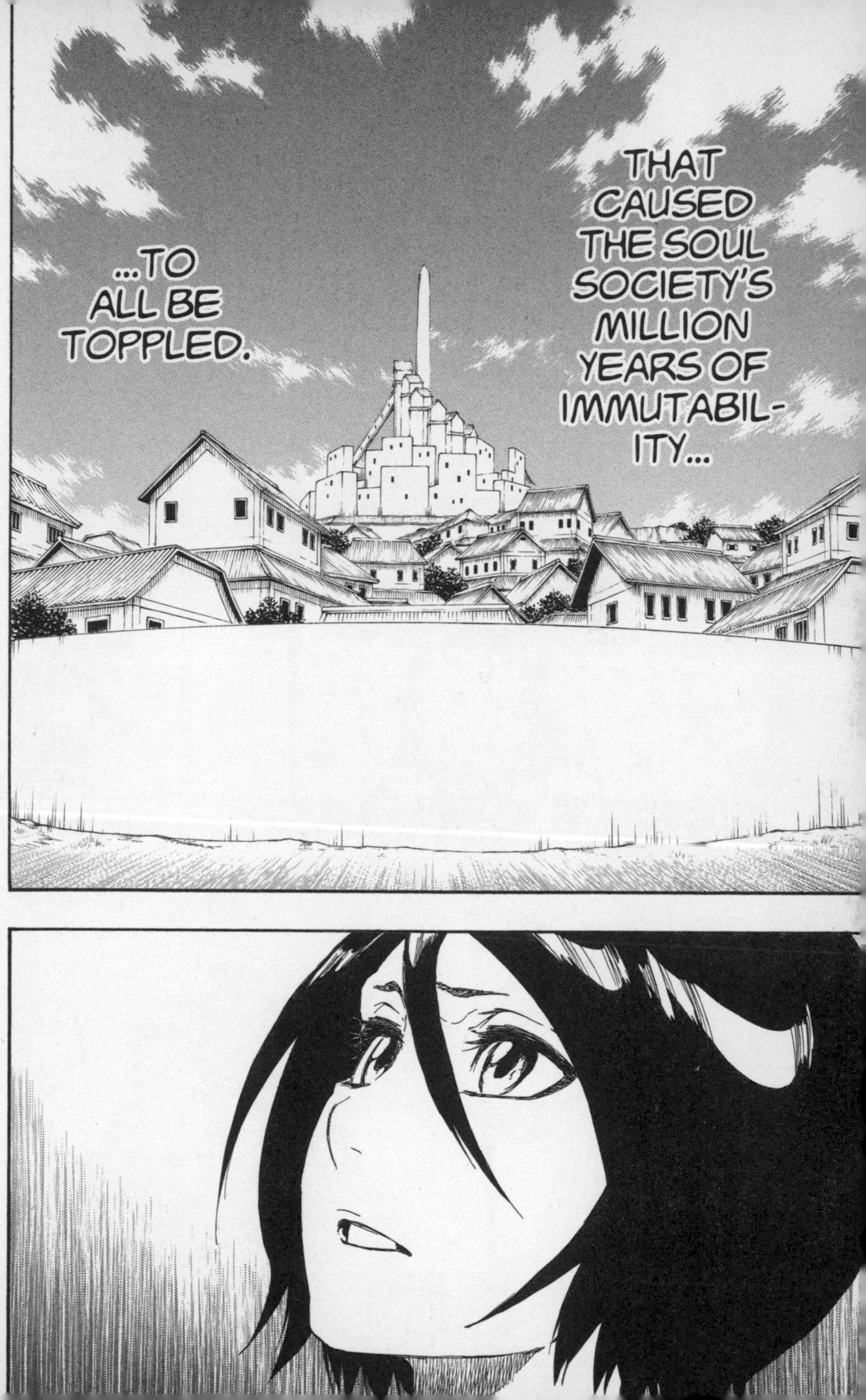
THAT CAUSED THE SOUL SOCIETY'S MILLION YEARS OF IMMUTABIL-ITY...
...TO ALL BE TOPPLED.

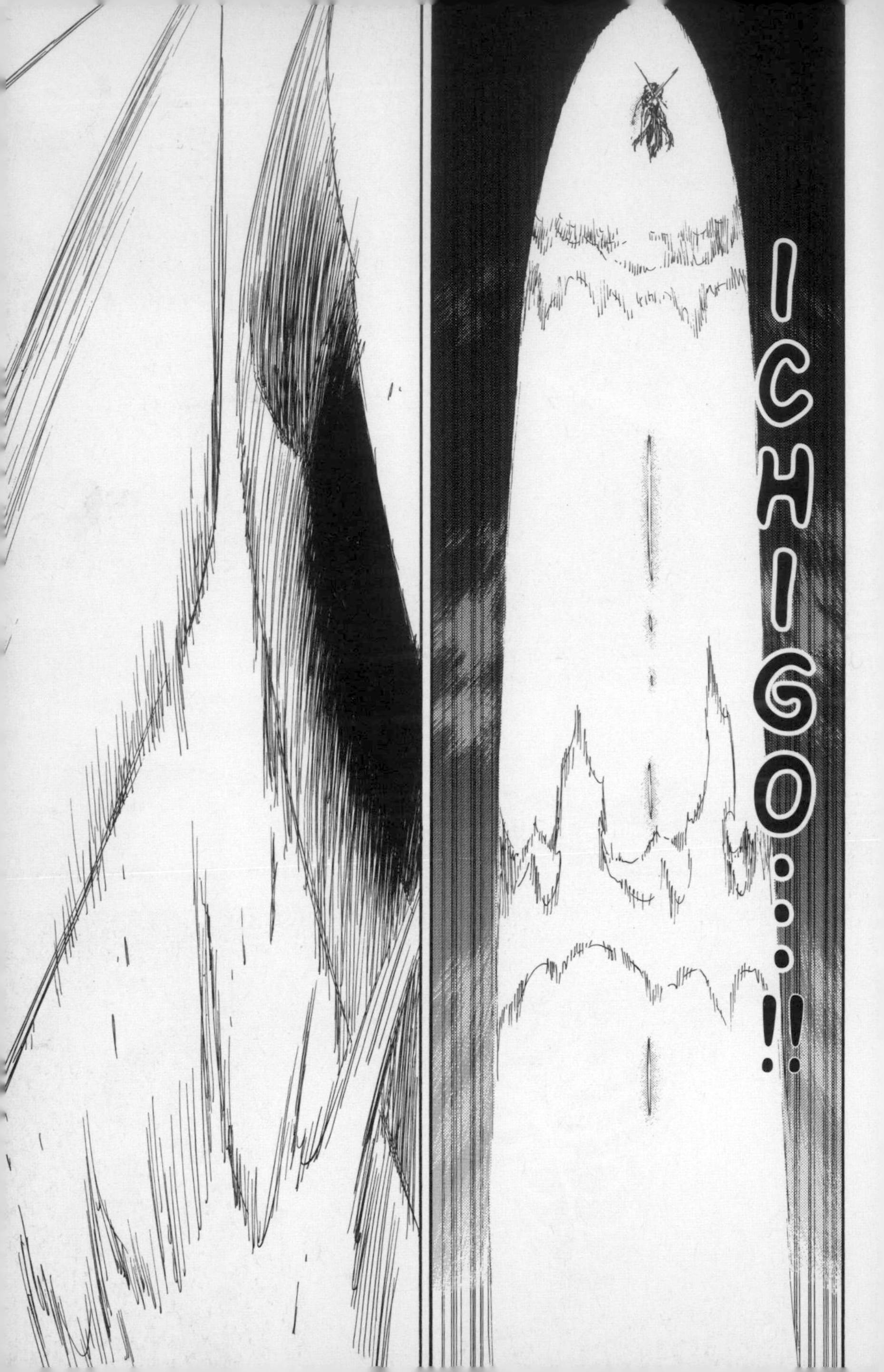
ICHIGO...!!

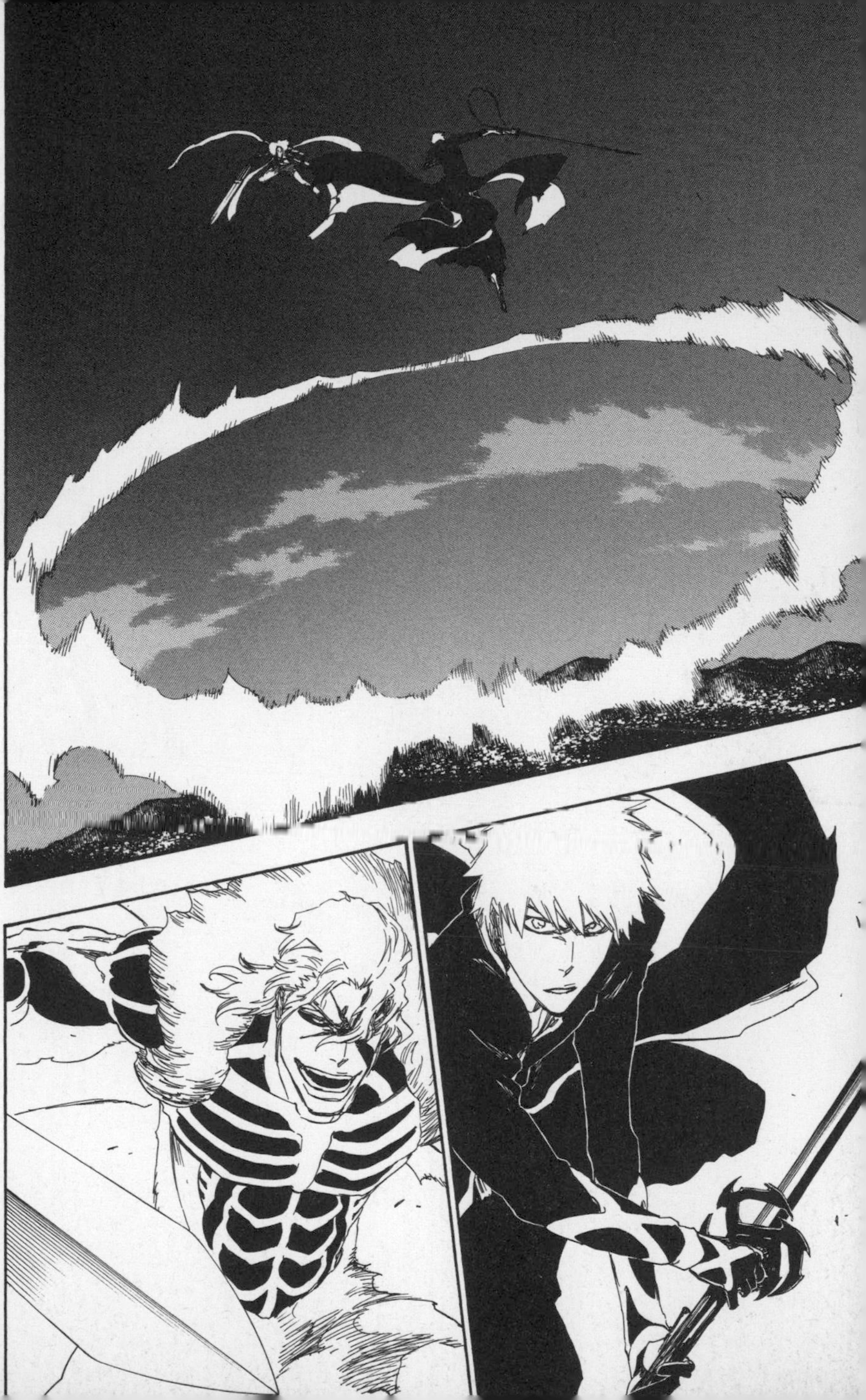

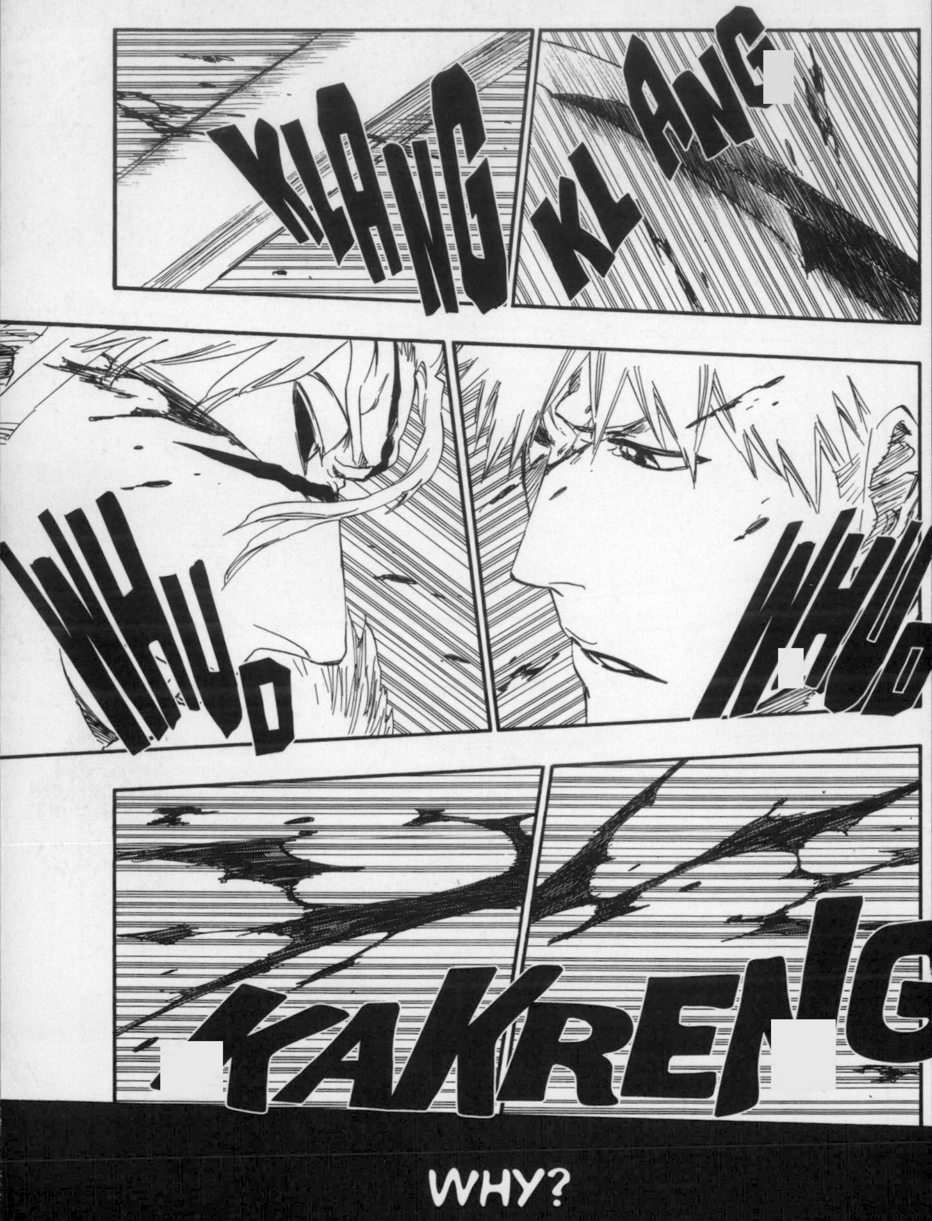
KLANG
KLANG
WHUD
WHUD
YAKRENG
WHY?

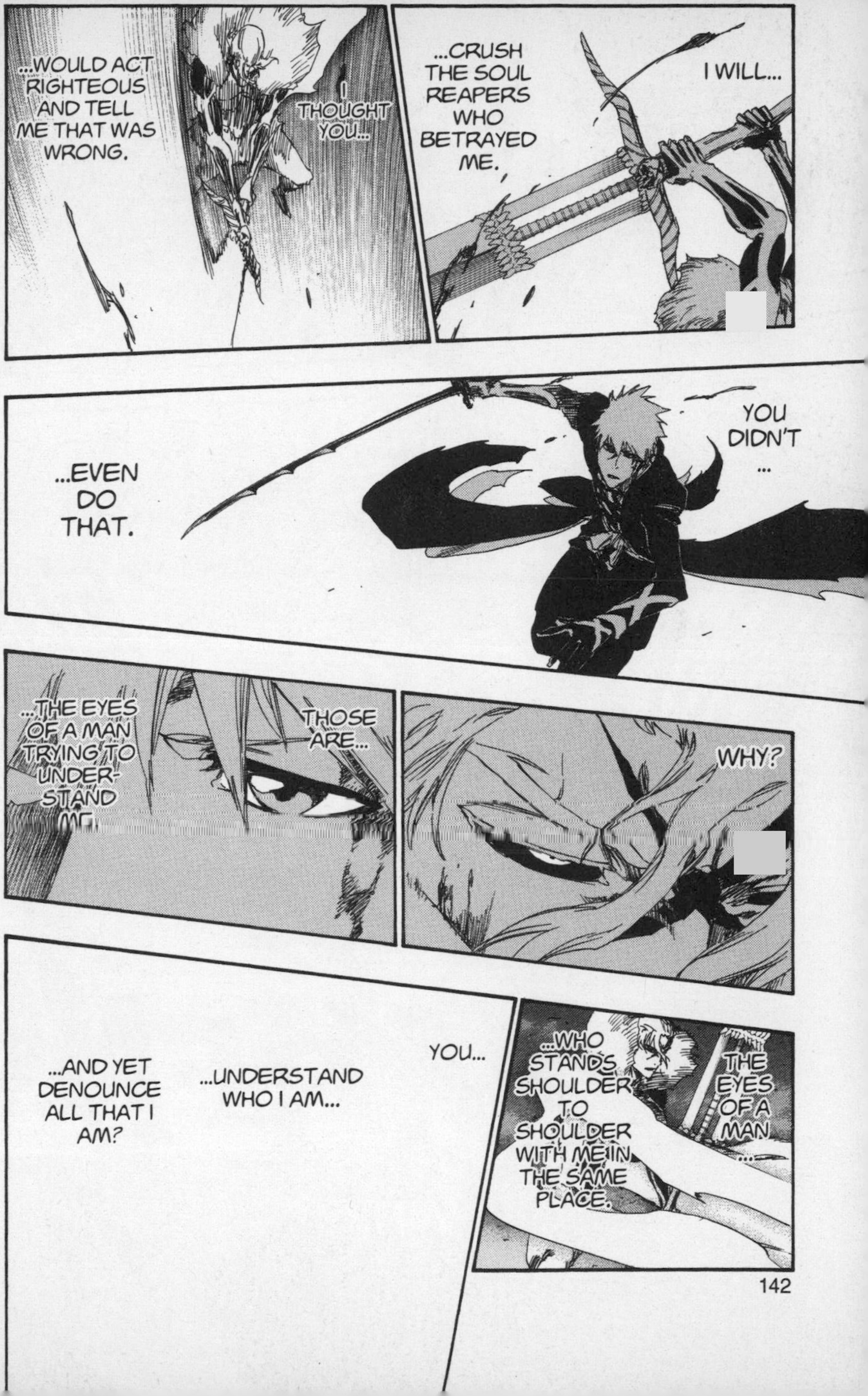
I WILL...
...CRUSH THE SOUL REAPERS WHO BETRAYED ME.
I THOUGHT YOU...
...WOULD ACT RIGHTEOUS AND TELL ME THAT WAS WRONG.
YOU DIDN'T ...
...EVEN DO THAT.
WHY?
THOSE ARE...
...THE EYES OF A MAN TRYING TO UNDERSTAND ME.
THE EYES OF A MAN ...
...WHO STANDS SHOULDER TO SHOULDER WITH ME IN THE SAME PLACE.
YOU...
...UNDERSTAND WHO I AM...
...AND YET DENOUNCE ALL THAT I AM?

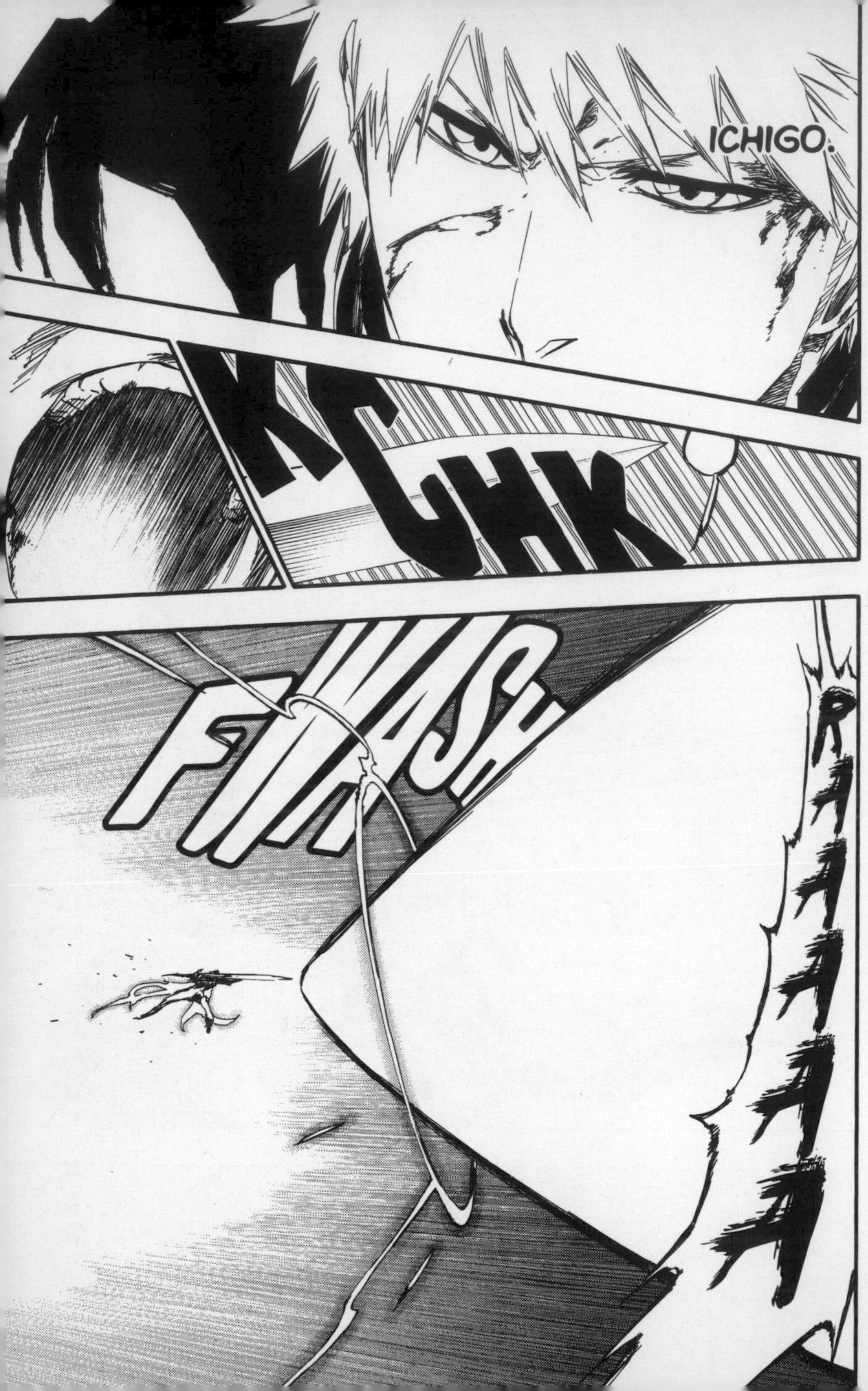
ICHIGO.
KCHK
RAAAAA
FWASH

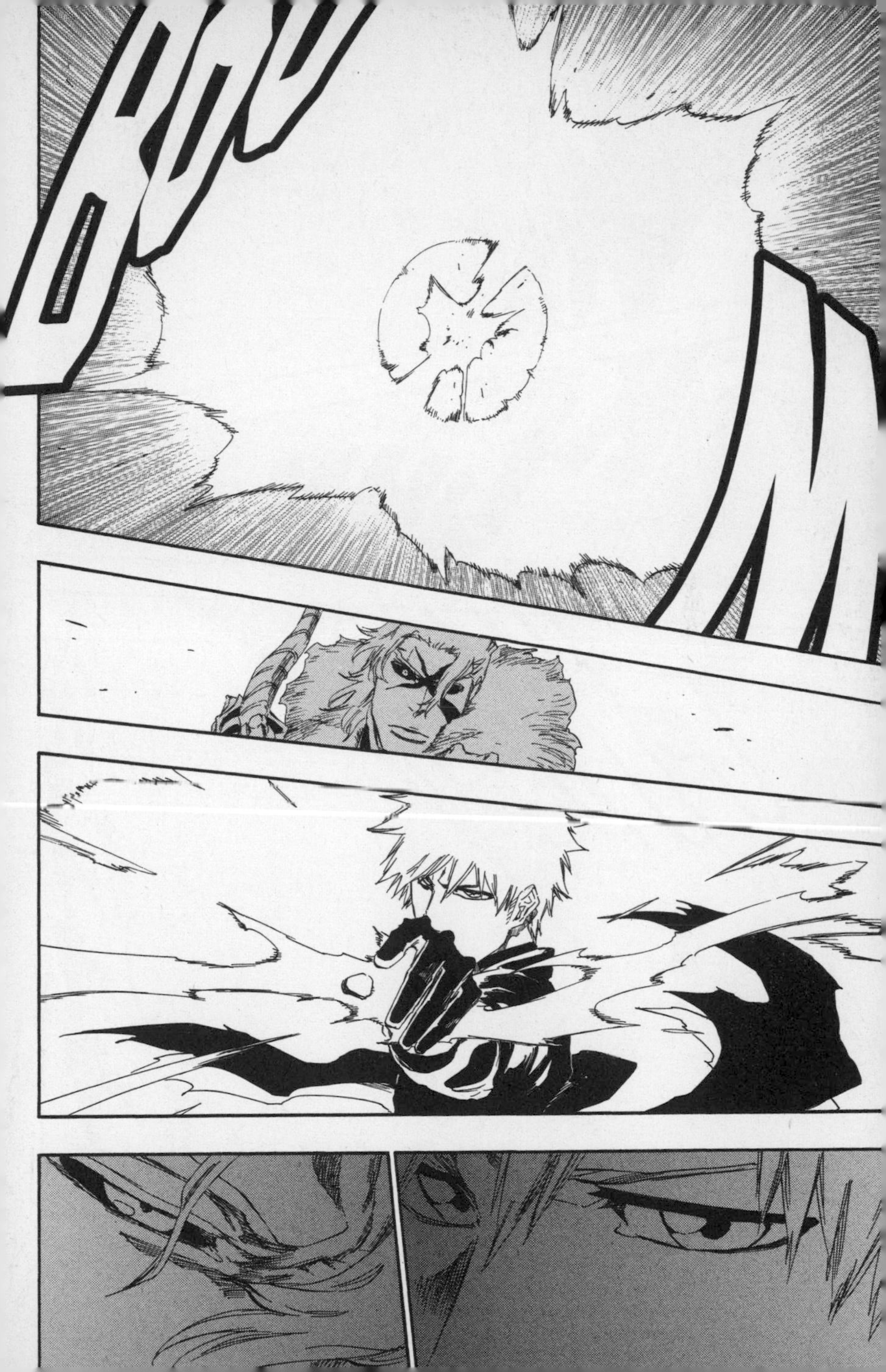

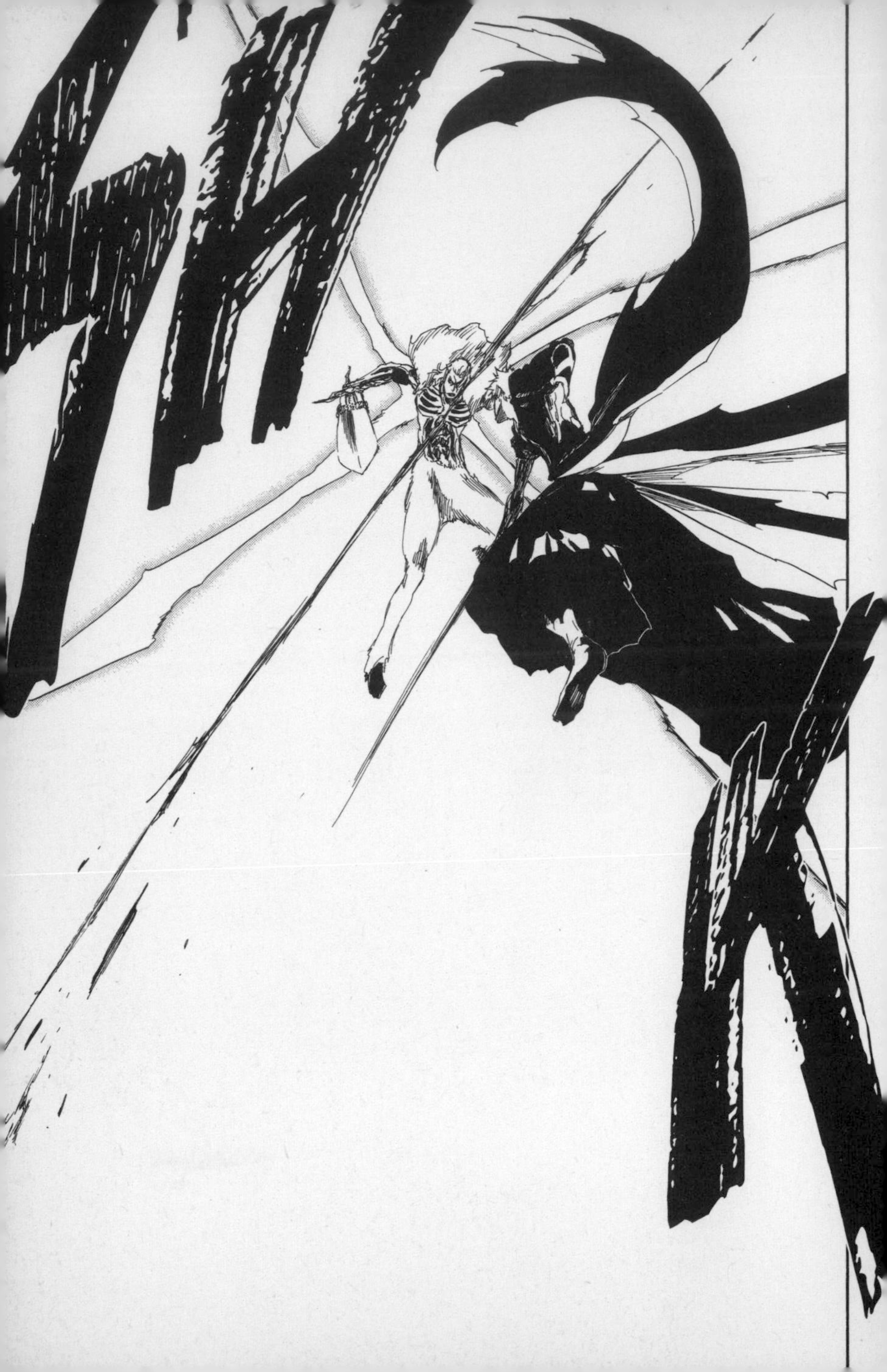
SHNK

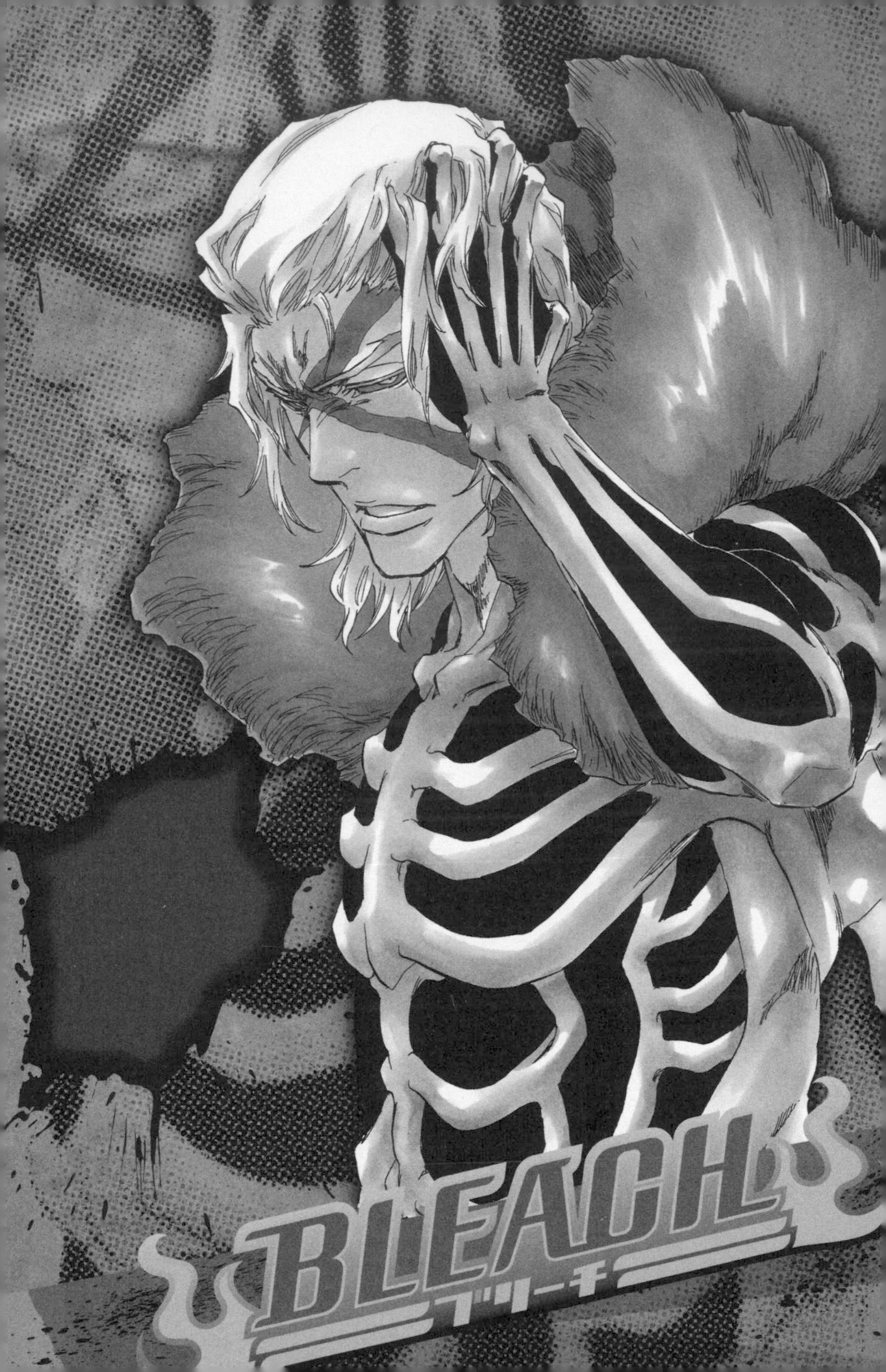
BLEACH
ブリーチ

BLEACH

ブリーチ

READ THIS WAY

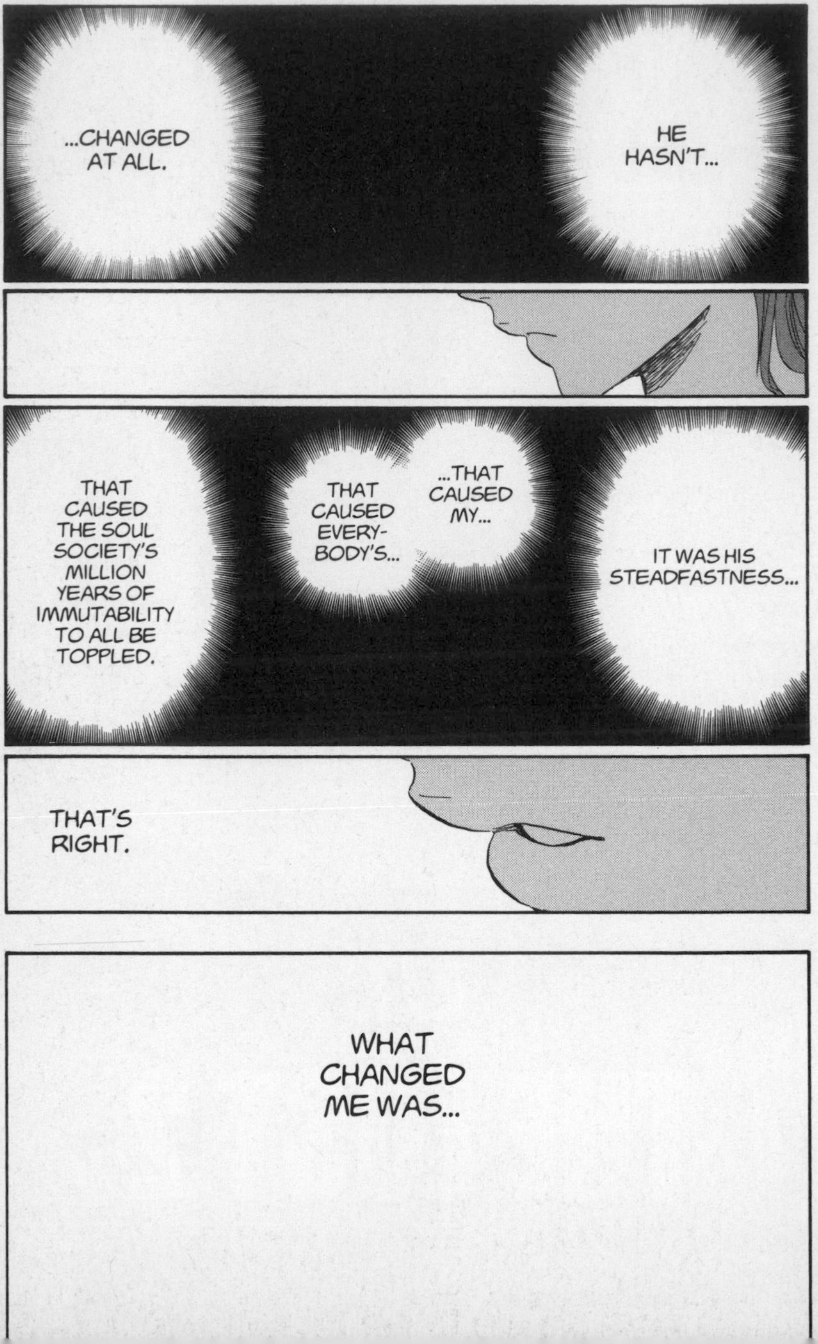
HE HASN'T...
...CHANGED AT ALL.
IT WAS HIS STEADFASTNESS...
...THAT CAUSED MY...
THAT CAUSED EVERY-BODY'S...
THAT CAUSED THE SOUL SOCIETY'S MILLION YEARS OF IMMUTABILITY TO ALL BE TOPPLED.
THAT'S RIGHT.
WHAT CHANGED ME WAS...

BLEACH

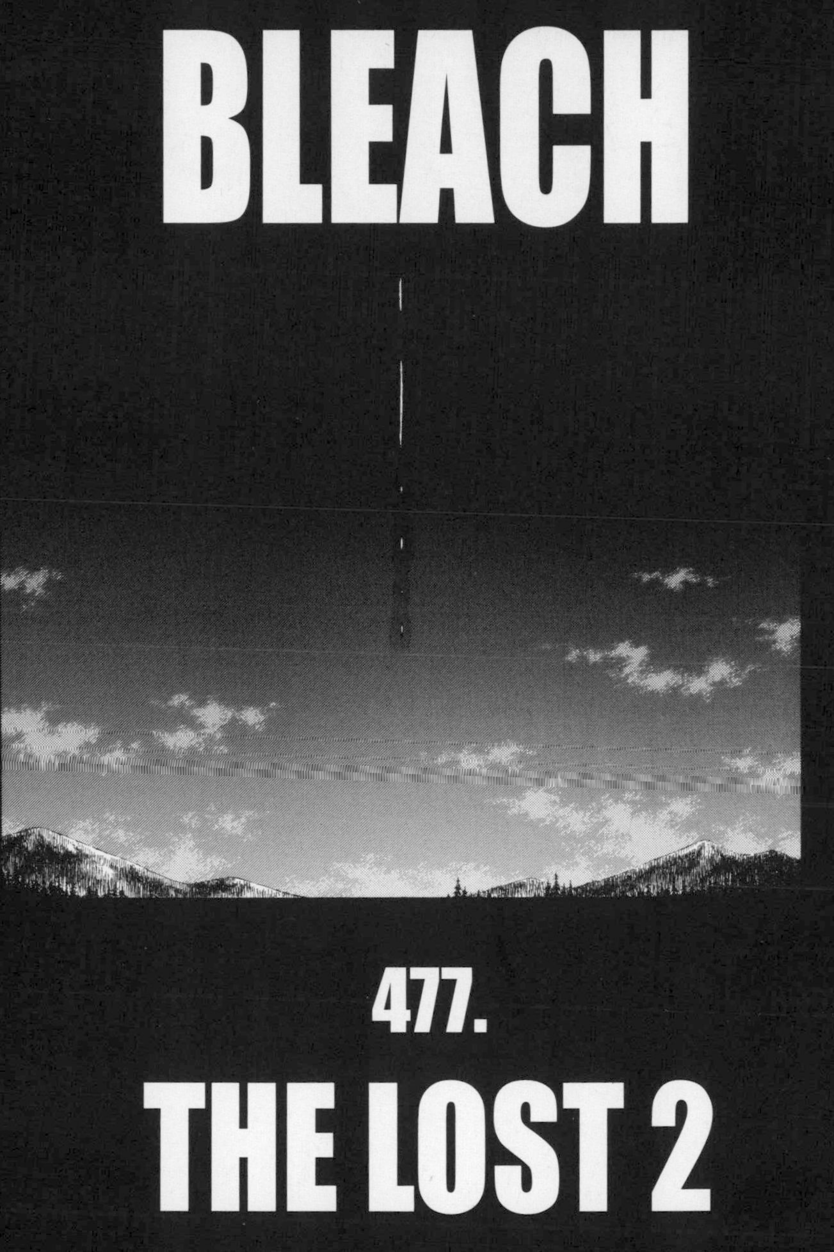

477.

THE LOST 2

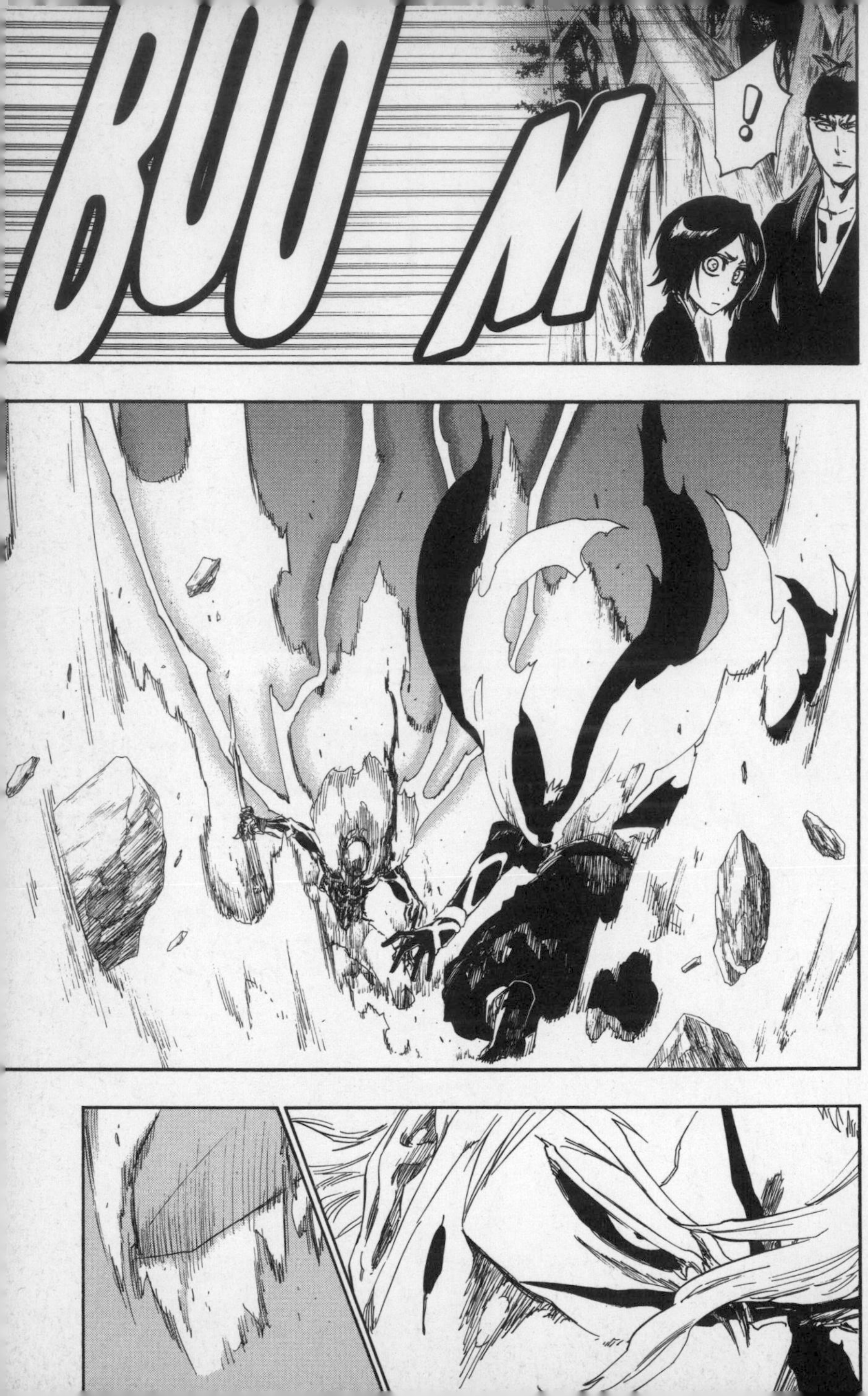
!
BUUM

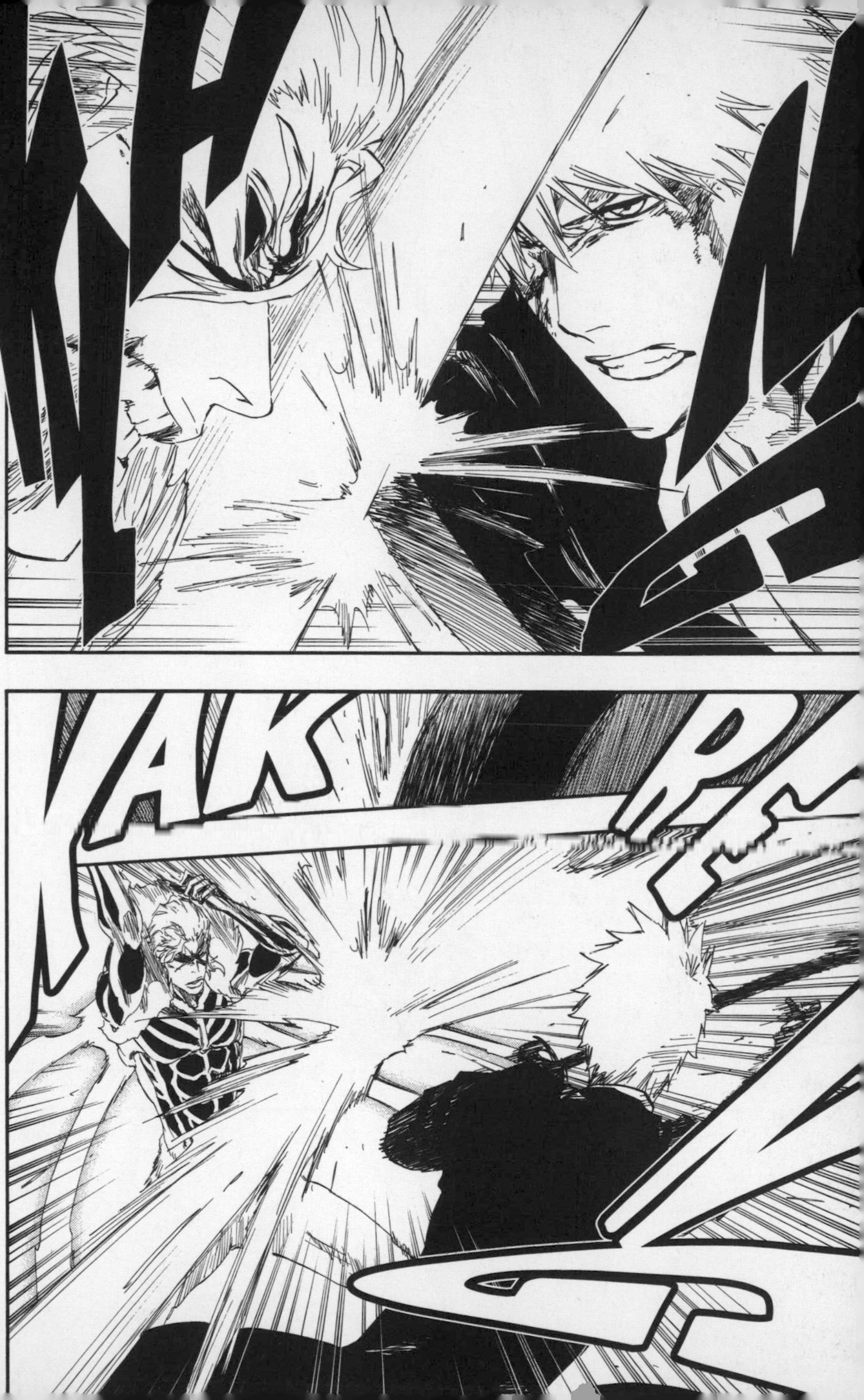

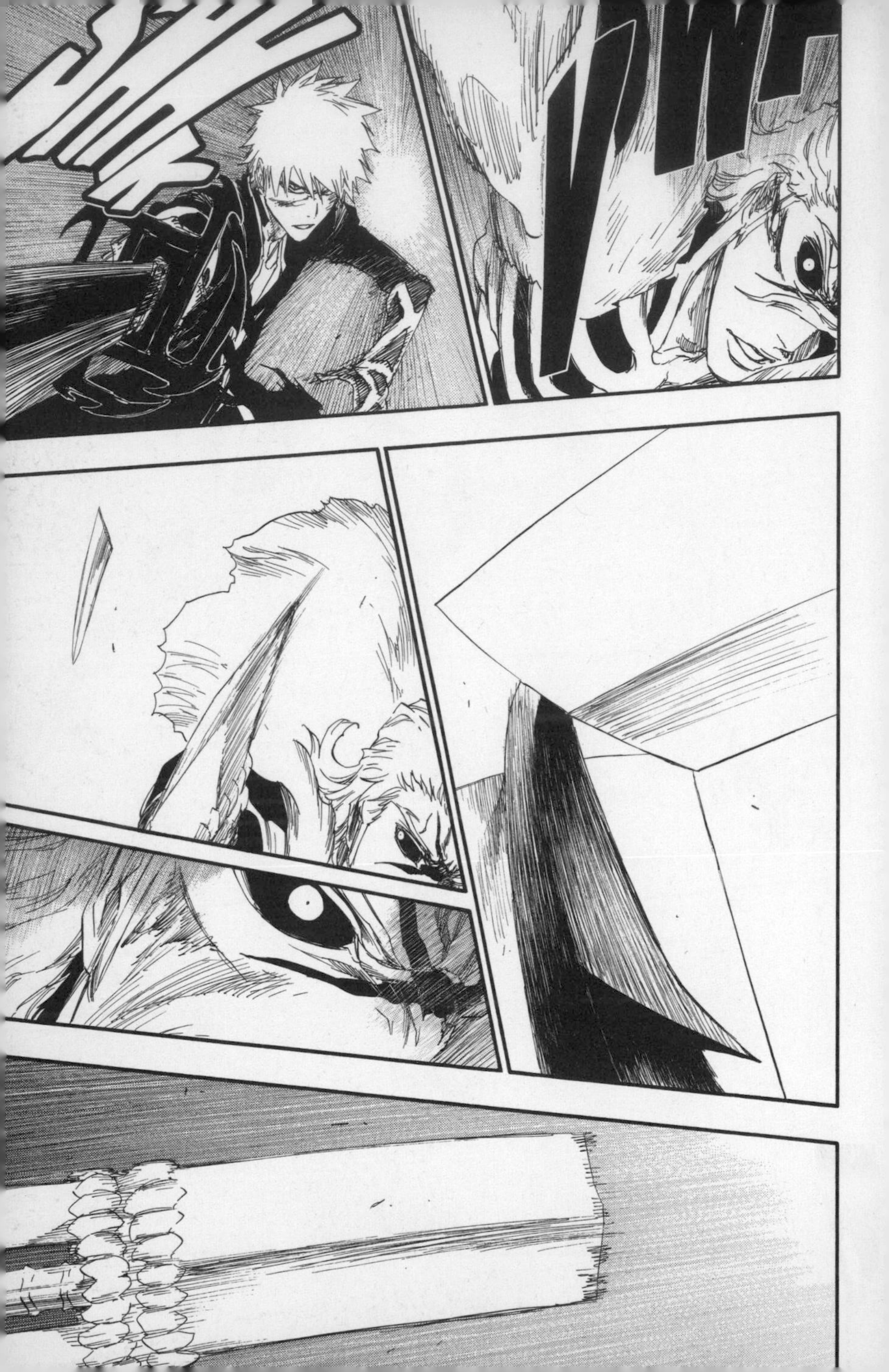

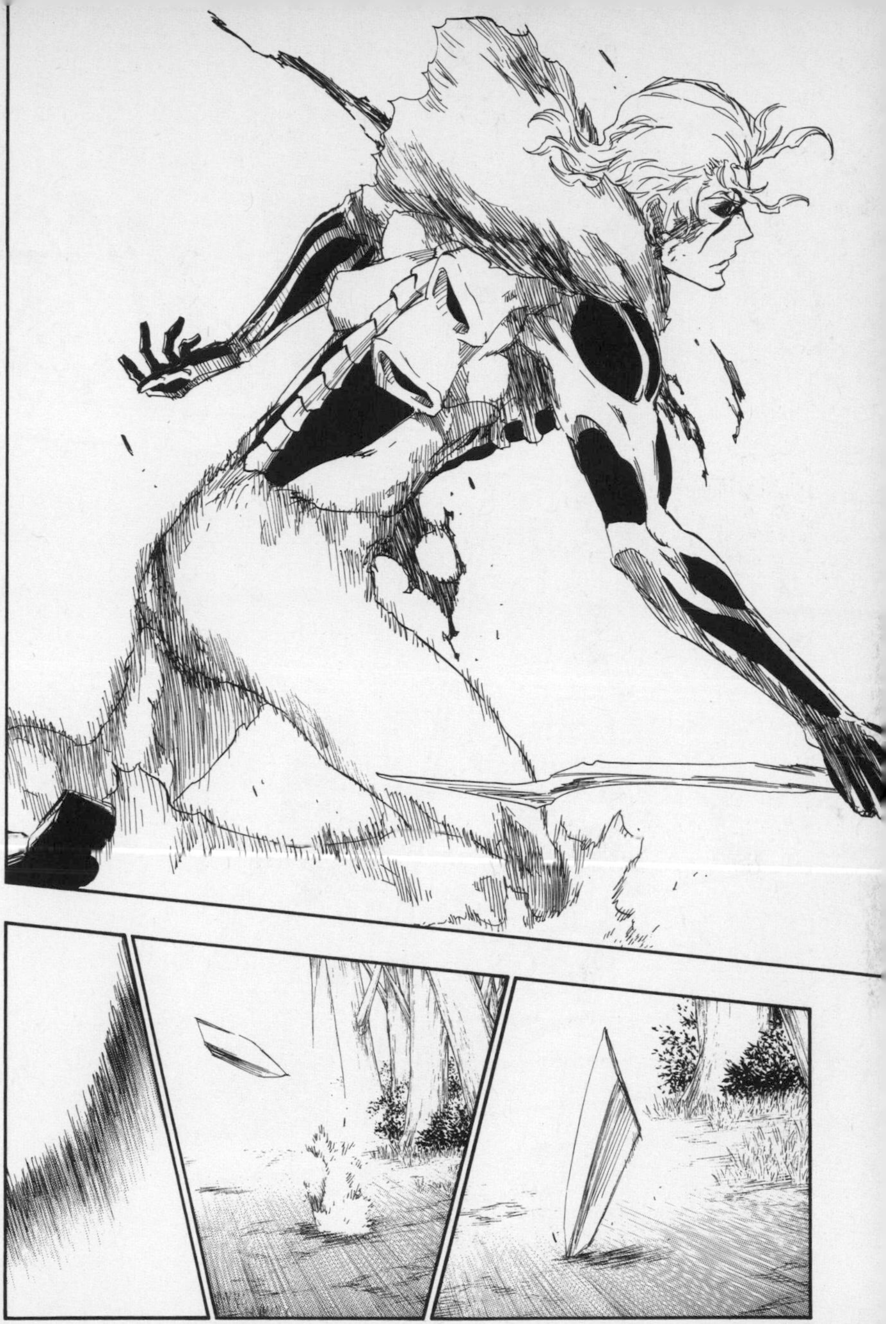

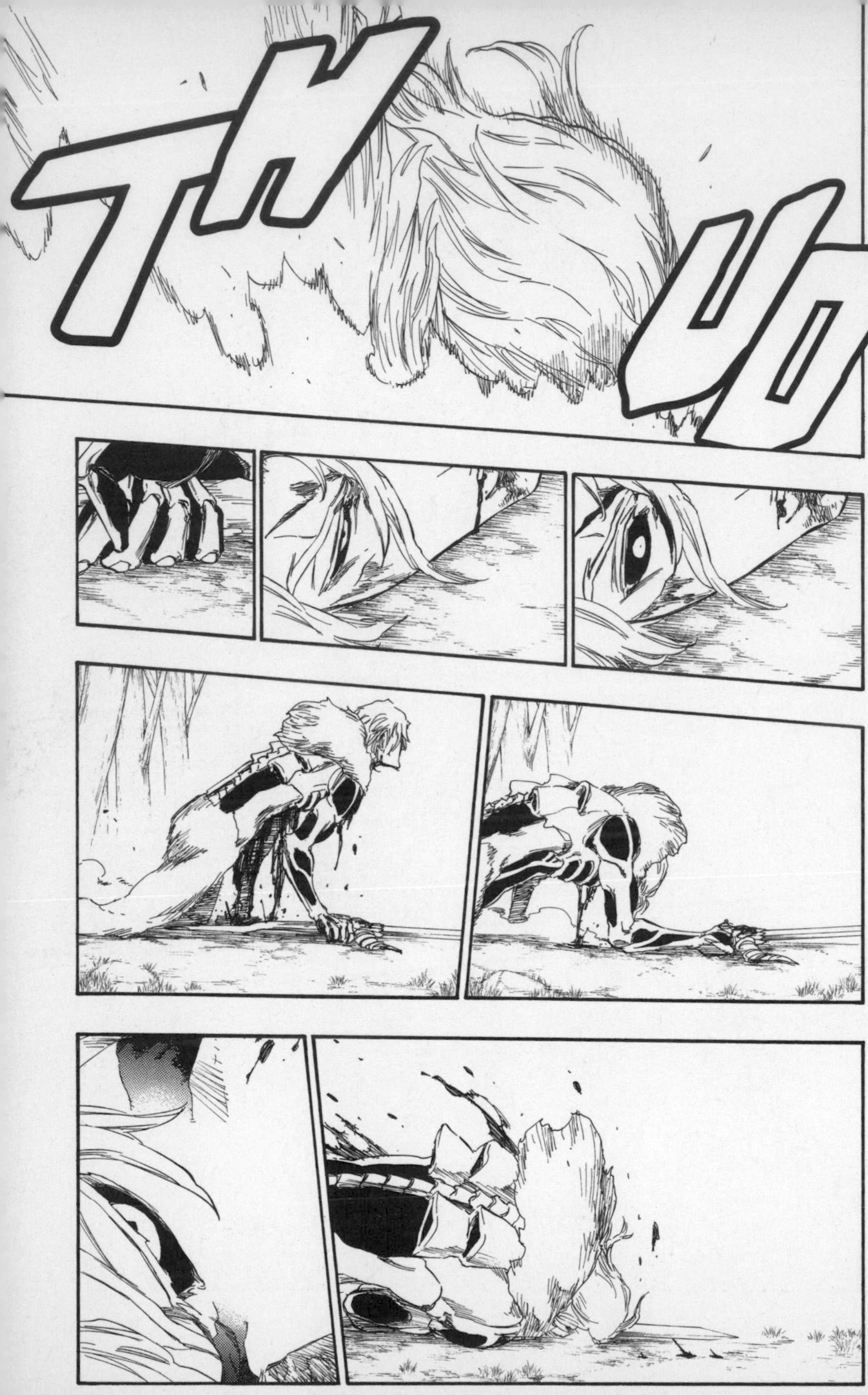
THUD

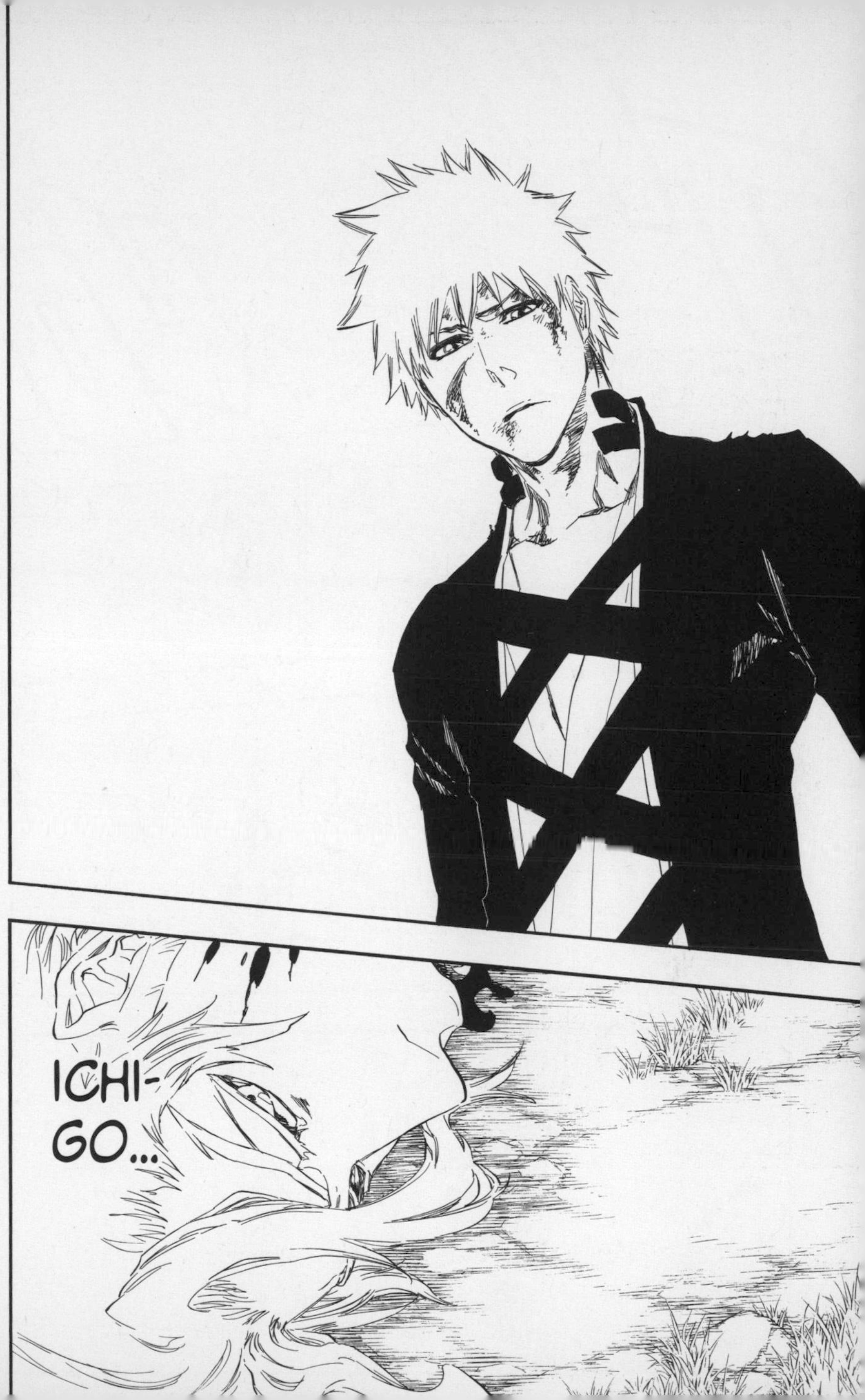
ICHI-
GO...

IF OUR ORDER HAD BEEN OPPOSITE...
...WOULD OUR POSITIONS BE REVERSED TOO?
WOULD YOU...
...HAVE ENDED UP LIKE ME?
HEY, ICHIGO.
IF WE WERE THE OPPOSITE...

WOULD WE HAVE BEEN...

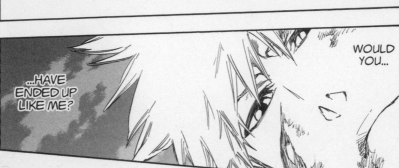

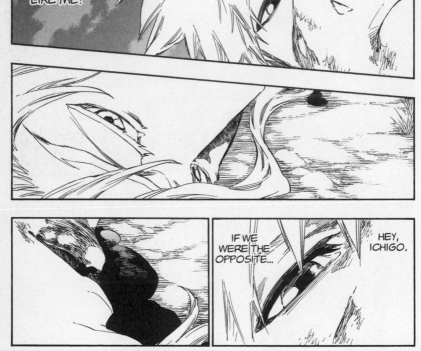

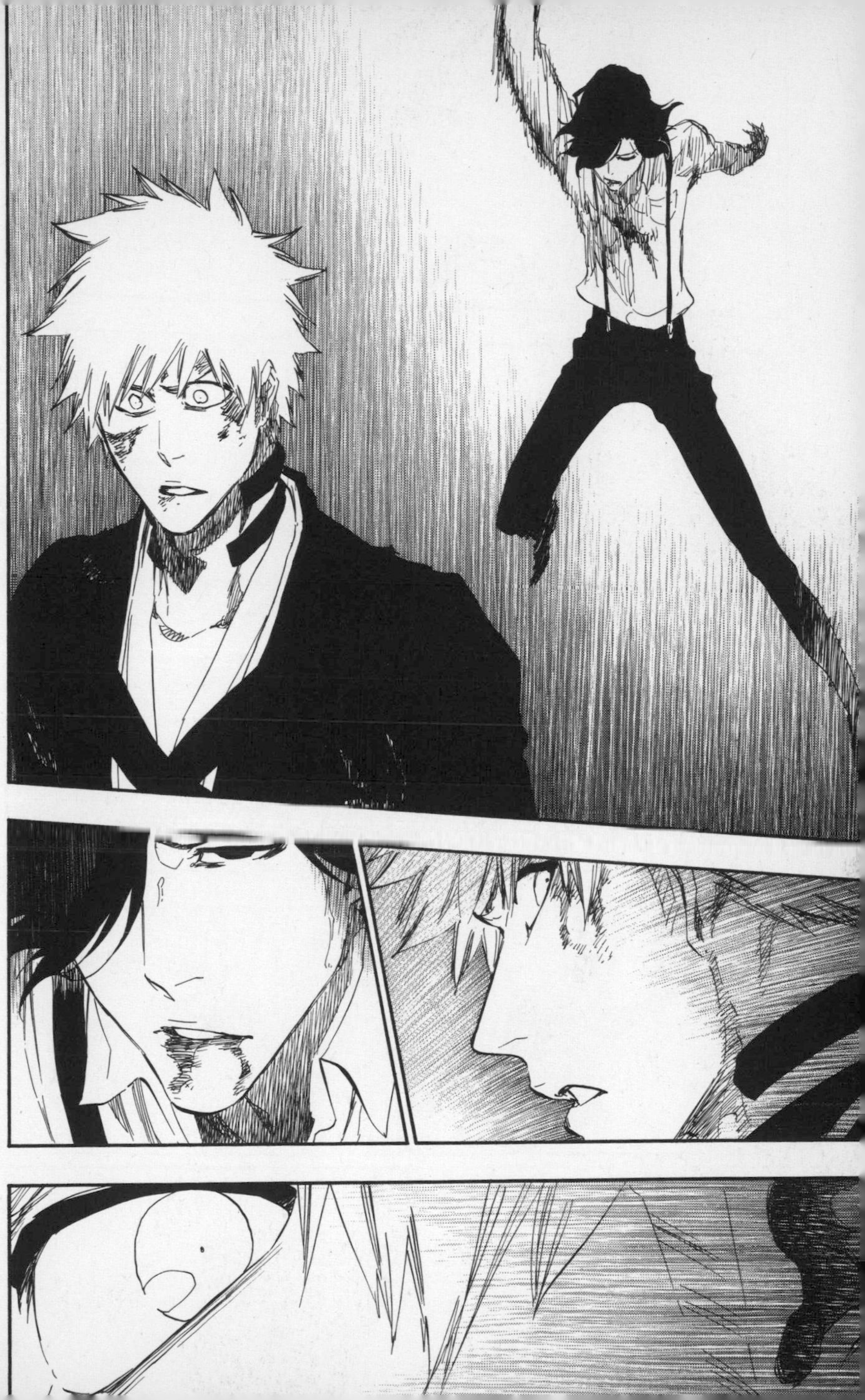

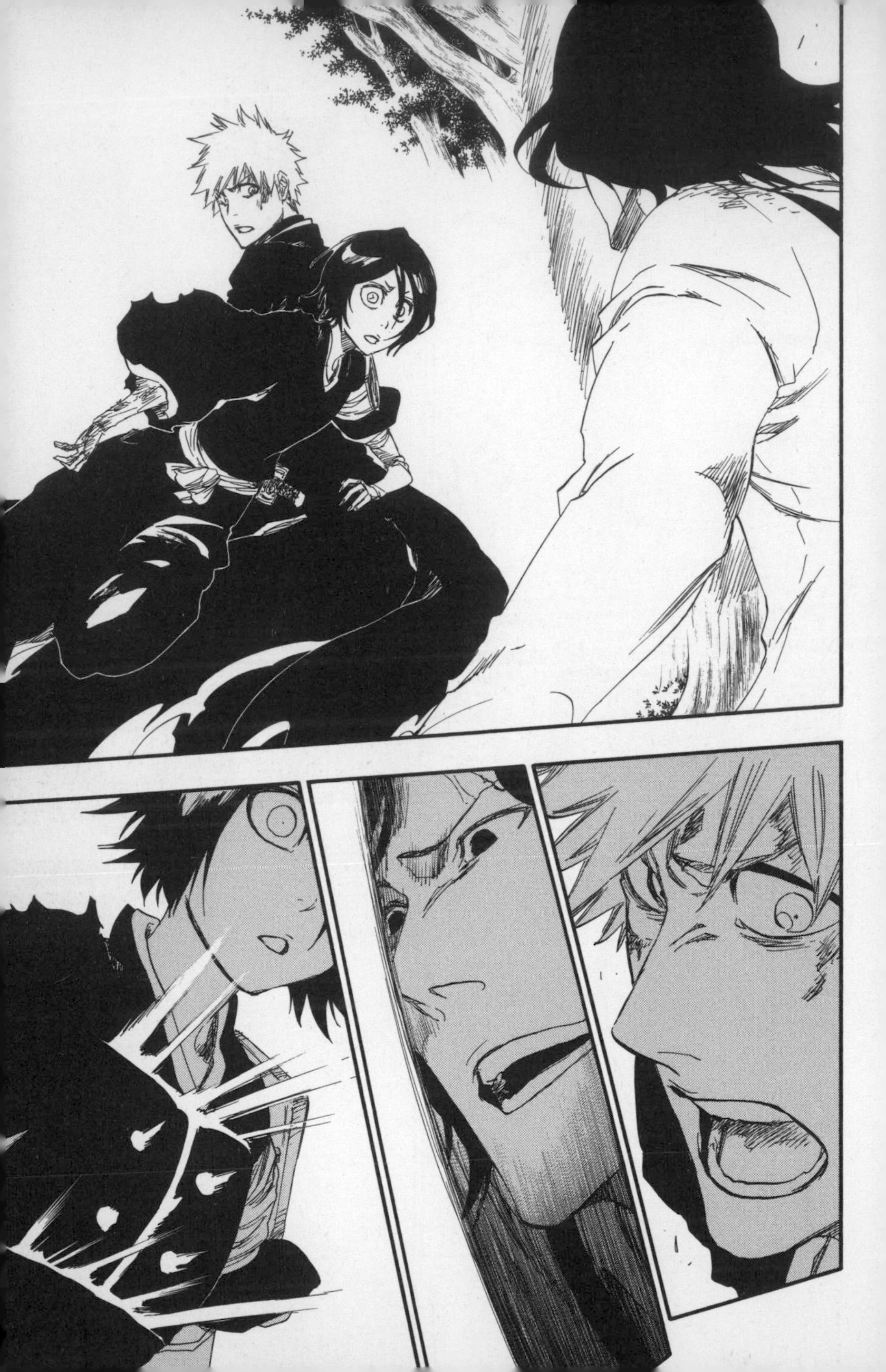

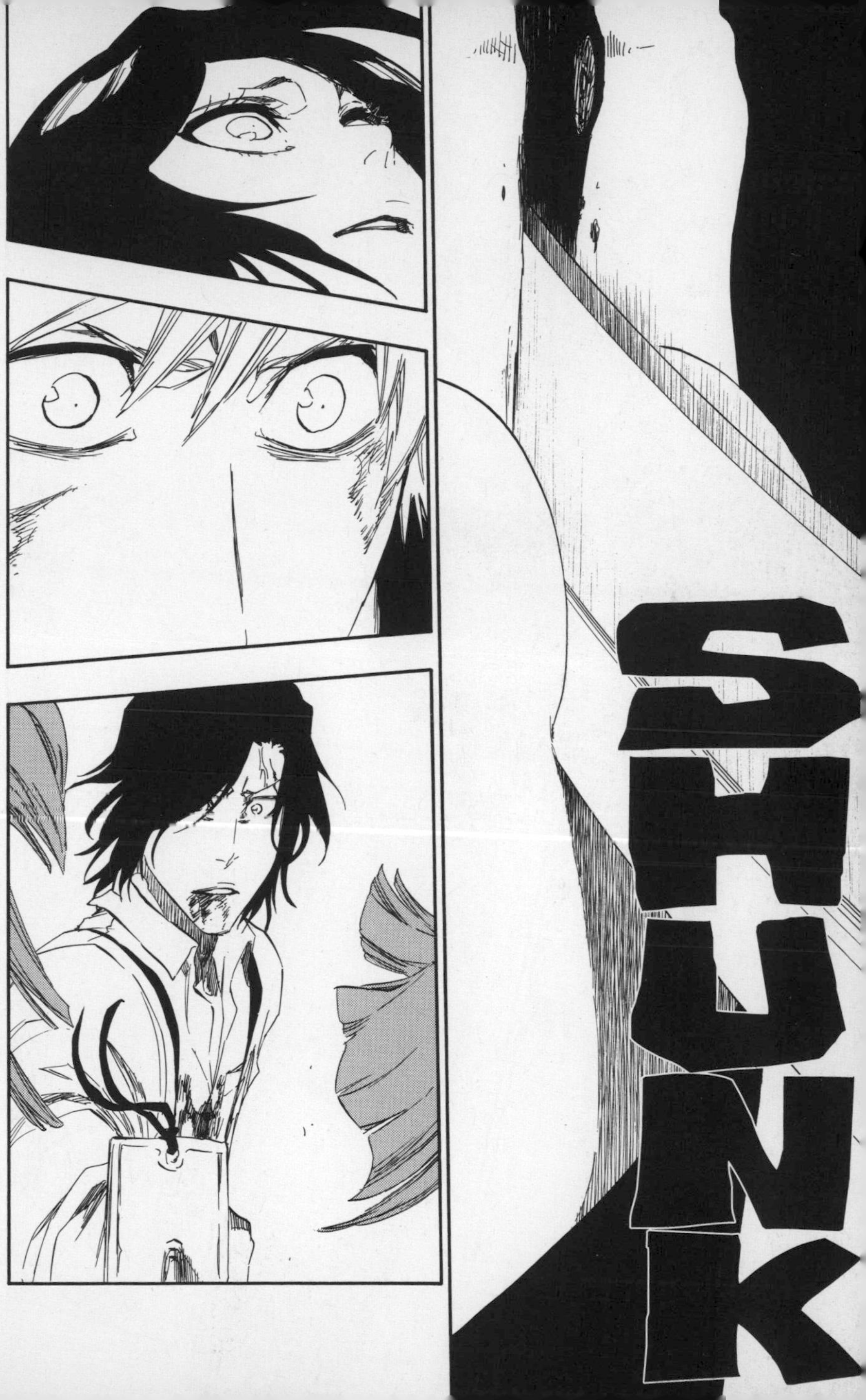
SHUNK

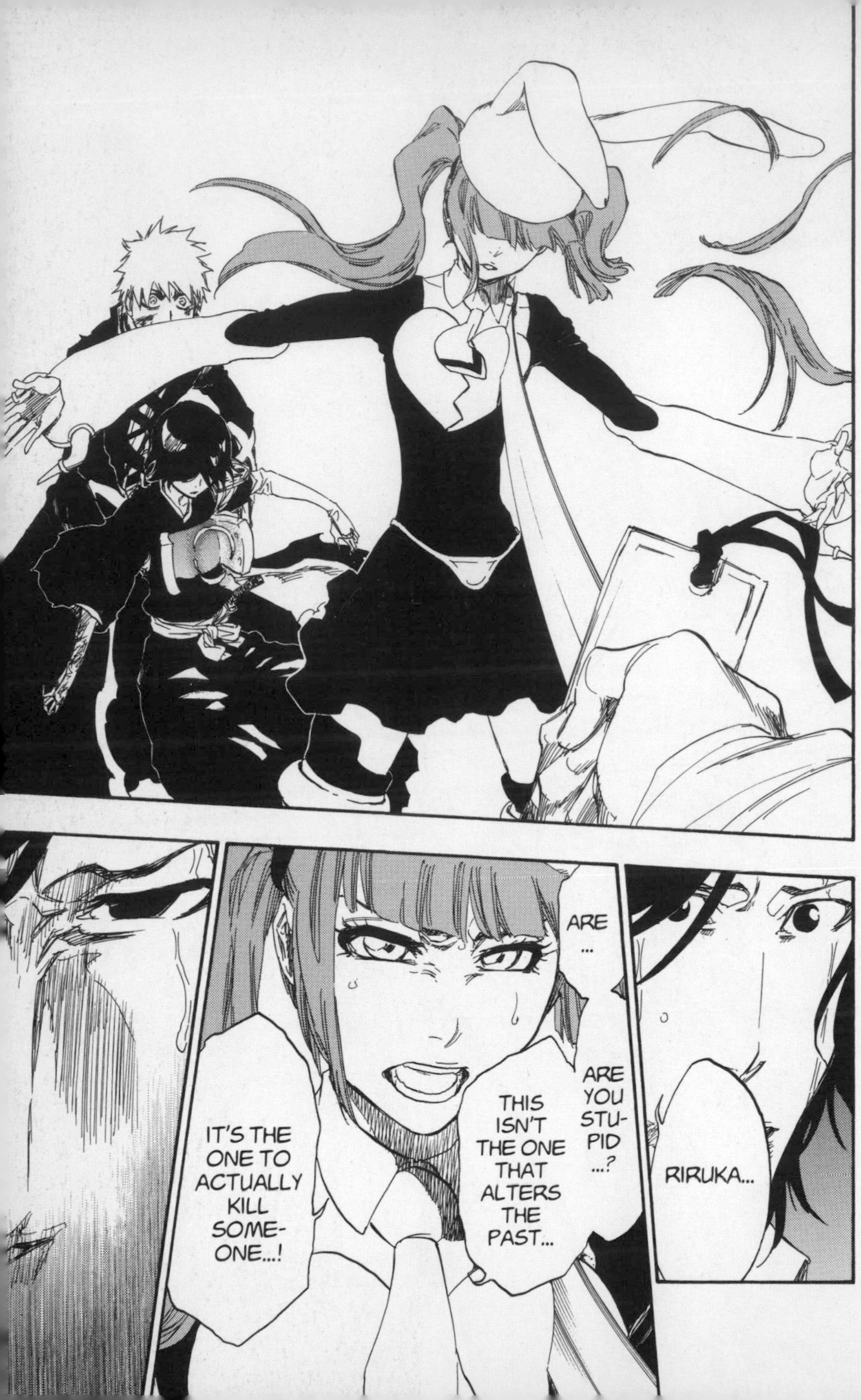
RIRUKA...
ARE...
ARE YOU STUPID...?
THIS ISN'T THE ONE THAT ALTERS THE PAST...
IT'S THE ONE TO ACTUALLY KILL SOMEONE...!

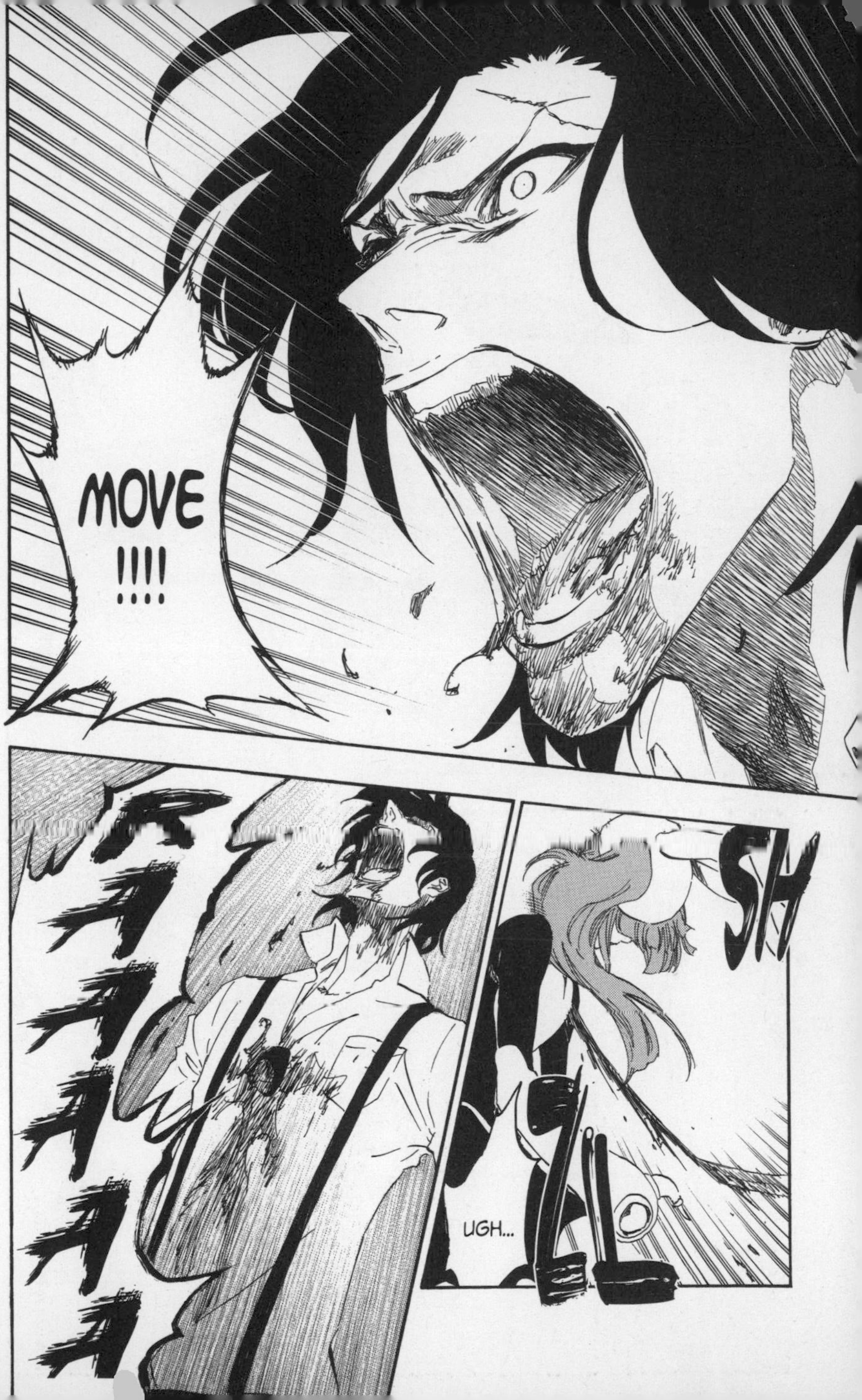
MOVE !!!!
SH
UGH...

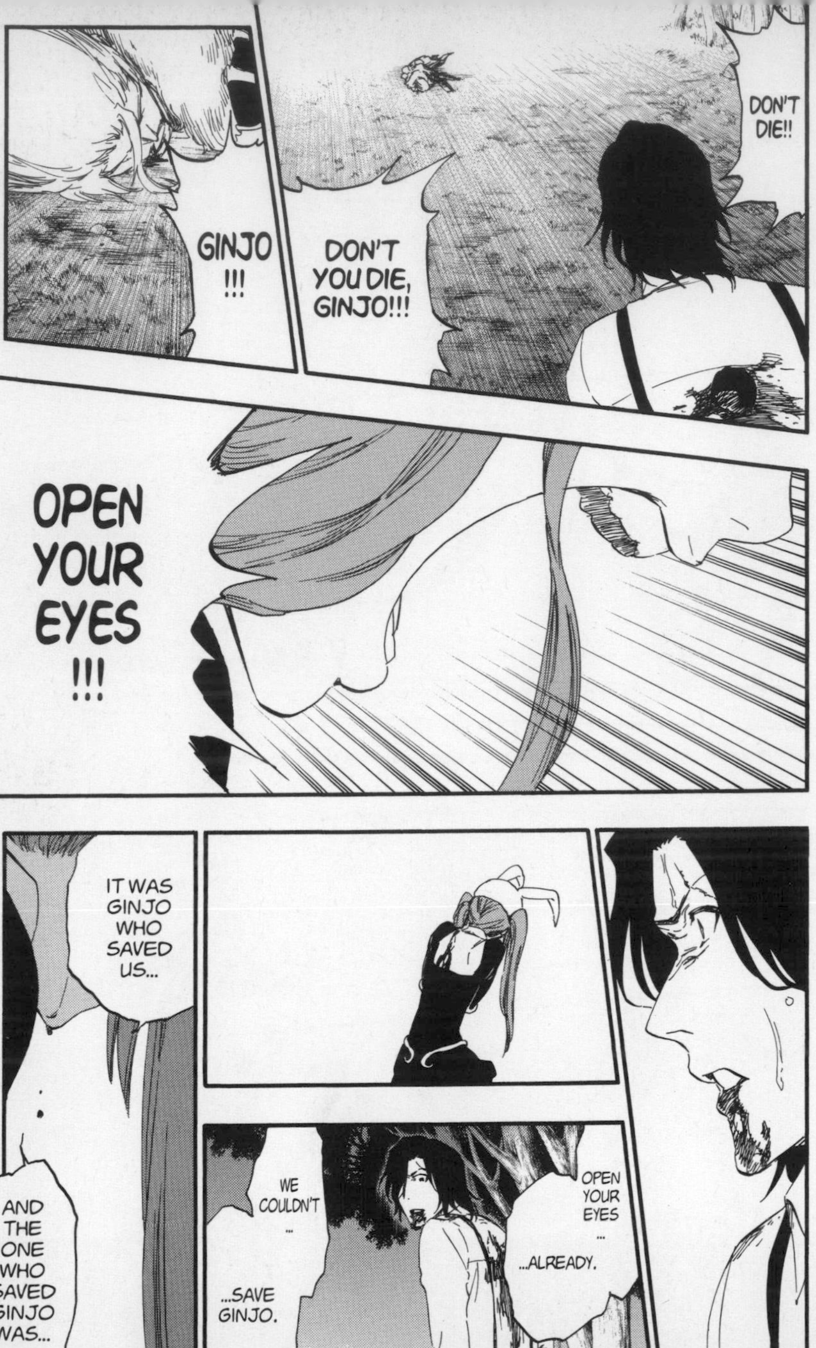
DON'T DIE!!
DON'T YOU DIE, GINJO!!!
GINJO !!!
OPEN YOUR EYES !!!
OPEN YOUR EYES ...
...ALREADY.
WE COULDN'T ...
...SAVE GINJO.
IT WAS GINJO WHO SAVED US...
AND THE ONE WHO SAVED GINJO WAS...

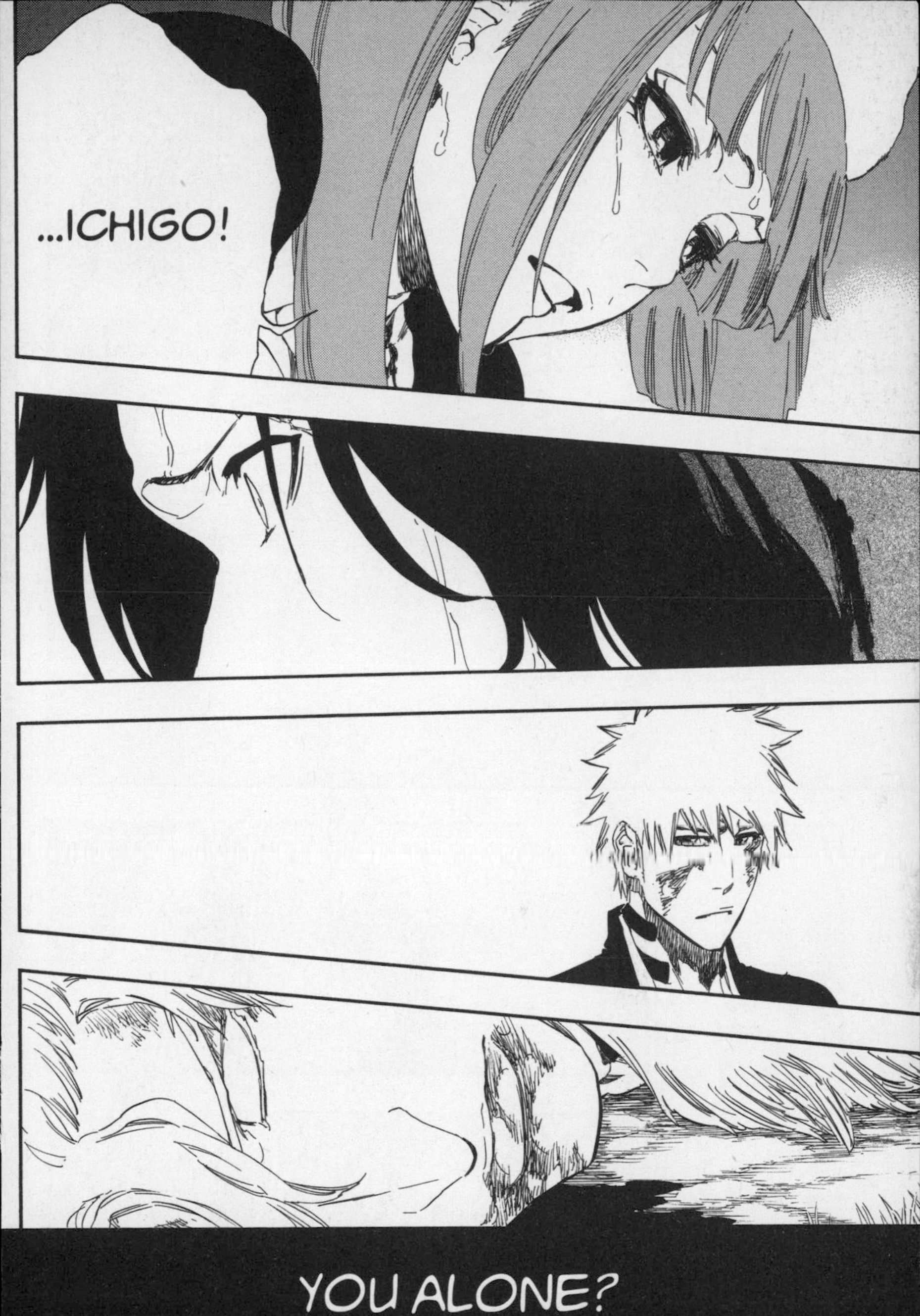
...ICHIGO!
YOU ALONE?

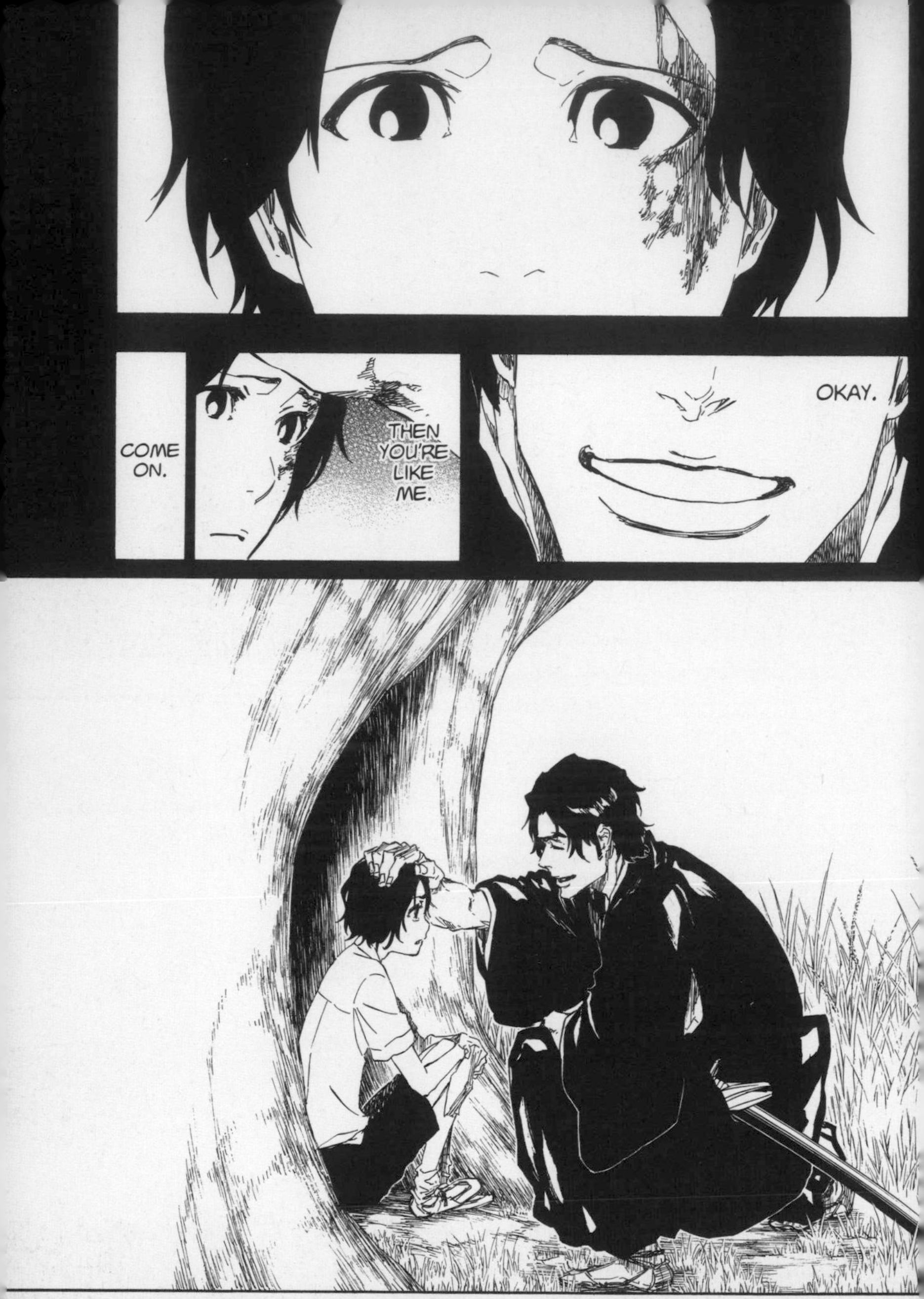
OKAY.
THEN YOU'RE LIKE ME.
COME ON.

STARTING TODAY, WE'RE TOGETHER.

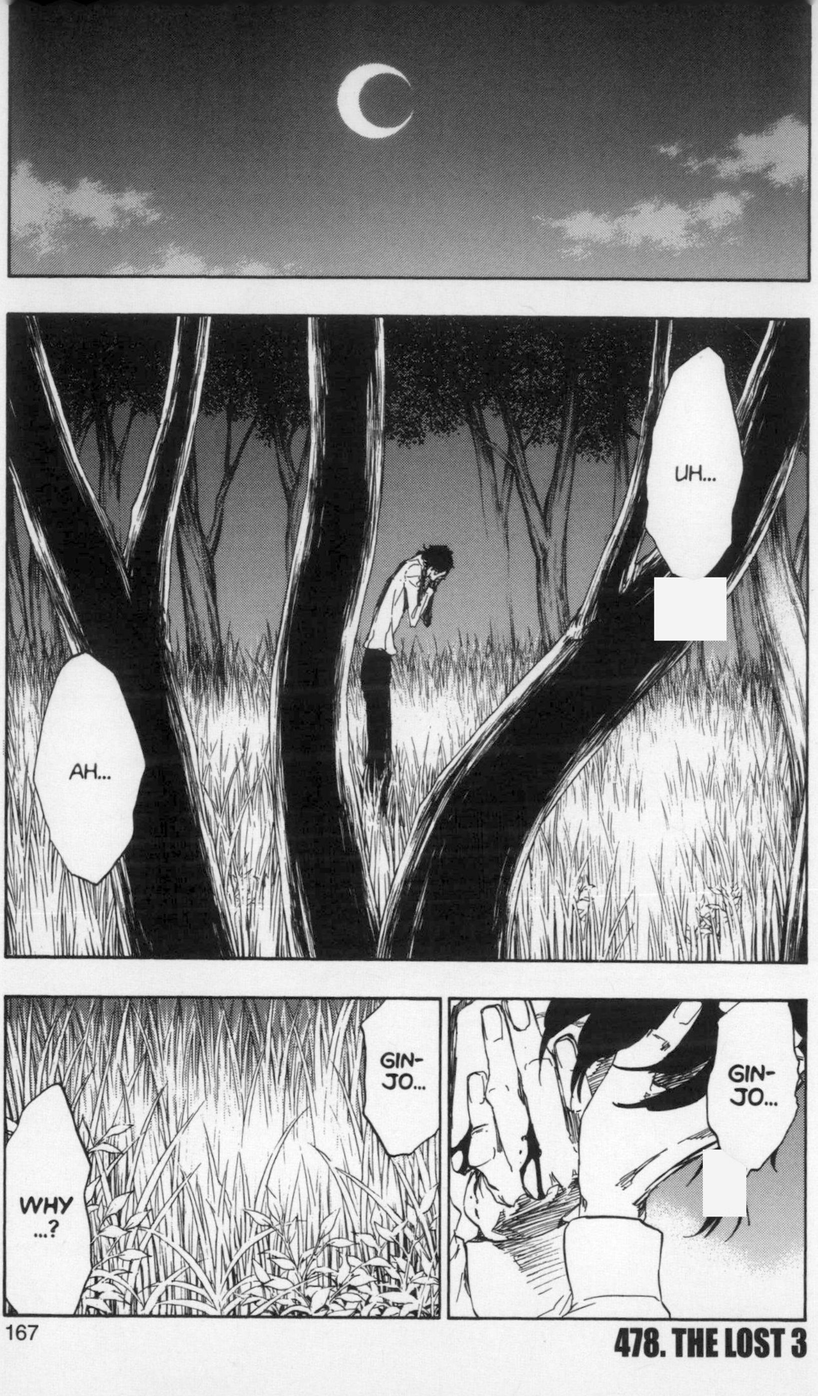
UH...
AH...
GIN-JO...
GIN-JO...
WHY ...?

478. THE LOST 3

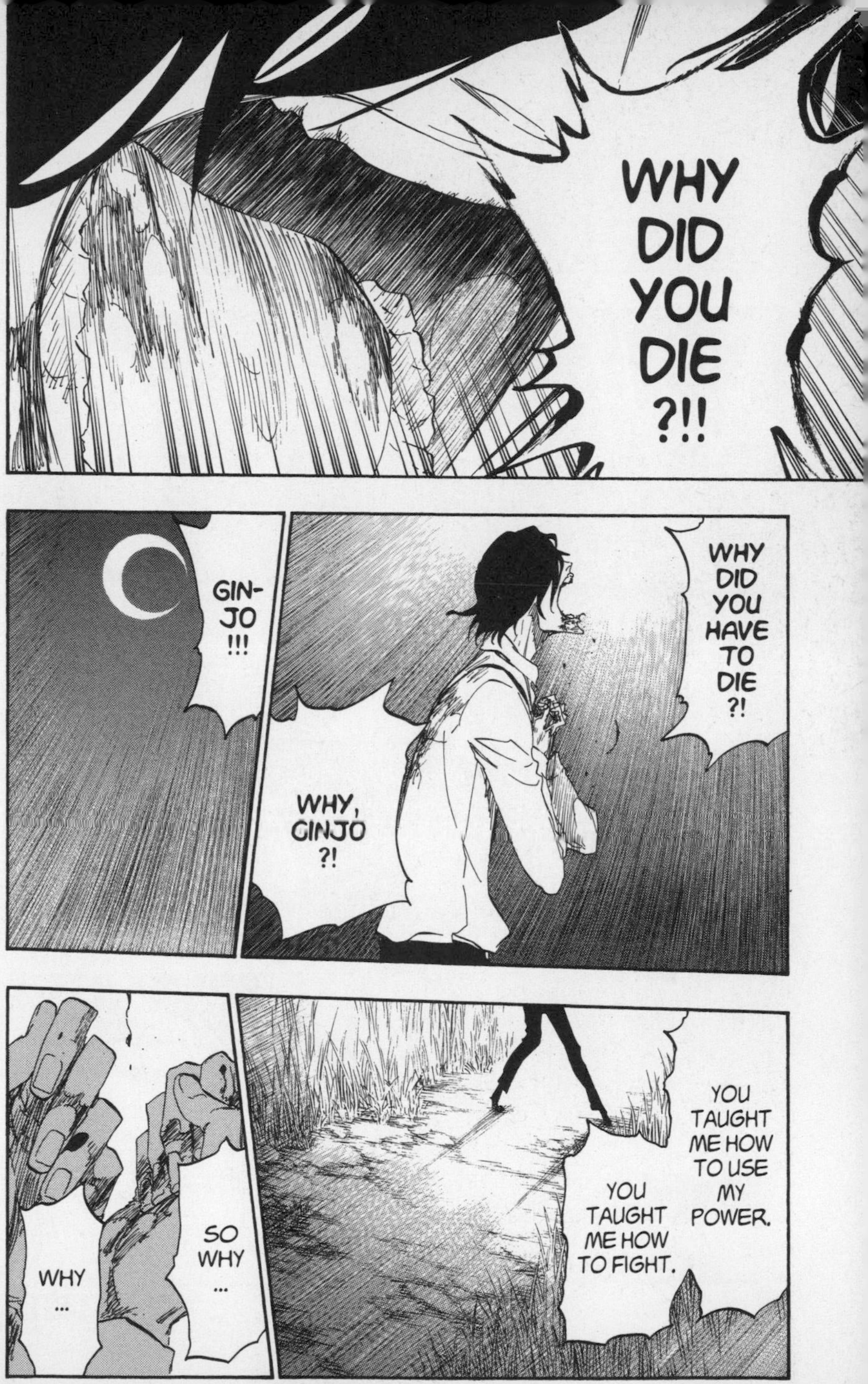
WHY DID YOU DIE ?!!
WHY DID YOU HAVE TO DIE ?!
WHY, GINJO ?!
GINJO !!!
YOU TAUGHT ME HOW TO USE MY POWER.
YOU TAUGHT ME HOW TO FIGHT.
SO WHY ...
WHY ...

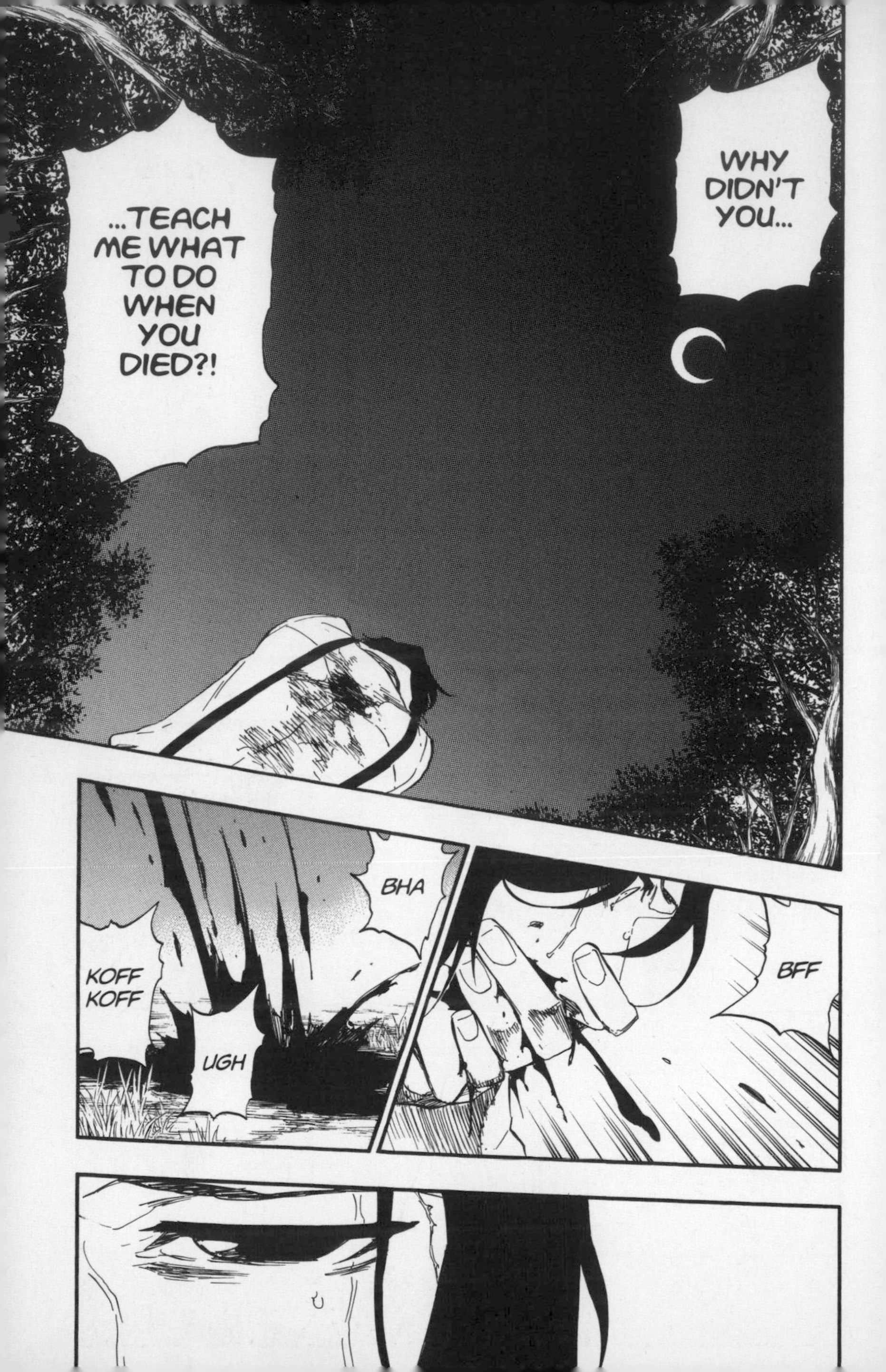
WHY DIDN'T YOU...
...TEACH ME WHAT TO DO WHEN YOU DIED?!
BFF
BHA
KOFF KOFF
UGH

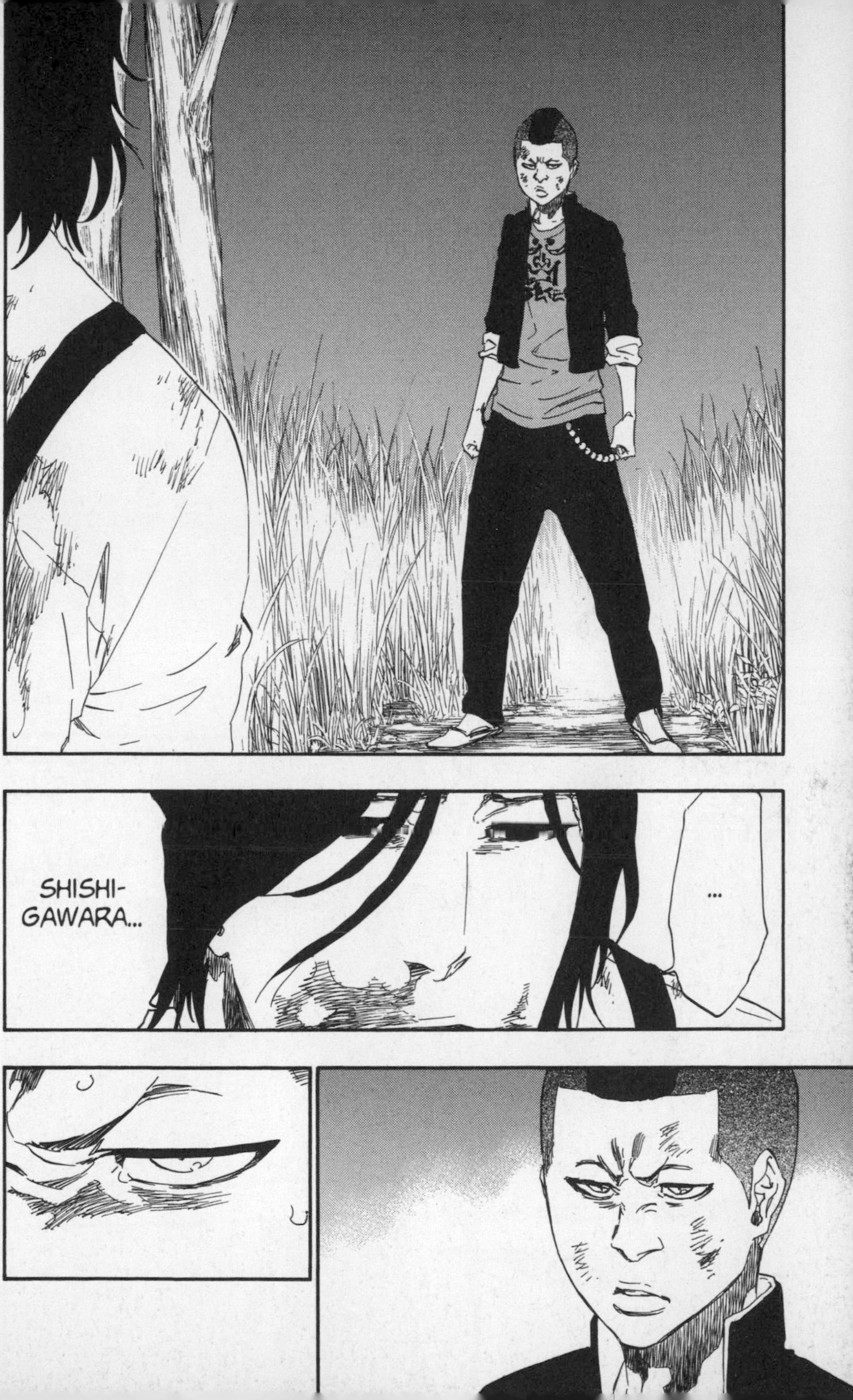
...
SHISHI-GAWARA...

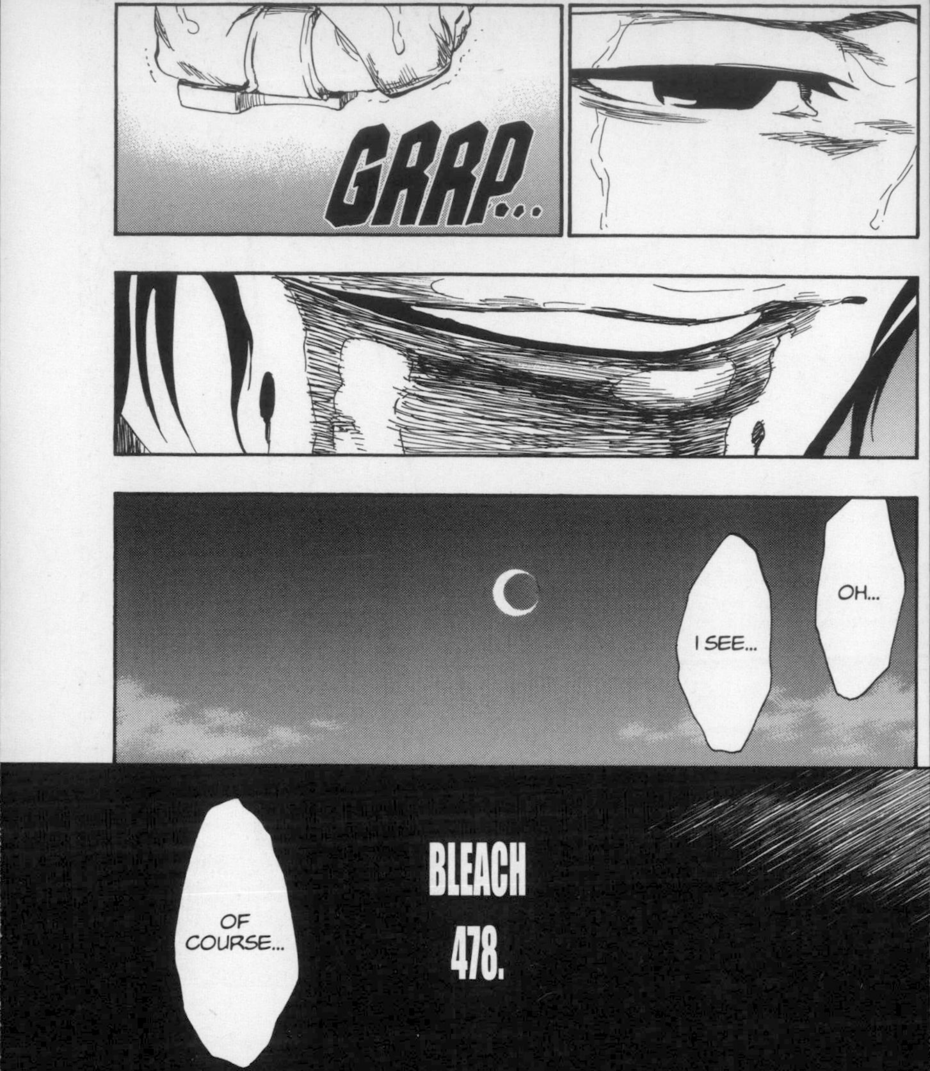
GRRP...
OH...
I SEE...
OF COURSE...
BLEACH
478.

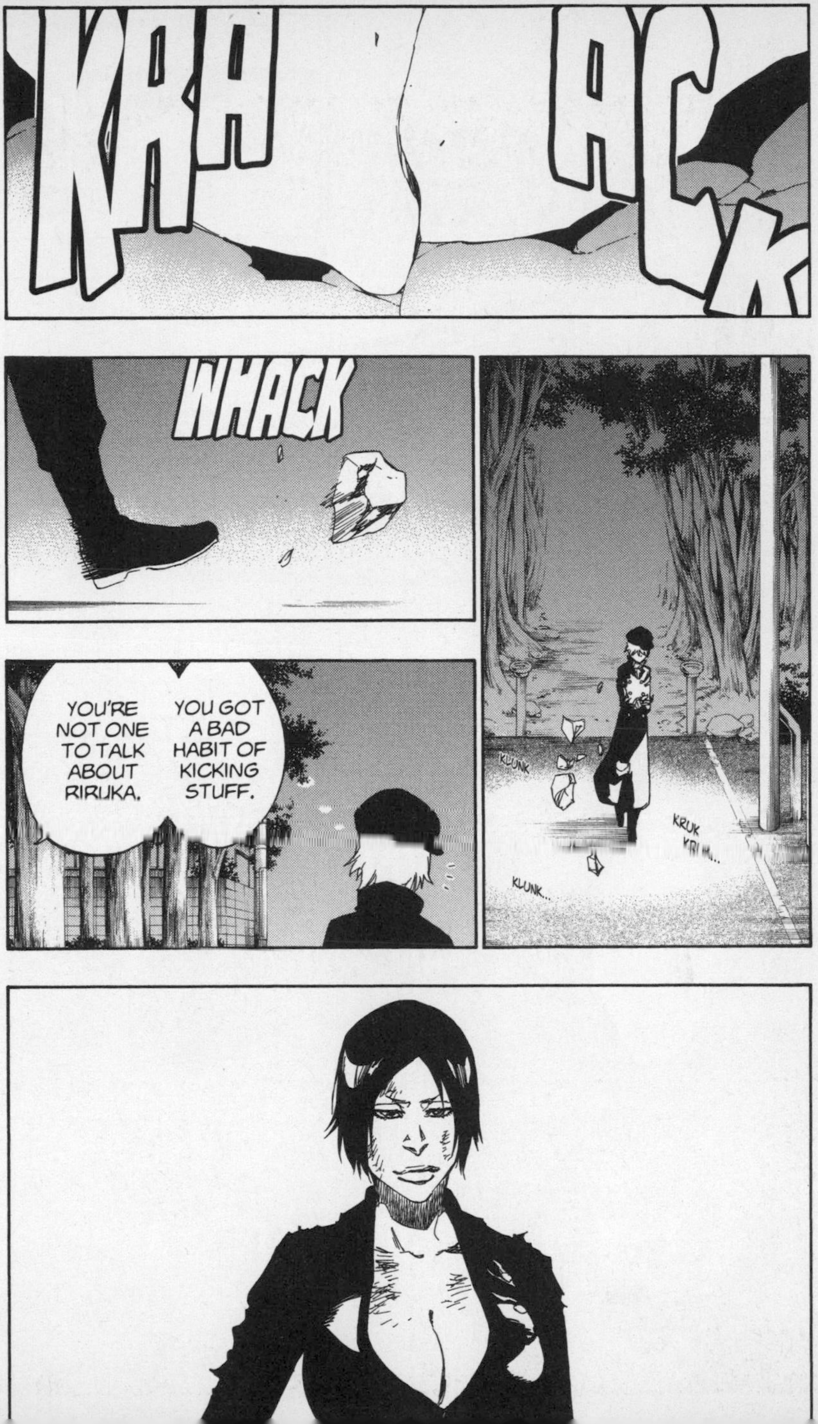
KRA ACK
KLUNK
KRUK KRI...
KLUNK...
WHACK
YOU GOT A BAD HABIT OF KICKING STUFF.
YOU'RE NOT ONE TO TALK ABOUT RIRUKA.

READ THIS WAY

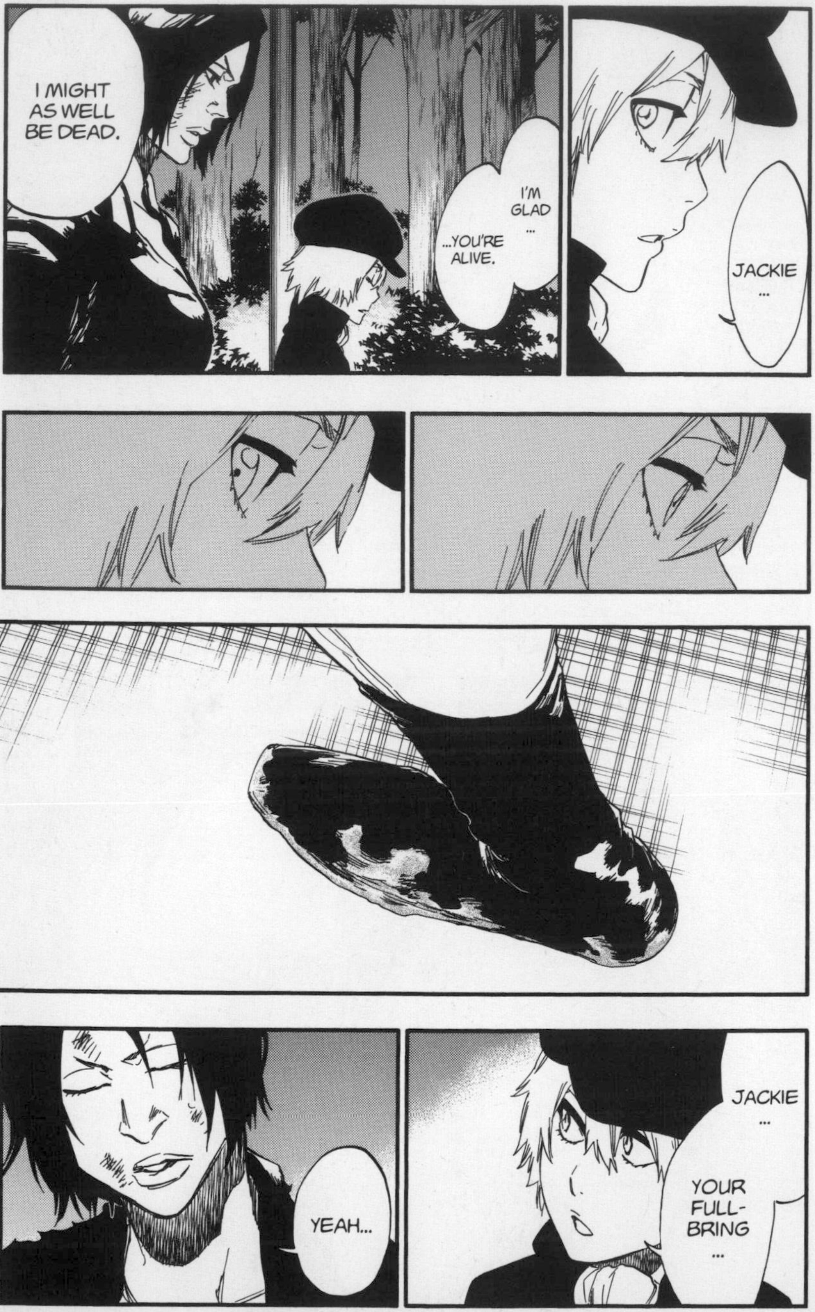
JACKIE ...
I'M GLAD ...
...YOU'RE ALIVE.
I MIGHT AS WELL BE DEAD.
JACKIE ...
YOUR FULL-BRING ...
YEAH...

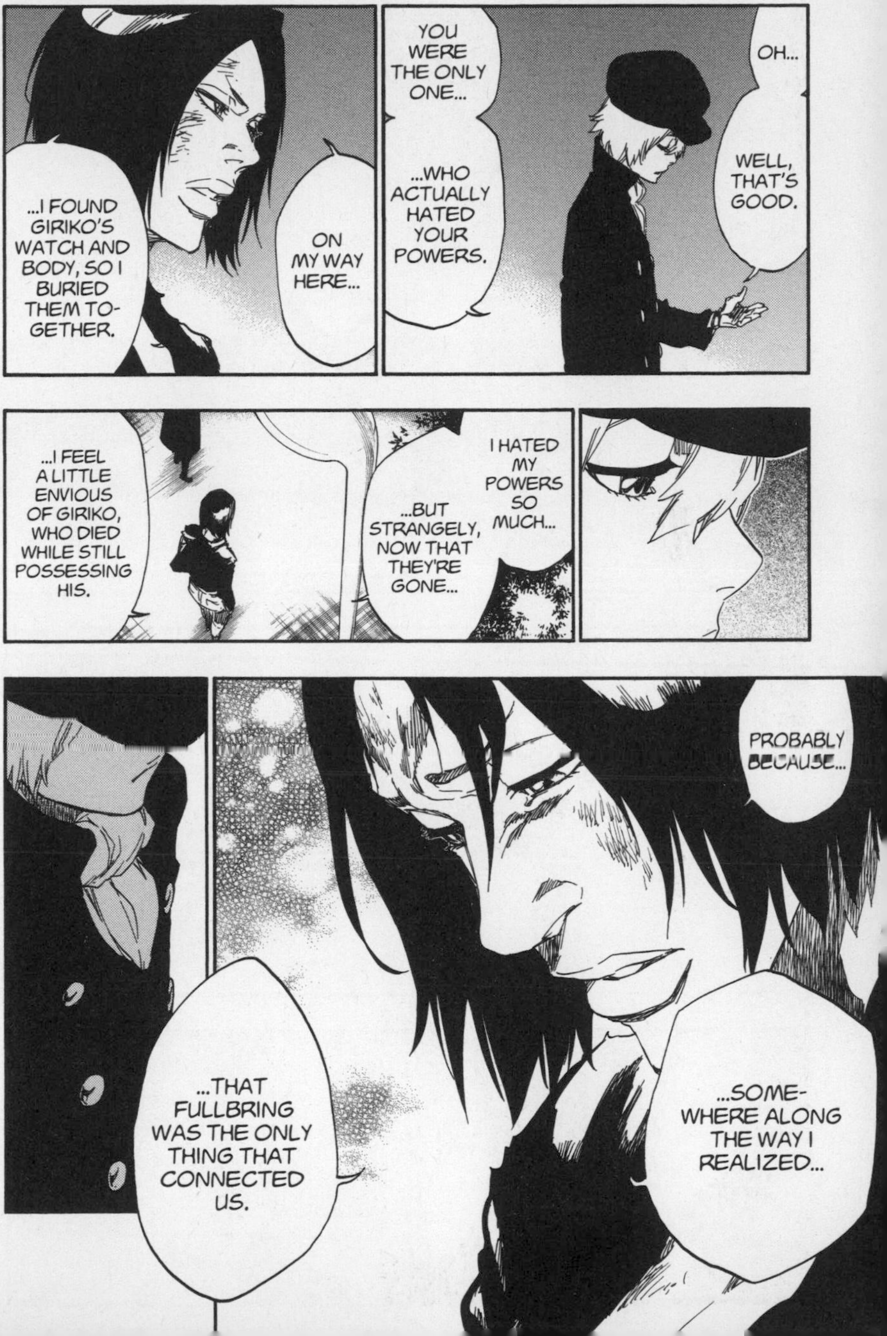
YOU WERE THE ONLY ONE...
OH...
...WHO ACTUALLY HATED YOUR POWERS.
WELL, THAT'S GOOD.
ON MY WAY HERE...
...I FOUND GIRIKO'S WATCH AND BODY, SO I BURIED THEM TO-GETHER.
I HATED MY POWERS SO MUCH...
...BUT STRANGELY, NOW THAT THEY'RE GONE...
...I FEEL A LITTLE ENVIOUS OF GIRIKO, WHO DIED WHILE STILL POSSESSING HIS.
PROBABLY BECAUSE...
...SOME-WHERE ALONG THE WAY I REALIZED...
...THAT FULLBRING WAS THE ONLY THING THAT CONNECTED US.

READ THIS WAY

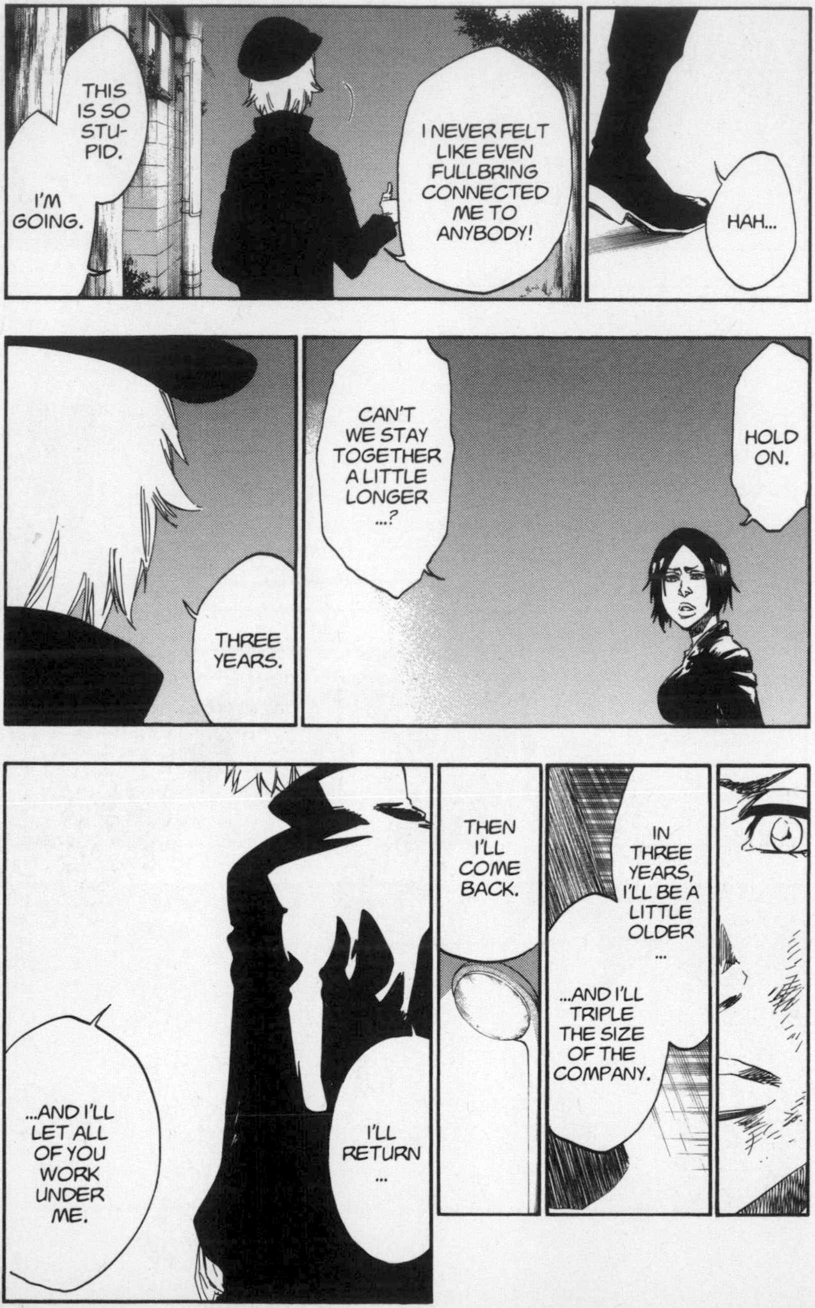
HAH...
I NEVER FELT LIKE EVEN FULLBRING CONNECTED ME TO ANYBODY!
THIS IS SO STU-PID.
I'M GOING.
HOLD ON.
CAN'T WE STAY TOGETHER A LITTLE LONGER...?
THREE YEARS.
IN THREE YEARS, I'LL BE A LITTLE OLDER...
...AND I'LL TRIPLE THE SIZE OF THE COMPANY.
THEN I'LL COME BACK.
I'LL RETURN...
...AND I'LL LET ALL OF YOU WORK UNDER ME.

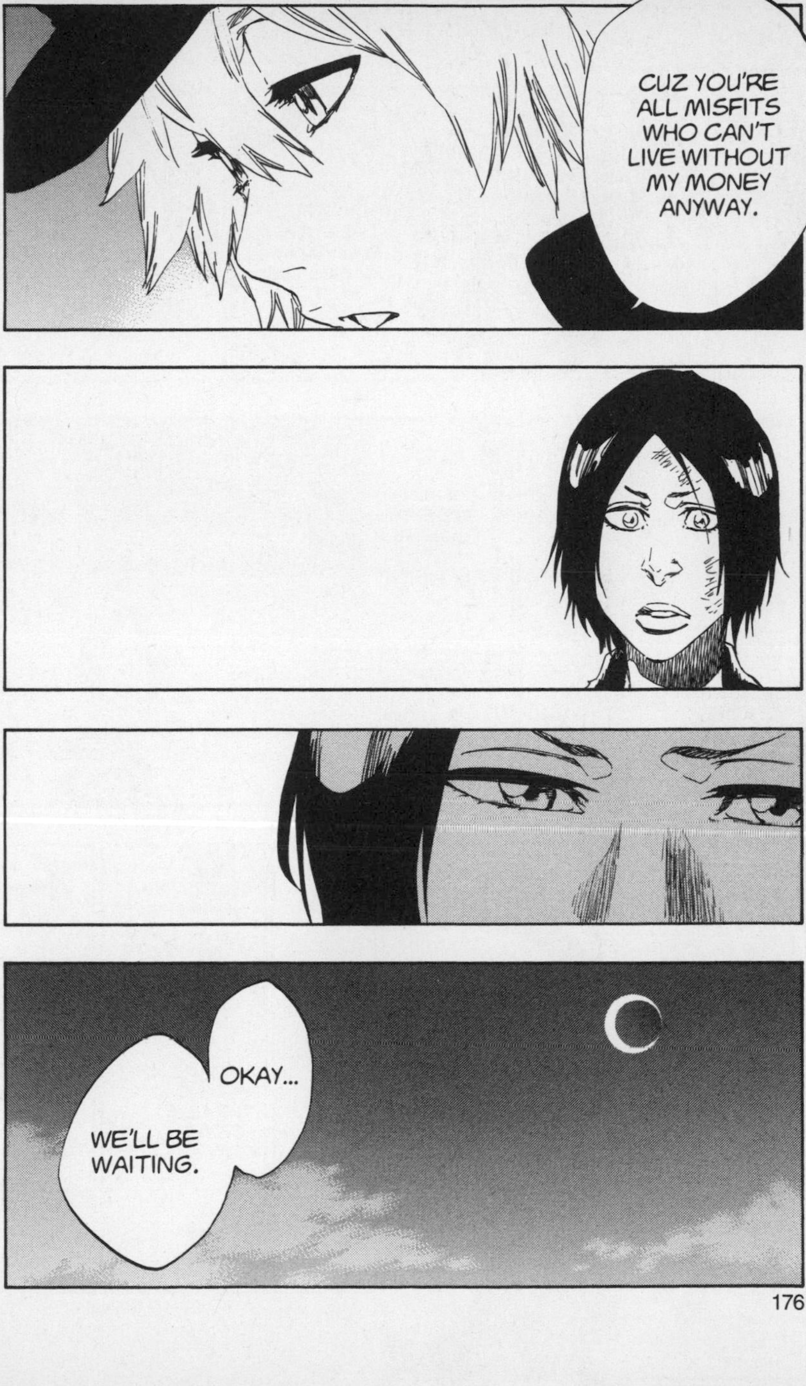
CUZ YOU'RE ALL MISFITS WHO CAN'T LIVE WITHOUT MY MONEY ANYWAY.
OKAY...
WE'LL BE WAITING.

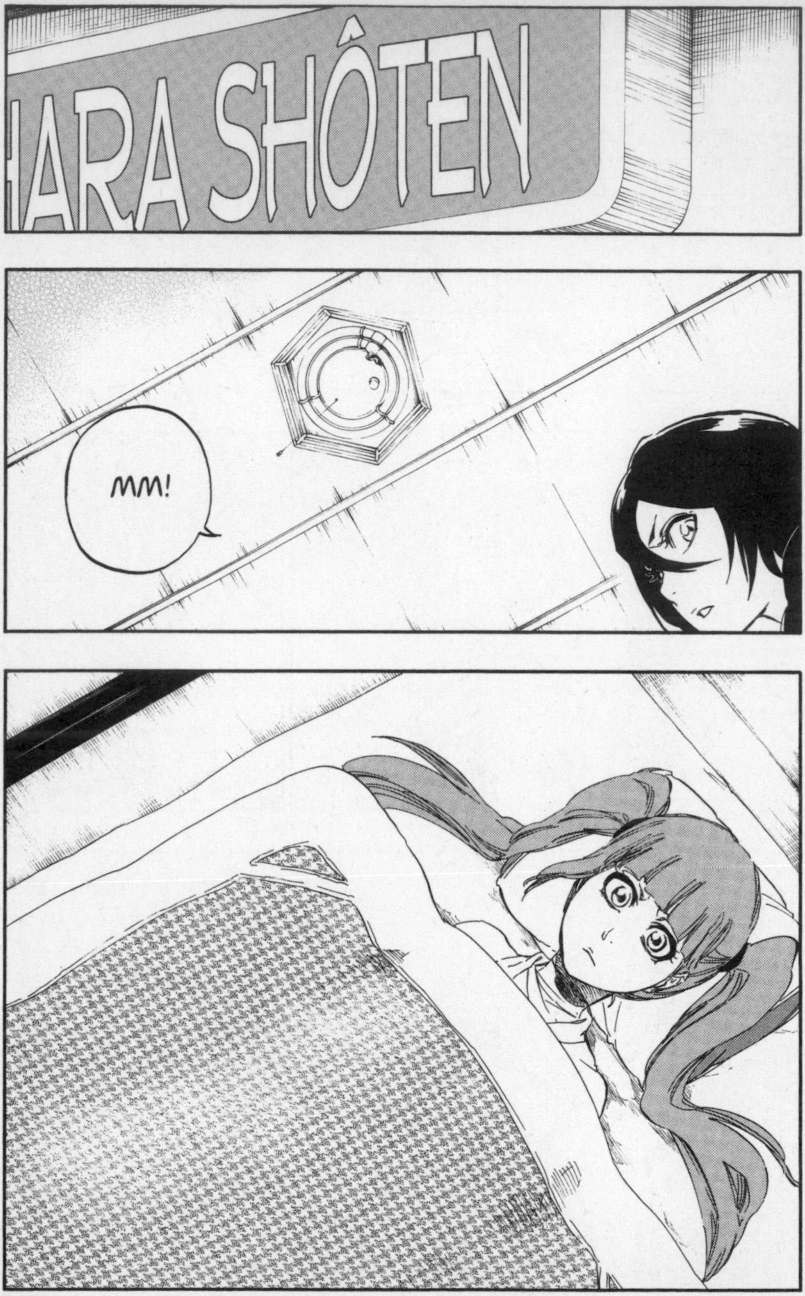
HARA SHÔTEN
MM!

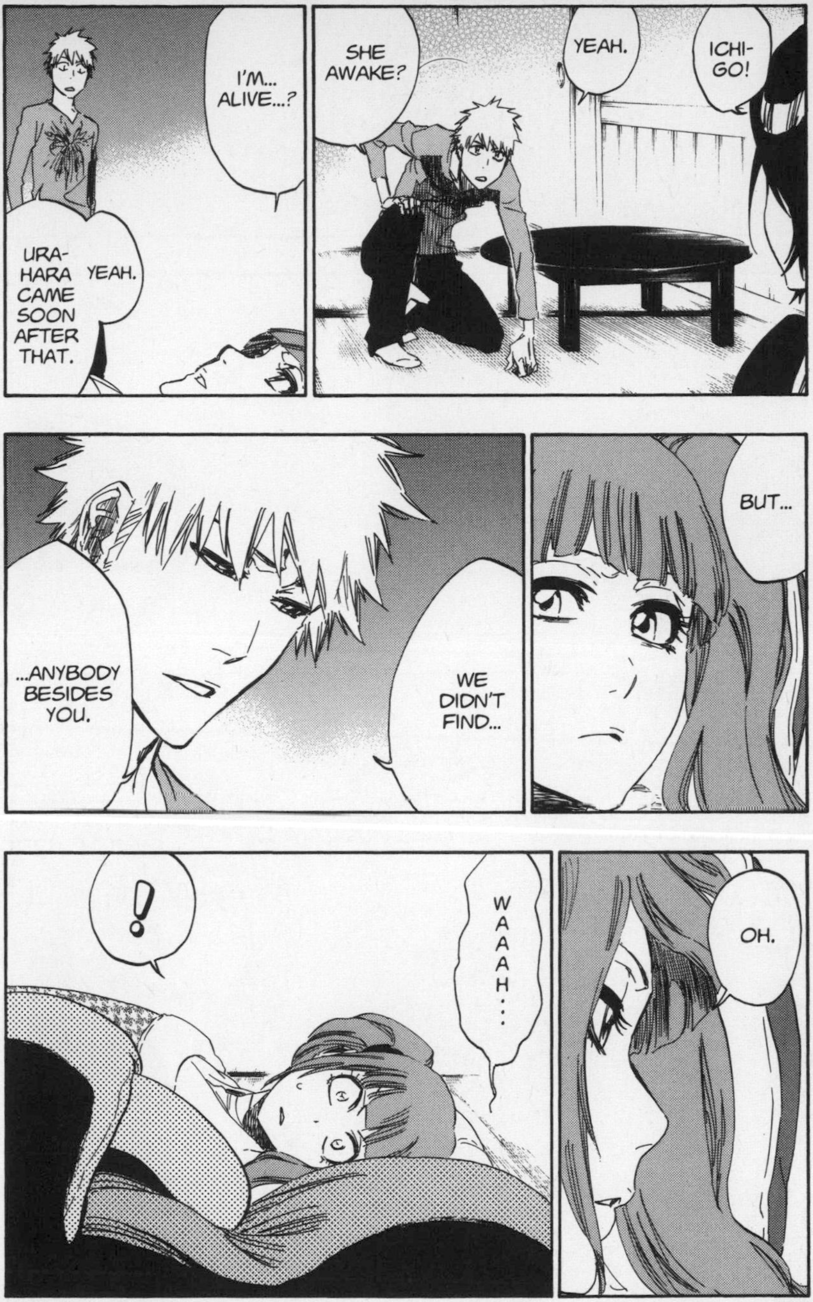
ICHI-GO!
YEAH.
SHE AWAKE?
I'M... ALIVE...?
YEAH. URA-HARA CAME SOON AFTER THAT.
BUT...
WE DIDN'T FIND...
...ANYBODY BESIDES YOU.
OH.
WAAAH...
!

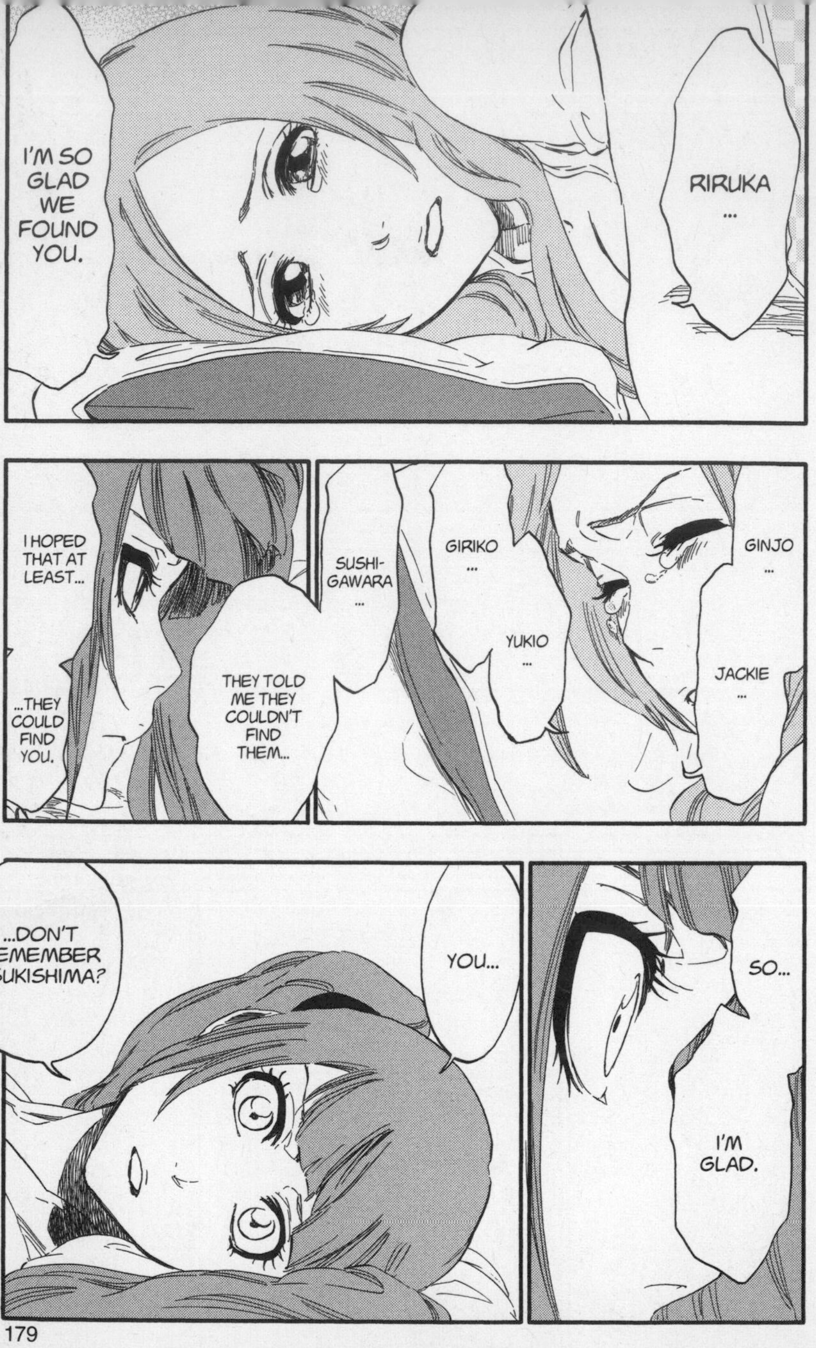
RIRUKA ...
I'M SO GLAD WE FOUND YOU.
GINJO ...
JACKIE ...
GIRIKO ...
YUKIO ...
SUSHI-GAWARA ...
THEY TOLD ME THEY COULDN'T FIND THEM...
I HOPED THAT AT LEAST...
...THEY COULD FIND YOU.
SO...
I'M GLAD.
YOU...
...DON'T REMEMBER TSUKISHIMA?

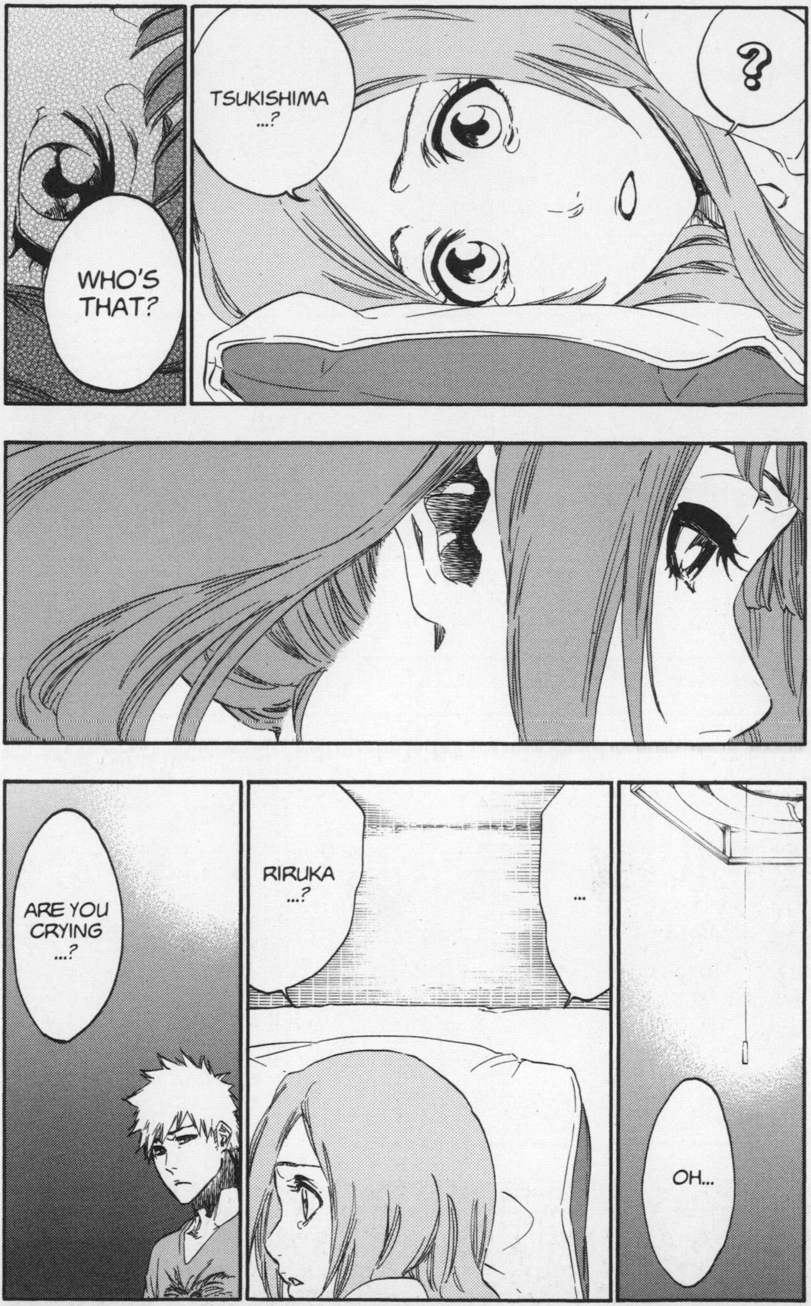
?
TSUKISHIMA ...?
WHO'S THAT?
OH...
...
RIRUKA ...?
ARE YOU CRYING ...?

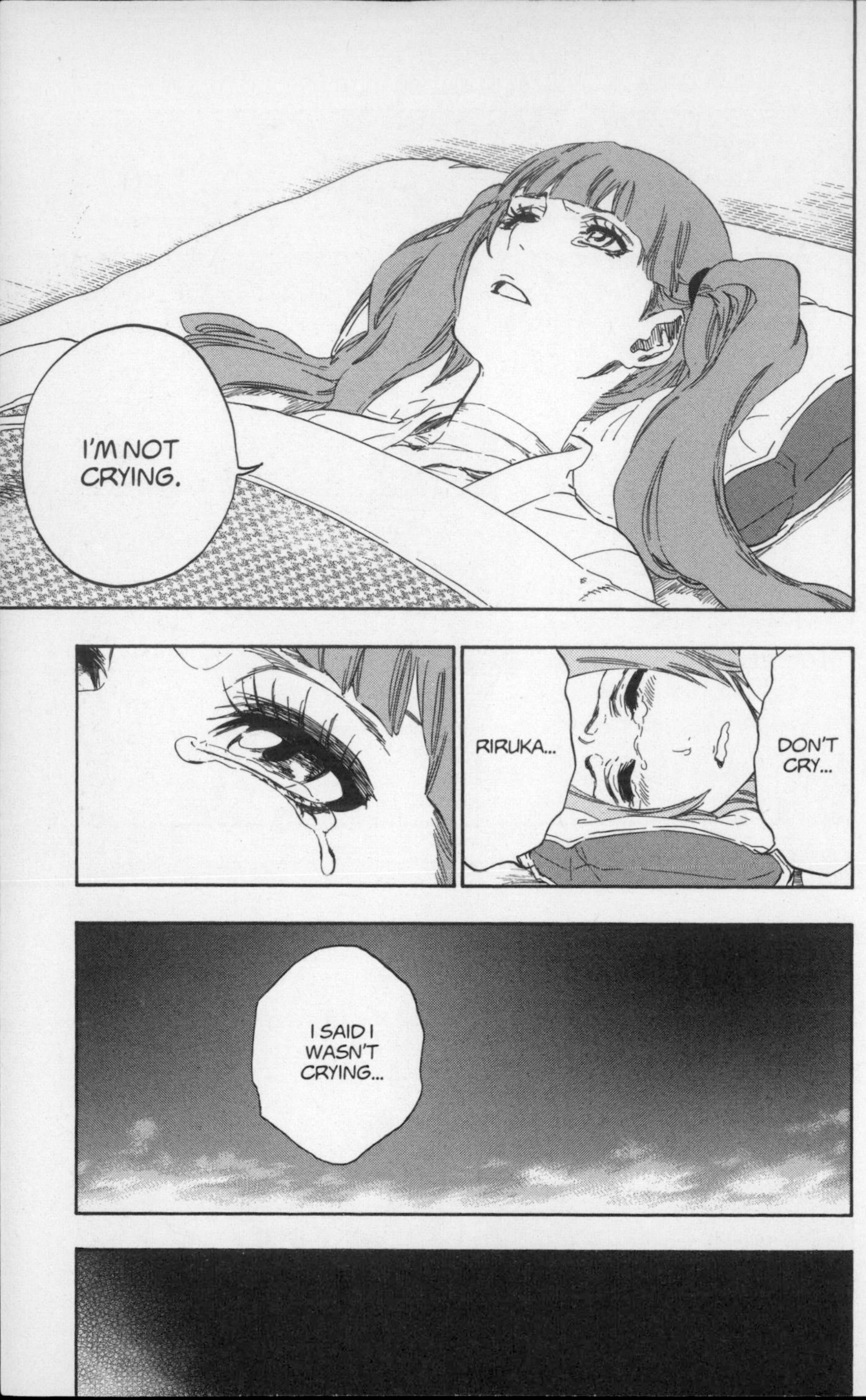
I'M NOT CRYING.
DON'T CRY...
RIRUKA...
I SAID I WASN'T CRYING...

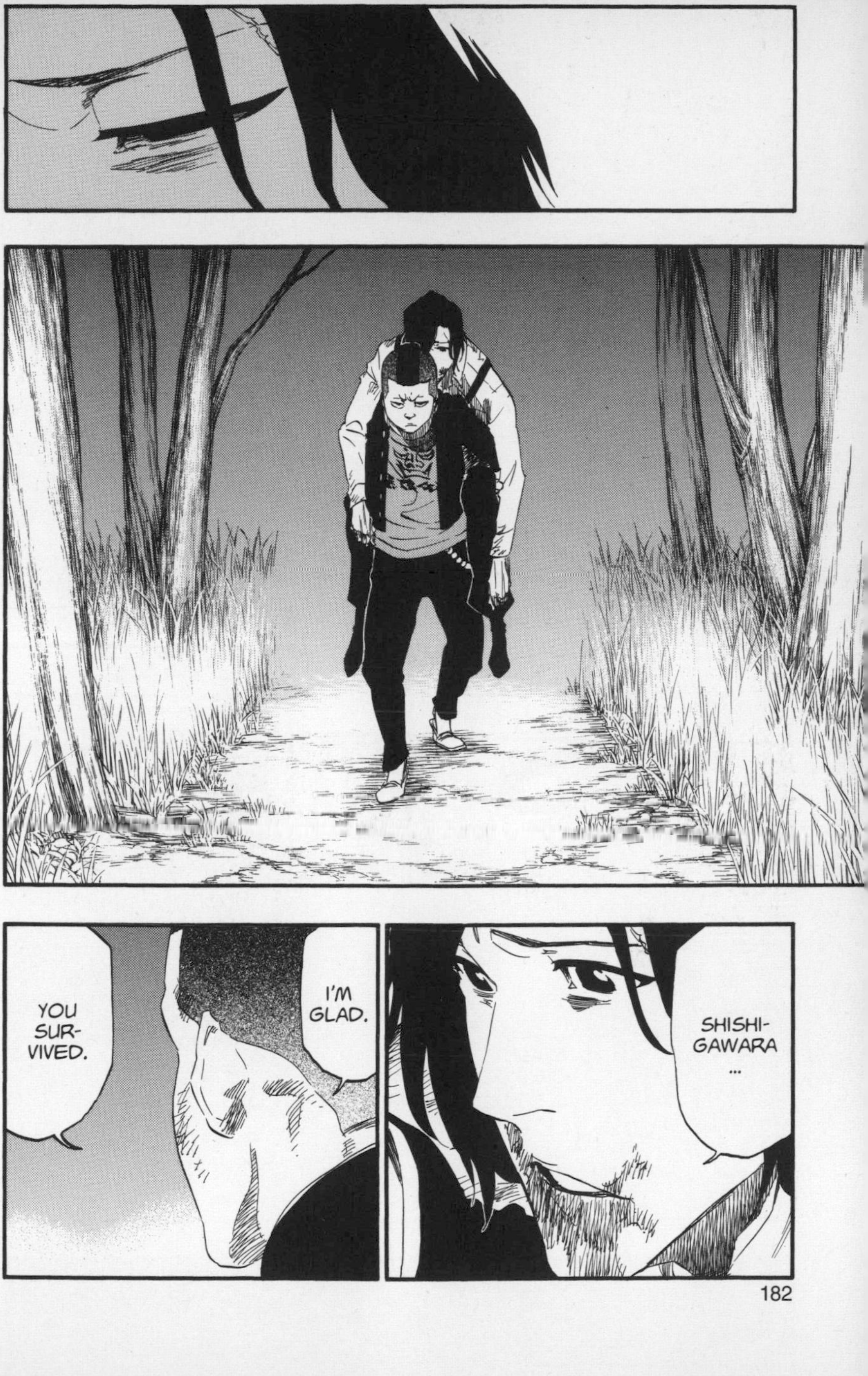
SHISHI-GAWARA ...
I'M GLAD.
YOU SUR-VIVED.

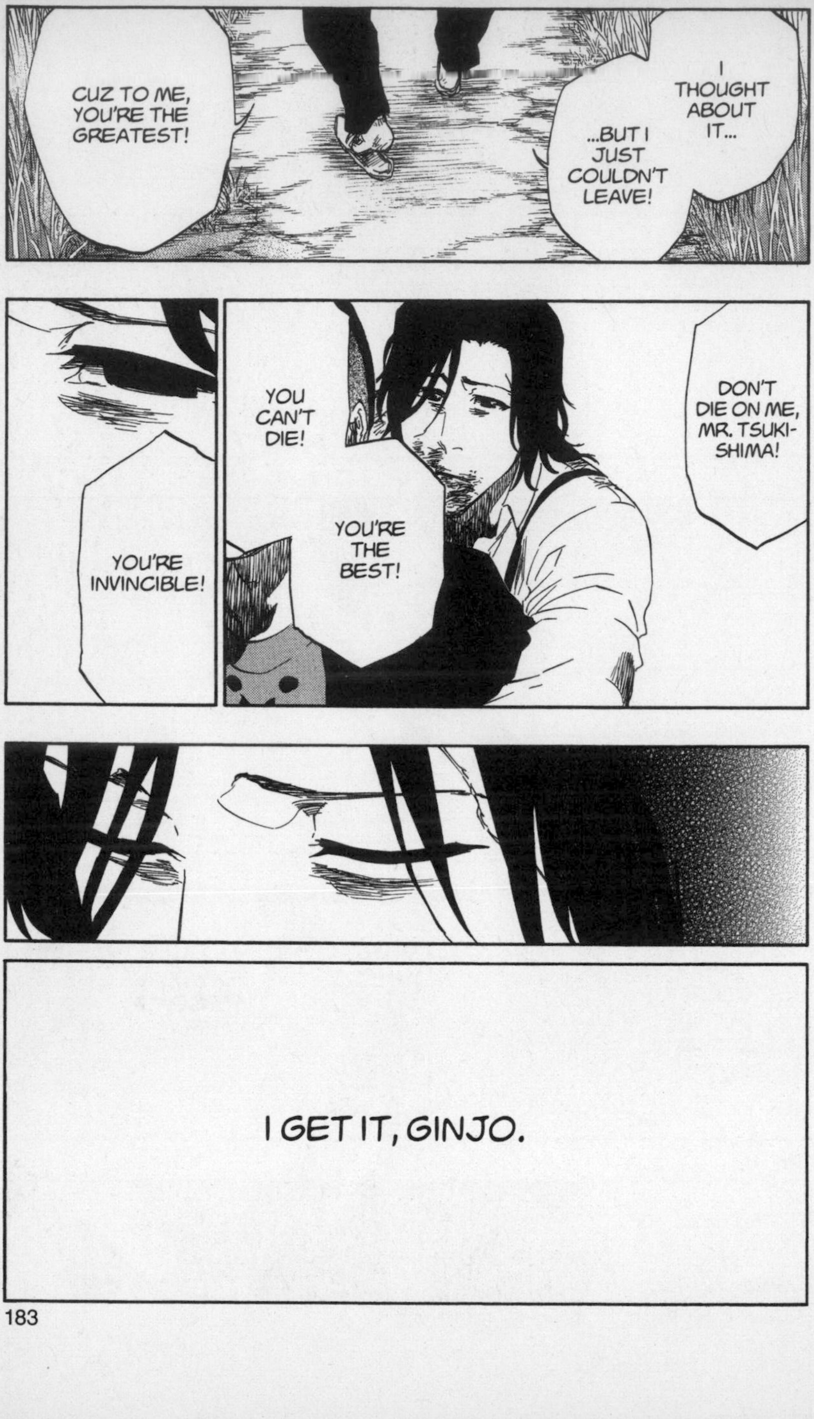
I THOUGHT ABOUT IT...
...BUT I JUST COULDN'T LEAVE!
CUZ TO ME, YOU'RE THE GREATEST!
DON'T DIE ON ME, MR. TSUKI-SHIMA!
YOU CAN'T DIE!
YOU'RE THE BEST!
YOU'RE INVINCIBLE!
I GET IT, GINJO.

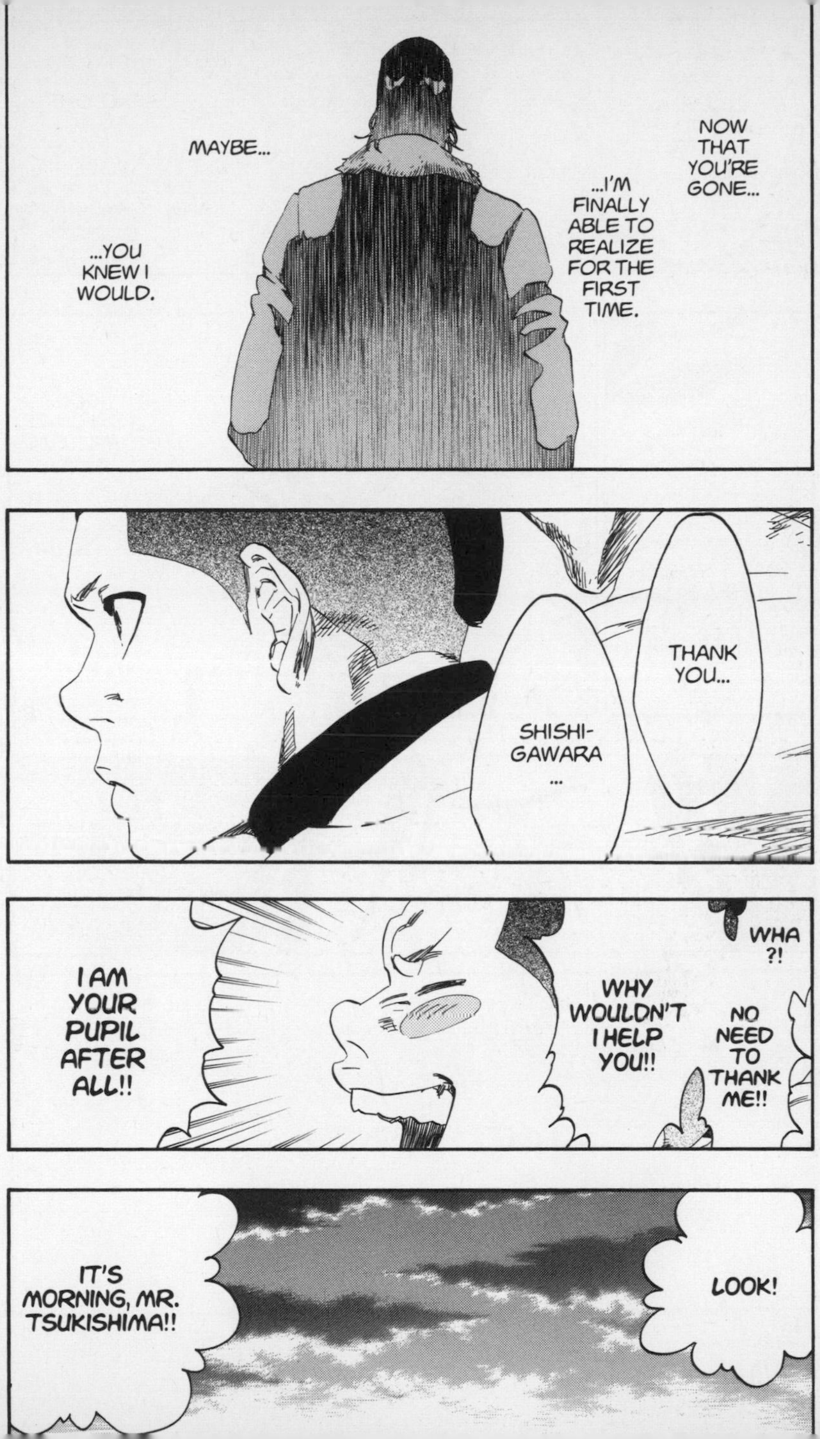
NOW THAT YOU'RE GONE...
...I'M FINALLY ABLE TO REALIZE FOR THE FIRST TIME.
MAYBE...
...YOU KNEW I WOULD.
THANK YOU...
SHISHI-GAWARA...
WHA?!
NO NEED TO THANK ME!!
WHY WOULDN'T I HELP YOU!!
I AM YOUR PUPIL AFTER ALL!!
LOOK!
IT'S MORNING, MR. TSUKISHIMA!!

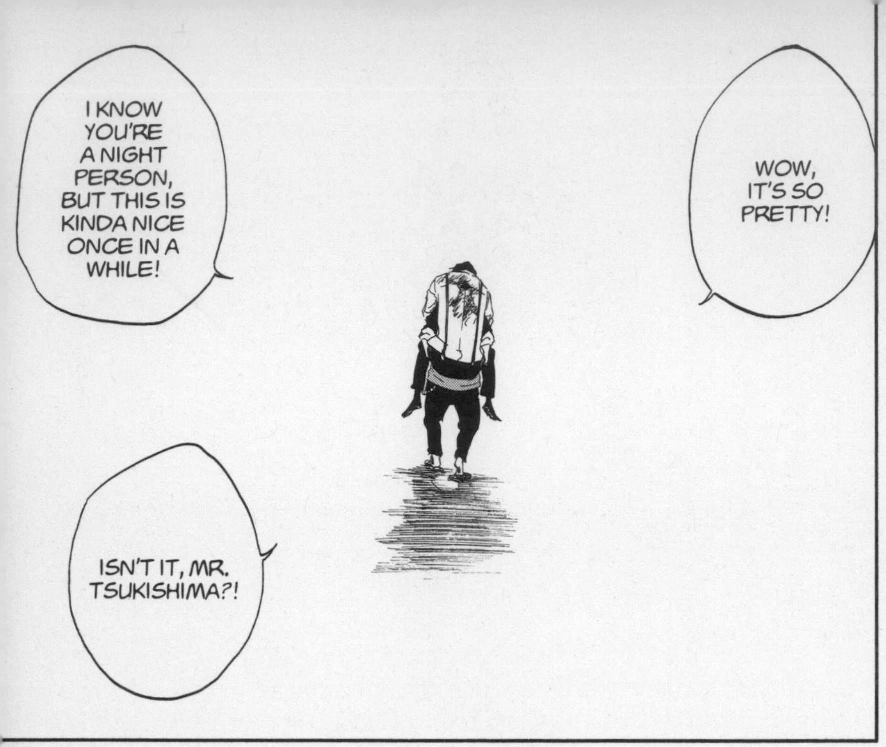
WOW, IT'S SO PRETTY!
I KNOW YOU'RE A NIGHT PERSON, BUT THIS IS KINDA NICE ONCE IN A WHILE!
ISN'T IT, MR. TSUKISHIMA?!

THANK YOU.

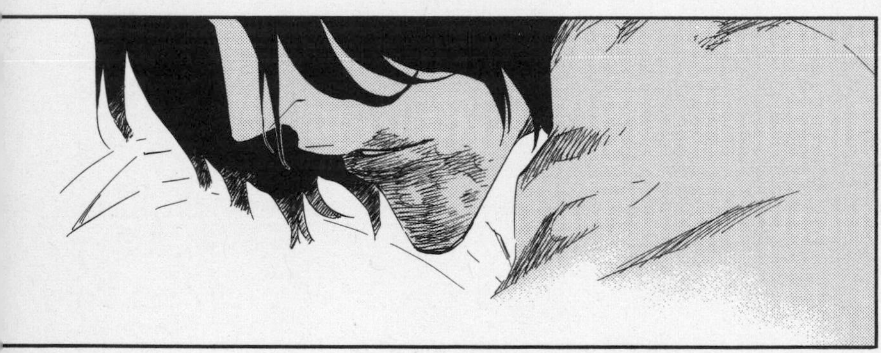

I WASN'T ALONE.

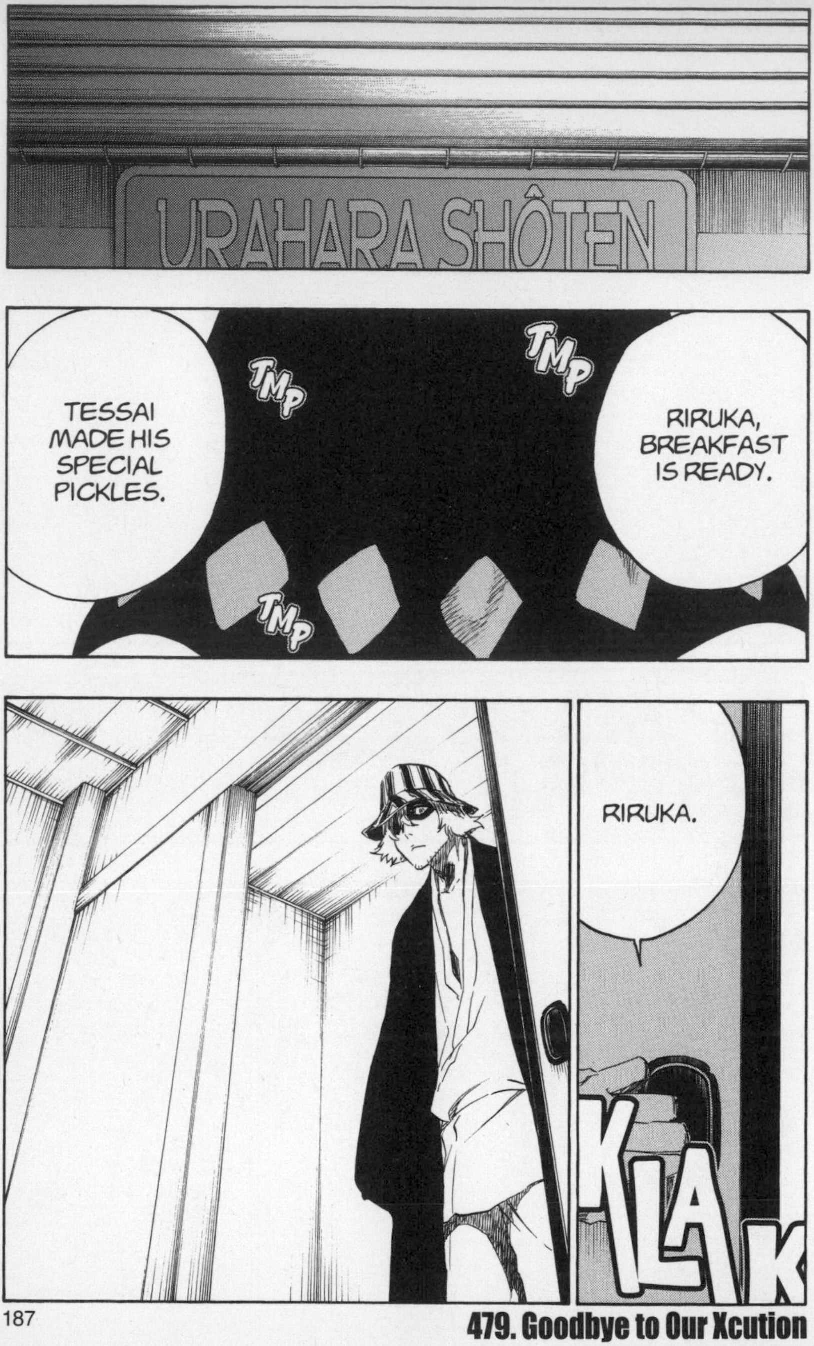
URAHARA SHÔTEN
TMP
RIRUKA, BREAKFAST IS READY.
TMP
TMP
TESSAI MADE HIS SPECIAL PICKLES.
RIRUKA.
KLAK

479. Goodbye to Our Xcution

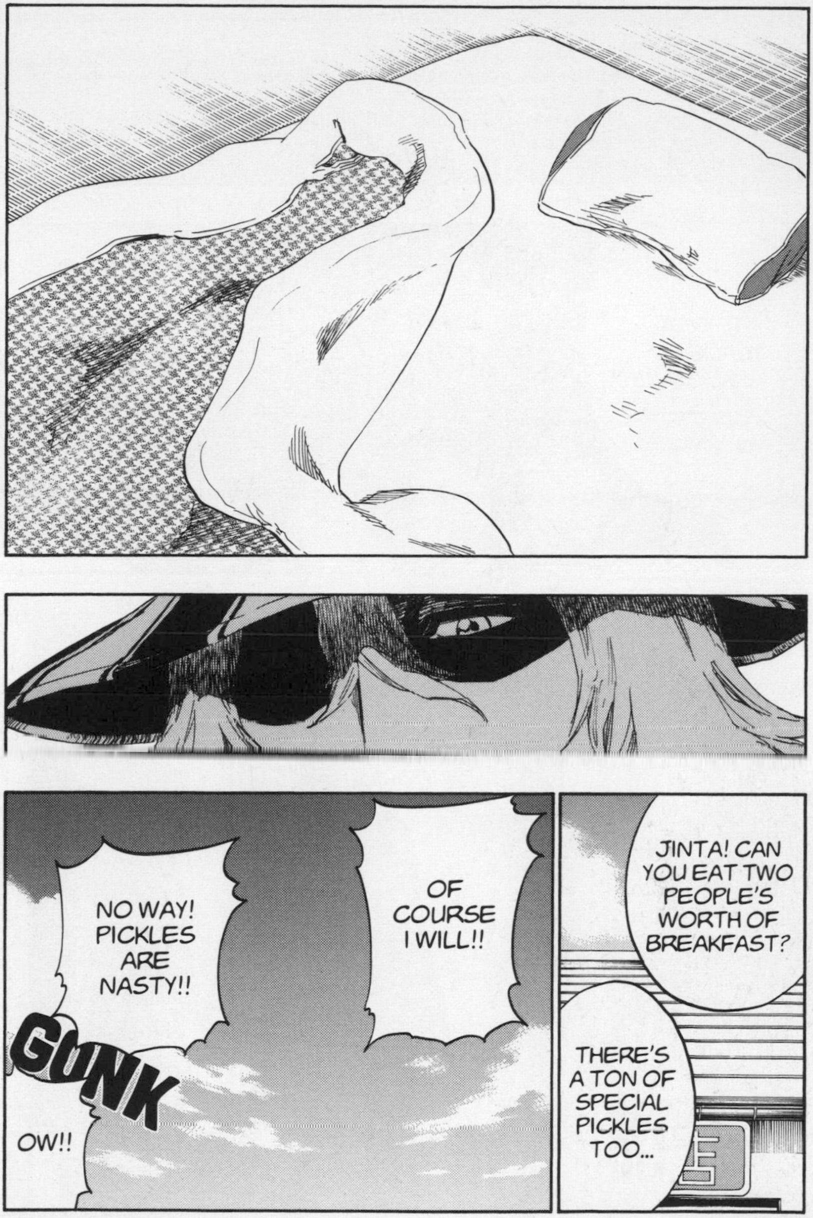
JINTA! CAN YOU EAT TWO PEOPLE'S WORTH OF BREAKFAST?
THERE'S A TON OF SPECIAL PICKLES TOO...
OF COURSE I WILL!!
NO WAY! PICKLES ARE NASTY!!
GONK
OW!!

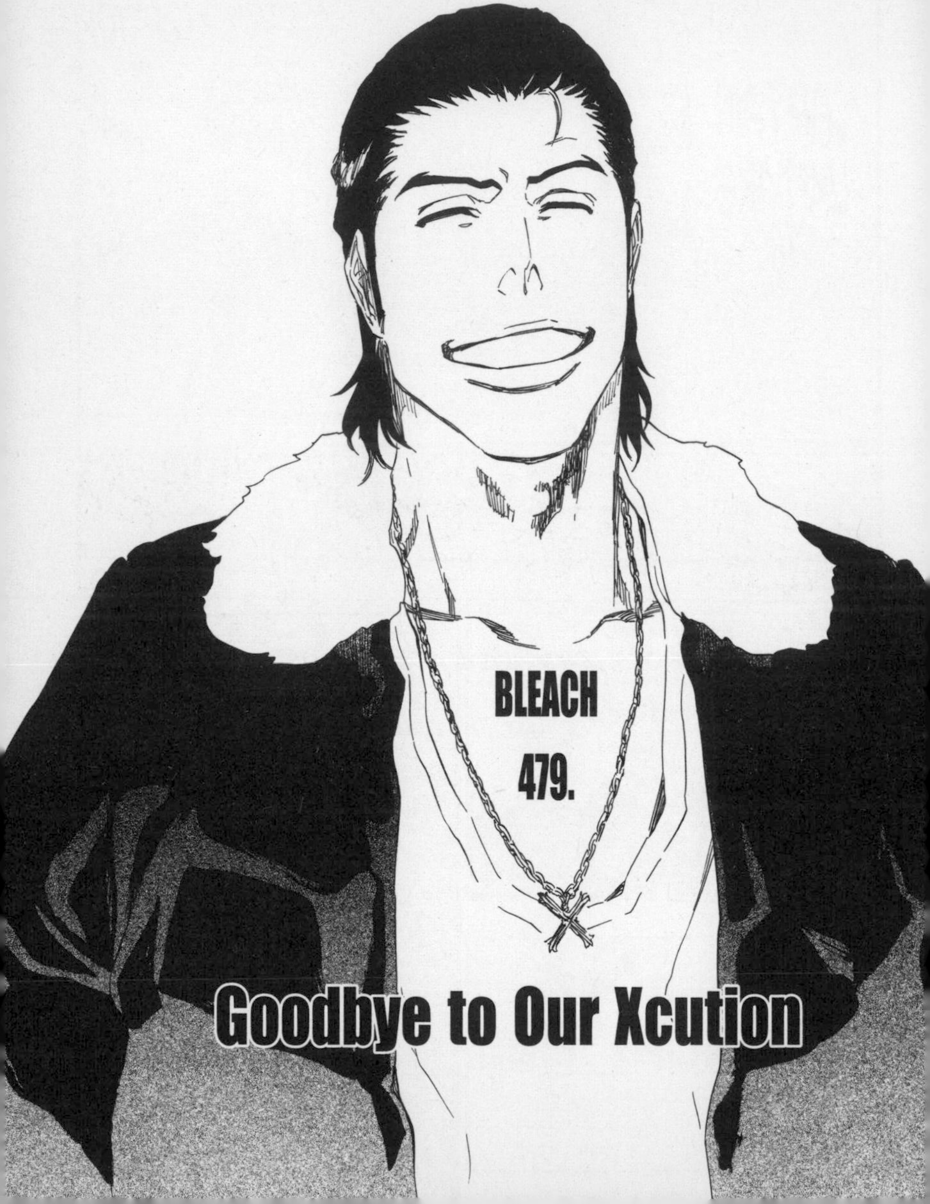
BLEACH
479.
Goodbye to Our Xcution

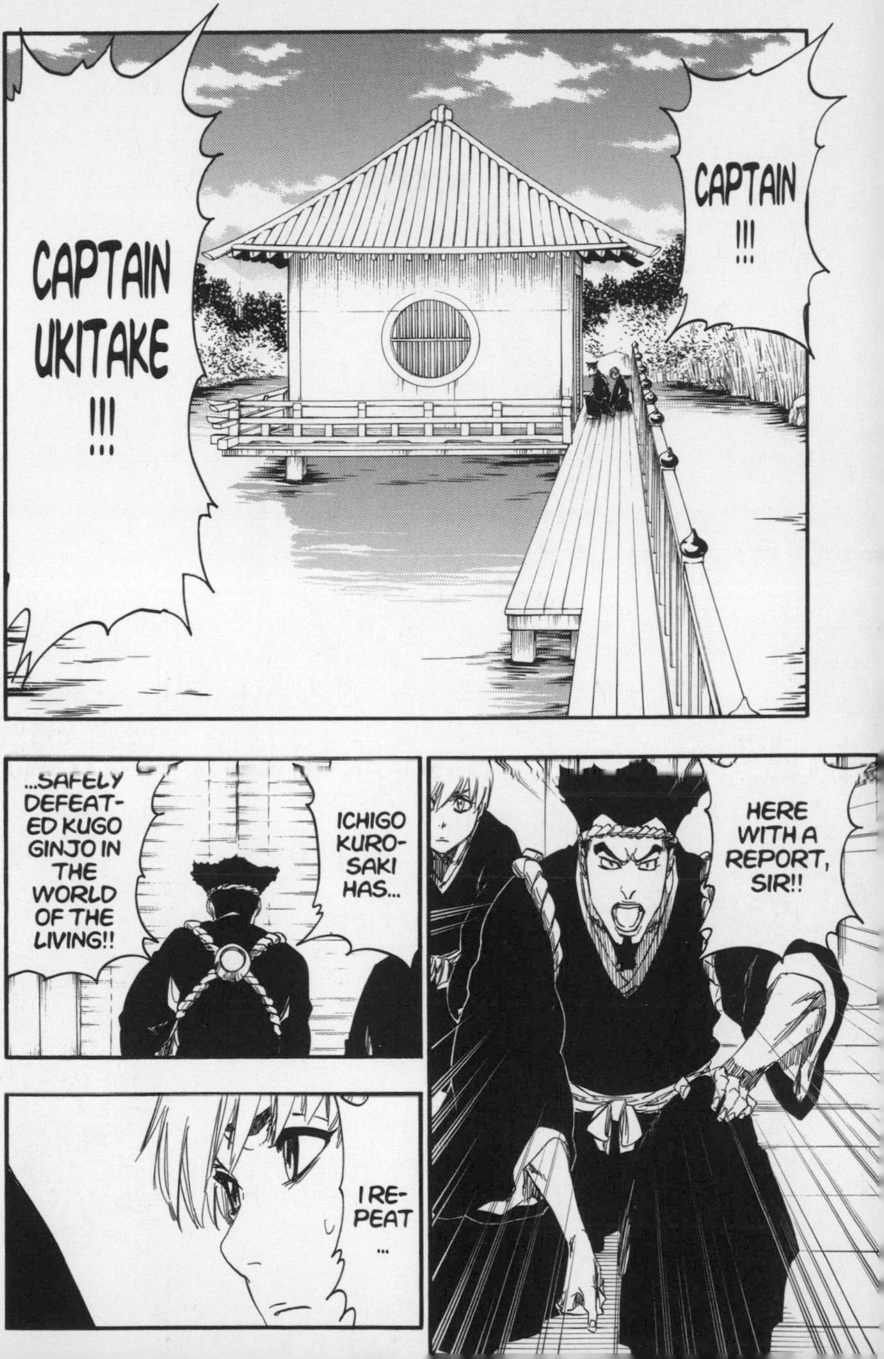
CAPTAIN !!!
CAPTAIN UKITAKE !!!
HERE WITH A REPORT, SIR!!
ICHIGO KURO-SAKI HAS...
...SAFELY DEFEAT-ED KUGO GINJO IN THE WORLD OF THE LIVING!!
I RE-PEAT ...

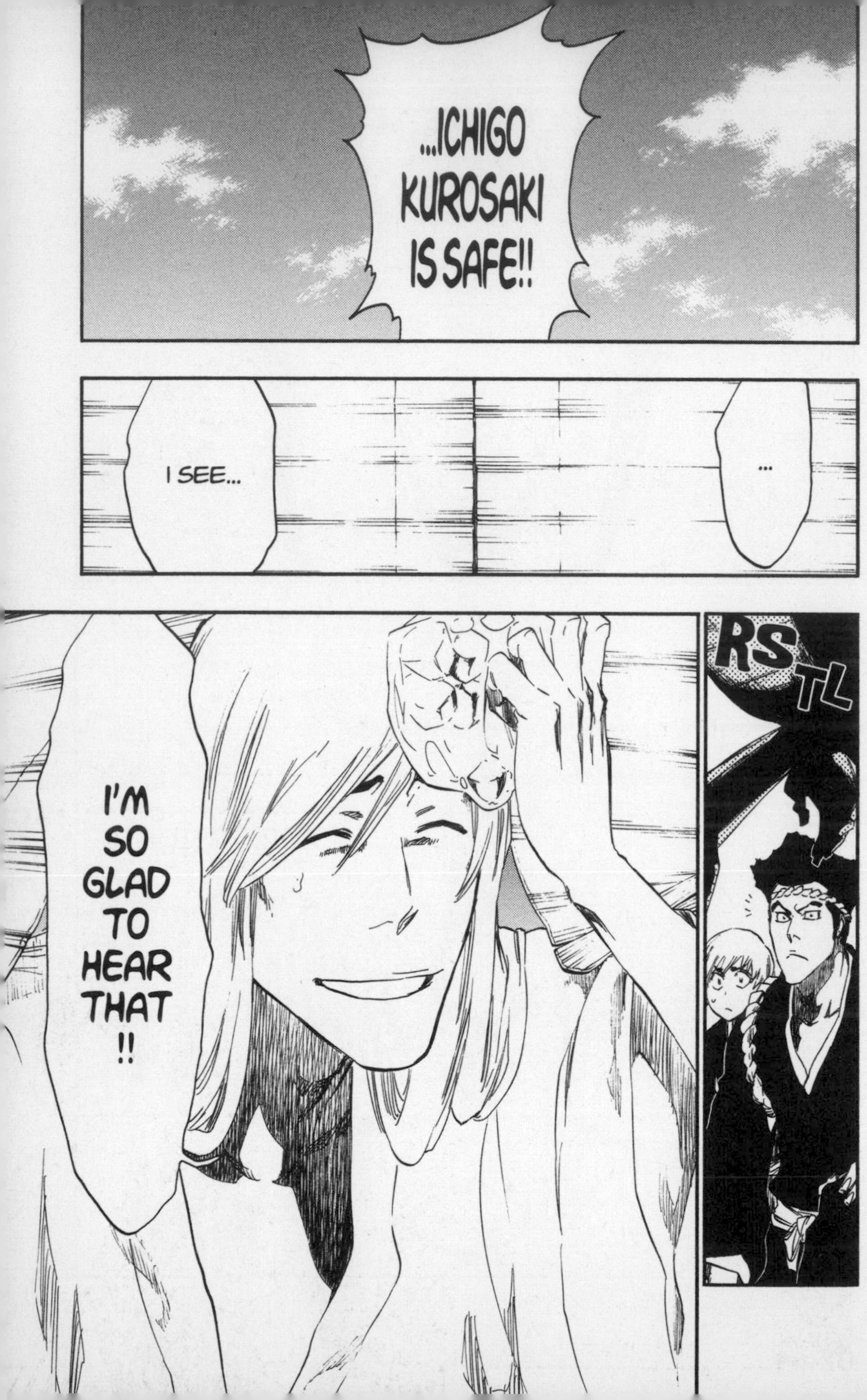
...ICHIGO KUROSAKI IS SAFE!!
...
I SEE...
RSTL
I'M SO GLAD TO HEAR THAT!!

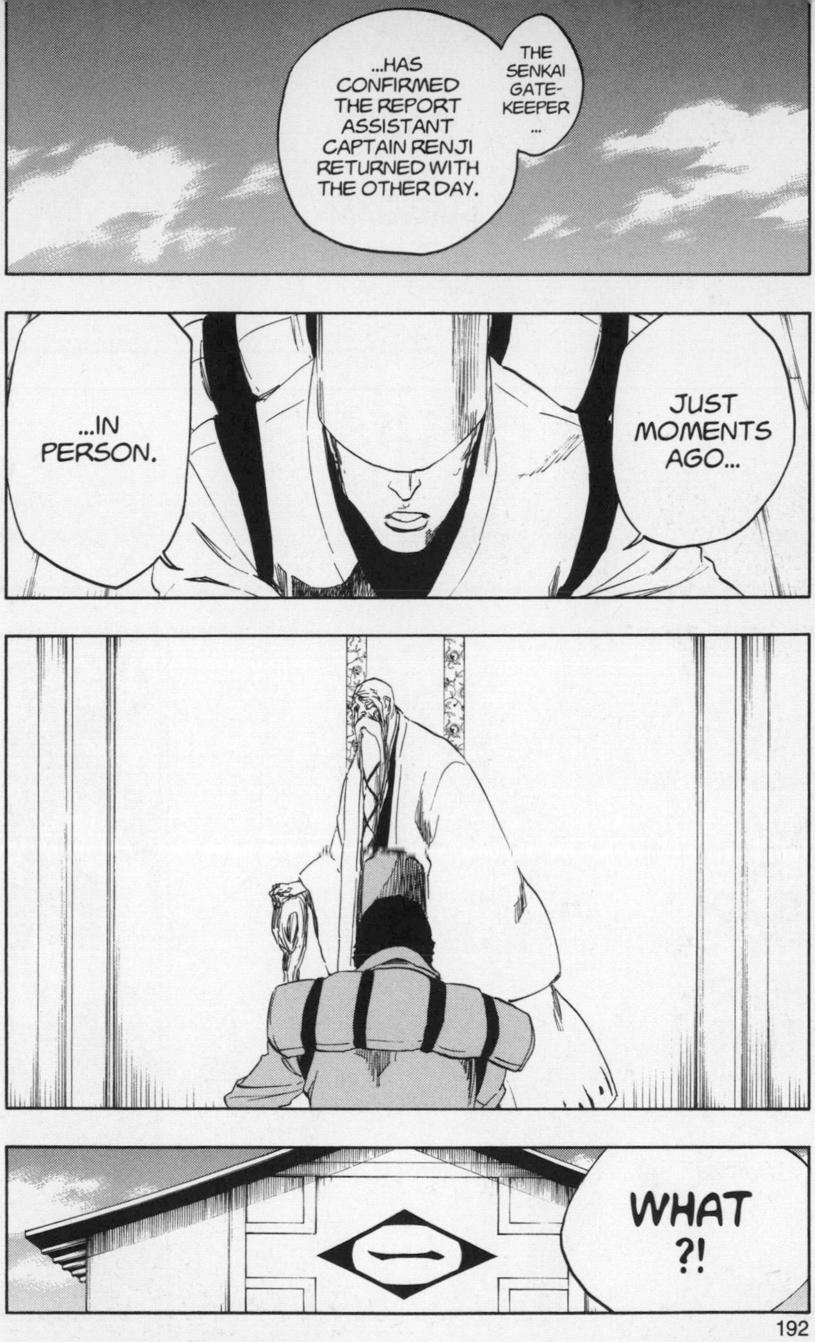
THE SENKAI GATE-KEEPER ...
...HAS CONFIRMED THE REPORT ASSISTANT CAPTAIN RENJI RETURNED WITH THE OTHER DAY.
JUST MOMENTS AGO...
...IN PERSON.
WHAT ?!

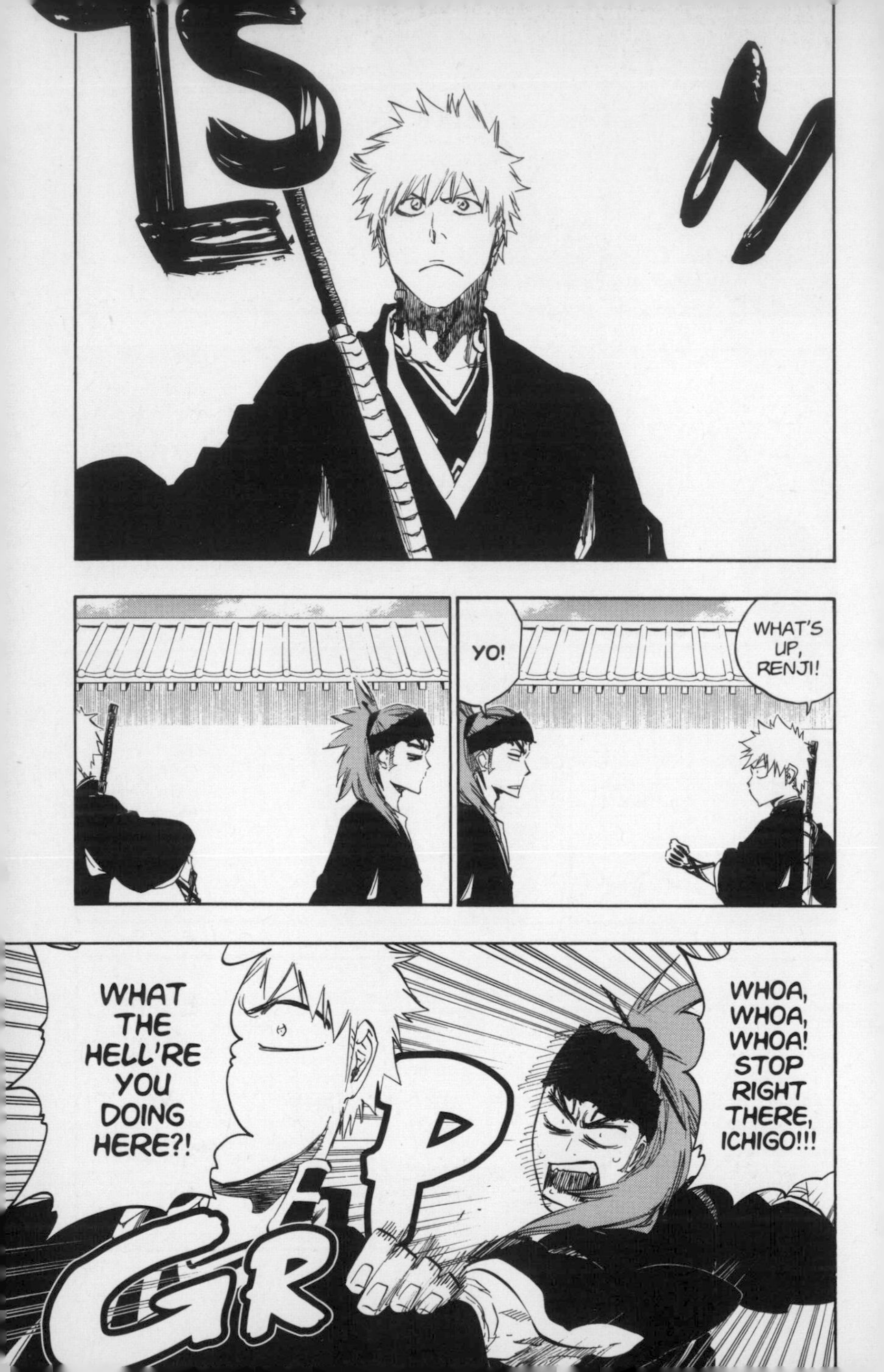
WHAT'S UP, RENJI!
YO!
WHOA, WHOA, WHOA! STOP RIGHT THERE, ICHIGO!!!
WHAT THE HELL'RE YOU DOING HERE?!

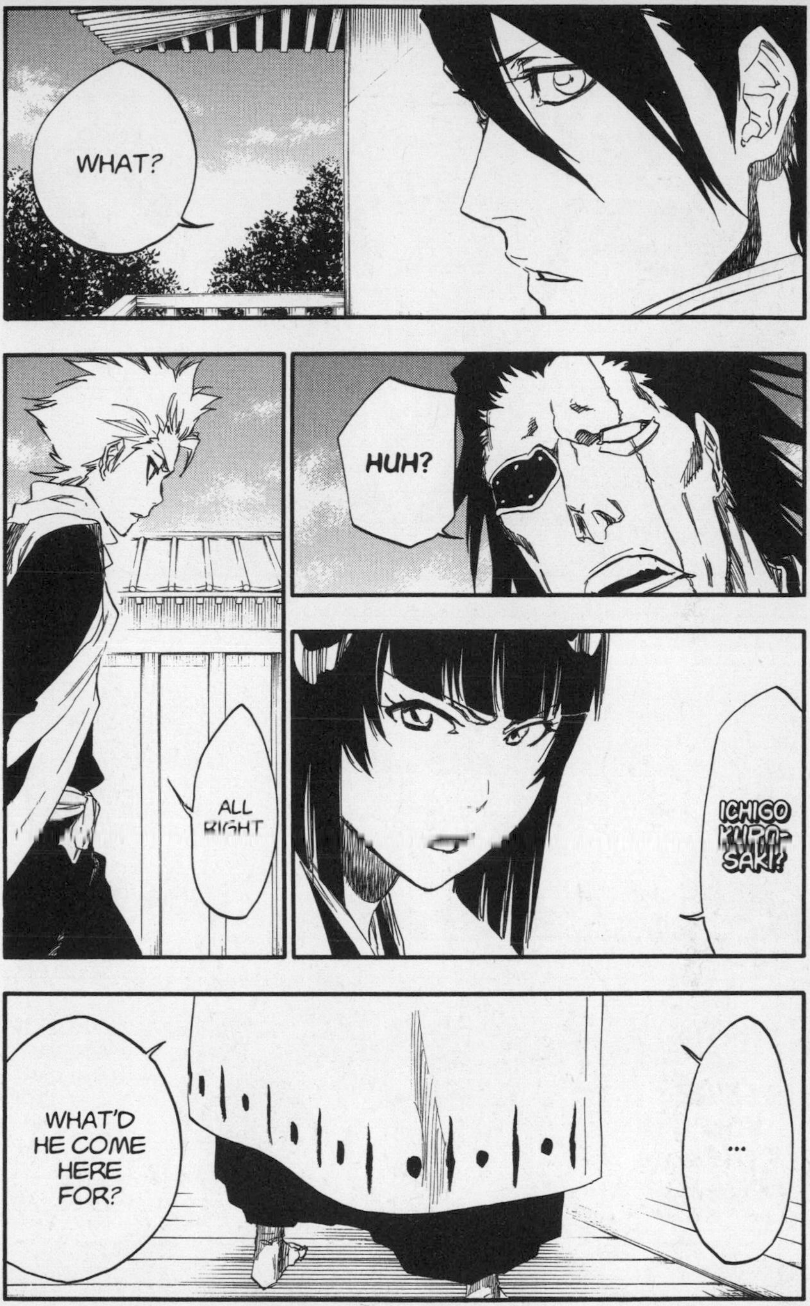
WHAT?
HUH?
ICHIGO KUROSAKI!?
ALL RIGHT
...
WHAT'D HE COME HERE FOR?

READ THIS WAY

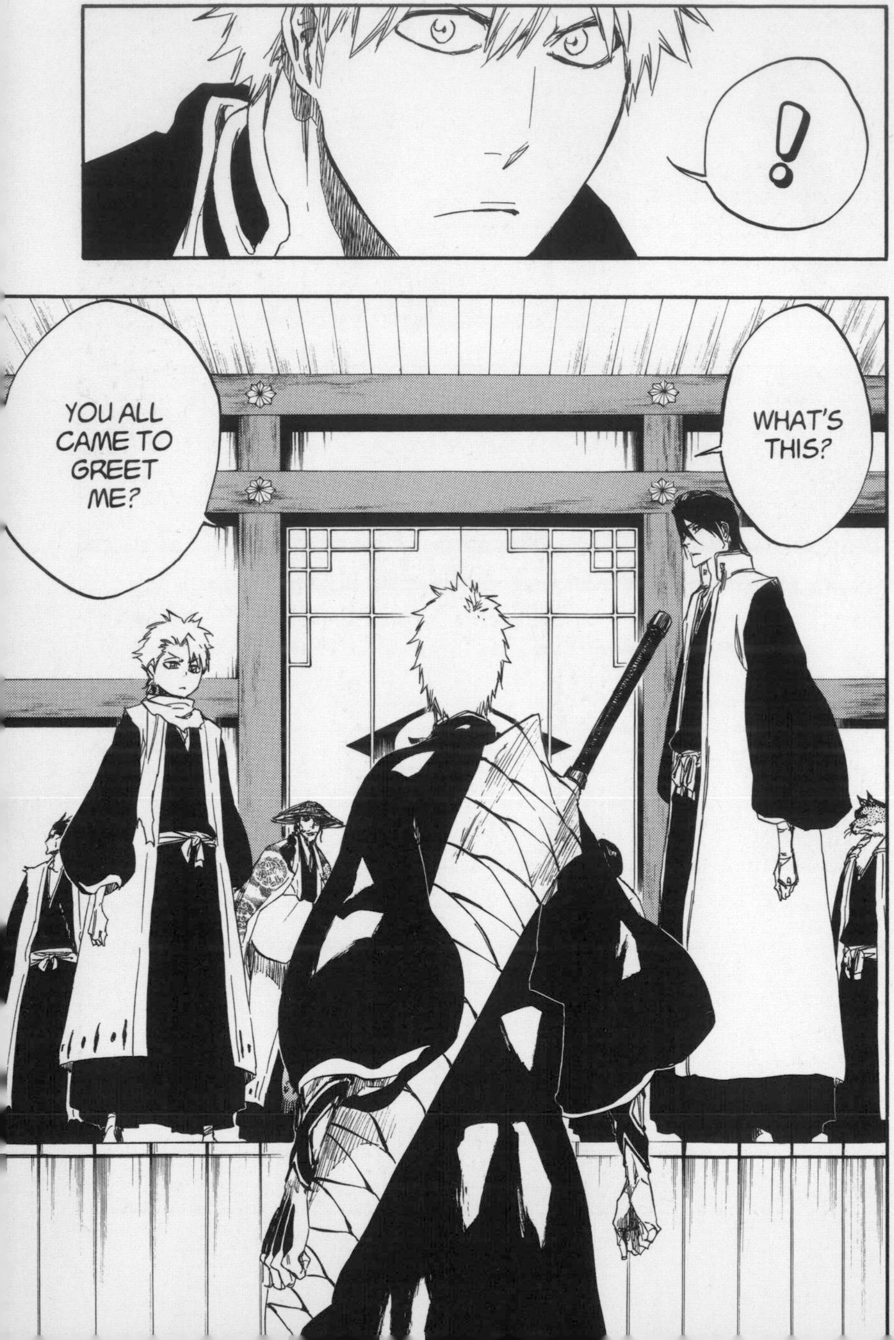
!
WHAT'S THIS?
YOU ALL CAME TO GREET ME?

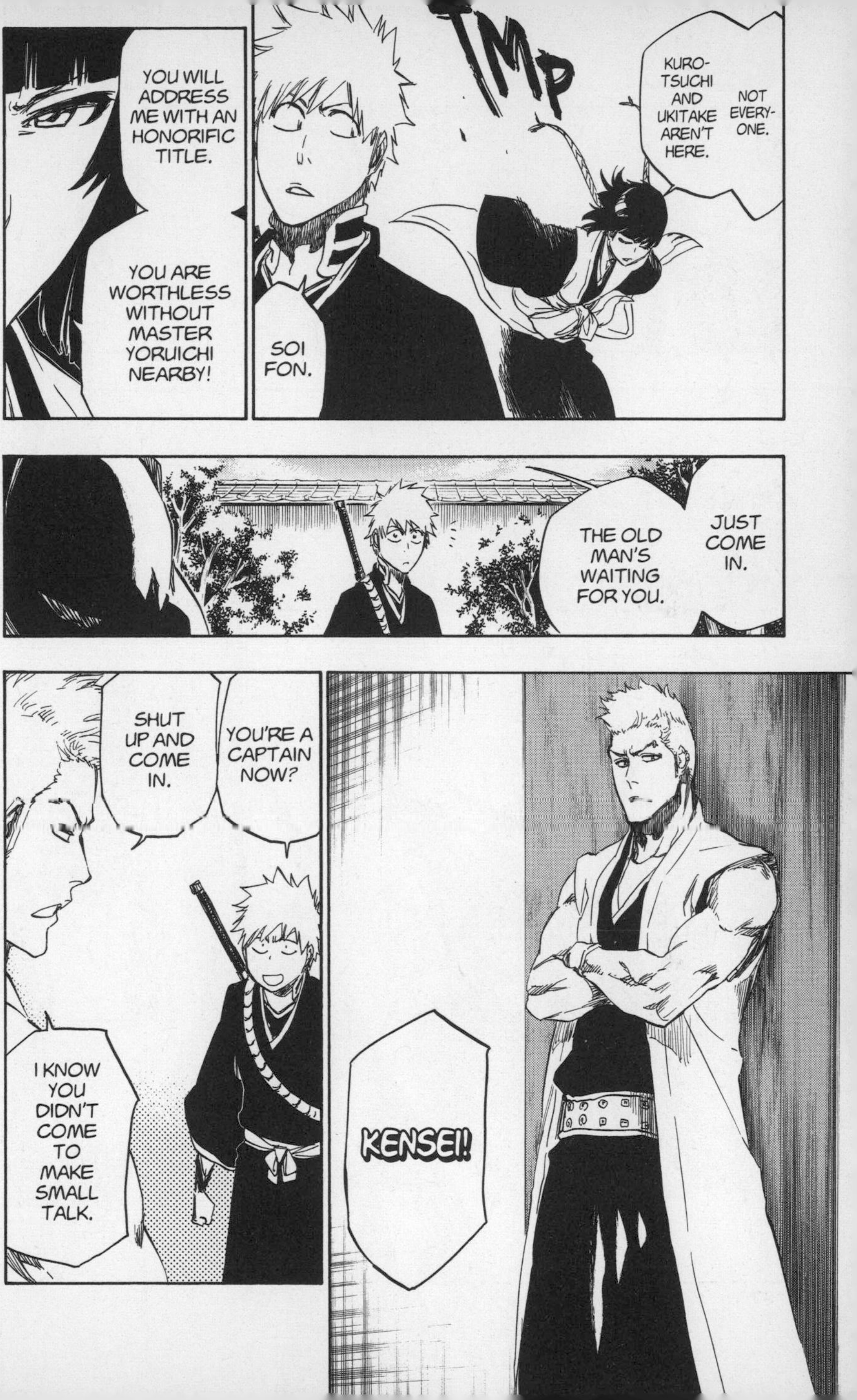
NOT EVERYONE.
KUROTSUCHI AND UKITAKE AREN'T HERE.
TMP
SOI FON.
YOU WILL ADDRESS ME WITH AN HONORIFIC TITLE.
YOU ARE WORTHLESS WITHOUT MASTER YORUICHI NEARBY!
JUST COME IN.
THE OLD MAN'S WAITING FOR YOU.
KENSEI!
YOU'RE A CAPTAIN NOW?
SHUT UP AND COME IN.
I KNOW YOU DIDN'T COME TO MAKE SMALL TALK.

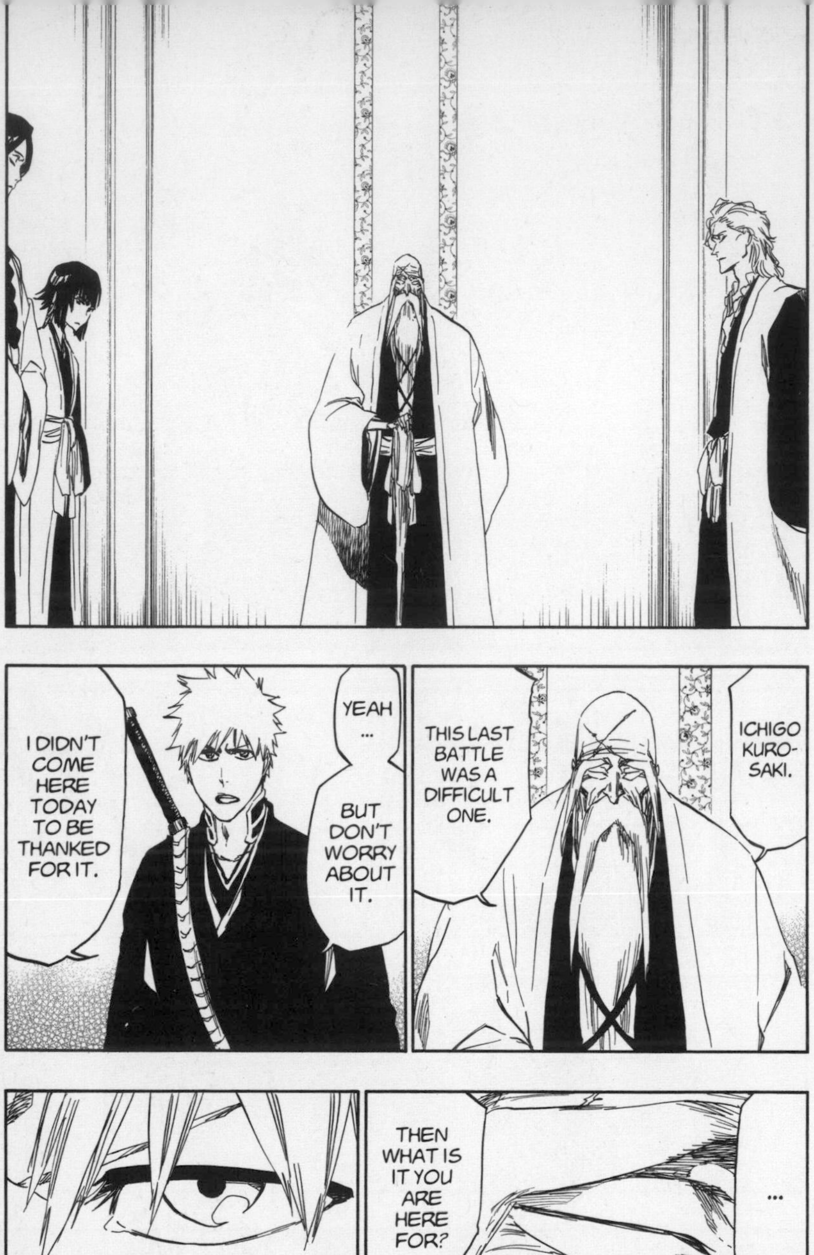
ICHIGO KURO-SAKI.
THIS LAST BATTLE WAS A DIFFICULT ONE.
YEAH ...
BUT DON'T WORRY ABOUT IT.
I DIDN'T COME HERE TODAY TO BE THANKED FOR IT.
...
THEN WHAT IS IT YOU ARE HERE FOR?

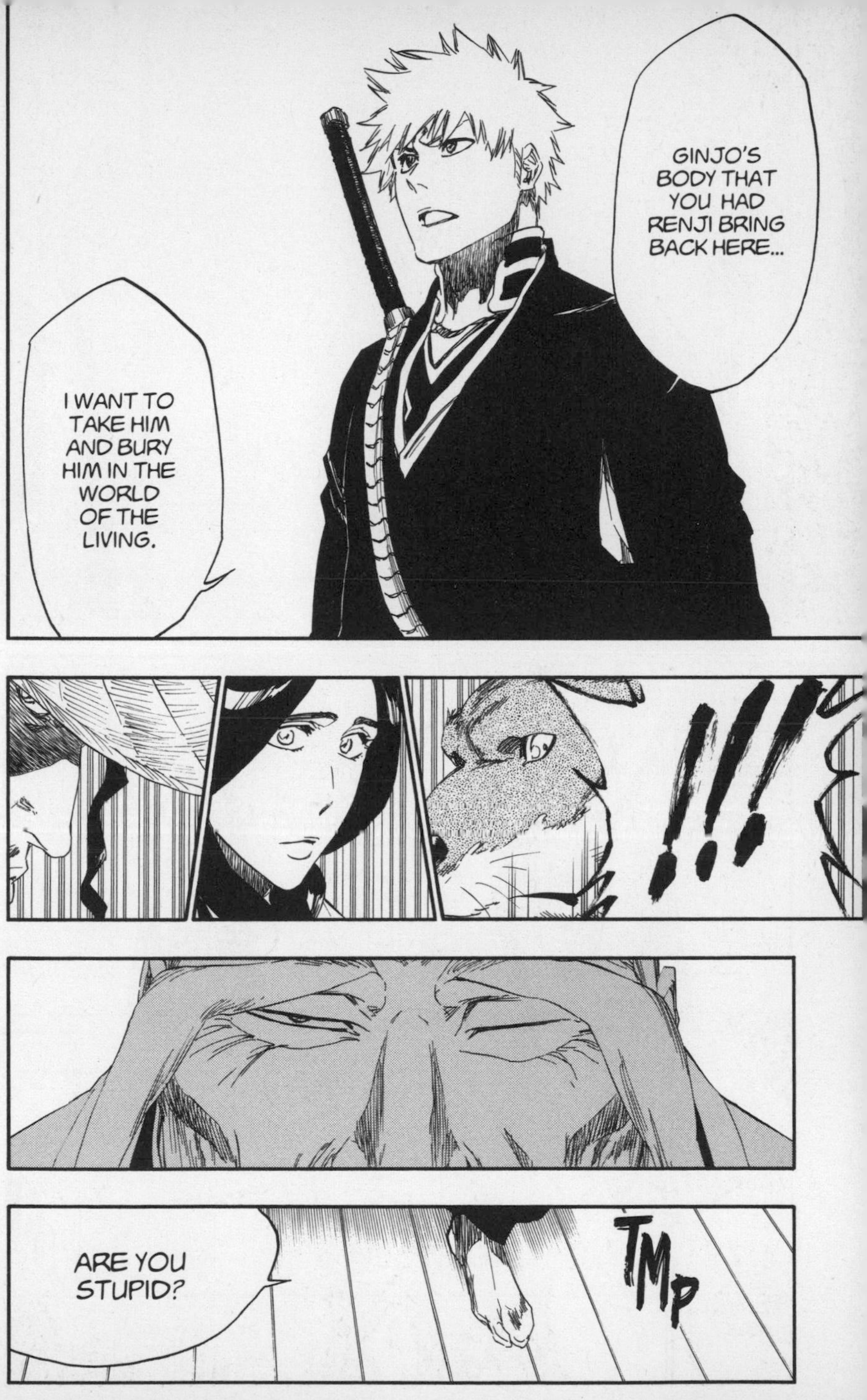
GINJO'S BODY THAT YOU HAD RENJI BRING BACK HERE...
I WANT TO TAKE HIM AND BURY HIM IN THE WORLD OF THE LIVING.
!!!
TMp
ARE YOU STUPID?

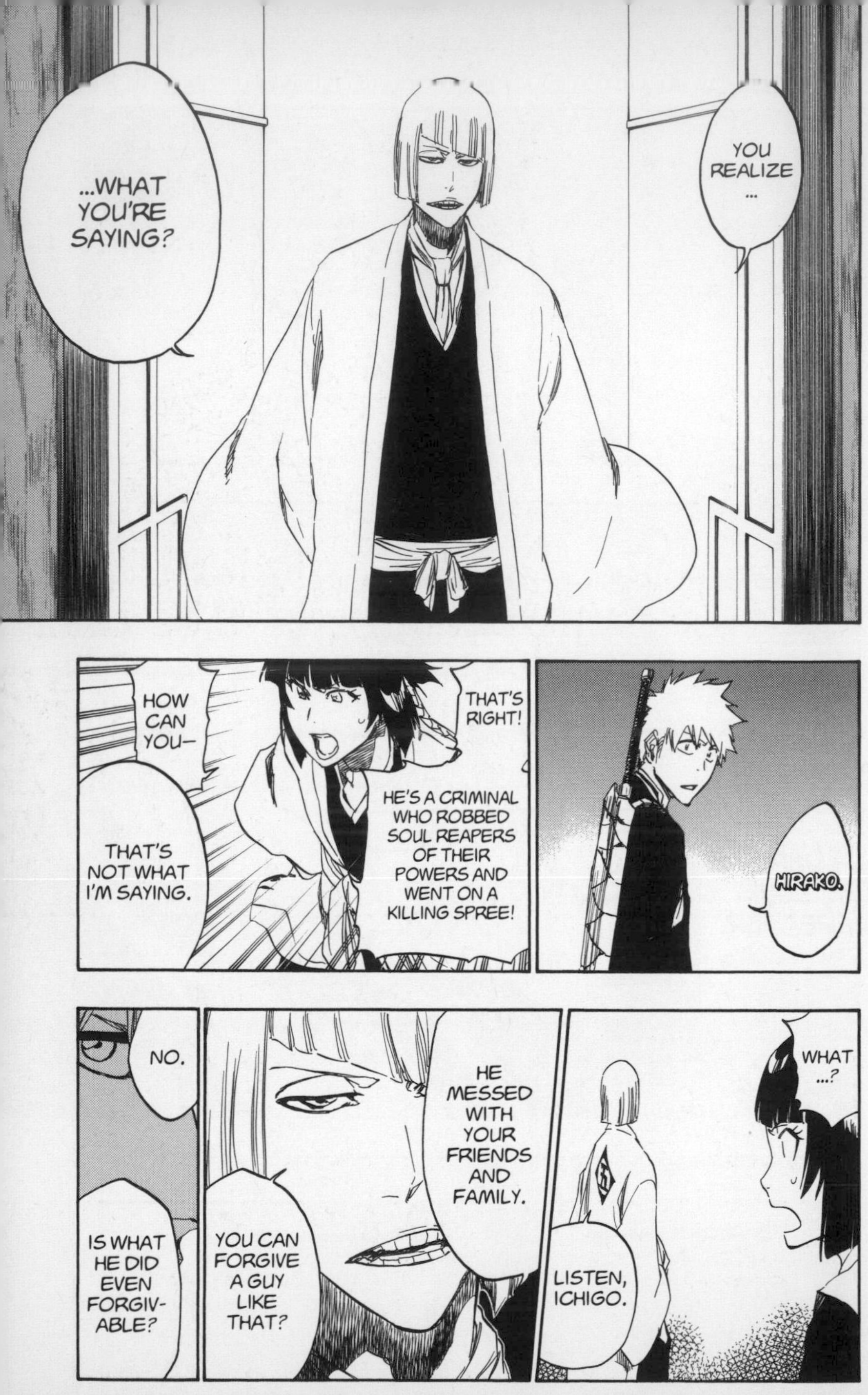
YOU REALIZE ...
...WHAT YOU'RE SAYING?
HIRAKO.
THAT'S RIGHT!
HE'S A CRIMINAL WHO ROBBED SOUL REAPERS OF THEIR POWERS AND WENT ON A KILLING SPREE!
HOW CAN YOU—
THAT'S NOT WHAT I'M SAYING.
WHAT ...?
LISTEN, ICHIGO.
HE MESSED WITH YOUR FRIENDS AND FAMILY.
YOU CAN FORGIVE A GUY LIKE THAT?
NO.
IS WHAT HE DID EVEN FORGIV-ABLE?

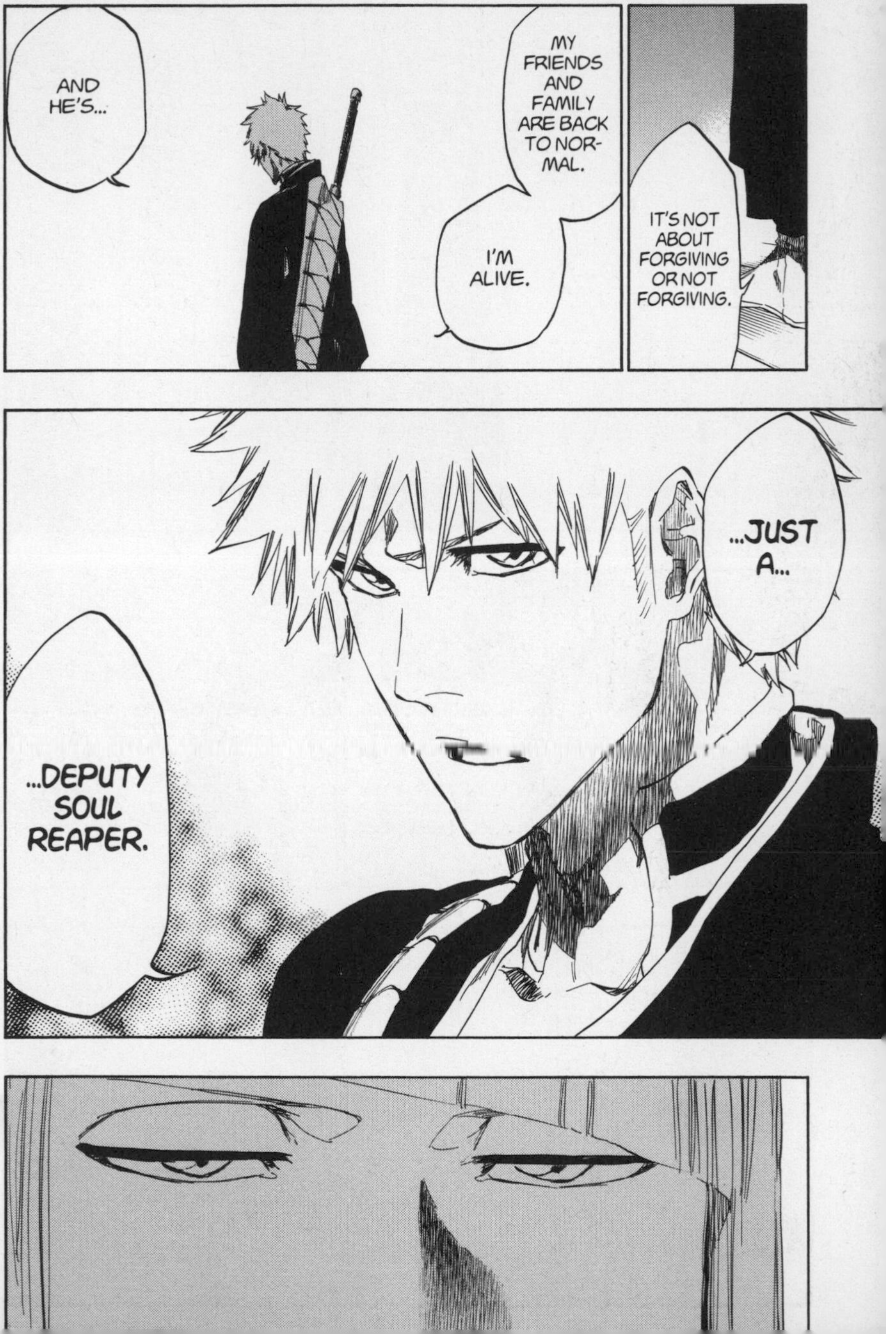
IT'S NOT ABOUT FORGIVING OR NOT FORGIVING.
MY FRIENDS AND FAMILY ARE BACK TO NOR-MAL.
I'M ALIVE.
AND HE'S...
...JUST A...
...DEPUTY SOUL REAPER.

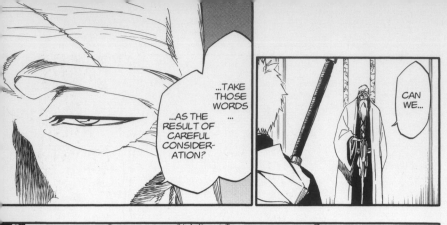

...TAKE THOSE WORDS...

...AS THE RESULT OF CAREFUL CONSIDERATION?

CAN WE...

I THOUGHT YOU'D BE HERE.

TMP

KYO-RAKU.

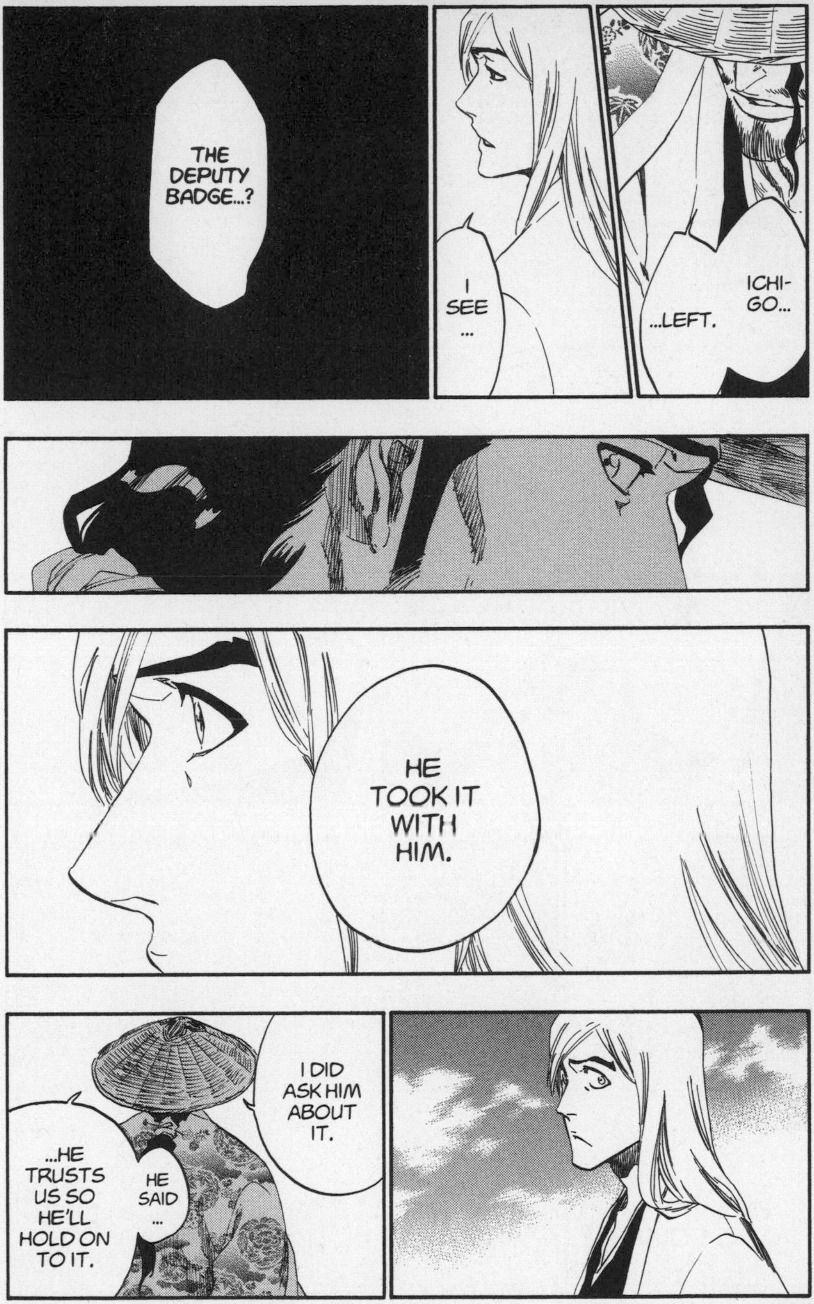
ICHI-GO...
...LEFT.
I SEE...
THE DEPUTY BADGE...?
HE TOOK IT WITH HIM.
I DID ASK HIM ABOUT IT.
HE SAID...
...HE TRUSTS US SO HE'LL HOLD ON TO IT.

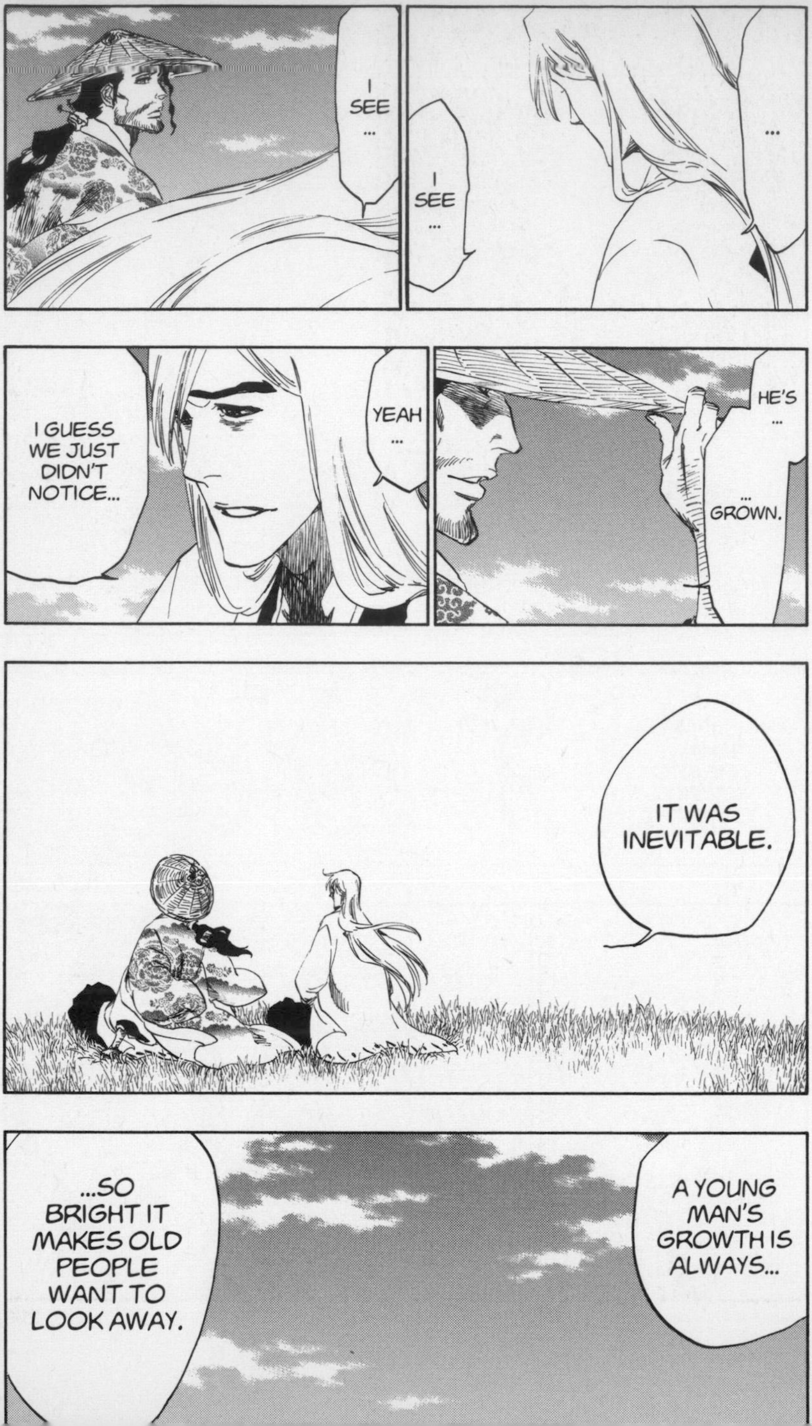
...
I SEE ...
I SEE ...
HE'S ... ... GROWN.
YEAH ...
I GUESS WE JUST DIDN'T NOTICE...
IT WAS INEVITABLE.
A YOUNG MAN'S GROWTH IS ALWAYS...
...SO BRIGHT IT MAKES OLD PEOPLE WANT TO LOOK AWAY.

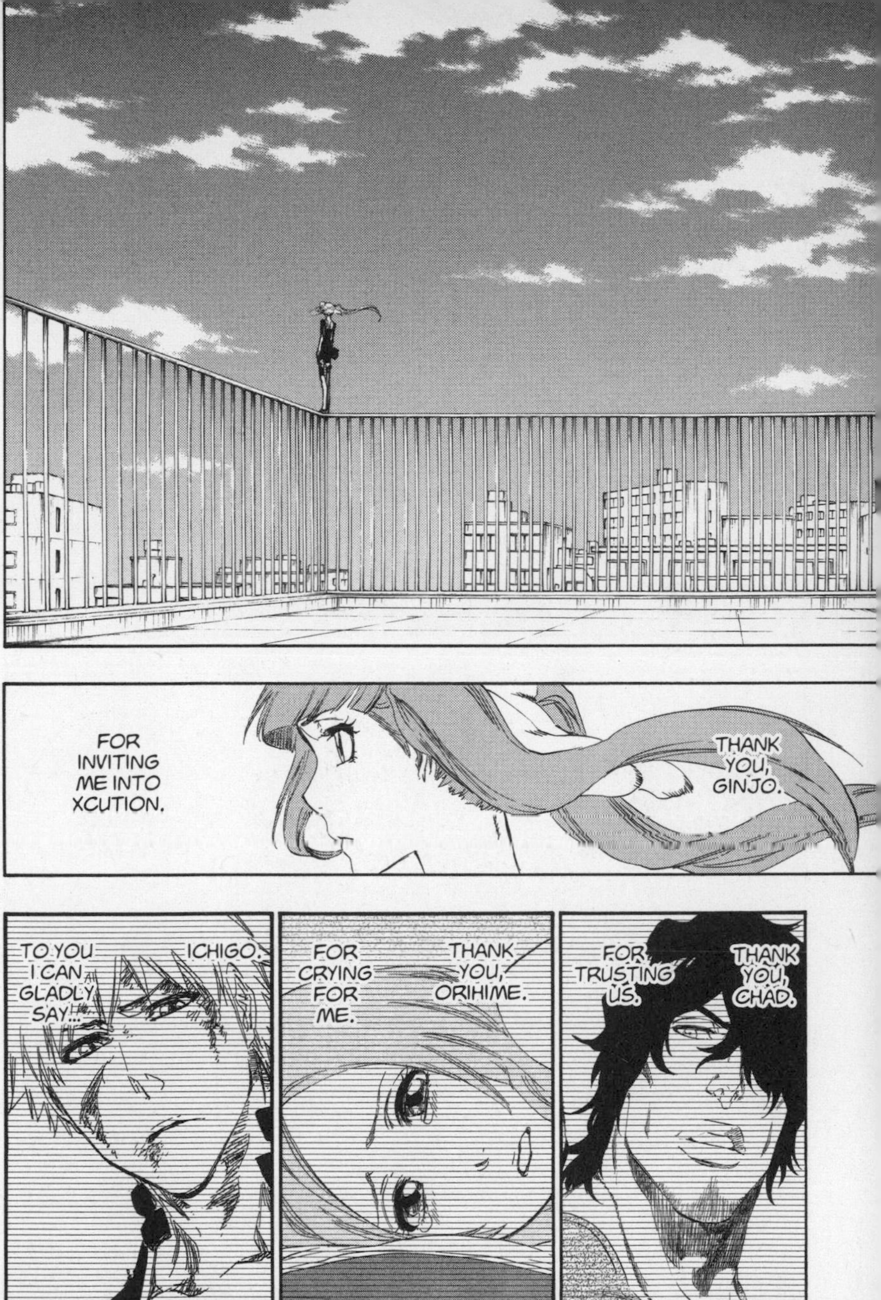
THANK YOU, GINJO.
FOR INVITING ME INTO XCUTION.
THANK YOU, CHAD.
FOR TRUSTING US.
THANK YOU, ORIHIME.
FOR CRYING FOR ME.
ICHIGO.
TO YOU I CAN GLADLY SAY...

GOODBYE.
PLEASE FORGET ABOUT ME.

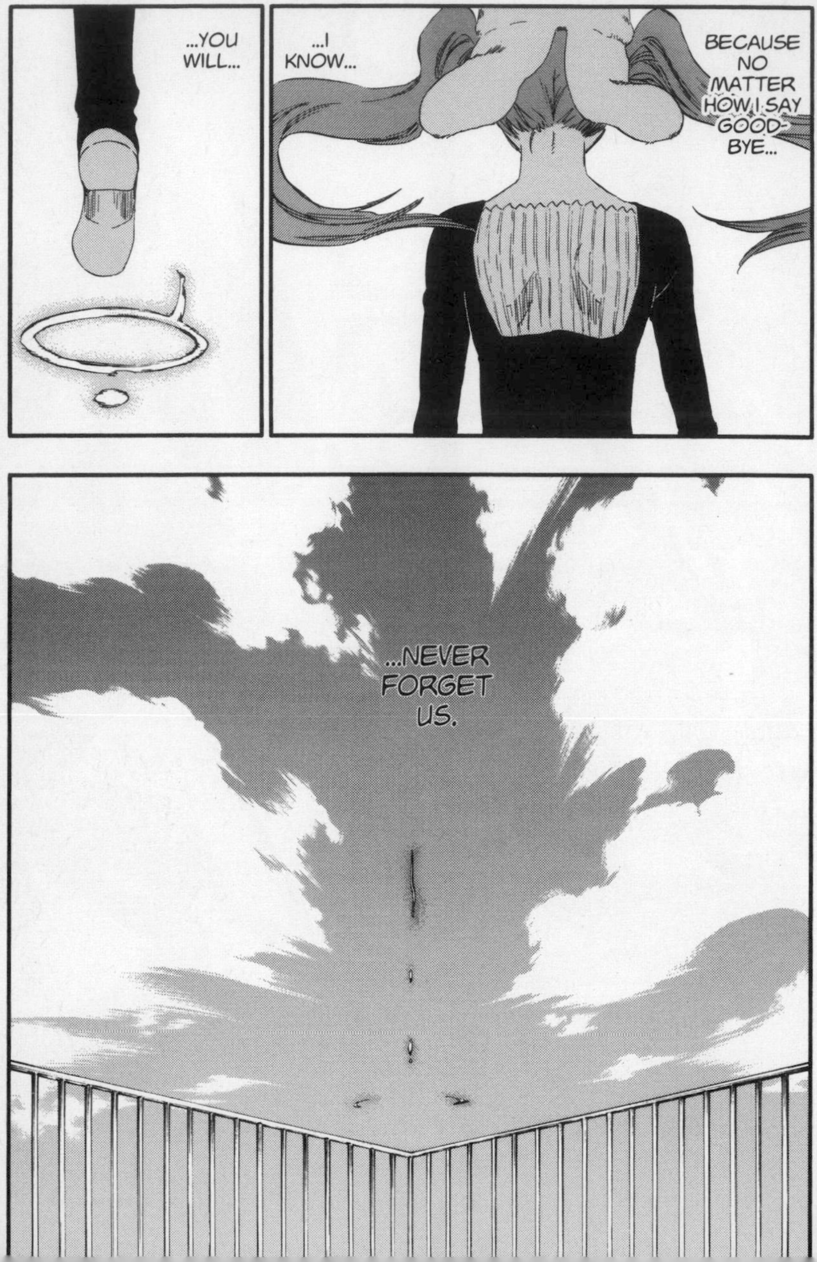
BECAUSE NO MATTER HOW I SAY GOODBYE...
...I KNOW...
...YOU WILL...
...NEVER FORGET US.

BLEACH

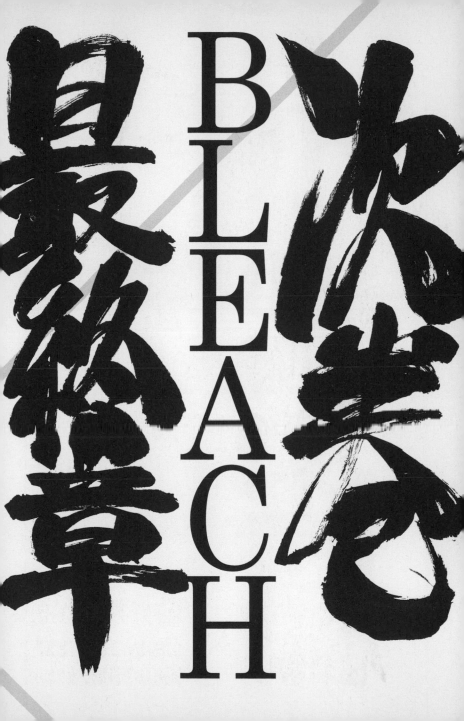

血戦篇

千年

Next Volume:
Thousand-Year
Blood War Arc

You're Reading in AR the Wrong Direction!!

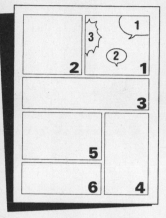

Whoops! Guess what? You're starting at the wrong end of the comic!

...It's true! In keeping with the original Japanese format, **Bleach** is meant to be read from right to left, starting in the upper-right corner.

Unlike English, which is read from left to right, Japanese is read from right to left, meaning that action, sound effects and word-balloon order are completely reversed... something which can make readers unfamiliar with Japanese feel pretty backwards themselves. For this reason, manga or Japanese comics published in the U.S. in English have sometimes been published "flopped"—that is, printed in exact reverse order, as though seen from the other side of a mirror.

By flopping pages, U.S. publishers can avoid confusing readers, but the compromise is not without its downside. For one thing, a character in a flopped manga series who once wore in the original Japanese version a T-shirt emblazoned with "M A Y" (as in "the merry month of") now wears one which reads "Y A M"! Additionally, many manga creators in Japan are themselves unhappy with the process, as some feel the mirror-imaging of their art skews their original intentions.

We are proud to bring you Tite Kubo's **Bleach** in the original unflopped format. For now, though, turn to the other side of the book and let the adventure begin...!

—Editor